GOVERNMENT AND THE ENTERPRISE
SINCE 1900

GOVERNMENT AND THE ENTERPRISE SINCE 1900

The Changing Problem of Efficiency

JIM TOMLINSON

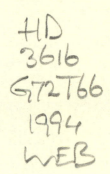
CLARENDON PRESS · OXFORD

1994

Oxford University Press, Walton Street, Oxford OX2 6DP

Oxford New York Toronto
Delhi Bombay Calcutta Madras Karachi
Kuala Lumpur Singapore Hong Kong Tokyo
Nairobi Dar es Salaam Cape Town
Melbourne Auckland Madrid
and associated companies in
Berlin Ibadan

Oxford is a trade mark of Oxford University Press

Published in the United States
by Oxford University Press Inc., New York

British Library Cataloguing in Publication Data
Data available

Library of Congress Cataloging in Publication Data
Tomlinson, Jim.
Government and the enterprise since 1900:
the changing problem of efficiency / Jim Tomlinson.
p. cm.
Includes bibliographical references.
1. Industry and state—Great Britain—History—20th century.
2. Great Britain—Economic conditions—20th century. I. Title.
HD3616.G72T66 1994 93–32725
338.941'009'04–dc20

ISBN 0–19–828749–6

1 3 5 7 9 10 8 6 4 2

Typeset by Pure Tech Corporation, Pondicherry, India
Printed in Great Britain
on acid-free paper by
Bookcraft (Bath) Ltd., Midsomer Norton, Avon

To
Kathryn, Isobel, and Eleanor

Acknowledgements

I am grateful to Richard Coopey, Marguerite Dupree, Terry Gourvish, Peter Howlett, Lewis Johnman, Malcolm Sawyer, and Grahame Thompson for helpful comments on various chapters. I have been especially helped by the comments of Nick Tiratsoo, and by him allowing me to draw on joint work on the 1940s and 1950s. Mrs Christine Newnham has typed and retyped the manuscript with her customary speed and efficiency, and once again I am extremely grateful to her.

This book is dedicated to my wife, Kathryn, and daughters, Isobel and Eleanor, without whom this book would either have been completed much sooner or not at all, in neither case a desirable outcome.

Contents

List of Tables

List of Abbreviations

AACP	Anglo-American Council on Productivity
BEC	British Employers Confederation
BIDC	Bankers Industrial Development Corporation
BIM	British Institute of Management
BL	British Leyland
BPC	British Productivity Council
BR	British Rail
CBI	Confederation of British Industry
CEB	Central Electricity Board
CEPG	Cambridge Economic Policy Group
CEPS	Central Economic Planning Staff
CIC	Capital Issues Committee
CPRS	Central Policy Review Staff ('Think-Tank')
DEA	Department of Economic Affairs
DSIR	Department of Scientific and Industrial Research
DTI	Department of Trade and Industry
EC	European Community
EEC	European Economic Community
EFTA	European Free-Trade Association
EPB	Economic Planning Board
EPT	Excess Profits Tax
EPU	European Payments Union
FBI	Federation of British Industry
GATT	General Agreement on Tariffs and Trade
GDP	Gross Domestic Product
GERD	Gross Expenditure on Research and Development
GNP	Gross National Product
HCP	House of Commons Papers
HLP	House of Lords Papers
ICI	Imperial Chemical Industries

IDAC	Import Duties Advisory Council
IFRB	Industrial Fatigue Research Board
IHRB	Industrial Health Research Board
ILO	International Labour Organization
ILP	Independent Labour Party
IMF	International Monetary Fund
IRA	Industrial Research Association
IRC	Industrial Reorganization Corporation
IRI	Instituto Ricostruzione Italiana
ITB	Industrial Training Board
ITC	Industrial Training Council
JIC	Joint Industrial Council
JPC	Joint Production Committee
JTS	Junior Training School
LPTB	London Passenger Transport Board
MAP	Ministry of Aircraft Production
MITI	Ministry of International Trade and Industry (Japan)
MMC	Monopolies and Mergers Commission
MSC	Manpower Services Commission
MTFS	Medium Term Financial Strategy
NCB	National Coal Board
NCEO	National Confederation of Employers Organizations
NEB	National Enterprise Board
NEDC	National Economic Development Council
NEDO	National Economic Development Office
NIC	National Industrial Council
NJAC	National Joint Advisory Council
NPACI	National Productivity Advisory Council for Industry
NRDC	National Research and Development Council
OECD	Organization for European Co-operation and Development
OPEC	Organization of Petroleum Exporting Countries
OR	Operational Research
PEB	Production Efficiency Board
PEP	Political and Economic Planning

PES	Production Efficiency Service
PP	Parliamentary Papers
PRO	Public Records Office
PSBR	Public Sector Borrowing Requirement
PUL	Percentage Utilization of Labour
R&D	Research and Development
SARA	Special Areas Reconstruction Association
SMT	Securities Management Trust
SWP	Sector Working Party
TEC	Training and Enterprise Council
TOP	Training Opportunities Programme
TUC	Trades Union Congress
TVEI	Training and Vocational Education Initiative
TWI	Training Within Industry
VAT	Value Added Tax
YOP	Youth Opportunities Programme
YTS	Youth Training Scheme

Introduction

For over a hundred years British governments have increasingly become concerned with the seeming inability of British companies to match the performance of those of competitor nations. Before 1900 such concerns were episodic and usually relatively minor parts of the political concerns of the day. Since the turn of the century the concern has become both almost continuous and increasingly central to public debate. Whilst 1900 is an arbitrary date with which to begin an examination of the character and consequences of this concern, it can be taken to coincide with a significant sharpening of worries about the state of the economy brought on above all by the failures of British arms in the Boer War (Friedberg 1988). To some degree the turn of the century conveniently marks the beginning of a period in which enterprise efficiency was never to be far from political concern.

This book is about the attempts by British governments to raise the efficiency of industry. The aim has been to give an empirical account of all the main policy issues which have come into play relating to that highly ambiguous notion of efficiency over approximately the last century.[1] The approach of most of the book is chronological. This is not just a matter of organizational convenience. Rather, it is intended to provide the framework for a particular perspective. That perspective starts from the belief that in analysing policy an interesting but under-utilized initial question is to ask, where do economic policy objectives come from? This is an approach previously used in discussion of macroeconomic policy (Tomlinson 1981, 1985) but in this book it is applied to the microeconomic problem of efficiency.

Whilst there is of course an enormous literature on Britain's relative economic decline in the twentieth century,[2] much of this

---

[1] Most of this material is drawn from secondary sources, but where particularly illuminating primary sources are known, these are cited.

[2] Recent interesting discussions can be found in Williams *et al.* (1983), Elbaum and Lazonick (1986), Newton and Porter (1988), Alford (1988), Oxford Review (1988), Collins and Robbins (1990), Dintenfass (1992), Kirby (1992), Supple (1993), Millward (1993).

is content to start from some standard measure of that decline, for example, the relatively slow increase in GDP per head. The effect of this to create a unitary problem which governments are then assumed to have addressed or, more often, failed to address. By contrast, in this book a primary question is, how was the problem of inefficiency seen at the time? Out of what elements was the problem constructed, and what did this imply for the policy measures taken? The approach then may be said to emphasize the conjunctural aspects of the issue and the policy response in this area, rather than the continuity of the problem. The hope is that such an approach will throw fresh light on the evolution of British policy in the twentieth century. On the other hand it is not intended to suggest a lack of links between the chronological periods, and this is addressed both by cross-referencing between the period chapters, and also by the two case-study chapters, on cars and cotton, as well as the chapter on public ownership.

Once the focus is put on how the problem of efficiency was constructed at different periods, the well-known ambiguity of that term becomes a major issue. Economists have long recognized that ambiguity, and even the most basic textbook will discriminate between allocative efficiency (maximizing consumer welfare from given resources) and engineering or production efficiency (minimizing the cost of a given output). But such a distinction does not take us very far in terms of the historical debates. Most of those debates, broadly speaking, could be put within the second category. But this issue of production efficiency in turn can and has been construed and measured in a variety of ways—as competitiveness or relative productivity, for example—each of these concepts in turn being open to conceptualization and measurement in a number of forms. Each chapter therefore begins with an attempt to situate and define the problem of efficiency in its particular historical context.

The central part of each of the chronological chapters is organized in a similar way. The structure, which borrows in part from Williams *et al.* (1983), assumes that industrial enterprises in capitalist economies have three broad areas where they must achieve a degree of success if they are to survive: market share, profitability, and productive efficiency. In turn the last of these can be schematically broken down into capital and labour, technical change, and company structure and organization. This division into factors of production needs to be used with some care. It tends to portray the production process as the consequence of the bringing together of autonomous elements, rather than emphasizing the key role of the particular form of organization and calculation of the enterprise in making production happen. But, with this qualification in mind, it does provide a convenient organizing device.

Finally, the achievements of economic policy in this area depend in part upon the context in which governments operate, which includes not only the macroeconomic environment, but also the political and economic ideas of governments and the institutions through which policy works. Hence each chapter has a section on state capacity and achievement.

The title of the book uses the word 'government' rather than 'state'. In part this is a minor linguistic preference. But it also reflects a certain desire to distance the approach from the connotations that 'state' often carries. 'State' is difficult to use without conjuring up all kinds of debates that I wish to avoid. Both in much Marxism and in liberal political economy (e.g. the work of Hayek), 'the state' stands apart from society as an entity which possesses certain powers which separate it from civil society. For orthodox Marxism, except at times of revolutionary rupture, the state has the capacity to deliver the conditions for the reproduction of the existing system of social relations (capitalism etc.). For liberal political economy the state has the capacity to do much harm to the functioning of the (market) economy unless tied down by strict constitutional rules. In both cases the state derives its powers from classes or interest groups in civil society, and acts on society, but its links to that civil society are basically unproblematic. Above all, the state's capacity to deliver its ends is not a major issue in this kind of framework. By contrast this book focuses considerable attention on the problems of the state attaining its objectives. This kind of focus fits better with the notion of 'government', which connotes much more a problematic political process than 'state' with its connotations of constitutionally defined and determinate capacities.[3]

---

[3] There is much political science literature of course on the government–industry relationship. For surveys of the more empirical material see Steel(1982) and of

Government is also a more congenial term because it fits with certain modern conceptions of how economic and social life is regulated in the advanced societies. Theorists such as Foucault have, if nothing else, alerted us to the extent to which that life is shaped by a whole range of practices (theories and institutions interwoven) whose origin-point cannot be found in government in the constitutional sense, but which are taken up by government in that narrow sense in its attempts to regulate everything from the number and health of the populace to the efficiency of enterprises. This is not in any important sense a 'Foucauldian' book, but it does try to take on board the extent to which in trying to regulate enterprise behaviour government is commonly trying to reorient existing interventions in enterprise practices rather than beginning with a blank sheet of paper.

Economists may wonder why the notion of market failure is deployed very little in this book. Economists have a well-established tradition of approaching industrial policy with this notion, in which government steps in where markets fail to deliver an efficient outcome. However this concept has been largely eschewed in this book for two reasons. First, whilst long-established in professional economics, the notion of market failure has played only a small part in policy formulation and discussion. It has certainly not been the framework applied in most twentieth-century discussions of government and industrial efficiency. Hence, in trying to recreate the terms of historical debate it has limited relevance. Second, it is a highly problematic and indeed highly tendentious theoretical notion. It starts from an idealization of 'the market' and then sees the government rectifying faults in that process. This necessarily biases the discussion, by assuming that the market can helpfully be discussed in a general way, rather than as always embedded in particular institutional structures and with specific effects. It also assumes that in an ideal world of fully functioning markets governments would not be necessary, which is not exactly a value-free place from which to start analysis of the government's role.

These points raise a general question about the use of economics in this book. Economic historians' use of economics comes in

the more conceptual, Wilks and Wright (1987): ch. 12. For one of the most interesting attempts to combine the two approaches in a comparative framework, see Hall (1986).

broadly two forms. On the one hand, there are those who use economics as their primary analytical framework and in effect accept economics as the social science best equipped to understand the past. On the other hand, there are the 'Jacks (or Jills) of all trades' (with its well-known corollary . . .), who see economics as just one amongst several competing frameworks. The approach of this book falls into the second camp. Of course, in the twentieth century and in discussion of economic policy, economics has played a key role, so obviously a book about twentieth-century industrial policy must contain substantial discussion of economics. A parallel would be a book on Gladstone and nineteenth-century politics. This would obviously have to say a great deal about evangelical christianity, since it is so important to the Gladstonian world-view. But it would not have to deploy a framework derived from that evangelicism. In the same way, whilst talking a lot about economics, this book does not derive its framework from that discipline.

The purpose of this book has not been to try to arrive at a definitive conclusion on the causes of British relative decline. The aim has been to 'historicize' that debate rather than to try to resolve it. Nevertheless implicit in some of the discussion are some assumptions about the causes of that decline. Perhaps most obvious is the relatively limited attention given to restrictive labour and trade-union practices.

The debates on these practices are not ignored. In 1901 Sidney Webb wrote that 'complaints as to the diminished quantity of energy and work, and of the tacit conspiracy to discourage individual exertion, have occurred with curiously exact iteration, in every decade of the last 100 years' (*The Times*, 6 December 1901) and the same could almost be said of the following 100 years. It would therefore be ahistorical to ignore the issue, and where it has been particularly prominent, for example in the debate about the car industry, it has been discussed (Ch. 14).

On the other hand, the popular belief that such practices provide a major explanation for Britain's relative decline seems extremely ill-founded (see also Nichols 1986). Attempts at broad and systematic empirical study of the issue have been surprisingly few. But those that have been attempted, notably those by Hilton *et al.* (1935), British Employers Confederation (1950), Zweig (1951), and the Ministry of Labour (1959) have all failed to find that such practices were widespread and significant across manufacturing industry (see also Richardson 1991).[4] It is therefore justifiable not to give such issues inappropriate prominence in this book.

---

[4] On this see also Tiratsoo and Tomlinson (1993*a*): ch. 8, and Tiratsoo and Tomlinson (1993*b*).

1

The Limits of *Laissez-faire*

INTRODUCTION

This chapter summarizes the development of government policy on industry up to the end of the nineteenth century. It might be thought this would result in a very short chapter: wasn't the nineteenth century the age of *laissez-faire* of the 'nightwatchman state', and therefore largely devoid of government policy on industry? Such a view is by no means absurd, but this chapter attempts to qualify it in three ways. First, by stressing that almost any sensible interpretation of *laissez-faire* recognizes that the state has to play some positive role and therefore necessarily has to take some actions which affect industry. Second, by detailing some minor but noteworthy shifts in policy towards the end of the nineteenth century. Third, by discussing the shifts in the intellectual, political as well as economic climate towards the end of the 1800s which are significant for what was to follow in the new century.

CONTEXT

Much historiography has traditionally seen the nineteenth century as the age of *laissez-faire* in Britain. Both the meaning and impact of this term have been widely debated for many years (Coats 1971; Taylor 1972). The development of this doctrine is usually associated with the work of the classical economists, running from Adam Smith (1723–90) to John Stuart Mill (1806–73). Besides these two it would include the work of Malthus, Ricardo, James Mill, Torrens, McCulloch, and Senior. Like everything about *laisse-faire* this list involves a degree of controversy, for example, as to whether it should also include Jeremy Bentham, the founder of utilitarianism.[1] Nevertheless most authors agree

---

[1] There is also a complex debate about how far the classical economists were utilitarians: see e.g. Robbins (1978): Lecture IV.

that the classical economists did form a school of thought united by broad principles. Whilst above all a group of economic theorists, they also shared a broad agreement on policy issues, which can helpfully be described as *laissez-faire* as long as we are careful in the use of that term.

This policy stance cannot be seen as simply derived from economic theory. It should rather be seen in sociological terms: Schumpeter remarked of the classical economists that their 'similarity of conditions of life and of social location produced similar philosophies of life, and similar judgements about social phenomena' (Schumpeter 1954: 470). But the classical economists shared not only a sociological location but also a quite comprehensive liberal philosophy which was concerned with much more than economics in a narrow modern sense. *Laisse-faire*, then, must be seen in this broader framework of ideas, and not just as an economic doctrine.

The broader framework may be christened 'liberal' in the sense that the political value of liberty was held to be primary. Liberty, or freedom from coercion, was held to be vital both to intellectual life i.e. by allowing the development of ideas, and also to economic life, by allowing the play of individual intelligence and action to generate new products and processes of production. Further, liberty was seen by most classical economists as secured best by a system of private property, giving (some) individuals the basis on which liberty could be securely founded. The classical economists were usually individualists—they held individual liberty to be the highest end but they also believed in individualism as a means. This meant individual private property and markets. However this broad-brush picture needs to be qualified, especially in the case of John Stuart Mill. Whilst clearly a liberal and individualist as to ends, Mill had a 'tendency to socialism' (Coats 1971: 12–14). This mainly related to his support for co-operatives as a desirable form of production organization. In later editions of his *Principles*, Mill advocated co-ops as vital to both the material and moral improvement of the working classes (Mill 1896: IV, ch. 7; see also Tomlinson 1986). However the crucial point is that Mill was never an advocate of *state* ownership of the means of production; whilst his liberalism could embrace co-operatives, like other classical economists he was quite hostile to socialism in that sense.

This leads on to what is perhaps the single most important feature of the classical economists views—their distrust of government: The classical economists as a group had a poor opinion of the wisdom of governments and a strong suspicion that, in fact, it was likely to prove the vehicle of special interests (Robbins 1978: 184; also Coats 1971: 5–6). However this suspicion of government did not mean that classical economists were advocates of a negligible and essentially negative view of government's role as anarchy plus the constable. Such a view may be attributed to the French school of Physiocrats but it would not apply to the classical economists. The former believed in a natural order of things in which economic freedom was laid down for all time; the latter were much more empirical in their approach. They were unprepared to lay down in advance prohibitions of state action resting on conceptions of a natural order of things at once simple and universally applicable (Robbins 1978: 46).

The classical economists believed in the invisible hand, that actions have unintended consequences, and that in economic life individuals pursuing their own ends may nevertheless secure the good of all. But the invisible hand for them was not some mysterious force before whose beneficience one simply bowed down. Rather

the invisible hand which guides men to promote ends which were no part of their intention, is not the hand of some god or some natural agency independent of human effort; it is the hand of the law giver, the hand which withdraws from the sphere of the pursuit of self-interest those possibilities which harmonise with the public good. . . . (Robbins 1978: 56).

So a market economy is desirable because it allows for the achievement of liberty and individual development, but it is not a natural phenomenon, rather it is a creation of human beings, a social artefact.[2] On the other hand, markets have their own internal logic, and once established these principles of working should be respected and allowed to function except where a very strong case can be made to the contrary. This position creates a

---

[2] This is a view to be distinguished from that which sees a complete incompatibility between a market economy and a natural order. In this view markets had to be created (and with only temporary success) totally against the grain of society, especially markets in labour, land, and money. A classic source of this kind of argument is Polanyi (1944).

potentially highly unstable view about how far an evolved order should be reformed by deliberate state action. This tension is particularly apparent in one of the major twentieth-century intellectual heirs of the classical economists, Hayek (Tomlinson 1991*b*: ch. 3).

The classical economists were essentially economic and social reformers, by no means celebrators of the status quo. Much of their reforming zeal was aimed at reducing the role of government, believing that the authoritarianism and paternalism of government was the major threat to liberty. But this anti-government zeal was not based on a desire for a 'war of all against all'. The doctrine of the invisible hand led the classical economists to believe that a society in which individuals competitively pursued their own ends could be both prosperous and free. But they believed such a result would only come about in the context of an appropriate legal and moral framework.

To take the latter first, Adam Smith was the first to put forward a systematic theory of the invisible hand in his *Wealth of Nations* (1776). But his analysis there presupposed that of his *Theory of Moral Sentiments* (1759) in which he argued that market or 'commercial' society worked because it developed individuals' sense of social sympathy and mutual dependence. The success of the invisible hand therefore rested not just on an absence of inappropriate government action, nor even legal framework allowing the pursuit of self-interest, but also and perhaps most importantly on a series of constraints derived from custom, morals, religion, and education. As Keynes (1926/1972: 279) remarked, 'Adam Smith's advocacy of the 'obvious and simple system of natural liberty is derived from his theistic and optimistic view of the world as set forth in the *Theory of Moral Sentiments*'. Absence of recognition of this dimension of Smith and other classical economists' thought is perhaps one of the major reasons why we can say that their opinions have so often been simplified to the point of misrepresentation. Smith in particular should not be canonized as the saint of free-enterprise economics (Winch 1992).

The classical economists were very much concerned with the appropriate legal framework for economic policy. On some issues this led to a straightforward and united position—for example, hostility to state-backed monopolies. In other areas their views were more complicated and less united—for example, on the early Factory Acts with their legislative restrictions on hours of work (Blaug 1958; reprinted in Coats 1971), or on the public provision of education (West 1965; reprinted in Coats 1971). Even in the case of free trade, which is commonly seen as a triumph for the classical economists, this reform was supported by them in a much more qualified and gradualist manner than, for example, in the work of real free-trade ideologues like Cobden (Coats 1971: 28–31).

On the more positive side the classical economists were supporters of the restoration of the gold standard in 1819 and the Bank Charter Act of 1844. These two government actions defined much of nineteenth-century monetary history in Britain. More than that, by imposing a form of automatic regulation of the money supply via the gold standard, the classical economists supported one of the three pillars of the anti-collectivist temple (Checkland 1983: 174), alongside free trade and low and balanced budgets.

The creation of a framework for banking and money supply is accepted by almost all strands of economic and political thought as a desirable aim of government activity. A similar point may be made about company law. But in neither case does the desirability in principle of such a framework determine what that framework is to look like. In the case of company law the major reform of the nineteenth century was the creation by a series of Acts between 1856 and 1862 of general limited liability, the ability of any company to obtain the benefits of limited liability by a simple act of registration, submission to a few regulations, and payment of a small fee.

General limited liability was significant deviation from *laissez-faire*. The state created a new type of economic agent: 'the joint stock company is the creation of the State, the creature of statutes' (Florence 1957: 69). Within this new entity a privileged body of shareholders was created, and one view would see the shareholder as thus receiving a defence against exploitation on a par with the Factory Acts and other measures defending the worker (Florence: 69–77).

Although later seen as a fundamental and almost inevitable institution for a successful capitalist economy, the emergence of general limited liability was hotly contested (Hirst 1979: ch. 5; Gower 1979: ch. 3). Interestingly, the attitude of most classical economists to this development was hostile. In this they followed Adam Smith who saw limited liability (available in his day only on a much more difficult and expensive basis), as largely a way for company promoters to defraud the investing public. His view of the ideal company was of what today would be called an owner-controlled enterprise, not a joint-stock company with a large number of anonymous shareholders with only a remote concern for the day-to-day running of the business.

The classical economists have been dealt with at some length because they form such an important reference-point in so much later doctrinal and policy debate. The question of how important they were for policy-making in the nineteenth century will be returned to below. But to complete the account of the broad development of economic doctrine in the nineteenth century it is important to say a little about the 'neo-classical' economists who followed the classical economists in the late nineteenth century.

The distinction between classical and neo-classical is a controversial one. The divide is based primarily on differences in the theory of value held to by each group. The classical economists adhered to some version of the labour theory of value, a belief that the objective value of goods derived from their embodiment of some quantity of inputs. Neo-classical economists, on the other hand, believed that value is fundamentally subjective, and that goods only have value in so far as consumers wanted them: usually such wants would be subject to decline as more of the goods were consumed—hence the name 'marginalism' often applied to such doctrines. These differences in the theory of value are not of concern here. But the transition from the classical to the neo-classical period at around the beginning of the 1870s does mark an important shift in the way in which economic issues were discussed by economists.

Modern economics from the time of Adam Smith has always had as a fundamental issue the proper scope of government. As we have noted above, the classical view, whilst complex, was distrustful of government but by no means advocated no government. Much of that distrust of government stemmed not only from a broad liberal philosophy, but also from the type of government as perceived in Britain. For much of the period that government was corrupt and inefficient, arbitrary in its actions and a poor channel indeed for any pursuit of the public good.

Almost all progressive opinion was therefore united in wanting less government

From the second half of the century this alignment began to break up. This was partly due to changes in the character of the government due to civil service reforms (Northcote–Trevelyan reforms of the 1860s) and the expansion of the franchise (the 1867 Reform Act) and the secret ballot (1872). Alongside this trend was the slow growth of the ideology of socialism or collectivism, which brought a quite different attitude to government both because of its rejection of the primacy of individual liberty as a political value and its belief that government could be an effective agent of reform and improvement.

Amongst the neo-classical economists in Britain the most important and also typical figure is that of Alfred Marshall (1842–1924). Whatever his differences with the classical economist over value theory, Marshall shared many of their liberal values and forms of economic analysis. He also shared their concern with the scope of government action. But in Marshall's time that concern was shaped by a quite radical shift in context. Where the classical economists had largely been concerned with the reduction in powers of corrupt, oligarchical government, the late nineteenth-century debate was increasingly about the response to socialist claims for a radical extension of the power of increasingly democratic government.

Marshall himself made this point forcibly when discussing his own view of the role of government in the economy. After stressing changes in the character of government between Smith and John Stuart Mill, he went on

Mill had seen a vast increase in the probity, the strength, the unselfishness, and the resources of Government during his life; and it seems that each succeeding decade has enlarged the scope of those interventions of Government for the promotion of general well-being which he thought likely to work well . . . this process has continued and . . . thus we can now safely venture on many public undertakings which a little while ago would have been technically unworkable, or which would have been perverted by the selfish and corrupt purposes of those who had the ear of Government (Marshall 1907: 18–19).

Given this perception of the changing character of government it is hardly surprising that Marshall was by no means a violent opponent of all extensions of government role advocated by socialists. Like most British economists towards the end of the nineteenth century he spent a great deal of time discussing socialism (Winch 1972: 36–42). This is very apparent in the pages of the first British professional periodical for economists, the *Economic Journal*, which first appeared in 1890. As Steedman (1991) shows, its early years were dominated by the discussion of socialism and related issues. In this discussion the predominant approach of Marshall and other mainstream economists was broadly one of sceptical sympathy with socialism. But this sympathy was much more apparent in relation to socialism's aims rather than its methods.

Marshall argued that in Britain there had been too much of a bias against a role for government: 'the problems of the economic functions of government have been studied in Germany with greater care, and with a bias that may be a healthy corrective to the bias in the opposite direction of the English speaking countries' (Marshal 1890: 48). Nevertheless Marshall's 'tendency to socialism' was of a very particular kind. Like John Stuart Mill he favoured co-ops (at least in distribution) for their improving moral as well as material effects (McWilliams-Tollberg 1975; Tomlinson 1986: 230–1). But as regards government, whilst willing to see its role extended in such areas as education and the 'provision of intelligence' to industry, his overall attitude was shaped by attitudes similar to those of Adam Smith. 'He was a little, but not very much, more enthusiastic about government involvement than the classical writers: Government involvement in enterprise was harmful to both managerial and innovative efficiency' (O'Brien 1990: 141). Marshall's attitude was that the dynamism of the private sector was its most important characteristic. This comes out very clearly when he discussed public ownership. He was not opposed to such ownership root and branch, but he argued it should be confined to areas where the business was routine, like the post office, and should certainly not be allowed in areas of competition where there was a need for continual adaptation to changing conditions—as, for example, in coal mines (Riesman 1987: 226–34).

A final component of economic arguments which needs to be reviewed in looking at this intellectual backdrop to policy discussions is the question of monopolies and trusts. The last two or three decades of the nineteenth century saw this issue come to the fore. The reason was not so much the internal development of the discourse of economics but the widespread perception that monopoly was growing and the question of how this was to be responded to: 'The study of monopoly in the second half of the nineteenth century was largely stimulated by debate over public policy' (Williams 1978: 121).

The late nineteenth-century movement to create trusts and monopolies was much more pronounced in the United States and Germany than in Britain, and the amount of debate over the issue was comparatively small in the latter country before 1900 (Williams 1990). For the mainstream economists like Marshall the theoretical legacy of classical economics in this area was quite small. Smith had been violently anti-monopoly but this was mainly in the context of companies enjoying direct government sanction, like the old trading companies, which he saw as leading directly to the exploitation of the consumer, rather than the kinds of industrial combinations that dominated debate in the late nineteenth century.

Mill had developed the concept of natural monopoly, where because of the extent of economies of scale only one firm could survive the rigours of free competition. Many economists in the United States took up this argument with enthusiasm in explaining and justifying the growth of trusts and monopolies in that country. It was also used by Marshall, but broadly speaking he emphasized the importance of the counteracting tendency of changes in consumer tastes in undercutting such monopolies (e.g. Marshall and Marshall 1884: 55; Riesman 1987: 222–6).

Before 1900 the trust issue in Britain had not attained the prominence it had in the contemporary United States or Germany, nor that which it was to achieve in Britain after 1900. This partly reflected the fact that contemporaries perceived, and probably rightly, that the pace of industrial combination was slower in Britain than in these other countries, though it seems to have sped up right at the end of the century (Hannah 1983: ch. 2, app. 1).

How far did policy reflect these preconceptions of the economists. If 'reflect' is not taken to imply a causal relation the broad answer would be to a large extent. A very broad-brush account of the nineteenth-century political economy would have to say that in the middle of the nineteenth-century the role of government was reduced, but that in the last decades of the century the tendency was somewhat the other way. But such a simple picture of ebb and flow would need to be qualified at once. As already noted, the limits of the state under *laissez-faire* were not clearly defined in theory, and it was similar in practice.

Though in theory *laissez-faire* limited the state to 'keeping the ring' around industry, policy as really practiced at the mid-century period of minimum state interference involved a much wider scope of state activity. State protection of property was always taken for granted. . . . In addition, the state set up and legalised the contestants in the ring, began specifically to protect adults from over work in industry, published information about industry and provided some of the public works, some of the demands, and some financial stability in the market (Florence 1957: 33).

Thus we shouldn't exaggerate the changes of the last decades of the century, as was done in the classic work by Dicey (1907), with its notion of a sharp break between the 'individualism' of mid-century and 'collectivism' after 1870. Nevertheless, as will be discussed in more detail below, policy in relation to industry did show signs of shifting in the last decades of the nineteenth century, however hard it may be to draw a sharp line between the ebb and flow of the interventionist tide.

The broad congruence between policy development and development of economic thought, to emphasize again, reflected no simple chain of causation. Much recent historical work has emphasized the limited impact of economics on policy, especially in the nineteenth century (e.g. Hilton 1988; Harris 1990; Supple 1990). But the impact of economic knowledge has typically been much more diffuse, erratic, and informal than historians of policy have sometimes suggested. 'Rarely has it consisted of the direct application of economic theory and data to specific societal problems; far more often it has consisted of gradual and often scarcely perceptible shifts in the wider climate of economic and political culture' (Harris 1990: 393).

Finally, in looking at the intellectual and political context of the period something must be said about the macroeconomy. The focus of this chapter and the book is on microeconomic policy, but this divide is always to a degree arbitrary and unhelpful, and certainly if we are to talk about *laissez-faire* and its implications the macro aspect requires brief attention (see Tomlinson 1990*a*: ch. 2).

The status of the gold standard as a 'pillar of the anti-collectivist temple' has already been noted. The important point about
that standard in the current context is that it embodied an
(allegedly) automatic means of regulating both the money supply
and the balance of payments. By so doing it obviated the need
for any management of the economy—the assumption was that
equilibrium in payments and stable prices would follow automatically if the standard were allowed to work. And the gold
standard, whilst long adhered to by Britain, only became a
widespread system internationally from the 1870s.

The second pillar of anti-collectivism was the low and balanced
government budget. There were many reasons for this combination, by no means all doctrinal, but it should be obvious that if
government is distrusted, and the benefits of individual enterprise applauded, the case for allowing individuals to decide on
the expenditure of most of their own incomes is a powerful one.
Couple this with a belief that governments should not in normal
conditions be able to borrow (and hence escape the political
pains of having to impose taxes) and the broad case for a low
and balanced budget seems strong. This budgetary policy was
challenged before 1900, but there were no substantial breaks with
such Gladstonian fiscal precepts until the early years of the
twentieth century.

Finally, free trade was brought into being for many reasons,
but one very important aspect in the current context is the way
it preserved competition in industry and restricted the scope of
monopoly. Initially this had been an important argument because of the old trading monopolies, but it became increasingly
an argument in relation to the growth of industrial combination.
So a *laissez-faire* attitude to industry, with its belief in the
benefits of competition, plainly fitted snugly with a commitment
to free trade. Free trade in Britain was challenged before 1900
(and again soon after that date) but was maintained effectively
unaltered until the First World War.

In sum, whatever qualifications to the idea of *laissez-faire*
in microeconomic policy may have to be allowed (as discussed below), it is difficult not to argue that Britain had a
laissez-faire macroeconomic policy before 1914, and this has to
be taken into account in looking at what shaped those micro-
policies.

MARKETS

The arrival of free trade in the middle years of the nineteenth century meant the British government gave up trying to secure the domestic market for domestic producers. Of course, government efforts continued to secure access to foreign markets by negotiation of trade treaties or the imposition of free trade on Imperial possessions. But at home at least there was a level playing-field, even if it was generally assumed that the intrinsic competitiveness of the home team would more or less always secure victory in trade rivalry.

Significant doubts about British capacity to retain this dominance of the home market first emerged in the 1880s. This is not to say that previously everyone in Britain had been totally ignorant of the growth of trade rivals. In 1868 a Parliamentary Select Committee recorded that 'nearly every witness speaks of the extraordinarily rapid progress of the Continental nations of manufactures. . . .' (Select Committee 1868: III, 2) and similar fears were quite common in the third quarter of the century.

But the first sign at government level of significant fears of loss of home markets emerged in the 1880s with the appointment of a Royal Commission on the 'Depression of Trade and Industry'. The fears that led to this Commission were diverse and by no means all concerned with trends in trade competitiveness. Indeed the immediate cause seems to have been the result of a sharp slump in 1885 and the associated unemployment and unrest (Harris 1972). But it was also the result of a wider feeling of depression, evident to a degree since the collapse of the boom after the Franco-Prussian war (Supple 1990: 330–1).

Modern economic historians have denied the existence of a 'great depression', which is the phrase an older generation of historians used to describe the period 1873–96 (Saul 1985; Crafts *et al.* 1990). But whilst the case for seeing any economic unity during this period seems very weak, the contemporary perception of a pervasive malaise, partly related to growing competition in the home market, seems difficult to deny. The Royal Commission itself accepted that the idea of a general depression was extremely dubious, it being mainly a problem either of redistribution of income from producers (especially profit-takers) to consumers, or periodic unemployment, rather than a trend decline in output (C.4893, Majority Report, para. 55). But the very existence of the Royal Commission is testimony to the fears of the period.

So, however far in retrospect we are sceptical of the existence of a great depression, it seems hard to dispute that in the 1880s there were widespread worries about the performance of the British economy, and that a significant element in this was the fear of German competition, including in the home market (Hoffman 1964: ch. 2; Friedberg 1988: 30–45). The Royal Commission's Majority Report suggested that 'we are beginning to feel the effects of foreign competition in quarters where our trade formerly enjoyed a practical monopoly . . . the increasing severity of this competition is especially noticeable in the case of Germany . . . in every quarter of the world the perseverance and enterprise of the Germans are making themselves felt . . .' (C.4893: paras. 74–5).

In this period from the 1880s right through to the First World War the primary worry about British markets was their loss to German competition. Periodically these fears come to the surface in scares, the best known being that in 1896. This was manifested most obviously in the big response to a series of *Times* newspaper articles (later a book) by E. E. Williams on the theme 'Made in Germany'. This attempted to demonstrate the worrying extent to which German goods had penetrated the British market. Williams invited the British middle classes to investigate the origins of goods they consumed: 'Roam the house over, and the fateful mark [i.e. "Made in Germany"] will greet you at every turn, from the piano in your drawing room to the mug on your kitchen dresser, blazoned though it be with *Present from Margate*' (Williams 1896/1973: 11).

Williams, like many who publicized worries about German competition, advocated a policy response of protection, or as it was commonly called in the 1880s and 1890s, Fair Trade. The strategy of the Fair Traders was to call for tariffs which were then to be used as bargaining weapons to get reductions in tariffs in other countries. Fair Traders were effective enough to be one reason for the setting-up of the Royal Commission on Depression. The majority of that Commission came out against any change in Britain's trade policy, arguing that whilst some ground had been lost to competitors such as Germany, the trends in trade were still expansionary. This line was supported by government officials, most notably Robert Giffen, who pointed out that whilst Britain might have a deficit in visible trade, it more than offset this by its insurance and shipping earnings and the returns on past investment (Giffen 1900).

Despite these worries policy changed little. The successive Liberal and Conservative regimes of the 1880s and 1890s maintained what Platt (1968: 104) has called a 'peculiar and sustained' official optimism about trade and economic conditions generally. Platt stresses the prevalence of committed free traders amongst civil servants in explaining this lack of policy responses, but it is clear that there was also a strong commitment by most politicians to free trade, even if that was weakening, especially in the Conservative Party, by 1900.

The Conservative Lord Salisbury, Prime Minister from 1895, seems to have become intellectually sceptical about free trade, but political calculation kept him from following the protectionist path. Above all he feared the loss of support of the Liberal Unionists (those Liberals who had split with the party in 1886 over Gladstone's proposals for home rule in Ireland, but remained committed to free trade) if he took a protectionist tack (Friedberg 1988: 43). Thus he successfully rode out Joseph Chamberlain's first attempt at combining British protection with the encouragement of Empire trade by the device of a 'British Zollverein', first proposed in 1896. Partly because of the concurrent trade depression this proposal made some impact, but it ran up against both Salisbury's political calculations and opposition from those (White) Empire countries which wanted tariffs against British goods to protect their own nascent industries. The campaigns of the 1880s and 1890s against free trade failed, though they were to be strongly revived after 1900 (see Ch. 2). The fears expressed about British trade therefore had very little direct effect on government policy. One view of the success of German competition was that it was based on sharp practices such as dumping, forging trade marks, conniving at violations of the Merchandise Marks Act, copying English models, and purposely striking at English trades by exporting prison-made goods (Hoffman 1964: 234). But there is no evidence that these factors were significant in the rise in German competition. Such fears had led to the Merchandise Marks Act 1862 and 1887, but as the previously cited quote from E. E. Williams suggests, the correct marking of German goods did not seem to stop British consumers buying them.

Some greater encouragement was given to the Consular Service at least to provide information for British traders and producers about foreign conditions, though it was not accepted that such people should actively promote British trade. In sum, before 1900, though scares and proposals for policy changes were plentiful, government action to secure markets for British goods was almost non-existent. Farrer's conclusion on the state's role in his *The State in Relation to Trade* of 1883 would have held for the end of the century: 'its chief praise in relation to trade has been that it has left as much scope as possible to the free energy and self-interest of its people' (181).

PROFITS

Government policy on profitability before 1900 may be quickly summarized. In line with the view that income should be left to 'fructify' in the hands of its recipients, governments imposed no taxes explicitly on corporate profits. In addition, for most of the time income tax paid on dividends was, like all income tax, negligible in impact. The pattern of taxation partly reflected the low overall level of tax to match the low level of public expenditure. But in addition it reflected the view that all citizens should pay taxes, so that a large proportion of Victorian tax revenue was raised from taxes on the consumables of the poor—tea, sugar, and alcohol most notably. Even those taxes which fell on income and capital were flat-rate, in line with the Gladstonian idea that progressive taxation was akin to confiscation (Roseveare 1969: 191). Only in 1894 were the first progressive death duties introduced, reflecting a growing concern with the incidence of taxation, especially of indirect taxes (Rees 1921: 170–1).

Within this general framework of low and mainly flat-rate taxation, the idea of taxing profits seems never to have been advocated, let alone implemented. Whatever else governments did for companies, they cannot be accused of discouraging private profit accumulation by the tax regime. On the other hand, one of the features of the 'great depression' was that profits fell. Feinstein calculates that the share of profits in the National Income fell from almost 30 per cent in the early 1870s to under 23 per cent twenty years later (cited in Saul 1985: 41–2). This fall underlay many of the industrial worries of the period, manifested in, for example, the setting-up of the Royal Commission of 1886. But it did not lead to any government action.

THE EFFICIENCY OF LABOUR

The classical economists, as we have noted, were divided on many instances of public intervention, including education. Broadly, however, the case for public regulation and provision of popular education was conceded as the nineteenth century progressed. The reasons were by no means entirely to do with notions of economic efficiency—for example some politicians linked the expansion of education to the need to 'educate our masters' in the face of the extension of the franchise. Also very important was the idea that education would make the Bible accessible to the masses. Before mid-century little was done by the state, partly because of the difficulties raised by the battle between the Church of England and Nonconformity, each of which was jealous of its own educational provision (Checkland 1983: 99–102). An annual parliamentary grant for school building was made from 1833, but basically elementary education was still regarded as a charitable activity. Following the Newcastle Report of 1862, and the founding of an Education Department in 1856, governmental concern with education grew, but its role continued to be one of monitoring and encouraging private effort until Forster's Act of 1870.

This act allowed for the setting-up of elected school boards where voluntary provision was deemed inadequate, supported by funds raised from local rates. However this Act was more a case of filling in the gaps rather than providing a wholly new national education system—not least because of the Church of England's decision to try to promote its own schools in competition with the Board Schools (Checkland 1983: 141–5). This provision at the elementary level was, of course, wholly separate from the provision for the moneyed classes in the so-called public schools. The Taunton Commission of 1868 reinforced the stark differences in educational provision with its notion of elementary, grammar, and public schools for the working, middle, and upper classes respectively (Evans and Summerfield 1990: 7–8).

In 1880 elementary schooling was made compulsory, and the minimum age for leaving was raised to eleven in 1893 and twelve in 1899; in 1891 the small charges previously made to parents were ended. From the 1890s school boards increasingly turned their attention to secondary education, but by the turn of the century there was growing disquiet with the inadequacy of the system. In 1899 a Board of Education was established to take over the Education Department's duties, but the major change was signalled by the Education Act of 1902 (Checkland 1983: 235–7).

How far this slow expansion of state provision mattered in economic terms is a matter of great disagreement. First, the scale of private provision is very much disputed. Much traditional literature in this area sssumed that in the absence of a large state role, provision would be thin and uneven. How far this was the case has been disputed, most notably by West (e.g. 1965, 1975, 1983). Similarly, revisionists have claimed that the Sunday schools of nineteenth-century Britain were centres for genuine education, not just for narrowly focused bible reading, and they probably involved 75 per cent of working-class children by 1851 (Pollard 1990: 164). Certainly it seems clear that the working class were not simply passive recipients of Church- or state-financed education, but at least amongst the artisan elements were able to shape educational provision to their own ends. This was, unsurprisingly, most striking where tax-funding was combined with local democracy, as with the board schools, which in many cases created 'central schools' with high levels of provision relatively immune from what was often a dogmatic central government attitude that the 3 Rs should be the staple diet of popular education (Vlaeminke 1990; Bailey 1990).

This leads on to the second issue in the relation between state provision and economic success: the content of the curriculum. To late-twentieth-century minds it is very difficult to comprehend the extent to which educational provision in the last century was dominated not by issues of the content of a secular curriculum but by religious and moral questions. So it would certainly be an error to suppose that the economic effects of education were ever the dominant element in policy-making on education in this period. It is also unclear what the most economically effective type of education is, in particular, how far should education for the working class be focused on basic educational skills, and how far on technical competences. This is an issue which continues to divide those who discuss education in poor countries today.

For both private and state-aided elementary education in the 1800s, most of the curriculum was taken up with basic skills alongside a large dollop of moral and religious indoctrination. Training in specific technical skills was still largely organized around apprenticeship. In the 1890s, for example, only 10 per cent of skilled engineering workers were affected by formal training (McClelland 1990: 31). Apprenticeship was an area almost wholly untouched by state regulation, its persistence being the result of its perceived advantages to employers and unions, with problematic implications for efficiency.

The state-financed local initiatives in education after the 1870 Act do seem to have led in a significant number of cases to the provision of technical education in a broad sense to the working and lower-middle classes, especially in some of the major industrial cities (Vlaeminke 1990). Similarly, it is becoming appreciated in the historical literature that the traditional stories about the grammar and public-school curriculum being almost entirely classics-based has been much exaggerated. Whilst no one doubts that the classics were important in British schools, this was offset to a significant extent by the growth of the natural sciences and engineering (Pollard 1990: 169-71). This means the common and unfavourable contrasts with German schools are overdone, and usually based on major misunderstandings about the German school system (Berghoff 1990).

A broadly similar point may be made about the curriculum of universities. Whilst Oxford remained committed to the classics as the gentleman's education, in Cambridge and especially in the provincial universities teaching in the sciences and engineering grew rapidly in the last decades of the nineteenth-century; as with the board schools this was partly a response to local perceptions of the kinds of education desired (Sanderson 1988). Overall, recent research has tended to undercut the story that British nineteenth-century education consisted either of the 3 Rs and religion at the lowest level and the classics plus religion elsewhere.

Technical education (in the wider sense) made substantial advances, albeit in a patchy and incoherent fashion (Wiener 1985 represents the old view; compare with Pollard 1990: ch. 3).

One of the reasons for these advances was undoubtedly a perception of loss of economic competitiveness. For example, money from the Great Exhibition of 1851 was used to supplement and aid voluntary efforts in broadly technical areas under the Science and Arts Department grants scheme of 1852, though its main function was as an examining rather than a teaching body. In 1868 a Select Committee on Scientific Instruction received much evidence that the progress in manufacturing of Continental countries was due,

besides other causes, to the scientific training of the proprietors and managers in France, Switzerland, Belgium and Germany, and to the elementary instruction which was universal amongst the working population of Germany and Switzerland . . . the facilities for acquiring a knowledge of theoretical and applied science are incomparably greater on the Continent than in this country, and that such knowledge is based on an advanced state of secondary education (Select Committee 1868: III, 2).

But despite such warnings, it was not until the 1880s that the worries expressed by various public bodies led to state action. The Royal Commission on Depression Majority Report (para. 97) remarked

In the matter of education we seem to be particularly deficient as compared with some of our foreign competitors; and this remark applies not only to what is usually called technical education, but to the ordinary commercial education which is required in mercantile houses, and especially the knowledge of foreign languages.

Such worries led to the Technical Instruction Act of 1889, 'the first significant state initiative in this area', though like so much Victorian educational reform, permissive rather than compulsory (Macdonagh 1975: 512). Nevertheless it did lead to a significant expansion of local technical colleges and technical education in schools. Thus, whilst Macdonagh (512–13) is right to say that Britain in this period lacked a national policy for science and technology, at the level of educational provision in these areas much did change in the late nineteenth century. Government had responded, if in a limited way, to the widespread belief that industrial competition was in part at least competition between the proficiency of workers based on their educational attainments. The key problem by the end of the century was caused more by employers' reception of the technically trained than by their inadequate supply (Sanderson 1988).

Technical education was developed primarily for efficiency reasons, and some developments in general education had a similar basis. But plainly there were many other reasons for the growth of the state's role in schooling in the nineteenth century. Education is always a form of social engineering, and this was often explicit in the debates around the reforms, such as that of 1870. Robert Lowe famously supported such reform saying 'we must educate our masters', and this view of education for the working class as a means of ensuring that they used their expanding enfranchisement 'responsibly' was a commonplace after the 1867 Reform Act. More generally education was about 'moralizing the poor', attempting to inculcate forms of behaviour and thinking deemed appropriate by the combination of State and Church which dominated policy-making. In part these morals may be seen as functional for economic efficiency, in so far as they aimed at inculcating habits of sobriety, punctuality, hard work, and thrift. But it would be grossly reductive of a highly complex phenomenon to suggest that the character of nineteenth-century educational expansion could be condensed to such a single function. (Equally, it would be wrong to exaggerate the success of such efforts, or to imagine the working class as a passive object of policy. The working class was neither putty in the hands of the educators, nor, in substantial part, itself indifferent to the potential benefits from such values for its own ends and ambitions.)

State intervention in the nineteenth-century labour-market went much wider than education. Indeed it is in many ways quite inappropriate to speak of intervention in a pre-existing market, and better to speak of the creation of a market which was therefore always in part the consequence of state action as much as an object of regulation. Symbolic of the early nineteenth-century drive to create a free labour-market were the Poor Law Amendment Act of 1834 and the Combination Acts of 1799 and 1800. The first of these was supposed to embody the key principle that relief could only be given to the able-bodied within the workhouse, thus destroying any notion that incomes would be provided which might provide a 'floor' to the wage-level. This was paralleled by the ending of a host of legal regulations concerning wage-levels, many of which had fallen into disuse, but which remained symbols of the idea that wages should have a moral and hence statutory basis, not be purely the result of market forces. Such notions of a moral economy in conflict with the laws of politics were to remain a potent basis for popular discontent in the nineteenth century (and arguably in the twentieth). But at the legislative level a clear position eventually emerged, that at least as far as adult males were concerned, the state should not intervene in wage determination. This, once established, was to remain the position throughout the nineteenth century, with only the minor exception of the Fair Wage resolution of 1891, which enforced the local minimum wage on government contracts (Phelps-Brown 1959: 197–209).

The Combination Acts were second only to the 1834 Act in symbolizing the opposition to interference in the labour-market, not by the public provision of relief in this case, but by trade unions. As with the 1834 Act, we must distinguish legislative intent from outcomes, but the intent clearly was to allow wages to find their market level by preventing interference in contracts between employers and individual workers.

Just as the 1834 Act was to a degree undermined by local action (see e.g. Foster 1974), so the Combination Acts could not prevent trade unionism, especially in the skilled trades (Wrigley 1982a: 135–8). The acceptance of trade unions as legitimate bodies was signalled to a limited extent by the repeal of the Combination Acts in 1824, though other anti-union legislation survived (Hunt 1981: 197–9). Much more important was the legislation of the 1870s, which gave some legal basis for strikes, most importantly by allowing trade-union officers some exemption from claims for damages for inducing breaches of contract. However, this legislative position (as was to happen several times in the twentieth century) fell foul of the judges, and by the end of the century 'the courts had made some strikes unlawful, and all perilous' (Phelps-Brown 1959: 191). Only in 1906 (see Ch. 2) was a new settlement achieved.

The legislative abstention from interference in wage-bargaining extended to an absence of provision for any statutory arbitration. Provision for such arbitration on a voluntary basis was on the statute-book for most of the nineteenth century, but in the 1890s when the issue was widely discussed, an Act was passed (in 1896) which still allowed arbitration only if both parties agreed. However, conciliation was possible at the request of only one party, and the 1896 Act did herald a big expansion in state attempts at such conciliation (Wrigley 1982*a*: 138–43).

This abstention by the state was part of a whole system of what came to be called 'voluntarism' in industrial relations. This voluntarism was not just grounded in the *laissez-faire* ideology prevalent in parliament and governments, but also reflected the predominant view of employers and trade unions, who generally favoured local bargains outside any political or legal system. This attitude is quite apparent from the Royal Commission on Labour of 1894–6 where even the trade unionists focused their attention on broad issues of social re-organization, not on the state's role in industrial relations (C.7421, Minority Report).

As with any general discussion of *laissez-faire*, this picture of the state creating the conditions for a free market and then abstaining from intervention needs to be qualified. At the very same time as Acts such as those of 1800 and 1834 were being passed a series of Factory Acts were passed which provided some protection for women and children, primarily concerning hours of work. Although doubtfully effective until well into the century, these Acts at least symbolically bounded the domain of *laissez-faire* to adult males. Not until the Coal Mines Act of 1908 were men's hours brought within the domain of state regulation (Florence 1957: 51–68).

The nineteenth-century accumulation of regulations under the Factory Acts reached its pre-war culmination in the Factory Act of 1901, largely a consolidating measure, which in Clapham's (1938: 431) words 'was the last great Factory and Workshop Act of the era; and its fine-meshed, wide-cast, and "bureaucratic" net was what the men of the day were learning to use or tolerate, if not always approve'.

THE EFFICIENCY OF CAPITAL

Technical training of labour remained largely a responsibility of individual firms via the apprenticeship system in the late nineteenth century. Similarly, most capital expenditure by firms was raised from internal sources (i.e. ploughed-back profits) rather than from formal capital markets. This was the position throughout the Victorian era, and showed little sign of change over that era (Cottrell 1980).

A large proportion of British investment in the latter years of the nineteenth century went into foreign investment, mostly by long-term issues in the London money market; but of the sums invested at home at most 20 per cent was channelled through the formal markets (Paish 1951). Perhaps only 10 per cent of net investment in British industry was financed through the London capital market in the period around the end of the century, though provincial stock exchanges were often locally more important (Thomas 1973: ch. 6).

How far this lack of linkage between British industry and London's capital markets was due to failings in that market has long been debated (for a recent survey, see Pollard 1990: 91–100). It seems hard to dispute that the London market was geared up for foreign issues and that its institutional structure reflected that fact. On the other hand evidence of unfulfilled demand for capital from British industry is sparse in this period (though intrinsically hard to document). Large issues for industrial purposes could be successfully made—providing the returns were high. Smaller issues were proportionately more expensive. Issues on provincial stock markets were a cheaper alternative, but their command of resources was limited. 'The firm with a local or regional reputation only, has therefore in the main been thrown back on its own resources if it wanted to grow: ploughed-back profits, mortgaged land, the entrepreneur's own savings and those of his own family and friends, or taking in money partners' (Pollard 1990: 95). Whatever the truth of the situation, there is little evidence of contemporary discontent by industrialists with the capital markets. Certainly the issue does not figure much in contemporary complaints about the British economy, which were increasingly aired before select committees and royal commissions. Even more certainly, this was not an area regulated by the government except by means of the Companies Acts.

As already noted, the coming of general limited liability in mid-century had been controversial. It was also taken up surprisingly little by industrial companies, despite the view that such

legislation was necessary precisely to finance larger-scale investment from investors likely to be scared-off by unlimited liability.
This was in part because of the poor record of such companies—
over 30 per cent of those formed between 1856 and 1883 ended
in insolvency, many within their first five years. It was also
reduced in its appeal to investors by the common use of partly
paid shares, which in effect made the liability less limited. So by
the 1880s 'perhaps only 5 to 10 per cent of those larger-scale
businesses which might have been expected to benefit from
outside investment had in fact adopted limited liability company
status' (Hannah 1983: 19).

This proportion rose quite rapidly in the 1880s and 1890s, but
even by 1900 the majority of industrial companies remained
private, with unlimited liability for investors. Government policy
on the Companies Acts does not seem to have been shaped
directly by a desire to expand the use of the form, and so to
encourage investment. Rather, the focus was on reducing fraud,
especially by company promoters who were often seen to have
gulled a naïve investing public (e.g. Select Committee 1877),
hence the general tendency of changes to company legislation to
be focused on tighter rules concerning disclosure in order to
reduce the scope for fraud on investors. Presumably such reforms aided the growth of the public limited liability form by
making it more attractive, but it cannot be said that government
played more than a permissive role in what was in any case a
slow growth of this kind of company.

THE EFFICIENCY OF COMPANY STRUCTURE AND ORGANIZATION

Governments in the Victorian period took little action in regulating how companies behaved, with the limited exception of
preventing fraud, as outlined in the previous section. However,
there was towards the end of the century increasing interest in
how far and in what ways the growth of monopolies and trusts
should be responded to by government. Whilst the main concern
in this section is this issue of the short-term response of government to the rise of monopolies and trusts, it is important to note
that this rise was seen by many writers as having very widespread

implications. Writers like Hobson (1894), Macrosty (1901), and the Webbs (1902) saw the rise of the trust as signalling a whole new phase in the development of capitalist industry. Macrosty (1901: 12), fairly typically, saw them as superseding a previous competitive phase of capitalism by something new: 'After a century of competition we find that a new motive is gripping the industrial world, the desire to put an end to competition while maintaining the private ownership and direction of industry.'[3]

Macrosty, again typically of many writers in this period, saw trusts and combinations as involving a higher, more efficient form of economic organization, but one whose benefits could be offset by their capacity of monopolistic exploitation of the consumer. From this could be derived what was to become a staple of socialist (including Leninist) argument in the twentieth century: 'The problem is, how to secure the benefits of combination withouts its disadvantages, and to this there is only one solution, the public ownership of monopolies' (Macrosty 1901: 283).

Such an iconoclastic view of the trusts was not typical, though it contributed significantly to the 'national efficiency' debates of the early 1900s (see Ch. 2). The orthodox economists like Marshall, and the governments of the late nineteenth-century were much less worried about the trusts as a general phenomena, though in particular fields concern was expressed and action taken. One monopoly which has always been the object of legislative attention was the railways. These had been regulated as to their fares and other parts of their operations from their inception in the 1830s and 1840s, and they continued to be an example of an industry whose monopolistic character led to periodic public pressure for the state to protect the consumer, though such pressure never achieved the intensity found, for example, in the United States.

In 1873 the Railway and Canal Commission was set up as a regulatory body for the industry, mainly concerned with rates and amalgamations. Railway rates were a significant complaint at the time of the 1886 Commission on Depression, and in 1888 a new act was passed which imposed maximum charges, strengthened

---

[3] Compare the Webbs (1902: xxi): 'the advent of the Trust almost necessarily implies an improvement in industrial organization, measured, that is to say, by the diminution of the efforts and sacrifices involved in production'.

by a further act of 1894 which put the onus on the companies to justify any rates above those prevailing at the end of 1892 (Ashworth 1960: 124–5; Parris 1965).

But Britain noticeably lacked any parallel to the Sherman Act of 1890, with its vigorous legislative approach to the perceived threat of the trusts across the broad spectrum of American industry. There were several reasons for this. First, the evidence available at the time suggested that whilst accelerating, the movement to monopoly was much slower in Britain than the United States. Second, the populist mainly agrarian politics of the USA found little echo in the predominantly urban working-class society of Britain, where the typical lower-class individual was a wage-worker not a small farmer concerned to protect his interests against 'big capital'. This was linked to the common socialist political view, noted above, that combinations were not inherently bad, indeed positively desirable as efficient forms of organization, if only they could be wrested from private hands.

The orthodoxy amongst both mainstream economists and ruling politicians was that the trust problem was not serious in the UK, and that its importance in Germany and the USA derived mainly from their tariffs and government meddling generally (Williams 1990: 104). Hence trusts were often argued to be just one more problem which arose from too much government intervention, rather than a reason for increasing such intervention. Overall, in Britain it can be said that by the end of the nineteenth century government action had made little direct impact on company organization, and there is no evidence that such organization had come to be regarded as an area where government should have a role.

STATE CAPACITY AND STATE ACHIEVEMENTS

By twentieth-century standards the British state by 1900 was a weak state. Central government was small both in terms of expenditure and personnel. Much government was done by local bodies, especially in the social welfare and education fields. As noted above, in the case of education those local agencies might well have a more progressive stance on areas like technical education than central government, but this inevitably meant that good provision was patchy and underfinanced. In many ways it is a misnomer to talk of a national education system before 1900—there was not much system and most of the provision was locally initiated and organized.

On trade matters things were different. Central government had long been concerned with trade, and this is shown by the fact that this is one area where decent statistics are available over a long historical period. But if the main agency, the Board of Trade, was in some ways well informed about British trade, and to a limited extent other parts of the economy, it was certainly not geared up to do much to shape the behaviour of that economy. It was small, and much of its approach was geared to minimalist assumptions about its functions. It slowly took on new responsibilities, especially on labour issues, in the late nineteenth century (Davidson 1985: ch. 2) but its character was not fundamentally altered.

As regards company structure and organization, apart from company law, which was assumed to have a largely permissive role, there was no attempt by government to intervene. In this particular sense *laissez-faire* may be said to have still been the ruling doctrine. However, as noted above, the consciousness of growing industrial rivalry and competition had touched political debate, and whilst this had rather little effect on policy, it would be a mistake to believe that the general perception of the government's role had remained unaltered since mid-century. On the Left socialist critics were taking an almost wholly new positive view of the possibilities of state action. On the Right the consciousness of a country and empire under strain had undermined the previous faith in the efficacy of unguided private enterprise. Whilst the centre had so far held, it was to come under even greater pressure at the beginning of the new century.

Further Reading

Coats, A. W. (1971), *The Classical Economists and Economic Policy*, London.

Evans, E., and Summerfield, P. (1990) (eds.), *Technical Education and the State*, Manchester.

Friedberg, A. L. (1988), *The Weary Titan*, Princeton, NJ.

Hannah, L. (1983), *The Rise of the Corporate Economy*, 2nd edn., London.

Macrosty, H. W. (1901), *Trusts and the State*, London.

Pollard, S. (1990), *Britain's Prime and Britain's Decline*, London: ch. 4.

2

1900–1914: National Efficiency and the Enterprise

INTRODUCTION

History did not stop at the end of the nineteenth century and start afresh in 1900. Nevertheless, beginning a book about the government and industrial efficiency at that date has a logic beyond convention and convenience. At the turn of the century Britain was at war, and as is so often the case war exposes the weaknesses of an economy and society as few other events can. On this occasion the Boer war, and especially the early defeats sustained by Britain in that war, served to crystallize perceptions of weaknesses and proposals to remedy them. Of course, if elements are to be crystallized they already exist, and the watershed aspect of the Boer war should not be exaggerated. But coming on top of two or three decades of growing worries about the strength of Britain's industrial economy, the shock of war led to a highly illuminating debate, and some little action, to try and address the economy's perceived deficiencies.

CONTEXT

The Boer war occurred in the context of a growing debate about Britain's relative power and place in the world. Friedberg (1988) has examined this debate in great and illuminating detail along four dimensions of power—economic, financial (i.e. budgetary), naval, and military. These, he persuasively argues, were the four connected but separable aspects of the 'great debate' that raged in Britain, especially between the years 1895 and 1905. The concern here is with the first of these.

As in the debates of the 1870s and 1880s, the focus of attention was Britain's alleged trading decline, especially in the face of

German and to a lesser extent American competition. Just as in 1896 Williams published his *Made in Germany*, so in 1901 a series of popular journalistic articles were published as a book entitled *The American Invader*, similarly aimed at rousing Britain from its alleged apathy because 'American brains, enterprise and energy are today ousting British traders in the battle for commerce in many lands' (Mackenzie 1901: 11).

But if alleged trading decline always remained central to the debate, the war brought into focus a range of other concerns about the efficiency of British society which were either directly economic in character or had economic ramifications. One of the most important of these was a concern with the physical health of the armed forces and by extension the populace as a whole. This worry led to the establishment of the Interdepartmental Committee on Physical Deterioration (1904), which is a famous landmark in linking an immediate policy concern with long-term worries of a Social Darwinist flavour about the 'quality' of the British race (Jones 1971; Harris 1972; Searle 1971: 60–70). It is of note that Rowntree's pioneering work on poverty of the same period defined that concept in relation to physical *efficiency*, and emphasized the importance of such efficiency for both military and industrial capacity (Rowntree 1902: 256–62).

Linked to the quality of the British race was the issue of education:

the blunders of the British army in South Africa seemed to be the consequence, not merely of the defective system of *military* education, but to reflect deficiencies in the mental training of a people incapable of reasoning, arguing or applying the 'scientific method' to the practical problems of life (Searle 1971: 73).

The organization of education raised issues about government capacity generally, and the Edwardian period saw a rising debate about the effectiveness of the British state, at local, national, and imperial level. One particular area of disquiet was the state's role *vis-à-vis* science. 'Science' here means not only the natural sciences, seen in a simple way as the basis of technological advance and efficiency, but also an approach to all aspects of social life. The war seemed to reinforce those views which saw British society as decadent, amateurish, and giving too little role for expertise and the expert (Searle 1971: 83–95).

As will be evident this range of concerns did not suddenly emerge freshly minted on the day after Ladysmith, nor did they form a tightly focused philosophy and programme of action. Nevertheless they did, temporarily at least, cohere into what has been called the *Quest for National Efficiency* (Searle 1971), which forms an important landmark in the development of British thought on politics and the economy.

It is important to note that the 'Efficients' who supported this movement were not concerned with economic efficiency in the way that was to become commonplace in late twentieth-century Britain. Their notion of efficiency was both less and more than such later notions. Less, because they were not much concerned with such issues as production and corporate organization which we have come to believe matter for industrial efficiency. On the other hand, they saw efficiency as embracing standards of health, physique, and the mental training of labour. That this was a widespread perspective, not limited to the Efficients, is suggested by Marshall's views (1899: 111): 'We have next to consider the conditions on which depend health and strength, physical mental and moral. They are the basis of industrial efficiency, on which the production of material wealth depends'.[1] In addition, the Efficients were concerned with general questions of state capacities which, together with the labour issues, implied a much broader agenda for efficiency than was to be apparent in other phases of the debate on Britain's economic decline.

The focus on the quality of the worker and the race also implied a considerable political ambiguity in the Efficients' approach. If that approach implied the need for policies to raise the quality of life of the poor then it could be seen as part of a socialist programme of state amelioration. This indeed was the basis on which many Fabian socialists, most notably the Webbs, came to embrace the Efficients' approach. Their programme of the National Minimum embraced minimum standards of wages, housing, and education. As such it fitted both the traditional socialist desire to raise working-class living standards, but equally

---

[1] This is not, of course, to deny that Marshall was interested in issues of industrial organization. Indeed of all the great names in economics probably none has been more concerned precisely with that subject. But even in his discussion of business management, Marshall put a great emphasis on the quality of the individuals involved, rather than on, say, systems of management (Marshall 1899: ch. 12).

as a basis for a more efficient labour-force for the national economy. Similarly, reform of the state apparatus could be seen as both a traditional socialist claim as well as something necessary to improve the efficiency of Britain as a world power in a competitive international system (Webb 1901*a*).

For Fabians like Webb these two elements are very difficult to distinguish. This was partly because in some respects they accepted the Social Darwinist notion of a battle between states in which only the fittest would survive. In 1891, for example, Webb indicted individualism for leading to Britain 'losing the race struggle' (1891: 378), and similar sentiments are very clear in, for example, a famous article by Webb ten years later which linked the claim for a national minimum to the need for reform 'to ensure the rearing of an Imperial race' (Webb 1901*b*: 375; Semmel 1960: 64–77).

The Quest for National Efficiency also embraced many of a clearly non-Socialist disposition, whose normal political home would be the Liberal and Conservative Parties. But what united these disparate positions above all was an opposition to the *laissez-faire*, non-interventionist state associated with traditional British liberalism and radicalism, and which it was claimed had been exposed in all its inadequacies by the failings of the Boer war. They saw these policies as causing Britain's Empire to be threatened and putting its very survival as a great power in doubt.

These, of course, were exactly the same worries as those entertained by the tariff reformers. Having lost the battles of the 1880s and 1890s the opponents of free trade found new opportunities at the beginning of the twentieth century to re-open the debate. The immediate opportunity was presented by the imposition of a corn duty in 1902 as a way of raising money to help pay for the war. Joseph Chamberlain saw this as an opportunity to push for a policy of Imperial preference (not the Imperial Zollverein of previous decades). This opportunity soon disappeared as the duty was abolished in 1903. But in that same year Chamberlain, like the Efficients taking advantage of the doubts raised about the British polity and economy by the war, launched his tariff reform campaign which was to be a central political debate down to 1906 (Zebel 1967; Rempal 1972; Green 1985).

Tariff reform and national efficiency drew upon similar discontents. Both can be seen as hostile responses to the failure of existing policies to give sufficient weight to the development of the national economy. Both attempted to grapple with the urgency of social reform as well as national power: the Efficients saw efficiency as embracing working-class improvement, whilst tariff reformers attempted to link the tariff revenues to the financing of social amelioration (Green 1985). But politically they were still divided on the issue of protection. Ultimately the Liberal Unionists who headed the Efficients found that their allegiance to free trade overrode all other issues, and the Efficients' idea of a policy alliance across traditional political divides evaporated as Chamberlain's campaign took off.

MARKETS

For the tariff reformers the crucial issue was the market—the protection of the British market against the foreigner and the need for privileged access to Imperial markets as part of a system of Imperial preference. For the tariff reformers (though not the Efficients) trade performance was the key issue in Britain's success and failure as a great power.

This focus on trade as the measure of economic success partly reflected the fact that figures on trade were the only systematic official data available on the performance of the economy, but even these were highly deficient by later standards, recording only visible items and thus heavily biasing the picture (Friedberg 1988: 54–68). As in the previous period there was a complex debate about the trends in the figures and their significance. Significance was very much in the eye of the beholder. This was especially the case where the decline of particular sectors of the economy was identified. Was this a sign of all-round problems or merely the expected, even desirable, consequence of shifting comparative advantage? (See e.g. Giffen 1900.)

Informed observers usually conceded some loss of trading competitiveness in the new century. A. W. Flux, for example, who periodically discussed the issue for the *Economic Journal*, wrote in 1894 that 'the evidence adducible in proof of a balance of loss of trade due to superior competing power on the part of our rivals receives absolutely no support from the official returns which furnish us with our figures'. By 1904, however, he accepted that trade to the United States had been hit by tariffs, and that the trade of the United States, France, and Germany was expanding faster than that of Britain (Flux 1894, 1904).

For policy-making it is contemporary perceptions that matter, of course, not retrospective analyses. In the case of trade it would seem to be the case that there was a wider agreement after than before 1900 about Britain's declining competitive power. Even those who defended the status quo were less likely than before to argue that all was well with British industry (Friedberg 1988: 73–4). Retrospective analyses bear out the view that in foreign-trade share Britain was losing out, though the trend rate of growth of trade was no slower than in the later 1800s (Tables 2.1, 2.2). It is important to note that the overall balance of payments position remained incredibly strong. Invisible items like profits and dividends, shipping, and insurance easily offset the visible trade deficit to allow an unprecedented level of capital export in this period, rising above the level of domestic investment in the peak years at the end of the first decade of the twentieth century (Table 2.3).

TABLE 2.1. *Britain's share of world trade 1860–1913*

	Exports of Manufactured goods (%)
1860	25.1
1870	24.0
1880	22.4
1891–5	18.0
1901–5	16.4
1913	12.2

Source: Pollard (1990), p. 6.

TABLE 2.2. *Growth of domestic exports at current prices, 1856–65 to 1907–13* (% p.a.)

1856–67	4.95
1865–74	3.12
1874–83	0.56
1883–90	0.89
1890–1901	1.08
1901–7	5.50
1907–13	4.96

Source: Pollard (1990), p. 4.

TABLE 2.3. *Britain's balance of payments 1900–14 (£m.)*

	Visible balance	Invisible balance	Current balance
1900	−129	+163	+ 34
1901	−136	+155	+ 19
1902	−141	+165	+ 24
1903	−144	+187	+ 43
1904	−140	+192	+ 52
1905	−118	+206	+ 88
1906	−106	+227	+121
1907	− 84	+246	+162
1908	− 93	+243	+150
1909	−111	+253	+142
1910	− 96	+270	+174
1911	− 75	+279	+204
1912	− 94	+297	+203
1913	− 82	+317	+235
1914	−120	+254	+134

Source: Feinstein (1972), T. 82.

Little information was available to contemporaries on output and income, certainly as regards any comparative data. Statements on the condition of particular industries were commonplace, but even more than with trade were subject to tendentious manipulation and highly questionable interpretation. Retrospectively we do know that Britain was losing ground in terms of both share of aggregate output and in particular industries. In aggregate terms, and wholly unsurprisingly, Britain's share of world manufacturing was falling, as shown in Table 2.4.

TABLE 2.4. *Percentage shares of world manufacturing production of various countries, 1870–1913*

	USA	Germany	Britain	France
1870	23.3	13.2	31.8	10.3
1881–5	28.6	13.9	26.6	8.6
1896–1900	30.1	16.6	19.5	7.1
1906–10	35.3	15.9	14.7	6.4
1913	35.8	15.7	14.0	6.4

Source: League of Nations (1945), p. 13.

Ground was also lost in particular industries, in the sense of share of world production and trade, though absolute levels of both continued to expand. Thus the tariff reformers tended to exaggerate the problems of the economy, as when Chamberlain claimed that 'our export trade has been practically stagnant for thirty years' (cited in Friedberg 1988: 70).

Chamberlain's challenge to free trade ultimately failed. The Conservatives, led by Balfour who had been converted to some kind of moderate protectionism, lost the 1906 General Election disastrously to the free-trade Liberal party. Whilst tariffs were not the only electoral issue, they do seem to have been the biggest reason for the anti-Conservative vote. Above all the presentation of the issue as a 'tax on food' seems to have ruined the tariff reformers chances (Rempal 1972).

But whilst free trade triumphed politically in 1906, its status was not as before. The Conservative Party had become a protectionist party, biding its time for a better opportunity to pursue the policy. (Its motives were largely related to a desire to raise revenue from tariffs to finance social reform without higher direct taxation.) Protectionism was undoubtedly gaining ground amongst industrialists, though the pattern of support was a complex one, and for many the key issue of party allegiance came before views on tariffs (Marrison 1983). Intellectually the argument for free trade also appeared less compelling than in the 1880s and 1890s. There was a much more general acceptance of a competitive problem even by those who rejected protection as a solution. Amongst the economists the case for free trade was put with notable moderation by the eminent. Both Marshall, and Pigou wrote on the issue, both coming to anti-protectionist conclusions, whilst accepting that some economic benefit might be achieved by judiciously arranged tariffs. However they believed that politically tariffs would encourage all kinds of 'pork-barrel' activity which was very unlikely to lead to the triumph of the public good (Marshall 1903/1926; Pigou 1903; Coats 1968).

Despite the weakening of the political, and intellectual sway of free trade, Britain's policies remained resolutely anti-protectionist until the First World War. But given the wide recognition that Britain's economy was not in the best of health, this meant all the more room at least for discussion of other remedies for those problems.[2]

---

[2] For an asessment of the likely effects of protectionism if it had been implemented see Cain (1979), and on the structure of British trade at this time, see Saul (1965).

PROFITS

Direct government regulation of profits by taxes or subsidies was no more apparent in the Edwardian than in the Victorian era. The general tenor of the fiscal system was shifting to a slightly more progressive basis, mainly for those on the highest incomes or with the greatest wealth, and direct taxes were becoming more prominent in overall tax income. But there was certainly no suggestion to treat companies as an appropriate object of taxation.

However, the Efficients' programme of a minimum wage enforced by statute where collective bargaining did not operate implied government action which might have a direct, and significant effect on profits. The idea of the minimum wage was not to redistribute profits to wages, but to give the worker sufficient income to be a healthy and hence efficient worker. It may be seen as one of the first versions of the 'efficiency wage hypothesis'—that wage levels may affect as well as reflect worker efficiency. The Fabian advocacy of the national minimum may be seen in part as a precursor of the 'high wage, high productivity' approach of later generations of socialists.

This was one area where legislation was passed. In 1908 the Trade Boards Act set up machinery for establishing minimum wages in a range of 'sweated' trades. The Liberal government's motives for this act were partly philanthropic but also embraced the idea of raising general living standards as part of a programme of increasing efficiency. The level of opposition by capitalists generally was small, presumably because of their unhappiness at being undercut by cheap labour in the sweated industries. The policy was not interpreted as a general attack on profits, and private property, and the evidence suggests that the claims of proponents of the Boards, that they would stimulate higher output, and therefore reduce neither profits nor employment seem to have been borne out (Sells 1923: pt. II, ch. 6). Interestingly, by being drawn into industrial issues by minimum wage legislation, government officials were placed in a position of offering advice on how to raise efficiency so that the wages could be afforded. They were placed in the position of industrial efficiency consultants, with some positive effects in generalizing best practice (Sells: 230–2).[3]

---

[3] Florence (1957: 64–7) cites this legislation as a nice example of where empirical evidence was almost entirely absent from the debate leading up to the

THE EFFICIENCY OF LABOUR

The Trade Boards Act was, then, in part about raising the efficiency of labour. Other measures concerned with the labour-market in this period may be seen in this light (Hay 1983; Whiteside 1979). The 1909 Labour Exchanges Act was not just about improving the mechanisms of the labour-market but was seen in part as about winnowing out the 'unemployables' as a prelude to restoring them to employability in a variety of ways (Harris 1972). Similarly, whilst the 1911 Unemployment and Health Insurance Act can be seen as a measure to relieve the suffering and maintain the health of workers, the unemployment provisions certainly aimed at keeping efficient the skilled worker in cyclical trades who might otherwise fall into inefficient casual labour (Harris 1977: chs. 5, 6). A similar gloss can be put on the Development Act of 1909, which provided for (small-scale) public works with the dual purpose of resource development, and employment maintenance. Welfare provision always carries with it elements of social control; it is always conditional on behaviour to some degree. It is unsurprising that the welfare legislation of the Edwardian period not only tried to increase the efficiency of the workforce by improving their physical quality, but also by seeking to 'reinforce industrial discipline, and the work ethic' (Davidson 1985: 16). In this it was no different from all subsequent welfare legislation.

Thus the Efficients' programme to some degree fused with that of the New Liberals, so that by the First World War the state had come to regulate the labour-market to an extent almost unimaginable half a century earlier. In addition to the measures noted above, there was also crucial legislation on industrial relations. The 1906 Trade Disputes Act established clearly the exemption from liability in tort for trade unionists engaged in a trade dispute, thus extending the principle first established in the 1870s and which has remained the basis of labour-disputes legislation in Britain to the present day. Whilst the 1906 Act does not have the significance attached to it by some writers (e.g. Hayek 1960) as marking the freeing of British unions from all

---

legislation, but was subsequently analysed in detail. This analysis seems to strongly support the case of the proponents of the minimum wage (Tawney 1914; Sells 1923).

legal restraint, it does emphasize the extent to which British industrial relations operated with a minimal degree of legal regulation (Wedderburn 1989).

However the sphere of action of the state in industrial relations was expanding in the period before the First World War. Most striking was the extension of legal regulation of hours and wages outside the peculiar conditions of the sweated trades into coal-mining. Where sweating, with its below subsistence wages, could be seen as inimical to proper competition and to the efficiency of workers, wages in coal-mining were above those in most manual occupations. The cause of the state's intervention under the Acts of 1908 and 1912 was straightforwardly to prevent industrial strife by forcing the employees to accede to the miners' claims. The minimum wage legislation of 1912 in particular can be seen as highly symbolic, Lloyd George going so far as to say that 'Asquith's declaration for a minimum wage sounded the death-knell of the Liberal Party in its old forms' (cited Wrigley 1982*a*: 149).

Central to the Efficients' programme was education. Rosebery, a leading Efficient but a committed free trader, asked 'How are we to fight these hostile tariffs? I believe we must fight them by a more scientific and adaptive spirit—by better education' (cited Friedberg 1988: 77). Education was also central to the programme of the Fabian national minimum, spearheaded by the Webbs: 'Sidney, and Beatrice more, and more became the advocates of "national", and, perhaps surprisingly "imperial efficiency" and they came to see education as the key instrument to that end' (Brennan 1975: 9). Sidney Webb was the Chairman of the London County Council Technical Education Committee (later Technical Education Board) from 1892 and increasingly urged the case for a new national policy on education. In a Fabian tract he said 'What that national well-being demands, and what we must insist upon, is that every child, dull or clever, rich or poor, should receive all the education requisite for the full development of its faculties. For every child, in every part of the country, at least a "national minimum" of education must be compulsorily provided' (Webb 1901*b*: 18).

For Webb, and the Efficients the question of education was intimately bound up with the issue of administrative reform. Education had always been primarily a local responsibility, but when the county and county borough councils were formed at the end of the 1880s the old school boards (like the poor law guardians) were left outside the new authorities. This, in the Efficients' view, led to administrative muddle which should be rectified by the subordination of education to the new authorities.

The 1902 Education Act brought into effect this change in administrative arrangements. Whether this had the effects suggested by Webb can be disputed. As noted in Chapter 1, some of the school boards had been very active in promoting high standards of technical education, and given the financial constraints on local authorities it is not obvious that giving them control of education necessarily encouraged a more ambitious approach (Searle 1971: 207–16).

The 1902 Act, as usual with education legislation, had no one origin, and much of the debate about it centred on the treatment of the church schools. But it is notable that when introducing it Balfour, the Prime Minister, contrasted the British system with that of rival states. 'Reasoning either from theory or from the example of America, or Germany, or France, or any other country which devotes itself to educational problems, I am forced to the conclusion that ours is the antiquated, the most ineffectual and the most wasteful method yet invented for providing a national education' (cited in Searle 1971: 213).

Whilst the reorganization of local authorities mainly affected elementary and secondary education, the Efficients were also involved in issues of higher education. Webb was, of course, the major initiator of the idea of the London School of Economics. He also played a wider role in the University of London, including aiding the creation of Imperial College, though here the prime mover was another Efficient, Rosebery. The Efficients did not have a philistine, Gradgrind attitude to education but they certainly wanted to see a modern curriculum with much less emphasis on the classics and more on commercial and technical subjects (Brennan 1975: chs. 5, 6). Such a view found wider support in the universities than many accounts of the alleged anti-business culture of British higher education would suggest (Winch 1990: 52–3).

In their concern with technical education the Efficients touched a national nerve. As in so many of the debates of this period the

German model was invoked, and the idea of the superiority of German technical education seems to have been widely shared. As Searle (1971: 74) notes, British backwardness in this came to be a staple of public speeches, 'Even members of the Royal Family began to make speeches on the subject: infallible proof that this viewpoint had attained the status of a platitude'.

The new local education committees did take some initiatives on technical education, but their main concern was with raising the quality of elementary education. But under the 1902 Act authorities were empowered to establish technical colleges and in some areas these did become flourishing sources of provision for both part-time and full-time students. At higher education level the growth of university provision outside Oxford and Cambridge and with a technological bias was notable. Between 1900 and 1910 the number of science and technology graduates tripled, from 378 to 1231 per annum. Most of these were in the provincial universities which had largely been founded to expand such scientific education. They also offered significant amounts of non-degree tuition in this area (Roderick and Stephens 1974).

Thus it was probably in education that the Efficient movement made its most direct and largest impact and came nearest to carrying through its programme of the national minimum. In part this reflected the fact that any direct government role in industrial research was almost inconceivable at this time, so an expansion of technical education was the nearest government could go to playing a role in technical change. (For the one exception to this, see the end of the section on Company Structure and Organization).

Of course, this governmental effort on training needs to be kept in perspective. Apprenticeship remained by far the most important route to skill acquisition in industry—there were around 340,000 apprentices in any one year in the early twentieth century, and numbers were probably increasing at least until 1914 (More 1980: ch. 5). The rise in technical education away from the place of work was particularly fast in London, where apprenticeship training seems to have been especially weak. Such education, overall, was more important to technical, and supervisory staff in this period than to ordinary manual workers. It was a well-recognized road to social mobility, 'a stepping stone out of the mill' (More 1980: ch. 10).

THE EFFICIENCY OF CAPITAL

In economic historiography the Edwardian period is perhaps most notable for the scale of capital exports from Britain, amounting to almost 10 per cent of national income at their peak, and in a few years exceeding the level of domestic investment (Feinstein 1990). The impact of this level of outflow on the British economy has long been a subject of intense debate (e.g. Pollard 1990: ch. 2). What is important in the current context is to record the absence of contemporary concern on any significant scale, let alone any attempt at regulation. The British economy to a significant extent had become a *rentier* state: 'Rome fell, Carthage Fell, Hindhead's turn will come' as George Bernard Shaw expressed this status in his play Major Barbara. On the eve of the First World War interest profits and dividends from abroad yielded directly 10 per cent of national income, leaving aside the indirect effects on other foreign receipts. There was no exchange control, Britain was an immensely rich country by the standards of the day, investment opportunities abroad were manifest, and British financial institutions were geared up to match British savings with foreign investment opportunities (Kennedy 1987: ch. 6).

The longer-term macroeconomic consequences of all this are not of concern here. But the scale of the capital flows does raise the question of how far it starved British industry of capital resources. Of course, in a neat neo-classical world of perfect information this could not happen. If demand for investible funds was unsatisfied this would bid up rates of return until demand was satisfied at the new equilibrium interest rate. In a world of particular national economies and institutions these effects would be nullified or at least weakened by different ways of calculating profits, and the institutions' specific criteria for lending. It is at least plausible that given the way that British financial institutions were geared up for foreign lending, the terms on which British industrial companies could borrow were unfavourable, though as usual most investment, it should be stressed, came from internal funds rather than banks or the stock market.

Kennedy (1987: 144–7) has argued that the bias in the market was not towards foreign investment *per se*,

Rather the bias was towards safe, well-known securities in general, a great number of which were foreign, and away from riskier, smaller, but ultimately from an economy-wide viewpoint, much more profitable ones. . . . The London stock exchange offered perhaps the best choice of essentially safe securities available anywhere in the world. As a consequence, less knowledgeable risk taking (in the sense of domestic, industrial capital formation in areas of advanced technology, the real risks) took place in Britain than in any of her advanced competitors (145).

Discussion of the financial system was not absent before 1914, and as in the area of education, unfavourable comparisons were drawn with the German system. But the issue never approached having sufficient importance to stimulate government intervention.

THE EFFICIENCY OF COMPANY STRUCTURE AND ORGANIZATION

The structure of British industry was undergoing significant change in this period. A merger boom took place at the turn of the century, peaking in 1899 and 1900 with 500 firms disappearing as a consequence of merger over the two years. Merger activity continued at a reduced but not insignificant level until 1914 (Hannah 1983: 175). By 1907 the 100 largest manufacturing companies in Britain accounted for around 15 per cent of output—a much lower level than was to be reached for the rest of the century, and lower than in other major industrial countries at this time (Prais 1976).

But in addition to mergers there was a great deal of co-operation amongst separate producers. One important example was the case of shipping, where the 'conference' system divided up the business by agreement amongst the major companies. This raised a deal of controversy, but the majority of the Royal Commission set up to look at the issue supported the conferences. This roused the opposition of economists, who saw the consumer interest being ignored, especially the effects of the rebate system (MacGregor 1909).

In neither the case of merger nor restrictive agreement was there an attempt by government to regulate firms' behaviour.

The trusts aroused a good deal of controversy, but no action. This was partly because, with the prevalence of Efficient ideas, a tough trust-busting approach was likely to smack too much of *laissez-faire* and too much of ignoring the alleged efficiency of the trusts. Macrosty, a prominent analyst of trusts in this period, and one who extolled their efficiency, published his first book (1901) in a Fabian series. Like other Fabians he saw the trusts as the product of evolutionary progress in industrial organization, even if they had unacceptable side-effects. His later work (1907) took a similar view, quite antithetical to any idea that trusts should be broken up (rather than nationalized).

Whilst the structure of British industry was changing quite rapidly in the Edwardian years, the typical enterprise was still a partnership or a family-owned firm. The smaller firm was probably helped by the provisions of the 1907 Companies Act which created the category of 'private company'. These companies could obtain limited liability as long as they did not trade their shares and the shareholders were limited to a maximum of fifty. Generally, company law continued to be guided by the objective of protecting the investor against the unscrupulous promoter. The effectiveness of this in encouraging the growth of public companies is unclear. Contemporaries noted that even after the changes of the 1900 Companies Act much greater freedom was given to promoters in Britain than elsewhere, and that the Act aimed at 'publicity rather than penalty: to give the death blow not so much to the fraudulent promoter as to the ignorant shareholder' (Barlow 1901). Overall it cannot be said that in this area government did much to encourage the public company as the ideal form of organization. The private company, with limited liability, remained the norm for industrial concerns up to the War.

Hannah (1983: 24–5) has stressed the extent to which the merger movement may be misleading about the real modernization of corporate organization in this period. Many of the mergers were in traditional areas of the economy, like brewing or textile-finishing, rather than modern sectors like cars or electrical engineering. By and large bigness in Britain did not denote rapid expansion to take advantage of new technologies, and their economies of scale.

Equally, whilst 'scientific management' became a big talking-point just before the War following the publication of

F. W. Taylor's book of that name in 1911, there is little evidence that such ideas had much impact in the factories. In a famous article in 1914 Cadbury, of the chocolate firm, offered a partial criticism of scientific management largely on the grounds of its unfavourable impact on the workers. Taylor himself replied, stressing how 'contented and happy' workers were who worked under his system (Taylor 1914).[4] Again, the idea of government having any role in encouraging or retarding such techniques would have been quite anachronistic.

The fear of German competition, which motivated so much in this period, also led to the 1907 Patent Act. This seems to have been very much the product of lobbying by one industrial interest, the chemical dyestuffs producers, who suffered particularly from German competition, but gained wide support. Its ostensible purposes were threefold: to make holders of patents work them in Britain; to prevent very wide patents from handicapping invention; to make licensing of patents available on reasonable conditions. This was a response to the belief that Britain was suffering from patents being taken in the country but being worked elsewhere, and stories were common of nefarious foreign syndicates abusing the system. Commentators at the time tended to draw non-interventionist conclusions from this piece of legislation: 'An examination of the circumstances of this particular law can only confirm the truth of the doctrine that to produce flourishing industries the growth must come from within, and external legislative provisions are powerless to create this' (Schuster 1909: 551). Of course, this begged the question of what was to happen if growth was not produced from within. Later commentators have seen this Act as moving some way towards 'economic nationalism, a sensible dose of it . . . and in its interests the state was occupying bits of economic territory which the mid- and late Victorian British state had been almost alone in leaving unoccupied' (Clapham 1938: 435).

As noted above, one of the features of the period was a growing belief in science in its broadest sense, and related to this, a belief that in matters scientific the Germans especially did things better. These kinds of influences led to the creation of the National Physical Laboratory, built in Teddington in 1899–1900.

---

[4] The practices of Cadbury's management are discussed in Rowlinson (1988).

This was a direct copy of the Physikalisch-Technische Reichsonstalt in Berlin, and according to Pollard (1990: 197) wiped out the lead of its German rival in a few short years'. However, detailed study of the early years of the NPL suggests that, as so often, Treasury parsimony restricted its activity (Mosley 1978). So this one example of a government role in research and development before the First World War was symbolic rather than substantive in its implications. It did symbolize a level of concern with research, which was having at least some impact on companies, where there were important steps towards establishing research laboratories (Sanderson 1972*a*: 109–10).

STATE CAPACITY AND STATE ACHIEVEMENTS

The capacity of the British state was significantly enhanced in the Edwardian period. Most notably the whole arc of labour regulation expanded, with the Trade Boards, Labour Exchanges, and the National Insurance system. The labour department of the Board of Trade, established in 1893, expanded, albeit slowly in the face of Treasury resistance (Davidson 1985). On the other hand the Poor Law remained largely intact as a patchwork local system subject to central scrutiny but not central control.

At one level all this can be seen as a nascent welfare state, and indeed many histories of the welfare state begin in this period. On the other hand, it should be clear that the reasons for this enhanced state machine were related to efficiency goals as much as welfare in a narrow sense—though part of the point of the Efficients was, of course, that these two things should not be assumed to be contradictory. In so far as these measures were effective in raising standards amongst the working class they can reasonably be seen as a successful policy of increased efficiency.

More unambiguously related to efficiency was the reform of the education system by the 1902 Act. Here the aim was fairly clear but the effects even more opaque—above all because the local basis of educational governance was hardly touched by the Act. Further up the education ladder more was achieved

the State was beginning to shed its reluctance to spend money on education, and science. . . The Government was devoting increasing resources to supporting secondary school, and university teaching, it helped to create the enlarged Imperial College of 1907, the London School of Tropical Medicine (1899), and the Medical Research Council (1913), and promised support for agricultural research in 1909 (Pollard 1990: 197).

The Edwardian state then was an active state by comparison with its Victorian predecessor. But this should not be exaggerated. In 1907 (19) Marshall wrote 'So I cry *"laissez-faire"*:—let the State be up and doing'. But it was clear from the essay that what the state should be doing was confined within strict parameters. Above all it should exclude any direct role in business: 'Governmental intrusion into business which require ceaseless invention, and fertility of resource is a danger to social progress and the more to be feared because it is insidious' (21).

In many ways Marshall's view represents where government had got to by 1914. It was 'up and doing'—but in ways which had little impact on enterprise practices. As always there are exceptions—for example, the creation of the state-owned Port of London Authority in 1908, but this was wholly exceptional for this period (Gordon 1938: ch. 2). Big changes in the regulation of labour and educational provision had come about,

Yet none of these changes, either in practice or in doctrine, seriously disturbed the presupposition that in *industry and trade* private enterprise was properly to be regarded as the rule. The state might introduce corrections at points where the system worked badly. But these were activities on the periphery. The heart of the system beat as before (Allen 1948: 5).

This position may be seen as measuring the limited inroads of anti-*laissez-faire* views by 1914. This is a reasonable point, but misleading if it obscures the particular character of the debate about efficiency and the particular kinds of challenge to *laissez-faire* that this debate raised. 'Efficiency' in this period had, as always, lots of connotations and opened up many lines of debate. Some contributors to the debate emphasized themes of great persistence; for example, Shadwell (1906) concluded his detailed survey of labour conditions in the textile and metal manufacturing industries of Britain, Germany, and the United States with a denunciation of the 'Gospel of Ease' to warm the heart of any popular writer on Britain's industrial decline in the twentieth century: 'We are a nation at play. Work is a nuisance, an evil necessity to be shirked and hurried over as quickly as possible in order that we may get away to the real business of life—the golf course, the bridge table, the cricket and football field' (454).

But whilst such views should not be ignored, this chapter has suggested that what is most interesting about the early twentieth-century period was the way efficiency was linked to the physical, and mental condition of the worker, and therefore intertwined with issues of welfare. In retrospect this period stands out as one when those two issues were not treated as alternative policy goals to be traded-off. Only perhaps in the 1940s, and on a more limited front, was the efficiency debate again to be constructed in this manner, especially with the human relations focus in the productivity drive (see Ch. 7).

CONCLUSIONS

If by 1914 Britain lacked a state willing and able to modernize the industrial structure, the question remains why this was so when states in other countries did seem to perform this role. Pollard (1990) follows many writers in seeing this absence as largely the consequence of the domination of financial and commercial interests in British politics. Manufacturing lacked the political clout of these other interests, and governments were able to ignore or even harm its interests with impunity. One particularly important argument he makes in this context is that the 'industrial interest' did little to organize itself, with employers organizations remaining weak, and divided (234–5).

Newton, and Porter (1988: ch. 1) try to link a similar broad analysis to the specific political features of the period. For them the crucial issue is the failure to forge a 'producers' alliance' to press for policies of modernization. As they rightly argue, the Efficients never had a significant mass political base, so that whilst they might permeate decision-making on specific issues, they were an implausible origin for a major shift in the political economy of Britain. Alternatively, tariff reform, the other reformist platform, was ambiguous as a modernization strategy. As Cain (1979: 49) plausibly argues, protectionism without a 'wider government plan designed to encourage the growth of newer sectors of industry' may end up simply protecting the inefficient. No such plan ever looked like emerging in this period. We must conclude then that neither the political nor the intellectual climate of the period seemed likely to provide a means whereby industrial organization and industrial efficiency generally would emerge as central policy concerns, despite the recurrent and. deeply felt worries on Britain's economic capacities as other powers came to challenge Britain's hegemony.

Further Reading

Davidson, R. (1985), *Whitehall and the Labour Problem in Late Victorian and Edwardian Britain*, London.

Friedberg, A. L. (1988), *The Weary Titan: Great Britain and the Experience of Relative Decline 1895–1905*, Princeton, NJ.

Hay, J. R. (1983), *The Origins of the Liberal Welfare Reform*, 2nd edn., London.

Pollard, S. (1990), *Britain's Prime and Britain's Decline*, London.

Searle, G. R. (1971), *The Quest for National Efficiency*, Oxford.

Semmel, B. (1960), *Imperialism and Social Reform*, London.

Webb, S. (1901), *Twentieth Century Politics: A Policy of National Efficiency*, Fabian Tract no. 108, London.

3

1914–1918: War and Wasted Opportunity

INTRODUCTION

'The war to end wars' did not, of course, do so, but it did mark the beginnings of industrial policy in Britain, from which the state has never entirely retreated. This was not, of course, an intended consequence of the war. It only emerged slowly and painfully from the undermining of initial belief that the war would be 'over by Christmas' and would be a war fought by professional soldiers and sailors without much affecting the rest of society. The transition to a total war which, at some remove, eventually meant nearly everyone was involved, brought an undermining both of the practices of the largely non-interventionist state and the ideas that underlay it. Above all, the state could no longer fail to be concerned with the capacity and efficiency of industry. In a world of competitive nation-states, such efficiency increasingly provided an unavoidable condition of success.

CONTEXT

The slogan of 'business as usual' is commonly associated with the government's approach to the economy at the beginning of the war, and its early actions were mainly concentrated on bringing in a war insurance scheme, taking control of the railways, and maintaining the financial system in the face of the crisis at the beginning of the war (Keynes 1914; Pigou 1947: 109–10).

'Business as usual' was not just a consequence of the prevalent *laissez-faire* ideas, but was also linked to the conception of the nature of the war. The emphasis on ideology of Lloyd's pioneering work of 1924 has been heavily qualified by French, who has argued that the military strategy of the British was crucial to the government's approach (French 1982). That strategy was based on the assumption that Britain's involvement in the war would be limited to the existing small volunteer army and the Royal Navy. Manpower and factories at home would therefore not require to be fundamentally reorganized to fight the war. All this changed when the growth of the army created shortages of men, machines, raw materials, and munitions. By the spring of 1915 nearly one-third of the total employed male labour-force had left their civilian occupations to enlist or to work in war-related industries. Business as usual was no longer possible.

The subsequent extension of state controls over the economy was piecemeal and *ad hoc*—there was obviously no pre-arranged plan to be implemented. From October 1914 the War Office began to purchase meat from abroad, and after this it found itself drawn into assuming responsibility for civilian supplies to prevent speculative price rises against government purchasing. Similarly a crisis over sandbags in 1915 led the government eventually to purchase the whole of the jute crop (Pollard 1992: 16).

After public disgust caused by the 'great shell scandal' of 1915, the Defence of the Realm Act of that year gave powers to the government to take over any existing factory or workshop making munitions. This soon proved inadequate to the demands for shells for the new British armies and the demands of the Allies. Under the Ministry of Munitions, established in May 1915, a whole new apparatus was created to try to remedy the problem. This included government-owned factories, the purchase and control of a range of metals and chemicals, and by extension a range of controls back to the raw-material supply. Just how far the Ministry of Munitions deserves the accolades later given to it is not clear (Wrigley 1982*b*). But certainly it played an economic role that would have been inconceivable before the war. Above all, it was to become involved directly in the functioning of enterprises in a manner wholly new in Britain (see below).

This piecemeal development of control was by no means successful in achieving all its objectives. Whilst the output of munitions rose, it still fell below government orders, while luxury consumption flourished. Price rises led to widespread profiteering, both of which caused labour unrest without seeming to deal with the shortage of supplies. Gradually in 1917 and 1918 such problems led to a much more comprehensive system of controls. These covered productive capacity, either by requisitioning, licensing, or direct ownership; widespread price-fixing and control of distribution; and control of labour. In sum

By the end of the war, the Government had direct charge of shipping, railway and canal transport; it purchased about 90% of all the imports and marketed over 80% of the food consumed at home,, besides controlling most of the prices. Direct or indirect control over industry and agriculture was virtually all-pervasive (Pollard 1992: 17–18).

Perhaps the most politically complex and fraught change in the economy brought about by the war was that relating to labour. War, as always, generated a problem of labour shortage and so shifted the balance of economic and political power in favour of labour. The state, driven by shortages of supply, had no choice but to negotiate with labour to try to obtain the co-operation necessary to secure output in the face of the major loss of workers into the armed forces. By a series of agreements (especially the Treasury Agreement) in 1914/15 the government negotiated a deal with organized labour which allowed women to work automatic machinery, semi-skilled workers to displace skilled mechanics, and the work of skilled men to be subdivided and simplified. Strikes by workers on war-related tasks were to be banned and unions agreed to arbitration in any dispute. These agreements were eventually embodied in legislation, but were explicitly accepted by the unions for the period of the war, as something reluctantly conceded for the duration, not part of a new long-term arrangement (Cole 1923; Wrigley 1976: chs. 4–14; Wrigley 1987).

On the other side of the bargain, the government accepted that welfare provision needed to be improved to make factory conditions acceptable, especially as controls were extended to tie workers to their jobs by use of 'leaving certificates'. A welfare department was established in the Ministry of Labour which encouraged the appointment of welfare officers, with the extension of rest rooms, canteens, and recreation facilities (Lowe 1982; Fitzgerald 1988; see also below, the section on Labour).

Many analysts of the First World War have seen the bargain struck between the state and labour as an example of the kind of arrangement which could have made all the difference to Britain's subsequent industrial performance if it had not been reversed at the war's end (Wrigley 1982a: 52). But this, of course, assumes the primacy of labour problems in the history of Britain's relative economic decline, a style of interpretation which has been disputed in the introduction to this book. In the event, the attempts at a consensual, even corporatist (Middlemas 1979) solution to Britain's economic problems were quickly wrecked on the reaction back to de-control soon after the war's end.

In a famous article Tawney (1943) argued that this de-control of the British economy demonstrated the weakness of the forces trying to use the war to significantly reconstruct the British economy. Certainly, he was able to point to evidence that during the war reconstruction, both social and economic, had been widely discussed both inside and outside government. A Ministry of Reconstruction had been created which had put forward ambitious plans for reform in health, housing, employment conditions, and a number of other areas of welfare (Johnson 1968). But in addition, there had been essayed the possibility of a reconstruction of the British economy—a programme of National Efficiency akin to that argued for at the beginning of the century. But this too was aborted.

The content and fate of aspects of this programme are returned to below, but it is important to note the macro-political circumstances in which the process of de-control occurred and hopes for reconstruction were dashed. As Cline (1982) has argued Tawney took too little note of the highly specific assumptions behind the economic approach of the wartime reconstruction movement. Above all, he argues, the driving assumption was that the war would end with Germany economically strong, and thus anti-German economic measures would necessitate significant changes in British policy. When the German polity collapsed and German competition looked likely to disappear for the foreseeable future, the whole politics of reconstruction shifted. Rather than trying to construct an economic anti-German alliance, Britain's attention switched to rebuilding the conditions (or alleged conditions) of the pre-war liberal economy once the immediate worry over wartime scarcities had evaporated.

If the war brought a crisis for the traditional practices of the British state, it was also the cause of a crisis in the ideas that underpinned that state. Traditional Gladstonian liberalism, however battered, had survived in large part to 1914. 'Business as usual' in part reflected mid-nineteenth-century views about how a modern state could and should behave. A belief in a largely naval strategy fitted closely with the idea of Britain as a far-flung Empire whose interests lay in keeping the sea lanes open to the free movement of goods, refusing Continental European commitments, and minimizing military expenditure. The military posture of pre-war Britain was closely enmeshed with its economic practice and thought. Hence a crisis of the military strategy was also a crisis of the liberal economy and liberal economic ideas. In a complex field of ideological shifts traditional liberalism was largely displaced by a patriotic, sometimes xenophobic, nationalism which embraced large sections of all classes. The patrician liberalism and cosmopolitanism of Asquith was displaced by the dynamic opportunism of Lloyd George, always ready to sacrifice principle to immediate national goals (Wrigley 1976). Politically the war marked the end of the Liberal Party, and though the closeness of the linkage should not be exaggerated, it also marked the demise of liberal ideas as traditionally understood in Britain.

MARKETS

The war had radical effects on both the quantity and direction of British trade. With the shortage of shipping, many imported raw materials, and the diversion of resources to war production, the value of exports in real terms roughly halved. (£547m. on average during 1914–18, compared with £578m. in 1911–12), whilst prices doubled. A significant proportion of this reflected loss of Central European markets as a direct result of the breaking of economic relations by the belligerents,[1] but it also included, for example, a large loss of Asian and Latin American markets for such items as cotton goods because of the non-availability of American cotton to Lancashire (Tomlinson 1979).

This weakening of the British position in many export markets was coupled to a sharp deterioration in the balance of payments as imports roughly maintained their real value, and despite the

[1] Britain continued to trade with Germany well into the war, including in crucial swaps of chemical dyestuffs for rubber for German instruments. Similar swaps for optical glass were mooted, but abandoned when British production expanded (Macleod and Macleod 1975: 174).

surprising strength of invisibles, this led to an unavoidable recourse to assets sales and borrowing to maintain the position.

TABLE 3.1. *British balance of payments during the First World War*
(£m. current prices)

	Visibles			Invisibles			Current balance
	Exports	Imports	Balance	Exports	Imports	Balance	
1913	637	719	− 82	405	88	+317	+235
1914	540	660	−120	361	107	+254	+134
1915	500	840	−340	440	155	+285	− 55
1916	630	980	−350	630	190	+440	+ 90
1917	620	1040	−420	740	270	+470	+ 50
1918	540	1170	−630	660	305	+355	−275
1919	990	1460	−470	720	295	+425	− 45

Source: Feinstein (1972), Table T.82

On their own the loss of markets and the deterioration of the
balance of payments would have been likely to raise again the
issue of protection. But this was coupled with two other factors
which greatly raised the force of this question. The war revealed
starkly the trading strength of the German economy. In a range
of goods, some of them vital to the war effort, dependence on
German imports was enormous. Almost all magnetos had been
imported from Bosch of Stuttgart (Cd. 8181: paras. 53–4), the
majority of optical glass (for binoculars, gun-sights, rangefinders
etc.) from Zeiss of Jena (Macleod and Macleod 1975: 170). Such
a position reinforced the general reawakening of a concern with
the penetration of the British markets by German goods. A
Board of Trade investigation of 1916, for example, found that
almost half of all domestic consumption of a range of consumer
goods came from Germany (Cd. 8181: paras. 10–12).[2]

Secondly, the war greatly reinforced Empire sentiment. Partly
this again resulted from a realization of the extent to which the
Empire was dependent on goods from the Central Powers (Cd.
9035: ch. IV). But more generally the role of Empire troops in the
war reinforced Imperial sentiment in Britain, and strengthened
the belief that Britain should respond to (some of) the Empire's

[2] For a characteristically astringent attack on these arguments, see Cannan
(1916).

calls for a changed economic relationship with the United Kingdom.

Thus the issue of protection again became a live one. A Board of Trade Committee in 1916 could record that 'Practically all the representative firms and associations consulted by us asked for a measure of protection' (Cd. 8181: para. 48). Undoubtedly there was a general shift towards protectionism amongst both industrialists and politicians, but this needs to be carefully contextualized.

The important background to much of the protectionist sentiment was the belief that at the end of the war Germany would be in a position to try to quickly recapture and expand her old markets in Britain and the Allied countries. In 1916 the Allied governments, at the Paris Conference, responded to this threat by proposing a period of severe restrictions on trade with Germany and the Central Powers after the end of the war. The idea was not one of permanent protection, but of providing a breathing space for the reconstruction of Allied trade and industry (Cd. 8271).

Nevertheless, government support for such measures reinforced the growing protectionist sentiment, especially amongst those who had suffered most from German competition before the war. To a degree this yielded a result in the McKenna Duties of 1915. These, named after the Chancellor of the Exchequer, were ostensibly aimed at saving foreign exchange and shipping space, and they imposed a $33\frac{1}{3}$ per cent duty on a small range of luxury items such as motor cars, cycles, watches and clocks, and musical instruments. Their main long-run impact was to protect the car industry (see Pollard 1992: 93 and Ch. 14, below), but in the short run they represented only a limited chink in the wall of free-trade policy.

Whilst this was the extent of actual protectionist policy, a consensus was established that further measures were required. The key committee on post-war trade policy, the Balfour of Burleigh Committee, seemed to capture this view quite accurately. It began its discussion of the issue by lamenting the reopening of old wounds over 'fiscal policy'. But, it argued, 'whilst the economic strength of the country has so far borne with remarkable success the strain upon our material and financial resources resulting from an unparalled war, certain defects in, and dangers to, the great fabric of British trade and industry have been revealed' (Cd. 9035: para. 212). The report argued that the 'early restoration of unrestricted dealings in the markets of this country and the world at competitive prices is essential to the re-establishment of British industry and commerce on a sound basis' (para. 119) and rejected general protectionism, but called for a range of measures falling short of this. These included the safeguarding of vital strategic industries, and a much vaguer call for the protection of a range of sectors 'important for the maintenance of the industrial position of the UK'. It also called for some moves towards Imperial preference, including, at least for a time, some restriction on German trade with the Empire (paras. 213–15).

This seeming advocacy of broad protectionism was in part offset by an emphasis on anti-dumping as the crucial measure in many sectors, and a clear recognition of the slippery slope argument, that once conceded, protection would be strongly demanded on all sides. To counter this danger it proposed a strong board to assess such demands, and to make sure they were only conceded when all other attempts to raise the efficiency of the industry had been exhausted (para. 255). This position seems to represent where the balance of argument (and political power) had reached by 1918. The Report was qualified by a call by six of its members for a general 10 per cent tariff, but the call was resisted.

Alongside the explicit protectionism of the McKenna Duties, import controls were used to restrict imports of goods in certain key industries, such as dyestuffs and other chemicals, scientific instruments, glasswear, and magnetos—all the goods of strategic importance mainly imported from Germany during the war (Cd. 8181; Cd. 9035: ch. V). Declared illegal in 1920, these controls were given legislative force by the Dyestuffs Act of 1920 and the Safeguarding of Industries Act of 1921 (see Ch. 4).

Protectionism lost one of its sources of support when Germany at the end of the war was much weaker than wartime fears had expected, and the apprehensions of an immediate post-hostility inrush of cheap German goods did not materialize (e.g. for steel, Tolliday 1984: 53). But the shift towards a more nationalistic political economy had been given a boost, and free trade never had quite the same religious status after 1918 as before the war, except perhaps amongst many economists. And even there the protection of strategic industries could be seen as a reasonable extension of the long-established infant-industry argument for trade controls (Supple 1990: 338).

PROFITS

In a supply-constrained economy, as the British economy quickly became during the war, the opportunities for profit generally increase. Couple this to a piecemeal and incoherent imposition of controls and the scope for profiteering is enhanced further. Whilst an ill-defined concept, profiteering was to play a large part in the politics of the war (and later discussions of its course; Boswell and Johns 1982). It was an issue on which government, anxious for public support, was to become increasingly sensitive. This sensitivity was given legislative form with, initially, the Munitions Levy, and then, much more significantly, the Excess Profits Duty which was brought in in 1915, and was to endure until 1921. It represented the first explicit tax on profits in British history, and was a source of a great deal of dispute, though its impact on profits was probably rather less than its promoters and opponents usually suggested.

Overall profitability in the war period is difficult to quantify. Feinstein's figures (1972: Table T.44) suggest a significant rise in the share of profits and self-employed income in total GDP from 1914 to 1916, but a fall thereafter. He does not have calculations of profit rates before 1920. The changes in the distribution of these profits is even more unclear. Boswell and Johns (1982) suggest that high profits were particularly common in textiles, clothing, and shipping, where there was excess demand and controls were introduced but in a slow and haphazard manner. Profits were probably at their height in the early period of the war when disorganization was at its worst, including in the munitions sector. Some producers of munitions undoubtedly did very well —Nobels, for example, the explosive-makers saw their profits increase at least threefold (Boswell and Johns 1982: 443–4).

Governmental attempts to control profits took two forms— taxation and price controls, though the latter had other purposes as well, not least to maintain civilian purchasing power and hence morale. This latter was especially true in the case of food, where a whole new Ministry was created to purchase, control, and ration supplies (Beveridge 1928). The Excess Profits Duty was introduced in 1915 at a rate varying from 40 to 80 per cent (average 63 per cent). Over the period 1915–21 it yielded £1,154.5m., or about 25 per cent of total tax revenue. However these figures probably exaggerate its impact. First, because of the scale of evasion, exemptions, and various pay-back clauses the actual incidence of the tax has been calculated to have been around 34 per cent. Secondly, most of it was paid by reference to a base-line determined by the best years just prior to the war, and for most firms the immediate pre-war years were very good years for profits (Hicks *et al.* 1941: 71–8; Boswell and Johns 1982: 426–7).

Control of profits via price control also seems to have been fairly generously administered. In this case one of the key problems was the determination of costs against which prices could be assessed. Generally cost data in British firms was rudimentary in the extreme, and the government had to call in teams of accountants to try to get some idea of the costs of many of the firms where they sought to regulate prices (Lloyd 1924: chs. 25, 27). In administering price control, government was faced with a fairly obvious trade-off of objectives. By and large it was keen to encourage production, so prices tended to be set to allow the least efficient firms to survive, even if this meant the aim of holding consumer prices and profits in check was compromised (evidence of G. H. Roberts, Cmd. 166: para. 1–28.7). Boswell and Johns (1982: 445) assert the 'liberal nature of price control, which reflected a mixture of the inherent problems of standard prices, deliberate political strategy and muddle'.

The political sensitivity of the issues of prices and profits was compounded by their mixture with a third issue—that of trusts. It was widely and probably correctly perceived during the War that one of its consequences was the growth in combinations, trade associations, and all kinds of co-ordinating bodies for firms. (The ramifications of this are returned to in the section on Companies, below). The central reason was seen as 'the novel circumstances of war under which the Government, acting through the Ministry of Munitions or other Departments, found it necessary sometimes to consult the most informed opinion in a trade, and sometimes to ration material through an organization representative of the trade' (Cd. 9236: para. 4).

This comment is drawn from the 1918 Report of the Committee on trusts set up in the face of widespread concern about the issue. Its conclusions were largely to suggest the benignity of the trusts, but accepted that there was widespread concern. It therefore suggested a body be established to investigate trusts and report back to the Board of Trade. Whilst noting the pattern of anti-trust legislation in many countries, it did not endorse such a radical approach, and was mainly concerned with conciliating public opinion rather than actual reform (Cd. 9236: paras. 6–12).[3] A similar tone is evident in a Ministry of Reconstruction pamphlet on the subject, 'Instead of combination being regarded as an organized conspiracy, it should be looked upon as a natural, inevitable, and in many ways beneficial development, but as one that creates a new order of problem for the community and the State' (PRO 1919a: Trusts, Combines and Trade Associations: 2).

Action along these lines came about, but in highly specific circumstances, just after the end of the war. The war was followed by a brief but frenetic boom from the middle of 1919 to the middle of 1920. A feature of this boom was a very rapid rise in prices (Pigou 1947: pt. I). This further fuelled worries about prices and profiteering. In July 1919 the government established a Select Committee 'to inquire how far the present high prices of articles of general consumption are due to excessive profits on the part of any person concerned in their production, transport, or distribution and to advise as to what action can usefully be taken in the matter' (CMD. 166, Introd.). Within a few weeks the government had gone much further and passed a Profiteering Act. Under this Act was established a complex of committees and Tribunals with two superordinate bodies—a Standing Committee to Investigate Prices and a Standing Committee on Trusts. Under these two prongs of policy a range of investigations was launched into various sectors where either excessive prices were perceived or combinations suspected (e.g. Cmd. 514, 983).

---

[3] An addendum by E. Bevin, J. A. Hobson, W. H. Watkins, and S. Webb reiterated the standard pre-war position of the Left on trusts—that they were a major threat to the public good, but that they were efficient, and so the solution should be tough price controls, not breaking them up.

This flurry of activity was highly conjunctural, and as the boom of 1919/20 rapidly became a slump, interest in profiteering, excess profits, and trusts rapidly declined. The legacy of government intervention was very limited—the political drive to de-control being added to from 1921 by the change to a macroeconomic context of slump and excess supply rather than excess demand.

Whilst the reaction of firms to the profit-making possibilities of the war and immediate post-war booms varied, many made lots of hay whilst the sun shone. In particular, the high profits were the basis for a great wave of amalgamations and flotations in 1919/20, which left many companies in very great difficulties in the slump that followed. What a later generation was to call financial engineering seems to have dominated over any major attempt to use the profits to change the pattern or organization of manufacturing capacity (Macrosty 1927; Alford 1986: 215–20).

THE EFFICIENCY OF LABOUR

As with all twentieth-century wars fought by Britain, the First World War gave considerable impetus to the reform of education. As in pre-war discussions, this was seen as a key determinant of economic and hence national efficiency. In school education, Fisher's Act of 1918 gave the Board of Education, working through the local authorities, strong encouragement to develop all aspects of education up to the new compulsory leaving age of 14. Local authorities could raise this to 15, or alternatively provide day continuation schools for those aged 14 to 16 for one day a week. However, much of this, like other reforms, was aborted by the cuts in public spending following the slump of 1921/2. However, it did provide a major impetus to the development of the idea of ending elementary education at 11 and building up a system of secondary schools for all purposes— a process which proceeded through the inter-war years (Sheringham 1981: chs. 3–7).

The apprenticeship system continued to dominate the acquisition of manual technical skills, and seems to have been left largely untouched by the First World War. The state did not intervene in the provision of lower-level technical education as it was to do on a massive scale in the Second World War. However

some further impetus was given to higher level technical education by the creation of the Department of Scientific and Industrial Research, which had amongst it aims the expansion of
studentships and fellowships for university technical education—
though this remained on a small scale by German standards
(Cd. 8005: para. 1).

How far the war changed labour practices affecting efficiency
is unclear. As noted already, policies of dilution were explicitly
negotiated for the duration of the war, and in most cases this
seems to have happened, as pre-war practices were reverted to.
In any case, the extent of dilution should not be exaggerated. For
example, for all the battles over the issue, little dilution seems to
have taken place in shipbuilding (Reid 1985: 46–74). Reid suggests that this conclusion can be generalized, 'With few exceptions, British employers stubbornly maintained conservative
attitudes and had little faith in proposals to rationalize labour-
intensive methods of production. Indeed it was frequently managements which put up the strongest opposition to dilution,
because each firm wanted to retain as much skilled labour as
possible' (66; see also Cole 1923: 196). This attitude was no
doubt reinforced by the extent to which wartime labour unrest
was grounded in craftsmen's opposition to dilution and the
belief that union leaderships were making too many concessions
on the issue (Wrigley 1979, 1982a: 82). However the scope for
dilution to be maintained after the war should not be exaggerated. First, much wartime dilution was on cost-plus contracts,
where the costs of displacing skilled men by dilutees was not
at issue. Second, many of the tasks dilutees carried out in the
war period were simply not required to be carried out, or only
on a much smaller scale, after the war (More 1980: 28–36).
Again, it is worth making the obvious link between the approach
to skill and training and macroeconomic circumstances. The
concept of 'manpower' was coined in the First World War,
reflecting the acute shortage of the commodity, especially the
skilled variety (Grieves 1988). But after 1920 this shortage was
replaced by a surfeit, with therefore little incentive for most
employers to regard economizing on skilled labour as the key
issue.

The tight labour-market and the desperate need to raise output
gave an opening for the state to impose a degree of welfarism on

British industry. In 1915 a Health of Munitions Workers Committee was set up signalling the recognition of the link between the munitions worker's health and his (and increasingly, her) output. From this stemmed a number of reports on Sunday working, fatigue, canteens, ventilation, and lighting (Whiteside 1980: 312–14). In many ways this wartime effort pursued the logic of pre-war ideas about efficiency. For example, the Final Report of the Committee summarized their approach: 'it is his individual health, mental development and moral well-being which is the guarantee of effective labour' (Cd. 9065: para. 11) and further 'without health there is no energy, without energy there is no output' (para. 533).

This work was paralleled by the appointment of Seebohm Rowntree to the head of Welfare at the Ministry of Munitions in November 1915 (Briggs 1961: ch. 5). Rowntree was a major figure in the pre-war welfare movement, both in the broad sense illustrated by his landmark study of poverty in York (1902), and more specifically in his role as a pioneer of factory-level welfare in the chocolate factory owned by his family. The decision to expand welfare provision was particularly based on the expansion in the number of female workers, though later attention extended to all workers.

Wartime legislation gave the Ministry of Munitions powers to impose welfare measures on controlled factories, though Rowntree preferred to try to act by persuasion. He argued to reluctant employers that welfare provision was not philanthropy but 'a paying proposition' (Briggs 1961: 122). This indeed was a central part of his creed—in his view wages were the key to welfare: high wages required higher productivity if they were to be afforded, but they were in turn one of the conditions for worker efficiency and therefore higher productivity (Briggs 1961: 128–33).

This message had made little headway before the war (Littler 1982: 90–2) and faced considerable resistance in the war. Rowntree's position with employers was not helped by his parallel advocacy of 'industrial democracy' in the form of works councils, and eventually his approach of voluntarism plus sympathy for trade unions was replaced by a higher level of compulsion without any emphasis on the union role (Whiteside 1980).

With the leverage given by being the buyer of output as well as the law, the Ministry of Munitions undoubtedly did bring about a major increase in all kinds of welfare provision in the war. Quantification of this is difficult (though Fitzgerald 1988: 89–92 has examples), but one index would be the number of factory 'welfare officers' which grew from around 60 in 1913 to around 1000 by 1918 (Niven 1967: 42).[4]

Wartime welfare expansion fitted into the reconstruction movement's hopes for the post-war world. As a Reconstruction Problems pamphlet argued 'To-day, more than ever it is realised that the welfare of the worker is not only a vital matter for the community, but also from the point of view of the employer as a matter of expediency. There is thus the double stimulus—the good employer profits by his "goodness" ' (PRO 1919*b*, Scientific Business Management: 1). But as in so many other spheres reconstructionists were defeated by restorationists (Littler 1982: 99–101), who did not believe in the high wage and welfare route to economic efficiency. How far a permanent mark was left on British industry by wartime welfare is unclear. The general macro-level conditions of the 1920s as well as the ideology of restoration told against such an approach, as of course did the end of the Ministry of Munitions, but Jones (1983; also Niven 1967: chs. 5, 6) has suggested at least something survived, and the movement found new impetus in the late 1920s. However, some of this was founded on a calculated desire to reduce state involvement in welfare, which seems to have been quite explicit in the foundation of the Industrial Welfare Society in 1918 (Whiteside 1980: 324–5; Fitzgerald 1988: 203–7).

THE EFFICIENCY OF CAPITAL

Wartime discussions of the efficiency of the British economy often reflected a highly ambivalent view of the German model. Whilst condemnation of Prussianism was common, there was also a reinforcement of the common pre-war belief that in key areas the Germans had found a pattern of economic organization which worked better than the British, and that to some degree this pattern should be emulated (e.g. Foxwell 1917*a*, 1917*b*).

---

[4] What was later the Institute of Personnel Management was founded in 1913 as the Welfare Workers Association, with 68 members (Niven 1967: ch. 3).

One area where this approach was evident is finance for companies. In 1916 a Board of Trade Committee argued that whilst British banks generally did well by traders,

> the British manufacturer may be frequently in want of finance of a kind which a British joint-stock bank ... could not prudentially provide, whereas the German banks in particular seem to have been able to afford special assistance at the inception of undertakings of the most varied description, and to have laid themselves out for stimulating their promotion and for carrying them through to a successful completion (Cd. 9346: para. 4).

From this argument they drew the conclusion that a new institution was required to help both production and trade-financing facilities. 'If industry is to be extended, it is essential that British products should be *pushed*, and manufacturers, merchants and bankers must combine to push them' (para. 14).

The Committee called for a British Trade Bank, complementary to the existing banks. This was established in the form of the British Trade Corporation the following year. This was a private body, and the idea of a state bank for this role was explicitly rejected by the Burleigh Committee as likely to 'lead inevitably to extensive government interference with the actual conduct of trade' (Cd. 9035: para. 200). The new Corporation was partly financed by the joint-stock banks, and seems largely to have been involved in the financing of trade, rather than in the role of a German industrial bank, as some of its proponents had hoped (e.g. Kirkaldy 1918: 300–4).

Trade finance was an area where the government did become directly involved just after the war. A system of export credit guarantees was established in 1919 partly to encourage exports for employment reasons, and partly to try to restore trade with Eastern and Central Europe (Pigou 1947: 139–40; Rodgers 1986). However this was about the only direct government intervention in domestic financial markets at this time. The traditional divorce of the joint-stock banks from industry remained unaltered. The stock exchange did become more important as a market for industrial shares, but this was largely a consequence of the financial engineering of the 1919/20 period, rather than the channelling of new money into industry.

Government did, however, break with the extreme *laissez-faire* attitude to foreign investment. Controls were exercised during the War and continued in more relaxed form into the 1920s (Atkin 1970). However, this change was brought about not in the name of diverting capital resources to domestic industry, but in the name of restoring and sustaining the gold standard. So it was a temporary policy aimed at restoring a pillar of Victorian economic cosmopolitanism, not a basis for a new nationally oriented economic policy.

THE EFFICIENCY OF TECHNICAL CHANGE

One area where government did take a significant initiative to improve the quality of British investment was the creation in 1916 of the Department of Scientific and Industrial Research (DSIR). This derived from a Board of Education Report, the opening paragraph of which it is worth quoting in full because of its summing up of so many of the ideas of the war years:

This is a strong consensus of opinion among persons engaged both in science and in industry that a special need exists at the present time for new machinery and for additional state assistance in order to promote and organize scientific research with a view especially to its application to trade and industry. It is well-known that many of our industries have since the outbreak of war suffered through our inability to produce at home certain articles and materials required in trade processes, the production of which has become localised abroad, especially in Germany, because science has there been more thoroughly and effectively applied to the solution of scientific problems bearing on trade and industry and to the elaboration of economical and improved processes of manufacture. It is impossible to contemplate without considerable apprehension the situation which will arise at the end of the war when our scientific resources have previously been enlarged and organized to meet it. It appears uncontrovertible that if we are to advance or even maintain our industrial position we must as a nation aim at such a development of scientific and industrial research as will place us in a position to expand and strengthen our industries and to compete successfully with the most highly organized of our rivals (Cd. 8005: para. 1).

The DSIR was one of the most long-lasting of the innovations of the war years. It provided funds for university research and financed fundamental research. But its most distinctive and important role was to encourage the creation or extension of Industrial Research Associations (IRA), co-operative bodies largely financed by firms in a particular sector. In this way, it was hoped, research would be encouraged that was closely tied to the priorities of the firms in an industry. The IRA movement spread quite rapidly at the end of the war, but stagnated in the period after 1923 when the government grant was reduced (Varcoe 1981: 434–4). Nevertheless, by most accounts it must be called a success, albeit on a modest scale.

The DSIR also took over and greatly expanded the work of the National Physical Laboratory, spending £150,000 on this by 1919/20. On parallel lines, the British Engineering Standards Association expanded, especially because of the impetus given to standardization by the long product runs of the war years (PRO 1919c, Industrial Research: 10–12). Probably quantitatively more important to British R & D than the DSIR was the stimulus to strategic research in dyestuffs, synthetic ammonia, and coal hydrogenation, which were major parts of ICI's research activities in the 1920s (Edgerton 1987: 91). And British R & D in the 1920s was heavily dominated by a small number of firms, such as ICI. But the war does seem to have given a general stimulus to private research and development, it 'provided not only the stimulus and the example of science, but also the profits with which to pursue this new development' (Sanderson 1972a: 115).

As with the founding of the National Physical Laboratory at the turn of the century, the foundation of the DSIR signalled a new research consciousness which, whilst aided by the direct state role, was taken up much more widely, so that some ground was made up on the research effort of the Germans, whose work in this area seemed to have been so clearly illustrated in their war capacity.

THE EFFICIENCY OF COMPANY STRUCTURE AND ORGANIZATION

The war brought an unparalleled level of state intervention into British industry. Whilst control of prices and profits and the government's role in the labour-market impinged on almost every enterprise, direct intervention on the production as opposed to the commercial side was much more limited (Lloyd 1924: 347–51). The major exception was in the area of the production of munitions, where the wartime state's concern was most immediate and compelling.

At the beginning of the war the direct role of the state in armaments production was limited to three Royal Ordnance Factories, most supplies being bought from a range of companies, each often receiving only a small part of government orders, and so maintaining competition in supply. These traditional arrangements were quite unsuitable for the scale of demand which the new type of war brought into being. By the end of the war the Ministry of Munitions had set up or acquired over 200 munitions factories at a cost of over £50m. In addition it was buying munitions from hundreds more factories, and as part of that relationship was cajoling and enforcing changes in company practices, on everything from welfare to costing systems (Ministry of Munitions 1922: vii, chs. 3, 4; viii, chs. 2, 4, 5).

Undoubtedly the Ministry in this way became a major force for modernization of industrial procedures. With long runs and guaranteed markets, plus dilution of labour, the way was open in many cases for mass production of standardized products, using automatic machinery on a scale unknown in the pre-war years.

There is no doubt whatever, that the result of Ministerial control was a general levelling up of standards of accomplishment in the engineering trade, more economical use of material and of labour, the increased adoption of labour saving and automatic machinery, more accurate costings, and a higher standard of accuracy, attained by the use of precision gauges on a scale hitherto unknown in England (Ministry of Munitions 1922: vii, 94–5).[5]

Spectacular increases in productivity were recorded in some munitions factories as a result of all these changes, perhaps above all the increased specialization of factories on large runs

---

[5] The emphasis on costing was partly because of the purchase role of the Ministry, but also reflected the emphasis on raising labour productivity. The Ministry of Reconstruction in advocating its important permanent role (in the home and garden as well as the factory), expressed this view in its own peculiar way: 'The foundation of costing is an attitude of mind which regards each "labour hour" controlled as a sacred trust, the unit of the nation's wealth, to be expended only with thought and care' (PRO 1919*b*, The Uses of Costing: 1)

of a small number of products (ibid.: 95). Yet the long-run impact of all this change is much less clear. As regards the national factories (sold off to the private sector at the end of the war) the official history is rightly cautious:

Large scale production, standardisation, scientific management, improved labour conditions, all the gains of these and kindred methods must leave some mark on industry. The experience gained cannot be lost. Yet the effects may be over-estimated, for to an important extent the wartime experience of the national factories is inapplicable to peace-time conditions (Ministry of Munitions 1922: viii, 84).

A similar point may be made about all those factories which, while remaining in private hands, were affected to a greater or lesser degree by Ministry of Munitions contracts. There is no doubt that few firms would have been unaffected by these contracts, and the Ministry enumerated areas where it saw particular gains. It believed that the Ministerial role had enhanced the spread of improved processes—for example, the open-hearth process in iron and steel improved the utilization of scrap and waste—from perhaps 15 to 50 per cent in the case of steel; and forced economical substitution of materials for more wasteful patterns (Ministry of Munitions 1922: vii, 90).

But whilst some of this must have rubbed off on company practices, the collapse of government purchasing, the restoration of pre-war labour practices, and the boom followed by massive slump greatly reduced the applicability of wartime methods. Not many companies could have continued to produce the large number of a few products which lay at the bottom of much of the wartime experience. It is striking how much scrutiny of British companies at the time of the next world war revealed how little had changed, for example in the areas of cost accounting and standardization, from before the First World War (see Ch. 6).

In a few industrial sectors the war did have a more lasting effect. Even before the war strategic concerns had led to the building up of particular industries. For example, in 1912 the Admiralty decided that in future the basis of its ships' motive power would be oil, not coal, and this led to direct state involvement (money and directors on the Board) for the Anglo-Persian Oil Company just before the war began in 1914. This attempt to build up a favoured supplier was greatly enhanced during the war itself, but after the war the same motive led to a favouring of an alternative company, Shell (Jones 1981: chs. 5–8).

In other sectors, even within the strategic perceptions operating before 1914, government had in some areas tried to play a more interventionist role, though not always very successfully (Trebilcock 1966). But the war, by highlighting the dependence on Germany for certain key supplies, greatly encouraged such a process. As already noted one such product was magnetos, and the Ministry of Munitions put a lot of effort into increasing output of this item, which in fact rose by a hundredfold in the war (Ministry of Munitions 1922: vii, 35). Similarly with optical glass, where the government financed existing firms as well as setting up national (i.e. state-owned) companies. From very little, by the end of the war this industry had large plant, modern machinery, techniques of mass production, and a significant design and innovation capacity (Macleod and Macleod 1975). Not all of such efforts were successful, and in one case at least they involved granting a monopoly of supply to dubious company promoters (Coleman 1975). But the government stuck to its policy in this area, these industries gaining tariff protection under the safeguarding and related legislation of the early 1920s. In another case, that of dyestuffs, where that protection proved inadequate to sustain the 'chosen instrument', the British Dyestuffs Corporation, the government encouraged it to become part of a merger which led to the creation of ICI, a company which owes its origins to government concern with supplies of war material (Reader 1977).

In these ways government had an impact on company organization and on Britain's industrial make-up. Another important impact of wartime government intervention was on industrial structure, linked in turn to the political representation of industry. The war's impact on industrial structure needs to be discussed with some care. Whilst combinations and associations undoubtedly expanded during the war, the scale of amalgamation is much less clear. Normally booms in amalgamation in Britain have been linked to high levels of stock-market activity, and this was absent during the war period. But it was very much present in 1919/20, when a further boost was given to the amalgamation of British industry by the seeming easy profits to be had from recapitalizing the booming staple industries. Alford

(1986: 219) suggests that these amalgamations were 'of a kind which included little alteration in business practices, since the primary objective was to achieve greater concentration of ownership and an increase in production along existing lines'. In the newer industries, he suggests, things were a little better, but 'in major respects their reactions to the pressures and demands of war fell a long way short of justifying an accolade for enterprise' (220).

So whilst the formal pattern of ownership showed further tendency to concentration, the impact of this on efficiency was probably limited. This is somewhat at odds with much official commentary at the time which tended to see a close and, by implication, necessary link between size, whether achieved by agreement or amalgamation, and efficiency. This, as noted, generated a benign attitude to trusts based on little more than a facile belief in economies of scale (Cd. 9035: ch. 7; Cd. 9236: para. 5).[6]

As noted above, the government's interventions in industry had as a major corollary the growth of combinations and associations to negotiate with government. Many trade associations began life in the First World War, effectively called into being by the state. But this was only part of the shift in government–industry relations. Many businesses were involved directly in government during the war, with results for government efficiency which remain highly disputable (Davenport-Hines 1984: ch. 5). More long-lasting was the creation of widely-supported employers' associations—notably the Federation of British Industry and the National Confederation of Employers Organisations.

The FBI owed its origins in part to the rise of commercial nationalism which was so much part of the war, and this was coupled to a desire for a new Ministry of Commerce or Ministry of Industry to press British interests. But it was also concerned to re-assert business interests, which it felt were losing out to the unholy alliance between government and trade unions (Turner 1984). The FBI can be seen as based on an attempt to create a producers' alliance (Newton and Porter 1988: ch. 2), based upon

[6] The benignity is also evident in the policy on retail price maintenance. An official committee reported in favour of this in 1920 on the basis of its effects in stabilizing prices and the incomes of producers and stopping speculation by middlemen (Cmd. 662).

the ideas of 'trade warriors' like Dudley Docker (Davenport-Hines 1984: chs. 5, 6). However it was weakened by, amongst other things, disagreements over tariff reform on which industrialists remained substantially divided, especially once the immediate threat of a renewal of German competition was removed (Turner 1984: 45–6).

The National Confederation of Employers Organisations was a body entirely concerned with wage bargaining and related issues. It grew largely out of a feeling on the part of the Engineering Employers Federation that it was being sidelined by wartime government–union negotiations. It was further helped by a National Industrial Conference in February 1919, when divisions amongst employers were only too apparent. The National Industrial Conference, called by the government, was part of what might be seen as the attempt to establish a corporatist political system in Britain, with the idea of establishing a consensus between the peak associations of labour and capital as well as government. But no such consensus was achieved, and British corporatism failed to flourish (Lowe 1978; Lowe 1986: 87–105). Whether such a consensus could have changed British industrial policy remains a moot point, but in retrospect the opportunity was small, given the political distance between unions and employers at this time.

STATE CAPACITY AND STATE ACHIEVEMENTS

In the short run the war had a major impact on the contours of the state in Britain. Wholly new Ministries—Munitions, Food, Shipping—appeared, and a more long-lasting Ministry of Labour. The Treasury lost its central role in the control of government expenditure, whilst finding new ones in international finance and monetary policy (Burk 1982).

Yet at the end of the war the changes wrought in the government machine appear rather marginal, and rather adverse to bringing issues of industrial efficiency to the centre of the political agenda. The Treasury eventually emerged strengthened, with a clear right and effective means to control public expenditure, coupled to the priority of restoring as much as possible of Britain's financial position of 1913 (Burk 1982; Tomlinson

1990*a*: 55–70). This agenda excluded the kind of policies favoured by the trade warriors of the wartime FBI, barring the limited scope of the safeguarding legislation. The FBI call for a new Ministry of Industry or Commerce was met by some very limited reforms to the existing Board of Trade. This was now divided into a Department of Commerce and Industry and a Department of Public Services Administration. The first was concerned with the 'Development of Trade, with vigilance, with suggestion, with information and with the duty of thinking out and assisting national commercial and industrial policy' (Cd. 8912: para. 2). As the tone of this suggests this was not to be a strongly interventionist role, and it is probably not entirely unfair to say that the Board of Trade's main contribution to Britain's industrial efficiency in the 1920s was, in line with these protocols, the Balfour Committee on Industrial and Commercial Efficiency (see Ch. 4). It was certainly not the dynamic Ministry of Commerce evoked by Dudley Docker and his kind (Davenport-Hines 1984: chs. 4, 5).

The only other reform of note was the creation of a joint Board of Trade/Foreign Office Department of Overseas Commercial Intelligence. This came at the end of a long period of bickering over the respective responsibilities of these two bodies in this area. The war provided sufficient impetus for these differences to be resolved (Cd. 8715). In many ways this small change is significant as signalling the emphasis to be put, especially in the early and mid-1920s, on restoring British trade as the prime economic policy aim. Whilst it broke with a certain nineteenth-century Foreign Office contempt for commerce, it hardly inaugurated a new policy stance in international trade.

Finally, the Ministry of Labour. Whilst this was a Department whose creation symbolized something of the wartime political clout of labour, it remained a 'still, small voice' in this period, barely surviving the political reaction and public expenditure cuts which accompanied the slump after 1920 (Lowe 1982).

How far was state policy on industry changed by the war? After noting some of the changes discussed in this chapter, G. C. Allen (1948: 5) wrote:

Yet none of these changes, either in practice or in doctrine, seriously disturbed the presupposition that in *industry and trade* private enterprise was properly to be regarded as the rule. The state might introduce corrections at points where the system worked badly. But these were activities on the periphery. The heart of the system beat as before.

This seems broadly correct, certainly as regards the ruling classes of the period. However amongst Labour and the Left the war had an important doctrinal impact: by and large it reinforced the movement to what was to become the dominant fissure in twentieth-century politics. This consisted of a Left which favoured more government intervention and a Right which favoured less. However oversimplified, this divide does represent an important truth about British politics, and it cannot be understood except by noting the widespread belief on the Left that the war had demonstrated the efficacy of state intervention in the economy (e.g. Furniss 1918). This view was then embodied at the heart of Labour's reconstructed constitution (Labour Party 1918).

CONCLUSIONS

As always, the big question is, 'Might it have been different?' Recent writers have seen the First World War and its aftermath as a lost opportunity to reconstruct British industry and project it on to a higher plane of growth and efficiency (Alford 1986; Newton and Porter 1988: ch. 2; Kirby and Rose 1991). Their views on why the opportunity was lost differ. Alford emphasizes the culpability of businessmen who learnt so little from the war; Kirby and Rose emphasize the limits imposed by the failure to permanently shift the pattern of labour relations and labour utilization. Newton and Porter have a more general approach, which emphasizes the conjunctural and political elements in the failure of the productioneers. All of these approaches seem to have their interest and relevance, but for all its rather general character, Newton and Porter's account is the one which fits best with the material in this chapter.

With the state machine largely unreformed there was little obstacle to the politics of 'return to normalcy', which meant trying to recreate the conditions of the Victorian economy. This is most evident in the restoration of the gold standard, carrying as it did a whole mountain of assumptions about Britain's political economy. It is also evident in the restoration of free trade, albeit with minor qualifications. It is less evident in public expenditure, which had been permanently raised by the war, but even here the rhetoric of the small and balanced budget continued to hold sway. Whilst the war had revealed weaknesses in the British economy, and some of these were addressed, it was after all a victorious war for Britain, which reinforced the view that except at the margins the pre-1913 parameters of policy should remain unaltered. On top of this, the slump after 1920 removed the threat from labour which had motivated so much change in the war period. And politically Labour was not able to offer a significant intellectual and political challenge to this restored hegemony (Booth and Pack 1985).

Further Reading

Burk, K. (1982) (ed.), *War and the State*, London.

Cd. 9035, (1918) *Final Report of the Committee on Commercial and Industrial Policy After the War*, PP 1918, vol. 13.

Davenport-Hines, R. (1984), *Dudley-Docker: The Life and Times of a Trade warrior*, Cambridge, chs. 4, 5.

Kirby, M. and Rose, M. (1991), 'Productivity and Competitive Failure: British Government Policy and Industry, 1914–1919', in G. Jones and M. Kirby (eds.), *Competitiveness and the State*, Manchester; 20–39.

Lloyd, E. M. H. (1924), *Experiments in State Control*, Oxford.

Ministry of Munitions (1922), *History of the Ministry of Munitions*, vols. vii, viii.

Pollard, S. (1992), *The Development of the British Economy 1914–1990*, 4th edn.: ch. 1.

Turner, J. (1984), 'The Politics of Organised Business in the First World War', in J. Turner (ed.), *Businessmen and Politics*: 33–49.

Whiteside, N. (1980), 'Industrial Welfare and Labour Regulation in Britain at the Time of the First World War', *International Review of Social History*, 25: 307–31.

4

1918–1929: Recession and Rationalization

INTRODUCTION

The immediate aftermath of the war was a frenetic boom, as outlined in Chapter 3. This was followed by an economic collapse which, measured by the fall in GDP (6 per cent), was the most serious of the twentieth century. Unemployment rose from 2 per cent in 1920 to 11.3 per cent in 1921. This in turn was followed by a period of 'doldrums' (Pigou 1947) and then a considerable recovery in the late 1920s, reaching a peak in 1929. However this recovery was never sufficient to take unemployment much below the 10 per cent mark.

This economic failure brought economic policy to a much more central place in political debate and government policy. But no sharp break in actual policy resulted. For much of the 1920s the predominant aim of policy-makers was to restore pre-1913 economic 'normalcy'. However this was compromised by the protectionist and Imperialist sentiment unleashed by the war, and later by the clear failure of that normalcy to be achieved. By the end of the decade the ideological ground of economic policy was shifting, but no major new policy orientation had emerged before the world slump arrived.

CONTEXT

The flow and ebb of economic activity was to a degree paralleled by a flow and ebb of policy. The 'khaki' election of 1918 had delivered a huge Conservative majority, albeit with Lloyd George still as Prime Minister. But with Bolshevism seen as an immediate danger, large-scale returns of ex-servicemen, and a tight labour-market, the government initially felt compelled to pursue policies aimed at sustaining the boom conditions. Despite the 1918 Cunliffe Report calling for the restoration of the gold standard, the government feared the deflationary consequences of such a policy, and in 1919 the wartime suspension of the gold standard was continued into the peace (Moggridge 1972: ch. 1). In line with this stance, policies of radical reconstruction continued to be discussed if not enacted, and the government convened a National Industrial Conference, in part to channel labour militancy into more constructive ends (Johnson 1968; Lowe 1978).

But these concessions to perceived political realities were short-lived. Fiscal policy was never lax, and the budget moved sharply into surplus in 1919/20. Monetary policy was tightened a little at the end of 1919, and then decisively in spring 1920 just as the boom was beginning to exhaust itself as re-stocking was achieved. The cumulative result was a sharp deflation with the major impact on output and unemployment already noted. The immediate reason for this change of stance was the fear of inflation, with consumer prices two-and-a-half times their 1913 level by 1920. This inflation unleashed a panic across the spectrum of informed opinion. Keynes was very much a 'dear money man' and his views typified many at the time: 'A continuance of inflationism and high prices will not only depress the exchanges, but by their effect on prices will strike at the whole basis of contract, of security, and of the capitalist system generally' (Howson 1973: 459).

This inflation and the fears it unleashed reinforced the desire for a return to the pre-1913 norms. Central to this was gold restoration, which promised automatic checks on inflation via gold loss and automatic adjustment of the balance of payments. This (alleged) automaticity of gold was its main attraction to its supporters—it seemed to promise a system where politicians could be denied any scope for their meddling and inflationary propensities (Moggridge 1972: 86).

Gold was the keystone in the arch of Britain's internationalist policy stance which existed before the First World War and which politicians wanted to restore in the 1920s. This internationalism was grounded in the belief that Britain's economic prosperity depended on the growth of the world economy, buttressed by stable currencies and exchange rates, free capital flows, and free trade. The rise in and persistence of unemployment in the 1920s could be interpreted in line with this stance as the consequence of the disruption to that international economy brought about by the war, and hence the restoration of the international economy became seen as the route to reducing unemployment. The restoration of gold in 1925 can be seen as the central achievement of this internationalism (Boyce 1987: chs. 1–5).

This policy stance was endorsed, with varying degrees of enthusiasm or reservation, by most major political and interest groups. It was in many ways a Conservative policy, and meshed in readily with Conservative enthusiasm for 'rolling back the state' in general and public expenditure cuts in particular. These latter were famously symbolized by the 'Geddes Axe' of 1922, which embodied highly contentious cuts in welfare expenditure, though much larger cuts in defence (Peden 1985: 76, 78).

But Conservative support for internationalism and normalcy was qualified by the Party's enthusiasm for protectionism, boosted by the nationalism of the war and then by the unemployment of the 1920s. Only electoral disquiet prevented a thoroughgoing protectionist policy by Conservative governments in the 1920s, and this did not prevent a nibbling away at free trade through the decade (see the section on Markets, below). In the late 1920s a progressive Conservatism was apparent, most notably in the work of Boothby *et al.* (1927). But whilst this moved some way from orthodox Conservatism in its advocacy of intervention in the economy and its emphasis on co-operation in industry, it did not advocate a break with the broadly internationalist stance of policy, refusing to pronounce on the issue of protection (Booth and Pack 1985: 56–8).

The Liberal stance in the 1920s, whilst more radical on domestic policy, was largely supportive of this internationalism. Free trade remained sacrosanct and was indeed the main element that bonded the diverse strands of liberalism together. The gold standard decision was of course attacked by the most famous Liberal economist, Keynes. But he and the Liberal Party tended to accept the *fait accompli* after 1925 and focused their attention on ameliorating the effects of this decision. Thus the famous Liberal Yellow Book (Liberal Party 1928) focused its attention on domestic policy changes whilst still adhering to the classical liberal tenets of free trade and gold (Booth and Pack 1985: ch. 2).

The Labour Party leadership in the 1920s was unambiguously internationalist. Its leader, Ramsay Macdonald, was economically illiterate, but his interest in foreign policy chimed in with seeing international negotiation and action as central to economic revival. Snowden, Labour's economics spokesman and Chancellor of the Exchequer in 1924 and 1929, was probably the most dogmatic internationalist amongst major political figures in the 1920s. He was fully behind the return to gold, and in the government of 1924 led the policy of reversing the small exceptions to free trade which had crept in over the previous decade (Boyce 1987: 14–18, 83–90).

However, within the Labour Party and its affiliates other currents were emerging. Oswald Mosley's *Revolution by Reason* of 1925 focused its attention on an expansionary domestic policy but linked this to a rejection of the gold standard and a call for a re-orientation of industry to domestic markets. The Independent Labour Party's *The Living Wage* of 1926 had considerable similarity with Mosley's view, though was less clear on the international implications of its expansionary policies (Booth and Pack 1985: ch. 1). But these arguments had almost no impact on the Labour leadership and Labour policies.

In all three main political parties a broad internationalism of economic policy was endorsed by the leaderships, the main qualification being the Conservatives' equivocations on free trade. But in each of the parties there was substantial unease about the domestic economic situation, especially as the 1920s wore on and demonstrated the failure of internationalist policies to bring a return to pre-1914 levels of unemployment. In all three parties a concern with the efficiency of industry was also much to the fore, at least among important minorities, and in all three cases this involved a larger though usually ill-defined role for the state. However the general acceptance of the parameters established by internationalism prevented this unease being translated into any coherent policy initiatives.

This policy stance was not seriously challenged by the major interest groups. The City was almost unanimous in its support for internationalism. The Bank of England was its powerful mouthpiece, and only a few mavericks like McKenna, chairman of the home-oriented Midland Bank, stood out against this opinion from within the ranks of finance (Pollard 1970: Introd.; Williamson 1984).

Amongst industrialists opinion was more divided. The Federation of British Industry, the main representative body on general issues, exhibited substantial unease on the restoration of gold and its deflationary consequences throughout the 1920s. But these doubts were never translated into a major attempt to change policy, partly because of divisions within the FBI's own ranks and partly because of the absence of a major political party with a stance hostile to gold (Boyce 1987: ch. 3).

Attempts to create a producers' alliance against the City and the internationalist stance of policy were not entirely absent in the 1920s. In 1927–9 the 'Mond–Turner' talks between a large group of prominent employers and the TUC included some questioning of monetary policy, though its main concerns were industrial relations and 'rationalization' (see below). Its questioning of monetary policy was in any event muted, its Report calling only for an enquiry into that policy and especially into the proposed amalgamation of the Treasury and Bank of England note issues, expected to have deflationary consequences (Macdonald and Gospel 1973; Gospel 1979).

Despite the General Strike, the general trend of TUC policy in the 1920s was towards a more conciliatory role *vis-à-vis* employers, and it was employers rather than unions who ensured the failure of Mond–Turner. However, the policy stance of the TUC was usually to back the Labour Party leadership's economic conservatism against the radicalism of the ILP and other dissident voices in Labour ranks.

If the political situation in the 1920s largely favoured a continuation, albeit increasingly uneasy, of economic internationalism, intellectual opinion, at least in so far as it can be said to be represented by economists' views, followed suit. Of course Keynes must be a major reference-point here, and he developed a devastating critique of the decision to return to gold at $4.86, arguing that it would entail industrial strife over wages and unemployment in the exporting industries (Keynes 1925/1972). But even his stance must be qualified in two ways. Once the return to gold came about in 1925, he focused attention on mitigating its effects and did not advocate a deliberate devaluation or departure from gold. Second, in the 1920s he remained a strong supporter of free trade, a position not given up (and then only briefly) until the early 1930s (Keynes 1981*b*; Eichengreen 1984).

Keynes coupled this position with a general scepticism about the sense of trying to recreate pre-1913 conditions, and announced the 'end of laissez-faire' (Keynes 1926/1972). This was a significant attempt to carve out a well-grounded position somewhere between state socialism and *laissez-faire*. But whatever the intellectual force of such arguments, the political force of the Liberalism they proclaimed declined throughout the decade of the 1920s.

However, Keynes should not be seen as an isolated battler against a reactionary economic orthodoxy in the 1920s. Most of the applied economics debate of the period focused on unemployment policy, and here the strands of thinking were complex. In the 1920s Keynes's own view on the issue was underdeveloped, and it was only in the 1930s that he became convinced of the need for a full-scale revolution in economic theory as a necessary prelude to adequate policies for unemployment (Clarke 1988: ch. 4). In the late 1920s his main emphasis was on public works and other what he regarded as second-best means of stimulating the economy whilst staying on gold. Other economists stressed the microeconomic basis of the unemployment problem, though there was no unanimity on whether this was mainly a problem of excessive wages, labour immobility, or unemployment benefit. Solutions were equally diverse, few advocating wage cuts, even when, as in the case of Pigou, they believed excessive wages were a major part of the problem (Casson 1983).

The great majority of economists remained wedded to free trade. Equally, they were not advocates of governmental intervention in industry. Their main interest in industrial organization focused on responding to the evident trend to industrial concentration and calls for 'rationalization', but whilst these issues excited much interest amongst economists, it cannot be said that economists had much of interest to say on them before the 1930s (MacGregor 1927, 1934; *Economic Journal* 1930). As to what went on within the enterprise, MacGregor aptly summarized the standard economist's view 'I do not know anything about it. I do not think anybody outside business does' (*Economic Journal* 1930: 352).

POLICY: MARKETS

As discussed in Chapter 3, wartime concern at Britain's lack of indigenous capacity in certain key industries, as well as the immediate desire to save foreign exchange, had inspired a number of protective measures. Industries deemed of strategic importance in war were deemed of vital importance for prosperity in its aftermath, and the 1919 Key Industries legislation allowed import licensing of a similar range of products as the wartime legislation. However this was struck down as unlawful in the same year, and the provisions re-enacted as part of the Safeguarding Act of 1921. This allowed for a 33⅓ per cent tariff on the same range of commodities.

The same piece of legislation also embodied a tariff defence against goods from countries with depreciating currencies. In practice this was only applied for a relatively short time (1922–4) and only against Germany. The Act also contained provision for protection against goods deemed to be dumped (sold below their prices in the producer's domestic market), produced by low-wage labour, or subject to subsidy. These very broad provisions were, however, largely inoperable and in practice the focus of protection was quite narrow. In addition to the key industries it covered dyestuffs, which had their own Act in 1919, and silk, which was protected by duties from 1925, though these were offset by an excise duty on home produced artificial silk. In introducing the duty, Churchill called it a 'sumptuary duty' (i.e. luxury tax) designed to raise revenue, and it may be seen as on a par with the McKenna Duties which had been continued into the peace, lifted by Labour in 1924, only to be re-imposed by the Conservatives the following year and slightly extended (to commercial vehicles) in 1926 (Balfour 1927: 399–427; Snyder 1944).

As Capie (1983: 41) summarizes all this legislative activity: 'the measures that had been taken in the 1920s were all rather insignificant in terms of the volume of imports they affected but they were of some importance for their inroads on free trade ideology' (see also Garside 1990: 149–59). As already noted those inroads had already gone a very long way in the Conservative Party, but the loss of the 1923 General Election to what was thought to be an anti-protectionist vote stopped the Conservatives pressing on to general protection even when returned to office in 1924–9.

The ideological implications deserve further comment. First, protectionism in this period usually embodied Imperial preference. Under the Budget of 1919 most protectionist legislation embodied a (variable) degree of preference, though not the key industry provisions. This was in line with the other (but equally limited) encouragement of Imperial economic links such as the Empire emigration scheme (of 1922) or the reorganization of the Imperial Institute (1925) to encourage exploitation of Imperial economic resources. This Imperial bias of policy was paralleled by a growing role for Empire markets and suppliers in British trade. But it seems doubtful if Imperial preference had much to do with this trend, which pre-dated the war and continued right through the inter-war period (Capie 1983: ch. 2). However it did set the stage for the intensification of Imperial protectionism in the 1930s.

Second, protectionism is not of course only encouraged by explicit legislation. It may also be encouraged by such bizarre events as the officially inspired 'Buy British' and 'British Shopping' weeks of 1925/6, the encouragement of local and central government to buy British-produced goods, through to the reform of the Merchandise Marks Act, extending it to advertisements as well as the goods themselves, in 1926 (Balfour 1927: app. B: 397–8, 423–7).

Rather more important was how the new policy objectives of the 1920s generated policy measures which helped to secure markets for British producers. The Export Credit Guarantee Scheme of 1919 was introduced as part of the policy of trying to restore the economic viability of Eastern and Central Europe, though it was extended to all countries in 1926 (Aldcroft 1962). The government also played some role in the creation of the Trade Indemnity Co. (Jamieson 1991: 166–7). The Trade Facilities Act was more significant, in that it offered guarantees for loans abroad which would lead to the creation of employment in Britain. Most guarantees were granted to the iron and steel, engineering, shipbuilding, and electrical industries. The take-up seems to have been very limited, resulting in Treasury expenditure of only £27,000 before the scheme was wound up in 1927 (Balfour 1927: 389–91).

This last Act, for all its trivial scale, raises the question why, in the face of persistent mass unemployment, more was not done to link employment creation to the advocacy of protectionism, as was done in the 1880s and early 1900s in Britain (and on a lesser scale in the 1970s), and is so often done in periods of high unemployment. The answer is that it was evident that most of Britain's employment problems in the 1920s arose in export industries and not from import competition (Table 4.1). So 'Made in Germany' or 'Made in the USA' were not the real problems causing unemployment, though some of the tariffs imposed were largely anti-German in character. By and large tariffs were therefore irrelevant to the unemployment problem. This was at least implicitly recognized by such measures as the Trade Facilities and Export Credit legislation, both aimed at expanding British exports rather than limiting imports.

TABLE 4.1: *Britain's export volumes in the 1920s*

Year	Export vol. (1938 = 100)
1913	173
1919	95
1920	123
1921	86
1922	119
1923	129
1924	132
1925	130
1926	117
1927	134
1928	137
1929	141

Source: Capie (1983), p. 18.

In addition, most export loss was not due to protection in potential markets, but to a failure of competitive power in largely free-trade markets (for the case of cotton, see Ch. 13).

Hence there was little pressure to impose tariffs as a bargaining counter, as had been proposed in the tariff debates of the pre-war period. By and large government and the major producer groups accepted that Britain was losing out on a level playing-field. The one exception to this was the attempt to get the general ratification of the International Labour Office's 1919 resolution in favour of the 48-hour week—but in the event this was not even ratified by Britain (Lowe 1982).

TABLE 4.2: *Balance of payments in the 1920s* (£m. current prices)

	Visible Balance	Invisible Balance	Current Balance
1920	−148	+485	+337
1921	−148	+341	+193
1922	− 63	+264	+201
1923	− 97	+280	+183
1924	−214	+292	+ 78
1925	−265	+317	+ 52
1926	−346	+328	− 18
1927	−270	+368	+ 98
1928	−237	+361	+124
1929	−263	+359	+ 96

Source: Feinstein (1972), Table T.82.

By the mid-1920s Britain was a significantly less foreign-oriented economy than before the war. For example, exports as a share of national output fell from 33 per cent in 1907 to 27 per cent in 1924, imports from 31 to 25 per cent. This process of domestic reorientation was by no means smooth and easy, and the balance of payments was under pressure through much of the 1920s, even with the help of mass unemployment and the improvement in the terms of trade (Table 4.2). It probably owed little to government policy, reflecting more the shift in the composition of domestic demand to domestically produced goods on the import side, and the loss of competitiveness on the export side. There was no concerted effort to switch resources from export to import-substituting sectors, so whilst domestically oriented producers could and did flourish in this period, the staple export industries mainly suffered a lingering decline (Table 4.3).

TABLE 4.3: *Staple exports in the 1920s* (£m.)

	1913	1920	1929
Cotton pieces (bn. yds.)	7.1	3.5	3.8
Coal (m. tons)	73.4	24.9	60.3
Iron and steel (m. tons)	5.0	3.3	4.4
Ships (000 tons)	340	846	260

Sources: Cotton: Robson (1957), p. 333; coal, iron and steel: Mitchell (1988), pp. 257, 301; shipbuilding: Jones (1957), p. 64.

For much of the 1920s the assumption of government and the main producer interests was that the staple export industries could be revived, and this was a central tenet of the internationalist orientation of policy (Garside 1990: 140–4). In the late 1920s this belief began to falter (Hancock 1970). This faltering was symbolized by the Industrial Transference Act of 1928, which reflected a belief that unemployment in the staples was never going to revive, and labour should be encouraged to move elsewhere. This meant that the markets that were worried about in the 1920s were mainly export not domestic. Government did what it could to secure the former, by monetary stabilization, encouraging capital exports (subject to qualifications—see the section on Capital, below) and working for international free trade. Electoral calculation more than intellectual conviction debarred a major effort to protect domestic markets, but this was no doubt reinforced by the compelling fact that the major economic problem of the period, unemployment, was largely an export not an import problem.

POLICY: PROFITABILITY

Like output, profits were subject to sharp cyclical movements in the 1920s. The collapse of 1920–2 was especially focused on both manufacturing output and profits, but the latter seem to have shown a sharp recovery. This recovery was sustained until the end of the late 1920s boom.

TABLE 4.4 *Profits in the 1920s: gross
trading profits of companies and public
corporations (£m. current prices)*

Year	Profit
1920	621
1921	343
1922	437
1923	456
1924	477
1925	468
1926	420
1927	478
1928	474
1929	485

Source: Feinstein (1972), Table T.30.

This cyclical behaviour seems to have been superimposed upon
a long-run trend towards profit decline which was noticeably
accentuated by the impact of the First World War. Table 4.5
compares the typical year of the decade, 1924, with 1913, and
whatever measure is used, gross or net, profit share or rate, a
significant decline is apparent.

TABLE 4.5. *Profits in 1913 and 1924*

	Gross profit share of trading income (%)	Gross profit rate (%)	Net profit share of trading income (%)	Net profit rate (%)
1913	33.8	11.8	29.8	14.9
1924	24.9	8.7	20.5	11.2

Source: Matthews *et al.* (1982), p. 186.

The causes of this long-run trend remain controversial. In part
it probably reflects the capital-saving nature of much twentieth-
century technical change. In addition, and perhaps particularly
accounting for the speed of change across the First World War,
there was a combination of tight labour-markets and the strength
of foreign competition. Whilst the former disappeared in most
industries in 1920–2, the latter remained throughout the 1920s
(Matthews *et al.* 1982: 195–7).

Against this background a constant theme of complaint by
industrialists in the 1920s was the level of taxation of profits as

an alleged source of the depressed state of the economy. Certainly profit was subject to higher tax rates than in the pre-war period, reflecting the general higher incidence of tax to pay for higher levels of public expenditure, especially on servicing the national debt (Morgan 1952: Table 9, 104). But the trend of taxation on profits was downwards. Income tax fell from 6*s*. (30p) in 1919 to 4*s*. (20p) in 1925/6. The wartime Excess Profits Duty was abolished in 1920/1. This was replaced by a Corporation Profits Tax in 1920–4 'to get some boom profits into the exchequer', but was then abolished (Thomas 1978: 85–6).

The Colwyn Committee on National Debt and Taxation set up partly in response to complaints about the impact of taxation on levels of economic activity generally discounted such views. 'Wider causes than taxation, however, and particularly the dislocation of our old export markets, must be held mainly responsible for the lack of buoyancy in recent years. Relatively, income taxation has not been a factor of high importance' (Colwyn 1927: para. 451; also para. 702).

The Colwyn Committee focused considerable attention on the impact of taxation on the supply of savings for investment, and argued that there was little evidence of capital shortage to suggest such a problem existed. This view is borne out by data on aggregate company savings which show them to be in excess of investment throughout this period. This is not true for individual sectors, especially the staple export sectors, but it does suggest that the problem of low investment was not a problem of capital supply but of rates of return. Here Colwyn accepted that 'in business generally, the existing taxes tend to discourage a sanguine outlook' (para. 694) but this did not disturb the general conclusion that it was heightened competition, especially in the staples, that was the main barrier to higher investment.

Overall, governments in the 1920s were highly sensitive to criticism of the higher taxation they imposed, but found themselves unable to restore pre-1913 levels of expenditure, not least because of the avid desire to reduce the war-induced national debt (Howson 1975: chs. 1, 2; Cronin 1991: ch. 5). In 1928 production industry was relieved of 75 per cent of its rate liability, and though this may have given some small help to firms in high-rate areas, the overall tax level was unaffected as local authorities were compensated by central government for loss of revenue (Hicks 1970: 77–8). Whilst periodic attempts were made to reduce total expenditure, the war had brought about a ratcheting-up, which brought with it higher levels of taxation that provided an element in the contemporary Conservative analyses of Britain's economic problems. But there is no good evidence that taxation's effects on profits should be seen as a major hindrance to economic activity in this period. In that area, government's concern with efficiency was not significantly compromised by their own tax-levying activity.

THE EFFICIENCY OF LABOUR

As noted in Chapter 3, the war induced a major input of training activity by the state, initiated mainly by the Ministry of Munitions. With the end of the war the Ministry's concern with the rapid creation of a new army of semi-skilled operatives disappeared (as did the Ministry itself). Policy for training now fell to the (newly created) Ministry of Labour. Its main concern initially was to make up the wartime deficit in training of those called up, and to assist the disabled ex-servicemen. But the coming of depression in 1920 meant their activity was soon confined to the latter. Activity was further reduced in 1922 with cuts in expenditure under the Geddes Axe. The 'work of the Ministry of Labour between 1917 and 1924 must be seen as an attempt to manage the aftermath of war rather than as part of a wider strategy aimed at enhancing government's role in the process of training the labour force' (Sheldrake and Vickerstaff 1987: 10).

The combination of public-spending economies and the downturn in the economy after 1920 ensured that even this role would be curtailed. But the depression of the economy also meant that government action on training in the 1920s became increasingly detached from issues of efficiency and concerned mainly to mitigate the worst effects of unemployment. This was not entirely the case. For example, the Ministry still regarded apprenticeship as the main route to industrial skill, and was worried by the shortage of apprenticeships. But, again, the main action which followed was to offset the effects of the war by initiating an 'Interrupted Apprenticeship Scheme' (Balfour 1927: 136–60).

Training schemes for the unemployed included Government Training Centres, which offered 6 months training where there was a reasonable chance they would find jobs as 'improvers' at the end of the period. The numbers concerned were trivial (about 6,500 in the 1920s). Similar small numbers in this decade were involved in 'Instructional Centres' aimed at the rehabilitation of the long-term unemployed, or 'Junior Instructional Centres' for the young unemployed (Sheldrake and Vickerstaff 1987: 13–17). All this amounted to a degradation of state-sponsored training into a kind equivalent to the relief of the able-bodied under the poor law. Training was mainly aimed at preventing the 'degeneration' of the unemployed rather than equipping them for largely non-existent jobs, though any role for the government in training, advocated by the Ministry of Labour in combination with Industrial Transference, was resisted by the Treasury, especially in the 1920s (Lowe 1986: 194–5).

Of course this macroeconomic gloom should not be overdone. In certain areas the demand for labour was strong for most of the 1920s, one good example being Coventry. Here the deficiencies of national provision for technical training were at least partly offset by local employers pressing the local authority to provide facilities. A reasonably successful system particularly of day-release style training was evolved which helped fill the skills gap created by the rapid growth of Coventry's engineering base (Thoms 1990: 37–53).

The other important agency for technical education was of course the Board of Education. As before the war, the pattern was of slow development at national level in some instances offset by local initiatives. The development of secondary education of any sort was very slow. In 1924/5 80 per cent of children went to elementary school, and of these 75 per cent went no further in education. The main school-age provision of technical education came in Junior Technical Schools, usually taking children from 13 to 16. In 1924/5 there were just 12,000 pupils in such schools, less than 1 per cent of the relevant age-group. Expansion of these schools was, like many of the reconstruction policies, torpedoed by post-war expenditure cuts. But beyond this JTSs suffered from the policy of developing secondary schools with an age of transfer of 11 and on an academic basis. They were adapted to a system of education covering post-elementary pupils up to the age of apprenticeship, and did not fit the new pattern. They also suffered from the Board of Education's belief that technical education was a local responsibility, whilst the technical associations largely acted as pressure-groups for the improvement of higher-level technical education (Balfour 1927: 160–71; Bailey 1990; Sanderson 1988: 43–4).

The Balfour Committee, like many others, recognized the weakness of the decentralized system of provision in this area. They recognized the need for co-operation between industry and the education system, but came only to the lame conclusion that 'it is desirable that some other organization which included a nucleus of energetic, enlightened and influential men should take the necessary action' (Balfour 1927: para. 190). It seems clear that the Board of Education was not the body to play such a role.[1]

On the broader industrial relations front the 1920s was most famously marked by the General Strike in 1926. This represented a dramatic dashing of the hopes of the reconstructionists at the end of the war of a new era in industrial relations. But by the end of the decade the defeat of the General Strike and the general failure of the economy to revive had led to the movements towards bi-partisan approaches to industrial modernization with the Mond–Turner talks.

Reconstructionist hopes for a new era in industrial relations were most obviously represented by the Whitley Reports, the results of a reconstruction committee enquiry into how to secure 'a permanent improvement in the relations between employers and workmen'. Its answer focused on the expansion of collective bargaining and underpinning of the Joint Industrial Councils where industry-wide issues could be discussed. They also proposed a system of works councils, and an expansion of (voluntary) arbitration. These were taken up with some enthusiasm by unions in weakly organized trades (Clegg 1985: 204–7). They also covered parts of the public sector, and it was mainly these whose existence was to be prolonged.

---

[1] The Ministry of Labour did undertake a major inquiry into apprenticeship (Ministry of Labour 1927) but this was explicitly limited to fact-finding not policy formulation. The Board of Education Percy Committee on technical education (1928) created some pressure for the expansion of technical education but this was a minority interest in the Board (Pavitt 1980: 70–1).

But they did not inaugurate a new relationship between capital and labour. Employers generally resisted the Councils as a threat to their prerogatives, and were effectively aided and abetted by the Treasury, which blocked strong promotion of the Councils by the Ministry of Labour (Lowe 1986: 92–7). A parallel negativism was apparent in the area of wage regulation. Trade Boards were expanded significantly by an Act of 1918, but in the reaction of the early 1920s were deemed to be going beyond their proper role of preventing sweating, despite the evidence of the favourable effects of such regulation on efficiency (Cmd. 1645; on the effects see Ch. 3).

The predominant perception amongst reconstructionists envisaged an expansion of the state's role in industrial relations, but certainly not general state determination of wages and conditions. For example a Ministry of Reconstruction discussion of the issue argued that 'the question of wages will never be allowed to return to the position of ten years ago when the Government had no concern in it', but was wary of suggesting extensions to state regulation beyond the expansion of Trade Boards in 'poorly-paid' industries (PRO 1919a: no. 19, State Regulation of Wages, 14, 3).

Voluntarism was still the desired system of most trade-union leaders and employers, though the two groups had different views of what its outcome was likely to be. As the depression ensued after 1920 the government was only too pleased to step back from any responsibility in wage bargaining, as the fall in output and prices brought overwhelming and successful pressures for cuts in money wages (Clegg 1985: 311–13).

Reconstructionists hoped that the new climate and institutions in the labour-market would have been a significant favourable effect on productivity: 'It had been common ground among the reconstructionists, and among the political parties in the 1918 election, that an increase in output per head would be necessary after the war, to allow Britain to provide the better life which all agreed could and should be enjoyed by the British people' (Clegg 1985: 263). But despite stated support for such views from unions and employers few deals were made to this end, partly because of the see-saw effects of the post-war boom and slump on the bargaining powers of the two sides.

Whatever the dramatic and indeed heroic aspects of the General Strike, in the current context its importance was rather limited.

Though lost by the TUC and miners, it meant wage cuts as a solution to economic problems were little applied, even in the slump after 1929. Once it had been absorbed by the trade unions and employers it sparked a 'new philosophy' (Clegg 1985: 461–4), particularly on the union side, which paved the way to the Mond–Turner talks. But the beginnings of the slump from 1929 put paid to this project—though, as Lowe (1986: 115–16) suggests, more might have been salvaged if government had been a little more supportive. But there was little evidence of the kind of political leadership required for such innovation in the late 1920s.

THE EFFICIENCY OF CAPITAL

As already noted, there is little evidence that capital supply was a major inhibition on the expansion and efficiency of British industry in the 1920s. Nevertheless conditions in that period probably did change so as to make financing less of a constraint than before the First World War.

First, any argument that foreign investment starved domestic industry of funds becomes less plausible. From the staggering heights reached in the Edwardian period, foreign investment fell back sharply, both absolutely and in proportion to home investment (Table 4.6). This partly reflected the reduction in attractiveness of investment in primary-producing areas in a period of depressed commodity prices. But in part it reflected the government's control of foreign investment, begun in wartime, and maintained thereafter. The purpose of this was definitely not to encourage home investment, but rather to aid the balance of payments in a period of aiming at, and then trying to remain on, the gold standard (Atkin 1970). As can be seen from the figures, this involved a favouring of Empire over non-Imperial flows.

TABLE 4.6. *Home and foreign investment 1911/12 and 1925/9* (£m. current prices)

	1911/12	1925/9
Home investment	38	165
Foreign investment (Empire)	67	67
Foreign investment (elsewhere)	95	48

Source: Pollard (1992), p. 92.

Second, the 1920s did see a significant reorientation of the stock exchange away from foreign to home issues. As noted in Chapter 3, this was partly stimulated by the desire to capitalize wartime gains evident in the stock-market boom of 1920. But over the decade as a whole home industrials rose from an almost trivial to a significant proportion of the market by the end of the 1920s (Hart and Prais 1956). Commentators have usually seen this change as reflecting the drying-up of some private sources of capital (e.g. because of death duties) coupled to the growing scale of the typical enterprise (e.g. Thomas 1978: ch. 2). However as Hannah emphasizes (1983: 57), this was not a process of the 'democratization of wealth' but rather one where the wealthy became much less often the sole owners of one enterprise and instead held a diversified portfolio of quoted shares.

This expansion of the significance of the stock market for domestic industry was accompanied by other changes, such as the rise of the unit trust. It was seemingly not linked to a major reorientation of established financial institutions, like acceptance houses, towards home industry. Rather, the main intermediaries in the stock market were company promoters, of highly variable degrees of honesty, who often helped create highly speculative waves in share prices, as was evident in both 1919/20 and 1927/9.

These bursts of speculative activity both had significant implications for company organization, as so often this being the main impact of the stock market rather than directly for provision of funds for new investment. The clearing banks do not seem to have altered their practices significantly in the 1920s, retaining an emphasis on liquidity. This may have helped maintain stability of the banking system but told against any activist response to problems of industrial competitiveness (Capie and Collins 1992: ch. 6; Ross 1990).

THE EFFICIENCY OF TECHNICAL CHANGE

A related case is that of industrial research. Here again the wartime worry at the poor research performance of British industry was not entirely forsaken in the 1920s. The DSIR continued its role as a state-funded supporter of industrial research, though the conditions of its grants were tightened in 1923, in line with the general tightening of public spending. Here, however, the main line of activity was explicitly non-interventionist, in the sense that it was aimed at creating Industrial Research Associations as co-operative ventures between firms, with only a temporary grant from government to get them started. In practice this was not a very successful policy, in that whilst over 20 IRAs were formed by the mid-1920s and 31 by 1934, only one had become self-sufficient in the expected five years. In addition, IRAs were noticeable by their absence in major industries like shipbuilding, railways, and steel[2] (Balfour 1927: 310–23; Varcoe 1981).

The importance of DSIR money for the expansion of research should not be exaggerated. Whilst the tightening of the grant conditions after 1923 was hardly encouraging, total DSIR spending did not reach a million pounds until 1933, a sum ICI was spending every year on research by 1930 (Varcoe 1981: 444, 447). Seemingly much more important in the general success of IRAs were the degree of industrial concentration, where medium concentrated industries fared best, the pre-existence of a research organization, and the stimulus of displacing a research-based import (Varcoe: 442–52).

The expanded role of the DSIR was only a small part of the total expansion of the research effort of British industry in and after the First World War. Company research laboratories seem to have benefited substantially from wartime profits, and the end of the war saw a major expansion. Where before the war the stimulus had come especially from German competition and German models, in the 1920s the inspiration was 'now not so much the old paragon of Germany, but the U.S. as a paragon' (Sanderson 1972*a*: 114). Whilst there was some falling back in the private as well as the public research effort in the slump of the early 1920s, Sanderson (1972*a*: 119) supports his belief that the trend was still upwards with figures showing a doubling of the number of laboratory assistants and an almost equal expansion of patents.

---

[2] A research association did appear in steel, after the Balfour Committee reported, in 1920 (Varcoe 1981: 438–9).

THE EFFICIENCY OF COMPANY STRUCTURE AND ORGANIZATION

The 1920s saw a highly significant rise in the typical scale of industrial companies. This is (imperfectly) measured by the rise in industrial concentration:

there was, in the decade following the First World War, a sustained and rapid rise in industrial concentration, as a result of which the largest 100 firms gained control of perhaps one quarter of manufacturing output. This level of concentration is very similar to the level achieved in the United States at the same time, though this high level had been achieved earlier in America (Hannah 1983: 91).

This process of concentration was largely the by-product of mergers rather than internal growth of firms. A measure of the intensity of such activity in the 1920s is that around 30 per cent of all investment expenditure by industrial firms in this period was on acquisitions (Hannah 1983: ch. 7).

The 1920s were then similar to the 1960s in that a great wave of merger activity was combined with a stock-market boom. The causal relationship between these two features would appear to run both ways. The desire to merge expands the market and raises the price of company paper, whilst the widening of the market in such paper makes possible mergers which would not be possible for unquoted companies. Later merger booms such as that in the 1960s (see Ch. 8) have been seen as doubtfully helpful to the efficiency of firms. The mergers were often driven by financial engineering rather than productive logic, or the newly merged companies found themselves unable to realize the economies of scale their new size supposedly made available. The picture of the 1920s is perhaps rather different. Although no parallel studies to those of the 1960s to assess the profitability of the newly merged companies seem to have been carried out, the impression is that they had more production logic and were better able to realize efficiency gains. This is perhaps suggested by the fact that many of the firms created by the merger movement of the 1920s remain central to the British economy today (Hannah 1983: 102–3, 120).

If this is correct, it would suggest that a major reason for the merger movement was technological change which made larger units imperative for efficiency. This would seem to be plausible for such industries as cars and rayon, which confirm most closely to the stereotype of the new mass-production industry. Merger may also have provided a mechanism for companies to shift the focus of their activities from old declining sectors to new growth areas—though this was not invariably achieved (Hannah 1983: 106–8).

The 1920s was certainly a period when there was widespread belief in the virtues of amalgamation and increases in the scale of industrial enterprises. Much of this belief was expressed through the idea of rationalization (Garside 1990: 209–15). As so often the very vagueness and generality of the term allowed it to be used with considerable abandon. At its broadest it could be equated with the 'scientifically based rational control of economic life' (Urwick 1929: 27). Vague as this is, it does bring out an important feature of the 1920s—a belief in the ability of Science with a capital S to solve both technical and social problems. However naïvely positivistic we may today consider this idea of science, it is an important background factor to the more specific meanings of rationalization.

Applied to industry these meanings had two major components. On the one hand it applied to industrial structure, i.e. to the size of industrial firms; on the other hand, it related to the internal organization of firms, or to what may broadly be called their management techniques. The former of these gets much of the attention in the rationalization literature—partly because much of it is written by economists who traditionally have had little to say on management. But one, perhaps the, great exponent of rationalization, Urwick, saw 'scientific management' as integral to, and even perhaps the larger part of rationalization. However not only has the literature on rationalization focused on the issue of industrial structure, but most government activity in the industrial sphere, our main concern here, has also had this focus. By and large government, like economists, obeyed a self-denying ordinance in relation to internal company organization.

Alfred Mond, one of the founders of ICI, defined rationalization as 'the grouping together of huge organizations which at one time would have been thought unmanageable and uncontrollable' (Mond 1927: 210). The model in such moves was often

American or German, perhaps especially the former as untainted with Prussianism. When Lincoln Steffans visited the Soviet Union in the 1920s and said 'I have seen the future and it works' he might have been one of the many British visitors to the USA in this period (Maier 1987: ch. 1).

The fad for rationalization was then part of the long-run trend of belief that economies of scale existed which were not being exploited by Britain's old-fashioned companies, with unfavourable comparisons being drawn with major competitors. But it also had more specific historical links. First, the 1920s were seen in a number of European countries as requiring a significant bout of economic adjustment to new circumstances—not least enhanced US competition. So rationalization was not just a British movement, but was taken up in international fora, such as the World Economic Conference of 1927 (Macgregor 1927: 521). Linked to this was the specific desire to pacify Germany by entering into international agreements in highly concentrated industries, thus providing a good reason to build parallel large-scale organizations (Maier 1988: 516–45). But above all rationalization was taken up as a way of responding to the problems of competitive failure and industrial depression. Most efforts to rationalize were responses to adversity rather than driven simply by a carrot of perceived profitable opportunities (*Economic Journal* 1930: 353). Perhaps this latter factor helps explain the scale of support for rationalization—the almost universal panacea for industrial problems in the 1920s. Few raised their voices against the movement, and even the economists' worries about monopoly and the impact on the consumer were strikingly muted (Macgregor 1934; Robinson 1931: ch. 12).

What was the government's role in this fashion for rationalization? Hannah (1983: 51) suggests that 'Essentially . . . the position of interwar governments was to eschew not only the role of trustbuster but also that of trust promoter'. Certainly the first half of this sentence seems unassailable: across the political spectrum anti-trust activity on the US model was regarded as inappropriate. The Left regarded trusts as technically desirable because of their efficiency, and believed their anti-social aspects provided a case for their nationalization. The Right by and large regarded anti-trust activity as a quite inappropriate meddling in private enterprise.

Government's role in the promotion of trusts is perhaps more ambiguous than Hannah allows. Certainly, as he notes, government's role in industry was more active and direct outside manufacturing. Most striking is perhaps the creation of a public corporation, the Central Electricity Board, to run the new grid and to buy electricity from local undertakings. This can clearly be seen in the mould of rationalization, not only because of the natural monopoly in electricity transmission, but in the way in which the CEB used its role to force rationalization on to larger generating units. Politically this was possible partly because the CEB as a public corporation was immune from a direct government role, and also because its output was sold to so many industrial consumers that the economic case for public ownership overrode political objections (Hannah 1979: chs. 3, 4).

A similar case is the compulsory amalgamation of the railways in 1921. Again there were specific circumstances which made this politically tolerable. The railway companies themselves were willing to trade amalgamation against de-control. And like the case of electricity, there was a compelling case for maximizing the efficiency of a sector which provided an input for so many other industries (Bonavia 1971: 3–35).

Strategic considerations also led to a government role in the encouragement of the creation of ICI in the 1920s, an involvement directly linked back to the wartime policy of creating a British dyestuffs capacity in competition with Germany. ICI was always an atypical company in Britain, with a strong element of 'public purpose' in its organizational objectives (Reader 1977).

In declining staple industries the political pressures for government to act were rather different. Here the decline of the industries brought unemployment. This in turn provided a case for rationalization as a means of raising efficiency, but also a danger that at least in the short run the problem would be exacerbated. In broad terms the government clearly favoured rationalization of such industries as coal, iron and steel, and cotton in the 1920s (on cotton see Ch. 13). In coal the desire to do something about the industry was strengthened by the terrible state of industrial relations that typified it in the 1920s. But the government's preferred route was to encourage the coal owners themselves to act to change the industry. This, however, the owners were reluctant to do. Frequent reports told of the economies of scale to be reaped by the

amalgamation of pits, but the first stage of government's intervention to this end in 1927 was extremely limited. By the Mining
Industry Act of that year compulsion could be applied to
minorities who opposed amalgamation, but the initiative for
change still had to come from within the industry.

However, the failure of the owners to take advantage of this
Act prompted the passing of perhaps the toughest and most
controversial piece of industrial policy in the period. The 1930
Coal Mines Reorganisation Act allowed for both the compulsory
imposition of amalgamations but more importantly state backing
for cartels. In practice it was the latter element which proved
most important, the pace of amalgamation being a subject of
dispute (see Ch. 5), but certainly falling below the hopes of the
framers of the Act (Kirby 1977).

In steel the picture is one of a government favouring rationalization, but relying on 'informality, personal contact and suasion'
(Tolliday 1987*a*: 293). Here the political issue was rather specific,
in that unlike most of the staple trades, the industry's problems
were partly the result of a considerable degree of import penetration, not just loss of export markets. Hence the question of
rationalization was bound up with the question of tariff walls, or
something to be done by the industry before it was allowed
protection. Until the coming of general protection in 1931 the
latter view prevailed. Governments in the 1920s were concerned
at the threat of inefficient monopoly from a protected industry,
and wanted rationalization before granting a tariff. As in coal
the owners themselves only moved tentatively down this road,
though the reasons for this were in some ways more complex
because different parts of the industry provided inputs for other
parts, so that simple horizontal amalgamations were less relevant
(Tolliday 1987*a*: chs. 8, 9, 12).

The fervour for rationalization also affected the banking sector.
Before 1944 the Bank of England was a private body, but one
with a significant if not always clear-cut public purpose element.
In the inter-war period the Bank was drawn substantially into the
rationalization arena both because of traditional banking concerns, and because of these more general concerns with industrial
efficiency. On the former side was the role in Armstrong Whit-
worth's, an armaments manufacturer and one of the Bank's
private customers. Here the Bank was instrumental in the take-

over of the firm by Vickers and the rationalization of armaments production. At one remove the Bank was also drawn into the attempts to rationalize cotton, by the threat cotton's bad debts posed to the commercial banking system. The Bank was also drawn into attempts to rationalize steel, and in 1929 created the Bankers Industrial Development Corporation to draw funds from a range of financial institutions to encourage rationalization (Sayers 1976: i, ch. 14).

In all this the Bank's relation to government was complex. Partly it had its own peculiar, banking, reasons to intervene. On the other hand it did see itself as having a general remit to encourage industrial efficiency. Governments in the late 1920s encouraged this role for the Bank, as a way of achieving policy aims without directly involving government. In some ways this fitted with the Bank's views—it saw its actions as pre-empting the need for a government role, especially if that government threatened to be Labour (Tolliday 1987*a*: 201).

The role of the Bank of England emphasizes the difficulty of answering clearly the question 'What did governments do to encourage rationalization?' They did quite a lot, but most of it indirectly is perhaps the fairest answer. And they only acted where the political benefits seemed likely to outweigh the general unattractiveness of interfering in the private sector. This mainly arose where a monopoly supplier (railways, electricity) seemed likely to damage the efficiency of major industrial consumers they supplied; where labour relations were close to breakdown (coal); or where a strategic industry was clearly in trouble (steel, chemicals). The limits of these actions are returned to in the final section below.

As emphasized earlier, ideas about rationalization sometimes embraced internal enterprise organization as well as simply industrial structure. Broadly speaking this was an area where government exempted itself from action. But it should be noted that this was not quite entirely the case. One small but not entirely trivial example would be that of 'industrial fatigue', an area which had originally engaged the attention of the Ministry of Munitions in the war (Ch. 3). The Industrial Fatigue Research Board (IFRB—Industrial Health Research Board from 1931) was created in 1916, and carried out studies on issues relating to worker health and efficiency right through the 1920s and beyond. Whilst only a research body, this is perhaps a case where the government was not willing to let private industry go entirely its own way even on internal matters (Balfour 1926: 171–8).

STATE CAPACITY AND STATE ACHIEVEMENTS

The Balfour Report argued that 'The promotion of manufacturing industry by means of direct financial subsidies is no part of the policy of this country. In the few cases where assistance has temporarily been given to industry some exceptional circumstance was present' (Balfour 1927: para. 384). This may serve as a general conclusion to the limits of government action in industry in the 1920s, though we might want to add that 'exceptional circumstances' were becoming more frequent as time went on. Given the widespread (though not, of course, universal) problems of British industry, why was more not done?

We can start with the general policy stance, and re-emphasize a point already made. Until quite late in the 1920s the general expectation across the political spectrum was that recovery would come to the staple industries by a restoration of the pre-1913 world economy. This hope was only slowly dissipated. Second, this commitment to economic internationalism was reinforced by the perilous state of British public finances, with a huge national debt and squeezed revenue base. This reinforced the *laissez-faire* bias against industrial intervention, as such intervention invariably cost money, and usually a considerable amount of it.

Alongside this broad policy stance we must also note state incapacity to deal with industrial issues. At the highest level there continued to be no focus for industrial issues. As Urwick (1929: 136) wrote:

The only Minister who can in any way be described as responsible to the Cabinet for measures affecting the general efficiency of British industry and commerce is the President of the Board of Trade. But if this Cabinet Minister should attempt to take anything like a synoptic view of the situation as a whole he would find himself sadly handicapped.

Urwick went on to point out the fragmentation of responsibilities, with the Ministry of Education dealing with training, the

Ministry of Labour with labour issues, the Home Office with factory legislation.

He might also have pointed out how innovation in such policy areas was handicapped by the reinforcement in this period of Treasury power and Treasury parsimony. This is, for example, a major theme of the historian of the inter-war Ministry of Labour (Lowe 1986). At a lower level there was a simple lack of knowledge about industry in the government departments. Only exceptions like the Mines Department of the Board of Trade slowly built up a competence to deal effectively with the complexities of their industry (Kirby 1979).

Finally, it is important to note that as always government intervention in industry depended in large part upon the organization of the employers in the industry concerned. In the case of the components of ICI, for example, a well-organized body of employers was able to present a united case to the government. In the case of steel the owners were often bitterly divided on most issues and unable to tell the government in a unanimous voice what they wanted (Tolliday 1987*a*: 290–1). So in assessing the limits of state action in this period it is important to note the rather disorganized condition of employers, which provided a major stumbling-block to government action, especially where the government machine was rarely capable of generating detailed proposals internally.

In sum, whilst depression and unemployment provided a strong impetus to government to intervene in this period, the political obstacles like to this were substantial. Hence the desire to act was rarely matched by a belief that this would be politically advantageous, and by the time of the slump of 1929–32 Britain had evolved nothing that could sensibly be described as an industrial policy.

Further Reading

Booth, A., and Pack, M. (1985), *Employment, Capital and Economic Policy: Great Britain 1918–1939*, Oxford: chs. 1, 2.

Garside, W. R. (1990), *British Unemployment 1919–1939: A Study in Public Policy*, Cambridge: chs. 6, 8.

Hannah, L. (1983), *The Rise of the Corporate Economy* (2nd edn.), London.

Lowe, R. (1978), 'The Failure of Consensus in Britain: The N.I.C. 1919–21', *Historical Journal*, 21: 649–75.

Newton, S., and Porter, D. (1988), *Modernisation Frustrated*, London: ch. 2.

Pollard, S. (ed.) (1970), *The Gold Standard and Employment Policies Between the Wars*, London.

Sanderson, M. (1972), 'Research and the Firm in British Industry, 1913–39', *Science Studies*, 2: 107–51.

Tolliday, S. (1987), *Business, Banking and Politics: The Case of British Steel, 1918–1939*, Cambridge, Mass.

5

1929–1939: Protection and Profits

INTRODUCTION

The economic history of the 1930s is dominated by the boom and the slump. From the peak in 1929 output fell until 1932 when a recovery began, fuelled after 1935 by rearmament. Table 5.1 shows the dimensions of this slump. Unemployment followed the same cyclical pattern, but, whilst falling in the recovery, remained well over the million mark into the beginnings of the war.

In comparison with many other countries the slump was relatively mild, and the recovery rapid. Output also grew quite rapidly from cyclical peak to cyclical peak (1929 to 1937). For those with work and especially in the South and East of Britain these were prosperous years as rising real wages fuelled a considerable expansion of expenditure. This forms one reason why despite the slump Conservative governments won successive elections with ease after the collapse of Labour in 1931. Nevertheless economic policy did change radically in the 1930s. The gold standard broke up and free trade disappeared. In addition the political and social pressures arising from unemployment drew government into acts of intervention in industry. Britain could certainly not be called a country of *laissez-faire* by 1939, though the best term to describe government's role in the economy by that date remains questionable.

CONTEXT

The 1929–31 Labour government was driven from office by the inability to combine fiscal deficits with maintaining international financial confidence. The Conservative governments after 1931 (called National until 1935) faced no such dilemma. The initial departure from gold in September 1931 was followed by a

TABLE 5.1. *Main economic indicators 1929–39*

	Output (GDP at Factor Cost; £m.)		Prices (consumer prices; 1913 = 100)	Balance of payments (current account; £m.)	Unemployment	
	(a) Current prices	(b) 1938 prices			(a) Numbers (000)	(b) Percentage
1929	4214	4216	161	96	1503	8.0
1930	4185	4210	155	36	2379	12.3
1931	3843	3980	145	−103	3252	16.4
1932	3746	4008	141	− 51	3400	17.0
1933	3776	4046	137	− 8	3087	15.4
1934	4016	4334	138	− 22	2609	12.9
1935	4197	4496	140	23	2437	12.0
1936	4389	4633	144	− 27	2100	10.2
1937	4708	4834	152	− 47	1776	8.5
1938	4959	4985	153	− 55	2164	10.1
1939	5225	5190	158	−150	1340	5.8

Source: Feinstein (1972), Tables 4, 5, 65, 15, 58, pp.T13, T16, T140, T39, T128

collapse of the pound down to 1932, but thereafter the relative economic and political stability of Britain led to capital inflows into London which put upward pressure on the pound. Desiring to keep the pound down, the authorities actively managed the currency via the Exchange Equalization Account, buying foreign exchange to hold the pound's rise in check. This was accompanied by low interest rates ('cheap money'), initially aimed at cheapening the burden of the national debt, later seen as aiding economic recovery. From the authorities' point of view through much of the 1930s, this happy combination of reserve accumulation and low interest rates was dependent upon the maintenance of financial confidence, a confidence which would be shattered by any departure from the fiscal norm of a balanced budget.

In practice budgetary policy was made to appear more conservative than it really was by window-dressing the accounts (Middleton 1985: 115). Nevertheless there was no recourse to Keynesian-style deliberate use of fiscal deficits to boost the economy, however much that may be one way of viewing the way rearmament impacted on the economy. If there was no Keynesian revolution in economic policy this did not mean the economy was unmanaged. As already noted the government managed the exchange rate and interest rates in the 1930s. In addition it erected tariff barriers around much of British industry and by these and various quotas attempted to manage British trade.

These various policies had no single objective or outcome. In part they were no doubt the *ad hoc* responses to changing circumstances rather than a well-planned package of policies. But it may be argued that there was more coherence in the government's approach than has often been granted. Booth (1987) has argued that much of the government's approach was based on the belief that the key need to revive the economy was to raise prices. In this view the slump was characterized above all by downward pressure on output prices unmatched by falls in costs. This led to a squeeze on profits as the central feature of the period. Treasury officials, Booth argues, 'very quickly had an analysis of the slump in terms of price movements, and a strategy of engineering a controlled price rise to restore profits to more acceptable levels' (Booth 1987: 506).

Such an approach was not confined to the Treasury, but was widely shared by economists and much informed opinion

(Howson and Winch 1977: chs. 4, 5). Thus in one part of the Macmillan Report accepted by all its members, it was argued 'We think that the recent increase in unemployment in every part of the world, accompanied by a decline in production, can in the main be attributed to the fall in the level of prices, unaccompanied by a proportionate reduction of money costs, however brought about' (Macmillan 1931: para. 197).

Whilst the diversity of policies of the early 1930s cannot be reduced to a single aim 'a range of economic policies at the beginning of the thirties was provided which would all have had, and were mostly intended to have, an upward pressure on price: a depreciating currency, cheap money, quantitative restrictions on commodity imports, import duties on manufactures and semi-manufactures' (Capie 1981: 141).

This desire to see prices rise without initiating a major inflation, combining expansion with fiscal conservatism, provides the framework for the style of macroeconomic management of the 1930s. Seen in the light of Keynesian analysis the resultant policies were ill-informed, conservative, and ineffectual, and certainly they did not deliver anything like a full recovery of the economy. But they did herald the coming of a more managed economy, and a loss of faith in the ability of a market system to recover by its own devices.

A similar political and intellectual shift was evident at the microeconomic level. There was much agreement by all forces outside the government itself on the need for planning in the 1930s—from the Communists through to progressive Conservatives like Macmillan (Marwick 1964; Booth and Pack 1985: chs. 3–8). This planning was often ill-specified. Sometimes it included a large dose of Keynesian macroeconomic management (e.g. Macmillan 1938, esp. chs. 9, 11, 13). But a theme underlying nearly all this belief in planning was that unaided private enterprise had proved incapable of changing as needed, and that some greater co-ordination of industrial change was necessary, though this very much left open how far there should be a large role for government, and how much could and should be left to industrialists with just a framework and a little prodding from government.

Whilst espousing no faith in planning, the Conservative governments of the 1930s also acted as if they had lost faith in the efficacy of market forces to solve industrial problems (Booth 1989*b*: 552). Building on the experience of rationalization in the 1920s, they intervened in a variety of industries, especially the staples, to try to improve their performance. This was done within no clear ideological framework, often by discreet negotiation with interested parties rather than by public pronouncement and legislation. Nevertheless it amounted in sum to a significant shift in the relations between government and industry.

POLICY: MARKETS

The tariffs of 1931 and 1932 mark a thoroughgoing departure from the free-trade regime of the previous eighty or so years. The emergency tariffs of 1931 were succeeded by the Import Duties Act of 1932, which imposed a 10 per cent general tariff on goods except those explicitly exempted, mainly primary produce from the Empire and most other food and raw material items. Most tariffs were doubled to 20 per cent later in 1932, and there were other changes for specific goods throughout the 1930s (Capie 1983: ch. 3; Garside 1990: 168–72).

These tariffs were imposed for a variety of reasons: to raise revenue, to bolster the exchange rate, to form the basis for Imperial preference, and to boost domestic output and employment. In part they represented the Conservatives' taking advantage of an electoral opportunity to pursue a long-desired policy. It also followed a long period of pressure from some industrialists (Capie 1983: ch. 4), and much agonizing amongst both economists and members of the previous Labour government (Garside 1990: 160–8).

Tariffs may be viewed from a macroeconomic or a microeconomic angle. From the macroeconomic side the difficulty of analysis is partly that the tariff was originally imposed at the same time as the pound was allowed to depreciate, and these measures have in theory similar economic effects. Both, other things remaining equal, increase demand for domestic output at the expense of imports. Hence the importance of tariffs to Britain's recovery in the 1930s has been much disputed partly because of the problems of disentangling these two causes (Capie 1983: 105–7; Kitson and Solomou 1990: ch. 4).

In addition, Eichengreen (1981) has argued that the beneficial effect was not felt via improvements to the balance of payments, but by raising domestic demand relative to output and raising prices. Kitson and Solomou (1990: 45–65) agree with this positive macroeconomic assessment of the tariff, but emphasize the impact of the tariff on investment and import substitution. In their view the tariff was important in reducing imports and therefore can be seen as raising the potential growth of demand and output. For them the view that tariffs were unimportant is based on neo-classical theories that assume perfect competition and its corollaries and full employment. Against this they want to argue that in a world of imperfect competition, increasing returns to scale, and mass unemployment, tariffs can and did both help the British economy to recover in the 1930s and put it on a higher growth trend. However they do note that by helping to revive the staple industries protection may not have helped longer-run growth because of the inhibition to structural change (101).

The hoped-for impact on Britain's Imperial trade links is also subject to dispute. Capie (1983: ch. 2) argued that the impact was very small given both the unwillingness of Britain to allow free access to all Empire food imports, and the unwillingness of the (White) Empire to allow free access to British manufactured goods. Hard bargaining at the Ottawa conference of 1932 seemed to produce only small concessions on either side, and not enough protection to seriously divert the course of trade. There was a growth of British Empire trade in this period, but this, he argues, dated back to before the First World War and cannot therefore be said to be due to Imperial preference. Kitson and Solomou (1990: 53–63) accept that many factors were at work, but believe Imperial preference did make a significant difference.

At the microeconomic level the issue is even more complex. The assessment of the impact of the tariff on particular industries depends on the rate of effective protection, not the nominal rate. The nominal rate such as the general 20 per cent of 1932 may be highly misleading as to the impact of the tariff, because what matters is how far producers price/cost margins are raised by the tariff. Effective protection calculations take into account the extent to which the tariff favours domestic value added, and this means in particular how far tariffs add to costs as well as to output prices. On this basis Capie has suggested that in some industries in the 1930s effective protection was much less than the nominal rates might suggest. In building, for example, he argues the effective rate was negative because output prices were not protected for this non-tradable good, whilst some imported inputs were subject to tariff. The iron and steel industry was also subject to much lower effective protection than it appears because the tariff raised input prices as well as output (Capie 1983: ch. 8; Capie 1991). Overall, Capie makes a strong case that the protectionist effects of the tariffs of the 1930s were considerably less than contemporaries or many historians have suggested.

However this view remains highly controversial (Foreman-Peck 1981; Kitson *et al.* 1991; Kitson and Solomou 1990). The theoretical grounding of the effective protection idea is that tariffs impact on the flow of resources between sectors of the economy according to the levels of such protection. But the difficulty is that in the 1930s, with mass unemployment and imperfect markets for capital and labour, such resource flows are unlikely simply to follow differences in the level of protection, even if these differences are understood by economic agents (Kitson and Solomou 1990: 36–8).

One of the intentions behind the introduction of tariffs was the idea of using them as a bargaining counter to get industries to reorganize themselves. This intention was expressed by Neville Chamberlain, Chancellor of the Exchequer. Tariffs, he argued 'provide us with such a lever as has never been possessed before by any government for inducing, or, if you like, forcing the industry to set its house in order' (cited Tolliday 1987*a*: 299). A similar tack was taken by the Import Duties Advisory Committee (IDAC), the body set up to distance the tariff-making process from political pressure. This policy was pursued especially in the iron and steel industry. This use of the tariff may be seen as forming part of the general attempt to get the staple industries to reorganize themselves, and is best discussed in the section on Company Organization, below.

If the overall substantive effects of the tariff are debatable, their symbolic significance still appears considerable. They marked the reversal of several generations of political and economic assumptions in British policy. More specifically, they signalled (and probably contributed to) a greater domestic orientation within British industry in this period. Having spent so much of the 1920s trying to re-establish the international economic system existing before 1913, the governments of the 1930s seem to have accepted that such a reconstruction was infeasible as the world generally became more economically nationalist (Garside 1990: ch. 6). Tariffs symbolized that turning inwards in economic policy orientation which is so marked a characteristic of the 1930s.

POLICY: PROFITS

The government's desire to raise prices in the early 1930s was based on a desire to raise profits. Whereas in the 1920s the government had seen the problem of profits largely as one of lowering costs, especially wages, in the 1930s the focus was on raising prices. This reflected the scale of price collapse (Table 5.1) and the inelasticity of costs, especially wages. Following the General Strike any general enthusiasm for wage cuts amongst either employers or governments seems to have dissipated, though public-sector wages were reduced by 10 per cent in the public expenditure cuts of late 1931 (which helped to provoke the Invergordon Mutiny). Increasingly it was accepted that money wages were inflexible in both directions, so that whilst money-wage cuts might be infeasible, rises in prices could cut real wages and raise profits. Keynes, who had of course opposed money-wage cutting in the 1920s, again dismissed it as a practicable

TABLE 5.2 *Gross trading profits of companies 1929–38 (£m. current prices)*

Year	Profit
1929	485
1930	411
1931	360
1932	321
1933	380
1934	464
1935	514
1936	627
1937	717
1938	687

Source: Feinstein (1972), T. 6.

solution in 1931, and said 'We prefer, therefore, to pin all our hopes on a recovery of world prices, and strain all our efforts to secure it' (Macmillan 1931: add. I, para. 53).

Certainly profits were squeezed hard in the depression (Table 5.2). As noted above, the government's policies in this period can be seen to have been highly sensitive to this issue, and the basis of a range of policies, both macro and micro. Prices and profits did eventually recover, though how much due to government policy is debatable.

In the later 1930s this recovery in profits was partly offset by a rise in the National Defence Contribution, a tax which raised the margin between pre-tax and post-tax profits. But overall the 1930s was a period when the government was perhaps uniquely sensitive to profit levels in its policy-making. Thus whilst a certain loss of faith in the efficacy of the market economy had undoubtedly occurred, this did not involve a loss of recognition that in a private-enterprise economy profit is the wellspring of output and employment.

THE EFFICIENCY OF LABOUR

As noted in Chapter 4, the enthusiasm for rationalization of the later 1920s included an attempt to come to a union–employer deal, leading to the Mond–Turner talks. One of the reasons for the failure of this initiative was the change in macroeconomic and hence labour-market conditions from 1929/30 onwards. By that time the original Mond–Turner approach had developed into formal TUC/FBI/NCEO negotiations. Ambivalence on the desirability of such talks with the unions on the part of the employers strengthened into hostility as the slump undermined labour's bargaining power. But beyond this short-term tactical element was a fundamental disagreement on the causes of the slump and therefore the relevant remedies. Whilst both sides could agree on criticism of monetary policy and the desirability of greater links with the Empire, there was a fundamental divergence on the central issue of why the economy was in such bad shape. For the TUC, the slump justified their view that private ownership was incompatible with efficiency, and that only in a framework of public ownership could the economy be put right. The FBI/NCEO reasserted the view that the key issues were costs and profits, and the need was for government to provide the proper environment for private enterprise to flourish (Dintenfass 1984; Booth and Pack 1985: ch. 4).

Thus the slump accentuated the divisions between employers and unions and undermined the idea that rationalization might be pursued with Labour's active involvement or at least aquiescence. Labour was largely excluded from the government's attempts to rationalize in the 1930s, and the unions were too weak to do much about this.

The 1930s provided an unpropitious environment for major action by the government on training. Labour-markets were slack, with a plentiful supply of most skilled workers, even in the revival of the late 1930s (Thomas 1983: 563–5). Public expenditure was subject to close scrutiny. Above all, the focus of attention was not international competitiveness, as had to a degree been the case in the 1920s. This does not mean the government was inactive—large numbers of people passed through training schemes of one kind or another. But these were part of social and regional policy rather than a strategy for greater efficiency via a better-trained work-force (Lowe 1987: 223–5).

Sheldrake and Vickerstaff (1987: 13–17) calculate that about 2 million people passed through the various government schemes from the late 1920s. But three-quarters of these went through Junior Instruction Centres for young people, where the emphasis was on rehabilitation and mitigating the personal and social effects of unemployment rather than providing significant skills training. Smaller numbers were involved but a similar conclusion applies to the Instructional Centres for Adults and the training courses specifically for women. A much better standard of training was given at the Government Training Centres, which provided a 6-month intensive training course, and seem to have been held in high regard. But the numbers involved were relatively small, the peak year being 1937 when 10,800 passed through these centres (Lowe 1987: 262).

One of the reasons for the small scale of this useful effort was the classic quandary of government training schemes in a slump—if the schemes are to be credible and attractive they have to lead to jobs, but jobs in a slump are in short supply. This was recognized by the Ministry of Labour, which therefore kept

numbers on the schemes low to maintain a high level of place-
ment. This was not the only reason for the small scale of the
efforts. The Ministry and the Treasury continued to believe that
training was basically a responsibility of managers. The Treasury
also provided funds explicitly because of the political pressures
arising from unemployment, and this meant the approach was
short term rather than far-sighted. There was also union opposition to any great expansion of the role of the state in areas where
apprenticeship in a context of collective bargaining had shaped
much training provision (Lowe 1987: 223–5).

In fact in this period traditional apprenticeship systems declined quite markedly, as 'employers neglected training and
systematically used apprentices as a source of cheap non-union
labour' (Gospel 1991: 24). Industries such as shipbuilding failed
to evolve any response to the weakening of apprenticeship or
training more generally (McKinlay 1991). Market failure of a
fairly crass kind was not compensated for by any strong government policy, though as in earlier periods individual local authorities could still evolve improved training provision, though the
political and fiscal environment was hardly conducive to such
efforts in the 1930s.

THE EFFICIENCY OF CAPITAL

Criticism of the City and finance generally in relation to British
industry had become common by the end of the 1920s, but it was
given a new impetus by the slump and the responses to that
slump. Most famously the Macmillan Committee of 1931 made
this point quite central to their report, albeit expressed in
typically restrained fashion:

In the last few exceedingly difficult years it would have been of high
value if the leaders, for instance, of the steel, or shipbuilding or other
industries had been working in the closest co-operation with powerful
financial and banking institutions in the City with a view to their
reconstruction on a profitable basis (Macmillan 1931, para. 385).

The Macmillan Committee is best remembered for its discussion
of the 'Macmillan gap', the gap in funding for small and medium
firms wanting to raise sums below £200,000. But as the above

quotation suggests, their focus was much wider than that. They suggested that 'there is substance in the view that the British financial organization concentrated in the City of London might with advantage be more closely co-ordinated with British industry' and called for a new institution to provide long-term industrial finance (Macmillan, 1931: paras. 397–403; see also Grant 1967: 204–5).

In context it is clear that whilst the Macmillan position involved a general worry about finance–industry relations, it was especially concerned with the staple industries. So the issue was not simply the provision of funds by financial institutions for industrial investment, but also the need for such institutions to play a larger role in rationalization (see e.g. para. 385). Thus it saw one way of creating a new institution to be a separation of the Bankers Industrial Development Corporation from the Bank of England and expanding its role both as a direct financing and intermediary body (para. 403). The BIDC, it will be recalled from Chapter 4, had been created by the Bank at the end of the 1920s to deal with its growing role in the rationalization of staples. As the next section outlines, this role for the Bank reached its peak in the early 1930s, but then declined significantly as the decade wore on.

Whilst Macmillan was important in spelling out the quite widespread consensus on the need for industry to be better served by financial institutions, not much happened in the 1930s to follow this criticism up. It is true that in the 1930s the City of London lost some of its international role and took a closer interest in domestic industry. The stock market became more important for domestic industrial issues, as alternative outlets became less attractive in the face of the international slump and demand revived once the slump had passed (Collins 1991: 67, 82–6). However there was no new issue boom in the 1930s, and allowing for price changes, new issues for 'general enterprise' at home only returned to 1929 levels at the end of the 1930s (Grant 1967: 149). In part the problem on the supply side of finance was the absence of institutions with sufficient expertise to properly advise and inform potential investors.

Certainly the commercial banks did not play that role, nor did they play an expanding role in direct industrial finance. At the Macmillan Committee they said they aimed to have 50–60 per cent of their assets as loans and overdrafts, but this target was not achieved in the 1930s, and in fact a decreasing proportion of their lending was to home trade and industry. Rather, the banks increasingly held government debt as a major item in their assets. 'Thus despite the widely perceived need for greater commitment to British industry the overall picture suggests, if anything, that the reverse happened' (Collins 1991: 75; compare Thomas 1978: ch. 3). However it may be argued that by being so conservative in their lending policies the clearers maintained the stability of the financial system, in contrast to developments in many countries (Capie and Collins 1992: ch. 6).

As in other areas, the main initiatives in financial provision came from the Bank of England rather than the clearing banks. The mid-1930s saw the creation of a number of institutions broadly aimed at filling the 'Macmillan gap'. These included the Charterhouse Industrial Development Corporation (1934), Capital for Industry (1934), and Leadenhall Securities Incorporated (1935). None of these was on a large enough scale to make much difference in aggregate. The same may be said of the creation of the Special Areas Reconstruction Association (SARA) directly by the Bank of England (the Bank subscribed 40 per cent of the capital (Sayers 1976: 548)).

This was created for political reasons partly in the context of measures for regional policy, and partly in response to the argument that financiers had been involved in rationalizing the staples without helping to create alternative employment. The SARA focused its attention on small firms, this emphasis arising from the fact that much of its capital was subscribed by big firms unwilling to finance competitors, and because involvement in big firms was thought likely to draw the Association into politics. Whilst the scale of operations and the impact of SARA hardly justify a major place for this body in the history of the 1930s, it does serve as an exemplar of much that was done or not done in this decade (Heim 1984). It was handicapped by a lack of Treasury enthusiasm for spending money, offset by a grudging desire to be seen to be doing something for the Special Areas of high unemployment. It was supposed to take a contentious issue out of politics by creating an independent body. Above all its approach was consistent 'with the prevailing uneasiness about government intervention: financial assistance, especially if organized by the Bank and City, could be regarded as an effort to make existing market mechanisms work more effectively, rather than to supplement them' (Heim 1984: 539). Its limited impact was also typical of other regional policy measures of the 1930s (Garside 1990: ch. 9).

THE EFFICIENCY OF TECHNICAL CHANGE

As for earlier periods, we have no accurate data for the level of industrial research in the 1930s. Authors such as Mowery (1987: 191–2) whilst rightly emphasizing the low levels of such expenditure in Britain relative to the United States, probably underestimate the level in Britain and simultaneously exaggerate the weight of publicly financed research in the total. This is readily explicable given the secrecy of privately owned companies on the subject of their research effort. Sanderson (1972*b*: 121–2), whilst accepting Britain's shortfall in expenditure compared with the USA suggests that private spending was at least ten times that by the government.

Government support for aviation R & D via Industrial Research Associations rose from £93,000 in 1930 to £177,000 by 1938, with the number of such Associations rising slowly from 18 to 22 over the same period (Hill 1950: 51–5). The FBI survey of 1943 found 422 firms spending £1.7m. in 1930, and 566 firms spending £5.4m. by 1938, though they accepted these figures were underestimates (FBI 1943: 7, 9).

These figures give some idea of the relative weight of publicly-financed civilian R & D in the total, but they also suggest that, however financed, R & D held up rather well in the 1930s. This may have been because of its concentration in the new domestically oriented industries, rather than the declining staples. Nevertheless the absolute levels of expenditure remained very low, and the FBI argued that both the state and private money for research needed to be expanded significantly, the DSIR, for example, needing to raise its expenditure to £1m. per annum. It pointed out that only one IRA currently spent more than £100,000 per annum, five in the £30–60,000 range, and the rest less than £20,000 (FBI 1943: 12–13). Even at a time when the average scientific researcher earned less than £500 p.a. these sums were clearly almost trivial.

THE EFFICIENCY OF COMPANY STRUCTURE AND ORGANIZATION

Rationalization first emerged from the growing loss of belief in the idea that Britain's staple export industries would be revived by the reconstruction of the international economy. This loss of belief was beginning to emerge just prior to the slump of 1929–32. It envisaged a reorganization of those industries both to gain economies of scale and to improve management, though it was the former concern that usually predominated (see Ch. 4).

This enthusiasm was reinforced by the slump and the further blow it gave to the fortunes of those industries. But the scale of the slump also tended to shift the emphasis in rationalization away from restructuring, amalgamation, and changes aimed at greater efficiency towards a more defensive posture of combination to protect prices and profits rather than defeat the competition, a 'shift from merger and growth of large firms towards the restriction of the market by collective agreements' (Hannah 1983: 135).

These two impulses are nowhere more evident than in attempts to rationalize the coal industry. These attempts, which stretched back into the 1920s, reached their culmination in the Coal Mines Act of 1930. As is evident from the date, this was passed whilst the Labour government of 1929–31 was in power, which, like its predecessor government, saw amalgamation as essential for the revival of the industry. But it was also concerned to raise prices, partly for the kinds of reasons already discussed, but also specifically to improve the welfare of the miners, notably by reducing working hours back to the level they had been before the General Strike (Supple 1988: 578–9). Thus the 1930 Act came to embody both the desire to amalgamate pits to raise efficiency and the desire to limit competition to raise the industry's receipts. Much commentary has seen these two elements as contradictory. Kirby (1977: 2) talks of the 'massively inconsistent Coal Mines Act of 1930, which instituted both the control of markets by cartel arrangements and a policy of compulsory colliery amalgamations.'[1]

---

[1] The combination of elements seems to have arisen from the need of the minority Labour government to obtain Liberal support. The Liberals were only willing to support the cartel aspect if provision was also made for compulsory amalgamation (Kirby 1977: 130–1).

The control of markets in coal was organized by district cartels which set quotas for individual pits. This seems to have been effective to some degree in raising domestic prices for coal, though it could not of course help the coal exporters (Kirby 1977: ch. 8). But the process of amalgamation was much less evident. The Coal Mines Reorganization Commission created by the Act at first tried for voluntary amalgamations, but with little response from the industry. A scheme initiated by the Commissioners, and with majority support of the owners in West Yorkshire, was deemed unlawful by the Railway and Canal Commissioners in 1935. When the legislation was amended in 1936 in response to this decision, hostility was met from the employers body, the Mining Association (Kirby 1977: 156–7; Thomas 1937: 240–5).

The unions, too, after supporting compulsory amalgamations in the 1920s became vehemently opposed to them in the 1930s, because of hostility to the consequences for unemployment. The government thus found itself in the position of supporting cartels without being able to push through the amalgamations which were supposed to offset the restrictionist and monopolist tendencies in the industry. Amalgamations continued to be sought right up to the Second World War, and the Coal Act of 1938 combined a nationalization of coal royalties with further efforts to encourage amalgamations. But overall the effects were minimal (Kirby 1977: ch. 9). Kirby's analysis of the 1930 Act remains the most detailed and his analysis of that legislation as embodying a conflict between cartels and restrictionism on the one hand and amalgamations and efficiency on the other has been widely endorsed, though Buxton (1970, 1982) has criticized the assumption that there were substantial economies of scale which amalgamations could have made realizable.

Fine has recently argued that whilst economies of scale were indeed available, the cartel did not successfully raise prices until 1936, and that after that date amalgamations did increase. The most important general point he argues is that the cartel arrangements still left an incentive for amalgamation and greater efficiency, as, given fixed prices, lower costs meant higher prices. At least, he argues, there is no evidence that the cartel impeded amalgamations (Fine 1990a, 1990b). These works at least challenge the rather common but surely unhistorical assumption that cartels are always and everywhere an obstacle to reorganization, even if it still remains a puzzle why there was so little amalgamation of coal-mines in the 1930s. Dintenfass (1988) from his detailed work on a number of coal companies, has shown that even where amalgamations took place this did not automatically realize potential economies of scale: 'The resistance to innovation that the industry displayed thus stemmed not from a predominance of small producers but from the conservatism of large concerns' (33). Coal, employing nearly 10 per cent of the British labour-force at its peak and acting frequently as a major flashpoint in economic and political relations, was perhaps unsurprisingly an industry which the government was most directly involved in trying to rationalize in the 1930s. More common was indirect intervention, especially via the Bank of England.

As discussed in Chapter 4, the Bank first became involved in the area through its direct banking role and then by its desire to support the banking system as a whole. These reasons had led to involvement in both the iron and steel and cotton industries. This role was extended right at the end of the 1920s into shipbuilding, when the Bank played a significant role in getting the National Shipbuilders Security Ltd. launched as a body aiming to eliminate excess capacity in the industry. The role in iron and steel was also extended at this time into Beardmores, a major Scottish steel company, and the Lancashire Steel Corporation (Sayers 1976: 320–33).

This growing range of interventions led in 1930 to the creation of the Securities Management Trust and the Bankers Industrial Development Company. SMT was wholly financed by the Bank and aimed at controlling the Bank's interests in coal and iron and steel. The BIDC also drew money from the clearing banks, and had as its aims 'to receive and consider schemes for the reorganization and re-equipment of the basic industries of the country when brought forward from within the particular industry, and, if approved, to procure the supply of the necessary financial support for carrying out the scheme' (Sayers 1976: 326).

The Bank of England thus substituted itself for a more direct role for government in private industry's affairs. The Bank saw this as in part a means of reducing the likelihood of a more radical government role. On the other side both Snowden, the

Labour Chancellor of 1929–31, and his successors seem to have been happy to stay at arm's length from most areas of rationalization (Sayers 1976: 324–5).

The founding of the SMT and BIDC looked like opening up a new era of more coherent interventionism by the Bank in the problem of the staples. But 'In the event these agencies proved not to be the engines of rationalization through a great array of industries; their principal task was rather to oversee the unwinding of commitments into which the Bank had always ventured, or into which it was about to be driven by political pressures' (Sayers 1976: 547). The reasons for this withdrawal remain opaque in Sayers's account, though there were always those who regarded such industrial interventionism as outside its proper remit as a central bank. This position probably only arose because of the marked lack of interest by the clearing banks in such issues: 'it might well be thought that this extraordinary central bank involvement was only necessary because the commercial banks failed to take the initiative' (Collins 1991: 79). The fact that the Bank's role peaked in 1929–31 suggests also the importance of the political calculation behind it, as a means of pre-empting a greater role for the state.

The effects of the Bank of England's interventions have been most closely studied by Tolliday in relation to the iron and steel industry. His broad assessment of the episode is that it failed to deliver a significant rationalization of the industry because the Bank was unwilling to use its position to discriminate between firms, a necessary condition for a major restructuring of the industry. It tried to play a strategic role but lacked the willingness to use the means to that end. The Bank's role, supported by the government, tended to entrench the vested interests of the participants in the industry in their existing positions and solidify them with cartels and tariffs (Tolliday 1986, 1987a: chs. 13, 14). This analysis would tend to support Garside's (1990: 219) sceptical summary of the Bank of England's role via the BIDC: 'In the absence of any agreed reappraisal of the relationship between the financial sector, industry and the government, its operations became increasingly dictated by the force of circumstance rather than the weight of principle'.

Alongside the direct role of government in coal and its (highly) indirect role via the Bank in iron and steel and cotton there was a third approach, usually christened 'industrial diplomacy' (Roberts 1984). In this arrangement, governments worked behind the scenes to try to encourage businessmen themselves to act, presenting their own initiatives as originating in business, and giving the impression of keeping clear of any direct subvention of industry. Much of this was handled at civil service rather than Ministerial level, officials acting to avert any suggestion of politicizing industrial decisions, or equally being seen to undermine parliamentary democracy. 'Industrial diplomacy avoided the direct threat to constitutional relationships but, at the same time, fulfilled the short-term needs of economic and social policy and party politics to help trade and industry, given the economic problems of the early 1930s' (Roberts 1984: 100).

However this approach to industry showed no clearer success than the more direct approach in coal and the route through the Bank of England. In truth, each of these three variants was within a narrow range of options. None of them involved a significant displacement of industrial decision-making away from the private firms. The government had no desire to displace these fundamental prerogatives of private enterprise. While interventions in the 1930s were *ad hoc* and responsive to circumstance, none of them threatened a major reduction in the autonomy of the private sector.[2] Indeed, by strengthening the importance of employers' organizations, legislating for tariffs, and providing support for cartels, the government strengthened the bargaining power of employers rather than gaining power for itself.

Of course private ownership was not universal. The creation of the CEB in the 1920s was followed by another public corporation, the London Passenger Transport Board in 1931, and just before the war, there followed the creation of the British Overseas Airways Corporation in 1939 (as well as the one-off nationalization of mining royalties in 1938). Of these the LPTB was the most important. Largely designed by Herbert Morrison under the 1929–31 Labour government, the nationalization legislation was passed little altered by the succeeding government. It represented the type of technocratic, consensual public ownership

---

[2] The one exception would seem to be the direct role of government in bringing about the merger between Cunard and White Star, and so making possible the resumption of work on the prestigous and politically sensitive *Queen Mary* (Tolliday 1987a: 339–40).

under a public corporation which was to become the norm for British nationalization (Morrison 1933; see also Ch. 8). In many ways it was Labour's own form of rationalization, and one which few could find good reason to oppose. But this was not a model which was to be employed in the major bastions of private enterprise in the staple industries. It augured much that was to come after 1945, but was not followed to any significant extent for the rest of the 1930s.

Finally, the stand-off between the government and the private sector and the public corporation type of nationalization together ensured that government stayed well clear of issues concerning the management of firms. Management and its practices remained forbidden areas to government, as such industrial policy as evolved was driven largely by a naïve belief in economies of scale and mechanization as panaceas, rather than any informed debate about how successful industrial firms could and should be managed.

STATE CAPACITY AND STATE ACHIEVEMENTS

The 1930s did not see the emergence of anything which could sensibly be called an industrial policy. Rather there were a series of *ad hoc* interventions, as much politically as economically driven. Politicians were keen to preserve the separation of politics from industry, and civil servants usually reconciled a continuing commitment to the market mechanism with interventionism by using that great stand-by for resolving tensions, the distinction between the long and the short run: 'In the long run the limited role of government was accepted, but in the short run, it was thought, intervention was needed by government to put trade and industry on the right course' (Roberts 1984: 98).

The most striking characteristic of government–industry relations in the 1930s was not the enhancement of government capacity to intervene but its willingness to support whatever producers seemed to want to revive their industries. This did not mean handing all powers over to industrialists, as suggested by, for example, Davies in 1940. Government did see itself as playing an advisory role, a role of persuasion even to the bodies newly strengthened by the state in the name of self-government. But, as

Tolliday (1987*a*: 342) suggests, 'In practice, the more effective the self-government, the less effective was the persuasion, and the new state-backed structures often meant responsibility without power'.

This outcome for policy was partly the consequence of party politics. On the Left, Labour largely focused its attentions on public ownership as the solution to industrial inefficiency and unemployment, this approach being embodied in *For Socialism and Peace*, a document published in 1934 which contained much of the blueprint for the governments of 1945–51, especially on nationalization.

For the Conservatives a policy of 'industrial diplomacy' (informal discussion) and 'industrial self-government' (strengthening producers' associations) were self-denying ordinances, intended to nudge industry in the right direction, hoping to stabilize and re-establish the credibility of private enterprise rather than by-pass it. Apart from general ideological predisposition, such a stance reflected a desire to avoid any blame for any unemployment that was likely to be the immediate consequence of industrial reconstruction (Garside 1990: 235–6). Employers, certainly as represented by the FBI (which tended to be dominated by firms in the staple sectors), were keen to involve government in trade bargaining, but were equally keen on minimizing its role in individual companies' affairs (Holland 1981).

These political pre-dispositions shaped the organization of a state machine which was not geared up for a policy of intervention in industry. The Board of Trade did not emerge as a major pursuer of industrial efficiency, and indeed in one major area, that of iron and steel, much of the initiative came from the Import Duties Advisory Council (as well as the Bank of England) rather than from any of the Ministries. In contrast the persistence of the Department of Mines in seeking amalgamation probably had some effects, but this was atypical of the level of activity by government departments.

Proposals for a Ministry of Industry were made by Labour Ministers in 1929–31. Attlee, for example, as Chancellor of the Duchy of Lancaster, made a cogent case for such a Ministry in 1930. He saw its role as planning rationalization, and especially mobilizing credit for such rationalization outside the 'private hands' of the Bank of England (PRO 1930). But whether made by 'radicals' like Mosley or more mainstream Labour people like Attlee, such ideas never came close to fruition (Garside 1990: ch. 8).

Various schemes for government finance for rationalization were also put forward in this period, but usually with as little effect as those for a Ministry of Industry. This was part of the general financial stance of the time, 'all but very limited financial concessions to industry remained an anathema within Whitehall' (Middleton 1985: 75). The Treasury also foresaw extensive administrative complexities, with significant political implications, if the state became more closely involved in industry.

It should be noted that nearly all the interventions in industry in the 1930s were concerned with the staples (SARA was a very limited exception to this). The government did little or nothing to alter the behaviour of firms in the new, expanding industries, though in parallel with its attitudes in the staples, it put no obstacle in the way of cartels and combinations amongst such firms. The general drift of opinion was in favour of scale and combination if not outright monopoly, and governments went along with this view. Whilst industrial concentration seems to have been stable in the 1930s and 1940s (i.e. the share of the biggest companies in total output did not increase), cartelization seems to have expanded. By the late 1930s such cartels may have embraced the producers of 30 per cent of British manufacturing output (Mercer 1993). Many of these cartels were organized by trade associations whose numbers, given a fillip by the First World War, expanded rapidly in the slump of the 1930s (PEP 1957: 15–31). This distribution of effort strengthens the view that the government in this period had not broken fundamentally from the belief that in the main the private sector could be relied on to work properly and efficiently. The problems of the staples were seen as contingent and resoluble by minimal intervention, rather than as an indictment of the general operation of the British industrial system.

CONCLUSION

Overall the 1930s did see a closer relationship between government and industry than any previous peacetime period. But the characterization of the relationship is difficult, and its relation to 'efficiency' even more so. As already stressed, the government was concerned to avoid direct intervention in industry, whilst keen to nudge industry into action, a desire which often led to encouragement of greater degrees of co-operation between firms. *Laissez-faire* critics and those on the Left have often seen this encouragement as a sanctioning of monopolistic and restrictionist attitudes, which damns the decade as one of lack of competition and inefficiency.

In a typical piece, *The Economist* (15 June 1940) derided the philosophy of the Conservative Party in the past nine years as wanting an 'orderly organization of industry, each ruled feudally from above by the business firms already established in it' with 'high profits and low turnover' as the dominant slogan of British business (1033).[3] Such a theme is also present in recent work on the long-run growth of the British economy (Broadberry and Crafts 1990, 1992).

On the other hand it may be noted that the conditions of untramelled competition in the 1920s had hardly demonstrated the efficacy of competition for bringing about the changes necessary in British industry. Whether the 1930s in that sense represented a less efficient manner of addressing industrial problems than such competition therefore must remain a moot point.[4]

[3] On another occasion *The Economist* (28 February 1942: 277) argued that this desire for 'organized industry' had been given a substantial fillip by the Import Duties Advisory Committee, and its insistence that representations to the Committee for tariff protection had to come from 'representative bodies of the trade concerned'.

[4] In order to compare the level of economic growth in each decade we need to eliminate the effects of the sharp cycles of the early 1920s and early 1930s. When this is done the rate of GDP growth (1924–9 and 1929–37) is remarkably similar (Dowie 1968). Claims that the 1930s saw a superior performance have to rely on seeing the 1920s expansion as a (delayed) cyclical response to the slump of 1920/1 (Kitson and Solomou 1990: 9–10).

Further Reading

Booth, A. (1987), 'Britain in the 1930s: A Managed Economy?', *Economic History Review*, 40: 499–522.

Booth, A., and Pack, M. (1985), *Employment, Capital and Economic Policy in Great Britain 1918–1939*, Oxford.

Capie, F. (1983), *Depression and Protectionism*, London.

Garside, W. R. (1990), *British Unemployment 1919–1939: A Study in Public Policy*, Cambridge: chs. 6–9.

Kirby, M. W. (1987), 'Industrial Policy', in A. Booth and S. Glynn (eds.), *The Road to Full Employment*, London: 93–109.

Kitson, M., and Solomou, S. (1990), *Protectionism and Economic Revival: The British Interwar Economy*, Cambridge.

Mercer, H. (1993), *Constructing a Competitive Order: The Hidden History of Anti-Trust*, Cambridge.

Skidelsky, R. (1970), *Politicians and the Slump: The Labour Government of 1929–31*, London.

Tolliday, S. (1987a), *Business, Banking and Politics: The Case of British Steel, 1918–1939*, Cambridge, Mass.

6

1939–1945: Planning and Production

INTRODUCTION

The Second World War entailed a radical shift in the relations between government and industry as 'total war' required a mobilization of economic resources on a wholly new scale under the direction of a vastly expanded state apparatus. This led to a government interest in expanding production and economic and industrial efficiency of unprecedented force. Industry was scrutinized in exceptional detail, and its shortcomings exposed to the public gaze. Remedial steps were taken directly to aid the war effort. But in addition the exposure of weaknesses was linked to plans for the post-war world, and for the industrial reconstruction which was widely assumed to be a necessary part of that post-war rebuilding.

Much historiography has focused on the impact of the war on social welfare provision, as social ills came under public scrutiny and public pressure to prevent any return to the 1930s mounted, articulated and shaped by reformists like Beveridge (Addison 1977; Milward 1984). Equally, much attention has been given to the international aspects of the war, its direct and dire effect on the British balance of payments, and more broadly the subsequent attempts designed to create a new international economic order (Pressnell 1986; Clarke 1982; Booth 1989a: chs. 5, 9). The primary concern of this chapter is rather different. Whilst not ignoring either the change in the domestic balance of forces brought about by total war, nor the major changes in the international economic environment, the focus is on the response of the British government to the pressures to raise industrial output and efficiency, both for immediate war reasons and to improve the position of the British economy in the post-war period. This is a relatively neglected topic, though it has recently been the basis of a (highly tendentious) work by Barnett (1986).

CONTEXT

In many ways the British economy was much better prepared for a coming of 'total war', i.e. a war involving a mobilization of the whole economy, in 1939 than it had been in 1913. Some of the lessons of the earlier conflict had been learned, and at the beginning of the war a whole new apparatus of government was created, and new ministries with the remit of controlling imports and raw materials came into being. As in the First World War these controls tended to expand through the war period, but without the same degree of controversy. In particular, controls over labour coupled to conscription had nothing of the political difficulty they raised in the First World War.

Central to the war was a new 'politics of labour' in several senses. Labour came to be regarded as the key resource, and so was granted a new economic and political status. The appointment of Ernest Bevin as Minister of Labour in 1940 symbolized the new situation where labour was given a political role to match the new conditions of labour shortage (Bullock 1967). As the key resource labour or 'manpower' became central to the planning of the economy. For many, manpower planning was the key element in economic decisions: 'the golden rule of planning is to plan with the scarcest resource, and the scarcest resource in wartime was labour' (Robinson 1951: 57). Certainly manpower allocation became increasingly central to the decision-making apparatus of the war period, crucial decisions being based on how far different Ministries both civil and military could obtain the labour they required for their plans. At the peak of the war effort, in 1944, it was labour that was its binding constraint. The institutions of labour—the unions and the Labour Party— also became central to the running of the state for the first time. Union membership shot up, and the TUC aspired to, even if it did not quite achieve, equality with the FBI and BEC in the various tripartite governmental bodies which characterized the period (Middlemas 1986: chs. 1–3).

Labour was also central to the macroeconomic policy of the war period. The central macro problem for the government was to maintain a balance between consumption demands fuelled by full employment incomes and long working hours, and production for the war effort (Tomlinson 1990*a*: ch. 6). The most innovative mechanism to achieve this was the use of the budget to balance total demand and supply in the economy, taxing working-class incomes sufficiently to prevent either diversion of resources into consumption beyond an unavoidable minimum, or inflation. The 'first Keynesian budget' of 1941 saw this fiscal apparatus in place, though it did not prevent all inflation, nor preclude the use of rationing to secure an egalitarian distribution of scarce consumer goods.

For the duration of the war the balance of payments was not a binding constraint. In the period up to the American entry into the war Britain gradually threw caution to the winds in selling assets and using up foreign-exchange reserves, but once the Americans entered the war the problem was effectively dealt with, largely by Lend-Lease and also by the accumulation of sterling balances (sterling credits, paid for imports from countries like Egypt and India). The long-term consequences of this were extremely serious, with a cumulative current account deficit of around £10bn. over the war period (roughly twice the British national income in 1938), but for the duration of the war little attention was focused on the immediate balance of payments implications of policy decisions.

Overall, total war meant a new emphasis on planning and production. Planning, in the sense of physical controls, permeated the whole economy (Hancock and Gowing 1949: 319–24, 329–37, 456–63, 494–8, 502–4). Production was a priority in an economy where not enough could be supplied to satisfy the demands of fighting the war and keeping civilians clothed and fed, especially given, of course, the diversion of over 5 million people into the fighting forces. Planning and the search for more production provided the vital immediate context of the government's interest in efficiency in the war period.

MARKETS

As noted already, the balance of payments constraint was lifted for the duration by a range of expedients. Given this, and the urgent desire for output for domestic purposes, exports were purposely reduced. Not only did this aim to direct resources into other uses, but also followed American pressure on Britain relating to Lend-Lease. The Lend-Lease agreements were concerned with supplying Britain with materials for the war effort, but there were recurrent American worries that some of what they were supplying was being used to produce goods which competed with American exports in third-country markets. In response Britain made a clear commitment to cut back on exports so that such fears would be pacified. A White Paper of 1941 (Cmd. 6311) set out the details of this, and by most judgements it represented a very considerable concession by Britain to US feelings (Pressnell 1986: 10, 21). Some indication of the overall effect of the war on British exports is given in Table 6.1. Exports were also constrained by the availability of shipping space, which also affected the import of goods used for producing exportables.

TABLE 6.1. *Britain's exports to selected markets 1938–44* (£m. current prices)

	1938	1944
Africa	73.6	65.9
India	48.2	35.9
South America	34.2	10.1
North America	44.0	41.2
France and N. Europe	140.0	46.4
TOTAL	470.8	266.3

Source: Statistical Digest (1975), p. 166.

On the import side, controls were used both to save scarce shipping space and foreign exchange, with allowed imports to be concentrated on raw materials. Total imports fell a little over 60 per cent from their pre-war level (Cairncross 1985: 8). All this meant, of course, that 'efficiency' in the sense of Britain's capacity to compete internationally was not an issue in wartime—British production faced little competition at home from imports, nor to a great extent in foreign markets, where demand was generally strong at prevailing prices. Judgement of the economy's performance was then made on different grounds from those commonly prevailing in peacetime, and largely focused on output maximization.

PROFITS

'Profiteering', that is the earning of excess profits, had been one of the cries prominent in criticisms of the conduct of the First World War, and in the Second World War there was a widespread political determination to prevent a recurrence. As Sayers (1956: 28–9) emphasizes there was a 'political compulsion' to 'take the profit out of war'. Initially an Excess Profits Tax of 60 per cent was imposed, effective from April 1939. In 1940 this was increased to 100 per cent. This rate was criticized for its efficiency effects, but although the government did alter some of the details of the tax, the 100 per cent rate was seen as politically immovable once imposed. The tax became a significant source of revenue, yielding at its peak £482m. in 1944, around 15 per cent of total central government revenue (Sayers 1956: 28–9, 46–8, 85–90, 118–26, 493).

The effect of this tax on efficiency is impossible to gauge. On the one hand a 100 per cent tax clearly offends the tenets of sound taxation of profits, in that it gives no incentive to increase efficiency (Postan 1952: 445).[1] On the other hand, the political hostility to wartime profiteering may have meant this effect was offset by a greater willingness to work on the part of those who would have been less happy if their efforts had contributed to higher profits for companies.

Profit levels in wartime were crucially affected by the government control of prices, especially where government itself was the purchaser. Cost–plus contracts predominated, and certainly did not bring any pressure on profits, as all cost increases could be passed on. Some fixed-price contracts were made to try to improve incentives to efficiency, but by and large government departments lacked the administrative capacity to monitor the costs of firms in the manner required by such contracts.

As regards its effect on the company sector's capacity to finance investment, the crucial point here of course is that in the war period finance was not the significant constraint on investment. Investment was limited by shortages of labour, steel, and other materials, rationed by the government. Hence companies

[1] The 100 per cent tax was offset by a 20 per cent repayment after the war, parallel to the 'post-war credits' of wartime income tax. Neither seem to have been regarded as much help to the impact of the tax on incentives (Balogh 1947).

earned profits which they could not reinvest, and so accumulated liquid assets instead. This was especially so because the level of distribution of profits seems to have been significantly cut across the war period 1938–49, partly presumably reflecting the high rates of income tax that were levied on dividend income (Seers 1950: 279). This was not true in all sectors, for example ship-building, where dividends were healthy throughout the war (Johnman 1992: fn. 110).

Overall profit's share of the national income seems to have been maintained over the war period, the total of profits rent and interest rising from 34.4 per cent of national income in 1938 to 39.4 per cent in 1945. Trading profits of companies rose up to 1943, then fell back slightly (Table 6.2). The combination of good profits (even allowing for EPT) and low distribution left many companies cash-rich at the end of the war—for example, Courtaulds had £40m., and Vickers £12.5m. in liquid assets in 1945 (Coleman 1980: ii, 11; Scott 1962: 301).

TABLE 6.2. *Trading profits of companies 1938–45 (£m.)*

Year	Trading Profit
1938	543
1939	715
1940	965
1941	1,105
1942	1,260
1943	1,290
1944	1,280
1945	1,225

Source: Statistical Digest (1975), p. 200.

THE EFFICIENCY OF LABOUR

In order to maintain consent for the war effort and maximize production enormous efforts were put in by the wartime government to conciliate labour and improve industrial relations. Legally government claimed enormous powers over labour, banning all strikes and having the ability to direct workers in and out of jobs. In practice Bevin, the Minister of Labour from 1940, concentrated on using voluntary methods to try to improve industrial relations as well as in the allocation of labour (Bevin 1942: ch. 5).

The war was not one of uninterrupted social peace at the factory level. Strikes, though illegal, occurred on a not insubstantial scale and disputes falling short of strike action were quite common. In 1944 the number of days lost in disputes in metal, engineering, and shipbuilding was higher than in any year since 1924, though the average number of days lost was much lower than in the 1930s (Inman 1957: ch. 12; Parker 1957: ch. 25). In this area, as more generally, it is important not to accept uncritically the mythology of wartime solidarity (Calder 1971). Nevertheless, enormous and unprecedented efforts were made to minimize worker discontent.

Much of this effort focused on improving welfare. This covered both physical welfare by provision of hostels, canteens, and medical services, and later on more general personnel and industrial relations issues. The Ministry of Labour was the spearhead in much of this, persuading often reluctant supply departments that such provision was necessary to secure increases in output. For the Ministry of Labour, responsible for the overall problem of labour supply, it was important to minimize labour demand at enterprise level by emphasizing the possibilities of better labour utilization, and how welfare provision was integral to that objective (Inman 1957: 223–8).

The issues of welfare and maximizing production were therefore always intertwined. In an important Report in 1941 the Select Committee on National Expenditure focused its attention on the 'Output of Labour' and reviewed the factors affecting output per worker. Their discussion of this covered a wide range of issues: they re-emphasized the lesson of the First World War that maximizing working hours does not maximize output, criticized management for poor labour utilization, and went on to list a range of welfare issues where improvement would help the expansion of output. Alongside the contribution of physical welfare to output performance, they emphasized that

many other difficulties which arise in the administration of a factory could be much more satisfactorily overcome if workers were taken more closely into the confidence of the management. At a time of when war conditions necessitate frequent changes of work and adjustments of personnel it is more than ever important that a spirit of co-operation should exist (para. 30).

This linkage between welfare and production was increasingly taken up by some Ministers. By 1942 Cripps, the Minister of Aircraft Production 'through visits to factories, public speeches and the departmental machinery, pursued and urged on others a policy which promoted the human factor in industry to at least as high a level of importance as the supply of raw materials and capital equipment' (Inman 1957: 230).

One consequence of this concern was a big emphasis on personnel management, which was very much a concern of the Production Efficiency Board, which Cripps created in the MAP to encourage efficient use of both labour and capital in aircraft factories. Personnel management was advocated as directly aiding production by reducing absenteeism and cutting labour turnover—both major problems of wartime industry (Inman 1957: ch. 9).

Another aspect of 'human relations' was joint consultation. Here a partly autonomous upsurge of enthusiasm for production led to demands for a greater say for workers in managerial issues, and this was taken up by the Ministry of Labour, who persuaded employers and union leaders, especially in engineering, to regard joint production committees at plant level as a desirable development for maintaining morale and encouraging a positive input into production by workers. Whilst the scope and level of activity of such committees varied enormously, they seem to have flourished in some sections, and represent an important conjunction of the 'welfarism' and 'productionism' of wartime policy (Inman 1957: 371–92; ILO 1944). At their wartime peak in 1944 JPCs were estimated to cover 4,500 factories and 2.6m. workers, though they declined rapidly at the end of the war.

Apart from physical welfare and human relations, other aspects of labour effort and deployment came under scrutiny in the war period. Wages were a problem for official policy from two aspects.[2] On the one hand some pre-war systems of piece-rates,

---

[2] On a broader front the taxation of wages was a policy problem because of the conflict between the need to restrict consumption for macroeconomic reasons (which meant high income-tax rates) and the need to keep taxes down to provide work incentives. There was a continuing debate on this conflict from 1941 till the end of the war, and indeed right through the 1940s.

especially in the West Midlands, proved highly expensive for wartime contracts and also led to poor labour utilization. The supply ministries struggled, without much success, to change these systems. On the other hand some forms of payment by results were seen as highly desirable where previously absent, and so, for example, payment by results on the Bedaux principle of group bonuses was used extensively in Royal Ordnance Factories (Inman 1957: ch. 11).[3]

The increased interest in issues surrounding the efficient utilization of labour led to an enthusiasm for 'motion study', especially in the MAPs Production Efficiency Board, whose members included Anne Shaw, a noted pre-war proponent of this technique. The PEB propagated such study widely, though was always anxious to keep it separate from 'time study', which obviously involved more contentious wage issues (Inman 1957: 429–31).

Overall the scale of effort by both the Ministry of Labour and the supply ministries on labour issues at the factory level suggests that Postan (1952: 438) understates the role of government when he says they 'did little to supervise or to direct the methods of production in the factories of its contractors'. The efforts may have often been *ad hoc* and uncoordinated, and spurred on by specific problems, but nevertheless in sum they amount to a notable achievement. Other, non-labour aspects of the government's attempts to raise efficiency are returned to below.

The government was also extremely active on the training front. Much of this drive came from the Ministry of Labour: 'If there was one subject on which Bevin continued to hammer as long as he was Minister of Labour it was the importance of adequate training' (Bullock 1967: 358–9). Over the war as a whole about 300,000 workers went through government-sponsored training schemes, either in industry, colleges, or the much-expanded Government Training Centres. The latter focused attention on raising workers from an unskilled to intermediate status, with the government meeting much resistance against higher levels of skill being taught outside industry.

---

[3] For details about the Bedaux system and its importance, see Littler (1982): 105–16.

Inman (1957: 73) emphasizes the 'ingrained prejudice in industry, amongst both employers and workers, against institutional training for skilled workers', and the scale of training fell short of government hopes both because of such opposition and because of problems with the supply of machines and trainers.

Training was intimately tied to the issue of 'dilution'—the use of unskilled workers for previously skilled tasks. This had been a major flashpoint in the First World War, and the authorities were very concerned to prevent a recurrence. Formal agreement was generally reached on dilution, on condition that this was only for the duration of the war. But the extent of actual dilution seems to have varied greatly, and certainly in the shipyards it does not seem to have been pursued as far as the agreements would have allowed (Inman: 1957: 141–5). Quite how serious the effects of this were may be disputed. Barnett (1986: 113–23) gives a typically hyperbolic account of the failings of British shipbuilding, whilst Milward (1987: 191), recognizing the slowness of action of the Admiralty in this area, nevertheless argues that eventually there was 'an extraordinarily rapid. . . . modernization of the equipment and methods in British shipyards with the particular aim of introducing the techniques of construction by prefabrication and welding' (for a more detailed discussion of this see Johnman 1992: 189–91).

As in other efficiency issues, the Ministry of Aircraft Production seems to have been the most innovative of the supply ministries in training. For example, it took up the American idea of Training Within Industry (TWI) for skills training which tried to combine the best elements of industry-based and education institution-based training. TWI for supervisors was similarly pursued by the Ministry of Labour, the competence of supervisors and foremen being one of the problems identified by the Select Committee in 1941 (Select Committee 1941: para. 33).

Overall, Britain ended the war with a significant increase in the level of skill of its work-force, though with a system for imparting skills which was still highly industry-based, and therefore subject to all the long-established problems of the too close intermixing of industrial relations, wage bargaining, and training in an apprenticeship scheme.

THE EFFICIENCY OF CAPITAL

Investment was subject to rigorous control in the war, both in financial and physical senses. Exchange control prevented capital outflow, and Britain underwent a major programme of foreign disinvestment—amounting to £4.2bn. over the whole war period. (£1.1bn. sales of assets, £2.9bn. in increased external debt, £150m. fall in gold and dollar reserves: Hancock and Gowing 1949: 548).

Domestic investment was controlled partly by the Capital Issues Committee control of new issues. Under the rules of the CIC all issues of over £5,000 had to be submitted for scrutiny, and only those for defence purposes or the maintenance of food supplies were generally allowed. But as nearly always in Britain, external finance was a small part of total investment finance in industry, and these controls were much less important than the physical controls over building, acquisition of plant, and labour.

Total investment was severely restricted in wartime, in order to free resources for immediate output ('consumption' in the sense of both civilian consumption and munitions). By 1943 investment was at its lowest at only about one-third of the 1938 level, having fallen from around 11.4 per cent of GNP to about 3.0 per cent in 1943 (Feinstein 1972: Table T89). At this level net capital formation was negative, as depreciation and destruction outweighed new spending—Hancock and Gowing (1949: 551) estimate the private loss as £1.6bn. over the years 1940–5.

TABLE 6.3. *British investment in wartime: gross domestic fixed capital formation at 1938 prices* (£m.)

1938	592
1939	540
1940	520
1941	480
1942	450
1943	360
1944	300
1945	350

Source: Feinstein (1972), Table T9.

The squeeze was particularly hard on buildings, where civilian house-building in particular suffered the biggest cuts, whilst plant and machinery expanded, at least in relative terms (Feinstein 1972: Table T86). This pattern reflected the priority that had to be given to expanding only war-related production, in such areas as machine tools and the production of alloy steels (Howlett 1993*a*).

The war thus led to an overall rundown of capital, either in a balance-sheet sense (including foreign assets and liabilities) or in the sense of physical capacity. But in certain sectors capacity was enormously expanded—most obviously in the capacity to produce armaments. Some idea of the scale of expansion (in the absence of data on investment by sector) is given by the output of various goods. Total aircraft production went from 7,940 in 1939 to 26,461 in 1944; tanks and self-propelled artillery from 969 to 8,611 in 1942 (the peak year); and bombs from 51,093 in 1940 to 309,366 in 1944 (Milward 1987: 91). Total munitions production rose approximately 6.5 times between 1939 and the peak in the first quarter of 1944 (Harrison 1990: Table 2), and this ignores the increase in the complexity of what was produced. Thus at the end of the war Britain had experienced a huge expansion of capacity in military-related areas, and this included capacity for intermediate goods like aluminium. The implications of this capacity for the long-run industrial performance of the British economy are unclear. Much of the capacity was highly specific and not readily convertible to civilian use, though there was undoubtedly a benefit in the capacity to produce more light, fabricated finished goods. Some of this development, perhaps particularly of the facilities for producing intermediate goods, must be set in the balance against the overall decline in investment (Hancock and Gowing 1949: 552), though aluminium is a case where wartime expansion was too large for peacetime needs and led to excess capacity after the war.

One area where this positive aspect of the war seems clear is in machine tools, where output rose from 37,000 in 1939 to 95,788 in 1942, as Milward (1987: 187–8) emphasizes 'Once they had an adequate market, and the protection which the rapid increase in the domestic demand for machine tools in the US in 1941 automatically provided, machine-tool manufacturers in Britain were able to manufacture a wide range of products which they had not made before the war' (see also Postan 1952: 206–7).

THE EFFICIENCY OF TECHNICAL CHANGE

The Second World War is famous for a variety of 'big science' inventions, such as radar, nuclear power, the computer, and the jet engine. But many of these were, at best, long-delayed in having any general impact on industrial output and efficiency especially in the civilian sector. Probably more important developments in the technological field at least in the short run were in the application of new technologies of production, as in the use of flow-line production in much munitions work, or in a new integration of design work into production. In part the war was not just a competition in terms of volume of weapons output, but also of weapons design. One of the key problems of war planning was precisely the conflict between volume and design change (Cairncross 1990: introd.; Devons 1950). Hence design and the whole problem of incorporating design changes into production gained a new prominence as an industrial issue. The war does seem to have given a fillip to R & D expenditure not only and obviously by the government, but also by at least some private-sector firms such as ICI who came to realize how far they had come to lag behind major foreign competitors in this area (Reader 1975: 432–3).

A major survey by the FBI in 1943 indicated how limited pre-war R & D had been in British industry. It suggested that the scale of the Industrial Research Associations' activities were generally 'disappointing' and called for a big expansion of the DSIR. It looked forward to much greater efforts by both the state and the private sector in research after the war (FBI 1943). Other stimuli to an expanded government research effort came from the widespread belief that scientific research in general had made a major contribution to the war, and that a much greater effort must be made to plan scientific effort after the war for civilian needs (Keith 1981).

Whilst the aspect of wartime discussions concerned with the 'planning of scientific manpower' came to little (Price 1978), the DSIR was expanded significantly and the National Research and

Development Corporation was created in part to exploit some of the many patents arising in the public sector from the war effort (Ch. 7).

A balance-sheet of the effects of the war on British R & D is not easy to draw up. On the one hand much more was spent in this area, both by government and by private firms. Some firms also clearly came to recognize the deficiencies of their pre-war efforts in this regard, and permanently expanded their effort with probably favourable effects in peacetime. But the focus of so much R & D effort on military and quasi-military areas was obviously a diversion of resources away from more civilian and commercially oriented R & D. This was no doubt unavoidable in wartime, but unfortunately seems to have left a lasting legacy for the post-war period (see Chs. 7, 9).

THE EFFICIENCY OF COMPANY STRUCTURE AND ORGANIZATION

Government policy had a major impact on the structure and organization of industry during the war. Most obvious perhaps was the creation of new and extensions of old capacity. Directly state-owned capacity was concentrated in the Royal Ordnance Factories, which expanded to employ 300,000 people at their peak. Also important were agency factories, where the government built and owned the plant, but where it was operated by the private sector. But most munitions—around 75 per cent of the total—were produced in the private sector.

This meant that the government impact on industry was in some ways indirect, though in war conditions the relationship became much closer in a variety of ways:

The Government was now the sole customer of war industry as well as its chief supplier of raw materials and components . . . the Government also became the chief source of new industrial capital. In some fields Government agencies designed the articles which industry made. Now and again they took a hand in planning factories, workshops and the layout of machinery within them (Postan 1952: 423).

Government leverage over the private sector was therefore considerable. But this leverage was deployed to varying degrees. The most active supply Ministry seems to have been Aircraft

Production.[4] Partly because of the central strategic role of aircraft, partly because of the ideological disposition of the Minister from 1942, Stafford Cripps, MAP was willing to take radical measures to change the companies it dealt with if it deemed such steps necessary. Thus it effectively nationalized one company, Short Brothers, and took over the management of several others, arousing considerable political controversy on the way (Edgerton 1991: 67, 78–9).

Cripps was also active at a more specific level, in creating bodies like the PEB, emphasizing the usefulness of OR techniques for production planning, and encouraging Joint Production Committees. He had himself been an industrial manager in the First World War, and had a more active and informed interest in the area than any other Minister, as well as being ideologically disposed to a willingness to interfere in the prerogatives of private ownership (PRO 1943*a*).

Postan argues against exaggerating the impact of the government on production methods in the aircraft industry. He notes work on production engineering in the Air Ministry from 1938, but argues that the emphasis in MAP was largely on programming production rather than getting much involved in the production aspects, except where these were seen to fall well short of acceptable standards. Overall the focus on programming 'prevented Government planning from penetrating at all deeply into the managerial autonomy of private business'. On the whole, he argues, government powers 'stopped short at the factory gate' (466, 452).

Despite this caution, it seems reasonable to argue that MAP represents an unprecedentedly detailed attempt by the state to improve productive efficiency, covering all the major issues from labour utilization, capital equipment, production engineering, and management competence. All this was to have a significant legacy in both general wartime discussion of British industrial efficiency and post-war industrial policy (see the section on Plans for Postwar, below, and Ch. 7).

The direct impact of this intervention on efficiency in the aircraft industry has been much debated. This debate was largely

---

[4] The Ministry of Aircraft Production has been much studied, especially from a planning perspective: see Devons (1950, and 1951) and Cairncross (1990); none of these deals directly with the issue of productive efficiency.

stimulated by the work of Barnett (1986: chs. 7, 8), who argued that the aircraft industry suffered from levels of inefficiency similar to much of the rest of British industry. However, his adverse comparisons with both German and American aircraft production seem ill-founded. Overy (1980, 1984) has shown that the German aircraft industry was highly inefficient at the beginning of the war, and only caught up and overtook Britain from about 1944. In the American case, Barnett's over-simple productivity comparisons ignore the central role played by larger production runs and bigger factories in the USA, which seem to account for the differences in productivity rather than differences in technology or the skills and effort of workers and managers (Edgerton 1991: 80). Barnett is here, as elsewhere, concerned to argue that it was the British worker who was the key problem for British industry, but as so often the argument is based on comparison with an ideal which does not match any actual country. Certainly German workers were just as attached to their craft privileges as those in Britain (Overy 1980: 174).

On the civilian side the war also saw significant changes in organization. In those industries deemed too large for the needs of wartime, a concentration-of-industry policy was pursued. This aimed to concentrate resources into the most efficient companies and to maximize the transfer of labour and other resources into war-oriented sectors. By and large this policy was conducted at arm's length by the government, with industrial associations organizing concentration schemes, though in some industries (e.g. cotton) ministers played a significant part in selecting which firms were to continue in current lines of production. Compensation was paid to firms closed under the scheme, and the intention was that they should be able to re-enter production at the end of the war period. Some saw this policy as paying too much heed to post-war rather than immediate production needs (Select Committee 1942: 11–12). In any event, this meant that the policy did not act as a forced rationalization programme even in industries where excess capacity was apparent before the war (Allen 1951; Oxford 1947: pt. 4).[5] The most important feature of

---

[5] A detailed survey of the smaller-scale industries in which concentration was prevalent concluded 'In general there is little evidence that wartime marriages of firms under the concentration scheme are likely to survive in considerable numbers, and from this standpoint the permanent effect on structure seems

the policy for industrial policy was not its effects on efficiency (except in the short run) but on the mechanisms of state intervention in industry. A clear division of task was established whereby 'the Government set out the objectives of policy, laid down the conditions that had to be satisfied and established sanctions; but the firms and industries to which the policy was applied were given the tasks of working out the arrangements in detail' (Allen 1951; 180). This was in fact quite a common and important pattern of government–industry relations established in the war (see the section on State Capacity, below).

STATE CAPACITY AND STATE ACHIEVEMENTS

Clearly, because of state purchasing, control over raw-material investment, and labour allocations, and provision of substantial capital funds, the government acquired enormous powers of control over industry during the war.[6] But equally obviously a substantial part of this control was for the duration only. Certainly peacetime would see the end of much of the government's customer role, even if physical controls over resources were continued. In that way the shift in state capacity was problematic with regard to long-run implications. In part the government would lose powers automatically with the end of the war, in other areas it would depend on the exigencies of post-war policy and politics.

More permanent in its impact was the boost given by the war to both employer (as well as trade-union) organization. Much of the wartime control apparatus was effectively subcontracted to employers, especially in trade associations, whilst the BEC and FBI played a major role in co-ordinating employers. In large part this was a question of administrative feasibility—only these bodies had the expertise and capacity to do the job. For exactly the same reason many of the control posts in the Ministries 'were very frequently filled by industrialists drawn directly from the

unlikely to be considerable' (Silverman 1946: xvi). The concentration process did evoke some discussion about the relationship between firm size and efficiency (Murphy 1945: ch. 3).

[6] For an analysis of this apparatus from a public administration approach, see Lee (1980): ch. 4.

particular industry to be controlled, and chosen because, as a rule, they were the only people in the country with the necessary knowledge and experience' (PEP 1952: 10).

This means that to talk of the war enhancing the government's capacity to intervene in industry is not necessarily very helpful. It might be more helpful to regard the war as causing a major intermingling of government and industry, within which government power depended on a high degree of consent and co-operation from industry, though they may have been extracted somewhat reluctantly from a private sector which often bent to political pressure only when it could not see an alternative. Where such consent and co-operation were not forthcoming the enhanced powers of industrial associations at all levels could be a powerful weapon in resisting government aims—as was to be clearly demonstrated in the late 1940s (Ch. 7).

Undoubtedly the political legitimacy of government intervention in the economy and in industry was enhanced by the perceived success of wartime intervention—though much of the debate about whether this perception was correct has focused on the issue of planning rather than the efforts to raise productive efficiency. In their standard history of the war economy written over forty years ago Hancock and Gowing (1949: 551) remarked 'It is to be hoped that before long some economist or historian will attempt a detailed study of wartime changes in industrial efficiency and of the underlying influences such as methods of management, rationalization and reductions in the number of types of particular products'. Alas, little of such work has been done, despite a massive recent expansion in the historiography of the Second World War (but see Howlett 1993*a*, 1993*b*; Tiratsoo and Tomlinson 1993*a*: chs. 2, 3).

Howlett (1993*b*) is one of the few to have attempted some quantitative assessment of the overall efficiency changes in the war, measured in part by labour productivity. His careful assessment on the basis of poor data suggests labour productivity peaked in the early years of the war, probably in 1941, when the political pressures to increase output were perhaps most intense (because of the absence of allies) and at the same time much of the expansion did not have to use unskilled, 'diluted' labour.

Howlett points out that Barnett's discussion of wartime productivity is in the context of the long-run performance of the

British economy, so that for him (Barnett) the war is the opportunity for an 'audit' but not in itself the main concern. Howlett also argues that Barnett's approach is misleading in so far as he focuses on productivity. Howlett suggests that the wartime government's fundamental concern was rather production, increasing the output of strategically required goods in whatever way possible. However, this distinction may be over-drawn. Certainly after 1941, with full employment and labour seen as the major constraint in many industries, a concern with production readily translated into a concern with (labour) productivity.

For example, the Select Committee on National Expenditure in August 1941 argued for 'The importance of securing the greatest output from the labour force in the war industries, as distinct from the problem of increasing the size of the force' and thereby suggested the logic of focusing on (labour) productivity as supplies of new labour dried up. The following month *The Economist* (27 September 1941: p. 380) was arguing that 'Since the net addition to the country's labour force that can still be expected is comparatively small, the emphasis of responsible criticism is rightly placed on expanding output by increased efficiency'.

In many ways there was a parallel shift in the debate in the war period as in the late 1940s (Ch. 7). Initially the focus was on maximizing labour supply, but as this reached its peak the focus switched to (labour) productivity. But in both cases productivity was normally seen not in the context of efficiency in the sense of competitiveness as, for example, became common in the 1970s, but of maximizing output with given (labour) resources.[7] How far this stated enthusiasm for productivity led to much effective action remains a matter of dispute, with detailed research on the issue only just beginning.

Issues of production, productivity, and efficiency came into focus in the war period not only because of the immediate problems of winning the war, but also because of the intense debates that occurred about the prospects for the British economy in the post-war period and the policies which might be

[7] Much of the wartime debate about the efficiency of production can be found in the numerous reports of the Select Committee on National Expenditure in PP 1940/1 vol. 3, 1941/2 vol. 3, and 1942/3 vol. 3.

needed to improve those prospects. This chapter therefore concludes with a brief survey of those debates.

PLANS FOR POST-WAR

According to Barnett's account, the British government during
the Second World War accurately diagnosed the weaknesses of
the British industrial economy but failed to suggest an adequate
remedy, and in the end did little to change things fundamentally
because of the priority given to 'building a New Jerusalem' over
the postulated alternative of a 'national industrial strategy'.

Looking first at the issue of diagnosis and the remedies which
flowed from this, it is apparent that the government did indeed
provide a detailed analysis of the failings of British industry as a
consequence of wartime concern with reconstruction, and especially the issue of how employment in the post-war period was
to be sustained. Much of this analysis seems to have been done
by the Board of Trade, which in 1943 produced a key paper on
'General Support of Trade' for the Committee on Postwar
Employment which summarized their policy proposals (PRO
1943*b*; Barnett 1986: 268–71).

These proposals were predicated on a diagnosis of Britain's
industrial ills with three major features. The first was a belief
that a major enhancement of the scale of industrial activity was
required—either by amalgamation or by trade associations combining separate units for common purposes. Here the Board
drew strongly on the inter-war rationalization movement, and
the belief that the largely voluntary movement for concentration
and amalgamation had failed and needed to be supplemented by
state action. The second feature was a concern with the low level
of investment, and the absence of sufficient willingness to scrap
old equipment and invest in new. And finally the third feature
was an inadequate level of research, especially of co-operative,
inter-firm research, given the small scale of much of British
industry.

This threefold diagnosis led on to proposals for government
action on all three aspects. On scale, the report proposed government encouragement for amalgamations and the creation of
industrial boards as a kind of super trade association to co-

ordinate activity amongst firms in fragmented industries. To guard against the restrictionist, monopolist possibilities of such institutions, the Board of Trade also advocated a strong anti-Trust policy. On the issue of investment, the report argued that the problem was more psychological than financial, but advocated the creation of new institutions, with government money, to finance industry and especially to make amalgamations possible. This might be best done by a Finance Corporation to help to pursue the policy 'without undue political influence'. On research, the proposal was for an extension of the Industrial Research Association system which had been initiated under the aegis of the Department of Scientific and Industrial Research in the First World War. The Board also saw the need for a new body to ensure the exploitation of British inventions, especially those made in the public sector.

In addition to these proposals, the Board of Trade proposed an Industrial Commission with a wide-ranging remit to encourage re-equipment, re-organization, the generation and propagation of new ideas, and possibly a role in monopolies and restrictive practices. Also advocated was an 'Advisory Bureau of Industrial Management' to raise management standards, and a 'Central Council for Design'.

For Barnett all this was 'mere tinkering' (271), especially as the issue of unions and labour restrictive practices was ignored. But this is surely to understate the radicalism of these proposals, and the significance of their being urged by a major department of state. The problem was not the weakness of the proposals, but the problem of political support for them. And here Barnett's analysis seems even wider of the mark. The opposition to such policies came not from New Jerusalem supporters, those allegedly obsessed with issues of social welfare. Rather, as Johnman (1991) argues, it came predominantly from employers and some sections of the Board of Trade who saw the short-term needs of expanding exports as running counter to such long-term plans for encouraging efficiency. Opposition also came from the Treasury, worried about 'excessive' government intervention in industry, especially that seemingly threatened by the broad remit of the Industrial Commission. The main proponents of New Jerusalem were also the main political supporters of this radical industrial policy—the Labour Party. The problem was that the

policy could not be realistically pursued in the face of employer opposition. Johnman (1991: 48) concludes that Barnett's
'positive vision of a national corporate strategy failed not because of countervailing pressure from "New Jerusalem" but
because the business community wanted little or nothing to do
with any such policy'. It might be added that this opposition
was aided and abetted by parts of the state apparatus, and also
by much Conservative Party opinion (Tiratsoo and Tomlinson
1993*a*: ch. 3).

This may be illustrated by the largely successful resistance to
some of these proposed measures—on industrial boards and
monopoly legislation—faced by the post-1945 Attlee Government
(see Ch. 7). Only relatively uncontentious elements like the
British Institute of Management, the Council for Industrial
Design, and the National Research and Development Corporation were established,[8] plus the new, but calculatedly non-govern-
mental, finance bodies, Finance for Industry and the Industrial
and Commercial Finance Corporation, created at the instigation
of the Bank of England to pre-empt any more radical action
(Fforde 1992: 704–27).

CONCLUSIONS

The war served to focus attention on British industrial efficiency
both because of the immediate need to maximize output with
limited resources, and because of worries about post-war prospects. The former concern stimulated a range of actions by
wartime Ministries to try to improve the operation of British
industry, in a context where this issue particularly related to the
skills and efficiency of labour, both because labour was seen as
economically the key resource by many, and also because politically labour had to be conciliated. This interventionism was
greatly facilitated by the status of government as the main
purchaser of industrial output and controller of the major
inputs. The effects of these interventions remain obscure, but
have probably been unreasonably ignored in much of the literature on the Second World War.

[8] On the origins of the BIM see Tiratsoo and Tomlinson (1993*a*), ch. 2.

As regards plans for post-war, the key point here is the gap between diagnosis and proposed remedies on the one hand and actual policies pursued. The problem does not lie with the former. Even Barnett is forced to concede that the wartime government did not ignore issues of industrial efficiency in the search for New Jerusalem. Indeed, in a paper which Barnett cites only in passing, the reconstruction debate had clearly accepted the point that New Jerusalem in the sense of social security could only be built on the basis of a much improved performance in Britain's industrial productivity (PRO 1943c). In this view efficiency and welfare were complementary not alternatives.

Overall the striking feature of the war period is the extent to which industrial efficiency became so central to the contemporary policy debate, a point obscured by much subsequent historiography. Reform of industry was much less radical than much of this debate hoped and anticipated, and the reasons for that were political. But 'political' does not mean because of the opposition between 'national industrial strategy' and New Jerusalem, a position which Middlemas (1986) in his own way seems to share with Barnett. Rather it was the political problem of mobilizing wide support within government and at the same time persuading the private sector to change its ways which were crucial.

Further Reading

Barnett, C. (1986), *The Audit of War*, London.

Chester, D. N. (1952) (ed.), *Lessons of the British War Economy*, Cambridge.

Hancock, W. K., and Gowing, M. (1949), *British War Economy*, London.

Howlett, P. (1993), 'The Wartime Economy, 1939–1945' in R. Floud and D. McCloskey (eds.), *The Economic History of Britain Since 1700*, iii, Cambridge.

Howlett, P. (1993), 'New Light Through Old Windows: A New Perspective on the British War Economy', *Journal of Contemporary History*, 28: 361–79.

Inman, P. (1957), *Labour in the Munitions Industries*, London.

Parker, H. M. D. (1957), *Manpower: A Study of Wartime Policy and Administration*, London.

Postan, M. M. (1952), *British War Production*, London.

Tiratsoo, N., and Tomlinson, J. (1993), *Industrial Efficiency and State Intervention: Labour 1939–1951*: chs. 2, 3.

7

1945–1951: Socialism and the Supply Side

INTRODUCTION

Labour came into power in 1945 with a clear programme of major economic and social reforms, many of which had been developed in the 1930s, especially in *For Socialism and Peace* (1934) and *Labour's Immediate Programme* (1937). These embraced a broad commitment to economic planning, especially focused on a National Investment Board, and a major expansion of the nationalized sector. By these means Labour aimed at providing greater economic and social security on the basis of full employment, greater industrial efficiency, and the creation of a welfare state. The 1945 manifesto *Let us Face the Future* broadly followed the ideas of the 1930s, but also reflected the legacy of war. On the one hand the war gave new urgency to some objectives, e.g. housing; on the other it had created a comprehensive system of economic controls which seemed to fit Labour's commitment to planning.

But this combined legacy of the 1930s and the war period, whilst crucial in shaping Labour's approach to policy, had to deal with quite new economic circumstances in the late 1940s. The standard assumption in wartime was that, as after the First World War, a short boom would be followed by a slump, a slump requiring a policy response to carry out the commitment of the 1944 White Paper (Cmd. 6527) to 'high and stable' employment. In the event the slump never came, and policy was focused on checking demand rather than its stimulation. In addition, the compelling force of the balance of payments deficits and shortage of commodities for home consumption and investment led to a quite new peacetime focus on expanding industrial output and industrial productivity. From this stemmed major innovations in the relationship between government and industry.

CONTEXT

To what extent there was a consensus at the time of Labour's accession to power has been much debated, especially in relation to issues of social welfare and the creation of a welfare state (e.g. Addison 1977; Jefferys 1987; Lowe 1990). Certainly there is evidence that public opinion accepted the need for a considerable expansion of the state's role in both social and economic areas. To that extent the Attlee government was the legatee of a shift in popular (and expert) opinion which had been generated in wartime. On the other hand, the idea that the 1945 Election result represented a semi-revolutionary tide of opinion in favour of something called socialism, seems much exaggerated (Mason and Thompson 1991; see also Fielding 1992).

The most frequently used word in Labour's 1945 election manifesto was 'planning'. As a general ideological stance this was grounded on Labour's long-held hostility to the market, and a belief that the war had demonstrated the efficacy of planning in a manner which would be equally relevant in peacetime. Some of the elements of that planning were clear enough—for example, nationalization, in large part, was seen as providing the foundations of a planned economy (nationalization is dealt with in detail in Chapter 8). But equally it was clear that for the foreseeable future the great bulk of industry was to be in private hands, and here Labour's policies were much less developed. The only seemingly unambiguous position on the private sector was a strong commitment to anti-monopoly policy (Mercer 1992).

If the private sector was, in Harold Wilson's later words, 'largely a vacuum in socialist thought' (PRO 1950*b*), in practical terms Labour had to come to terms with that sector. Its manner of doing so was largely shaped by the wartime legacy of controls. These embraced everything from foreign exchange to consumer rationing, but also extended to most of the industrial economy, with government controlling the supply of most major inputs, labour, raw materials, machinery, and building materials. This apparatus of controls was commonly regarded at the basis of a planned economy and

the machinery that was used by the Labour Government was largely a wartime creation. Most of the controlling departments, agencies and committees had been established during the war, and were retained afterwards. Similarly the system of controls and methods by which the controls were operated, originated, to a considerable extent, with the Coalition Government (Rogow and Shore 1955: 13).

Not only the mechanisms but the personnel running these controls often remained largely unaltered by the election of the Labour government, and this meant to a substantial extent that private-sector industrialists ran them. Effectively many controls in the civilian sector were subcontracted to industrial and trade associations (or industrialists acting as temporary civil servants), so that the private sector was in a very powerful position to shape these controls in ways in which they wanted (Rogow and Shore: ch. 3; PEP 1952: 155–60; Mercer 1991*a*). This position may, however, have been much less apparent in the military sector, where the Ministry of Supply was in a much more powerful position *vis-à-vis* suppliers of military equipment, and seems to have been willing to use those powers (Edgerton 1992: 108–10).

Central to Labour's approach to the private sector was a strong commitment to co-operation and consensus, to forms of tripartite government of industry. This was especially so of the most important figure in shaping Labour's industrial policies, Stafford Cripps. For him democratic planning was differentiated from the totalitarian variety by its commitment to consultation and co-operation. This was not just a rhetorical flourish, but was embedded in a range of bodies such as the National Joint Advisory Council (for industrial relations issues), the National Production Advisory Council for Industry, the Economic Planning Board (from 1947), and a host of other bodies. Whether this tripartism amounted to corporatism as suggested by, for example, Middlemas (1986) may be doubted. Labour's strong commitment to the doctrine of parliamentary sovereignty obstructed the delegation of real decision-making to these tripartite bodies (Tomlinson 1993*c*). Nevertheless tripartism was a central part of the type of planned economy Labour operated after 1945, though again much less apparent in the military rather than the civilian sector, and where the military sector extended across most of engineering.

Planning was seen by Labour as the basis for reconstructing the economy in pursuit of full employment and greater economic efficiency (e.g. Mayhew 1946). The first of these proved a non-problem, especially in the sense of a problem of deficient demand, anticipated to follow the post-war boom in demand. In fact employment was more threatened by supply constraints, above all the problem of securing sufficient energy and raw material supplies to maintain output. The first was basically a domestic problem of coal production, and led to the famous coal crisis of 1947 (Cairncross 1985: ch. 13). The second was a foreign-trade problem, part of the general problem of the balance of payments which was central to the economic issues of the 1945–51 period.

In part this balance of payments crisis was an economically straightforward legacy from the war, a war in which exports had been sacrificed to domestic output of war materials, the balance of payments only being sustained by Lend-Lease, the accumulation of sterling balances, and the sale of foreign assets (Ch. 6 above). Thus the balance of payments problem of the late 1940s could commonly be presented as a battle to expand Britain's exports to finance a level of imports sufficient to feed British consumers and supply British industry. But such a focus ignores the other elements of the balance of payments at this time— especially the scale of overseas military expenditure and foreign investment, which together accounted for a large part of the overall balance of payments problem of this period, and indirectly significantly affected the crucial dollar problem (Balogh 1949: 41–2; Cairncross 1985: 79–80, 90–1; Tomlinson 1991*a*).

Thus the balance of payments problem was in part politically determined by the twin desires to remain a world power in the political and strategic sense, and a desire to maintain the Sterling Area, within which most of the capital export flowed. These aims remained largely unchallenged in Labour's period of office, so that at the time the balance of payments issue was seen largely in terms of the current account alone, and it was this approach which shaped policy.

The urgent desire to raise exports as well as to supply domestic demand led to a degree of emphasis on raising output which had no peacetime precedent. A prosperity campaign was followed by a productivity campaign as government came to see its key need as raising production; 'few governments have proclaimed more insistently the need for higher productivity' (Cairncross 1985: 499).

With a fully employed labour-force and severe constraints on the expansion of the capital stock, the focus of the productivity campaign was labour productivity or output per man hour (OMH). This focus was reinforced by the forms of measurement deployed in analysing productivity. The foremost expert on British productivity at this time (and employed by the Board of Trade) was L. Rostas, who was strongly committed to the view that productivity should be measured in terms of labour inputs and output measured in physical rather than money terms. This view partly derived from the severe problems of measuring capital inputs and money measures of output, complicated further by the contemporary controls which distorted prices. He was fully aware of the potentially misleading nature of focusing on the labour input, but nevertheless saw OMH as the best measure of productivity available (Tomlinson 1993*b*).

The obvious difficulties with OMH are broadly twofold. On the one hand, it is simply not an acceptable measure of efficiency, because it ignores the major impact of capital on how much labour is able to produce. On the other hand, it reinforces the view, never far from the surface in Britain, that perceived deficiencies in labour productivity are labour's 'fault', due to low effort or trade-union obstructionism or some such nostrum. Thus the focus on OMH was problematic for a Labour government in the sense of potentially focusing attention on labour as the problem in the productivity drive. On the other hand, it did fit in quite well with the human relations emphasis of Labour's views on productivity, both seeming to highlight the potential that different attitudes on the part of labour could make.

This concern to raise productivity followed logically from compelling short-term economic circumstances. 'Output now' is a summary of the attitude prevalent in policy circles. But the undoubted immediacy of the problem did not mean longer-run issues of productivity and efficiency were ignored. Policy-making circles were well aware both that Britain had a long history of industrial deficiency, and that the current position where Britain could sell everything it could produce would not survive the revival of German and other war-damaged industries. Hence future competitiveness also entered into the debate about how to raise productivity in industry.

The problem of demand outpacing supply was attacked from both sides under the Labour government. The drive to boost production was matched, at least from 1947, by budgetary measures to control demand. Labour eschewed monetary policy as a way of controlling demand throughout the period (Howson 1988). But its initial lack of enthusiasm for budgetary policy shifted with the accession of Cripps to the Treasury in 1947, and the second budget of that year saw a return to the kind of Keynesian integration of budgets with assessment of aggregate demand and supply that began with the Kingsley Wood wartime budget of 1941.

How far this should be seen as part of a transition from planning in a traditional sense to a Keynesian regime of fiscal manipulation remains open to dispute (e.g. Tomlinson 1987*a*: ch. 5; Rollings 1988; Booth 1989*a*: ch. 9). Certainly at the time it was not generally seen in that light. Because so much of the attempt to contain demand focused on controlling investment expenditure it was also possible to regard the budget as 'a real beginning to economic planning' (Dalton) as previously investment had escaped effective control. Equally, budgetary policy was by no means seen as a simple alternative to planning and controls, and most Labour figures continued to regard some physical controls as integral to a democratic socialist approach to the economy (Rollings 1992).

One way of summarizing Labour's approach to economic and industrial policy would be through the dual objectives of stabilization and modernization. Undoubtedly the impact of the 1930s slump on the collective memory of the British population was to make a strong political force for economic stability and security, and in particular therefore full employment, especially in Labour circles. Full employment had an unchallenged centrality as the aim of policy in this period. But equally Labour had a rather under-recognized history of concern with industrial efficiency and modernization, and this was further stimulated by the discovery of the inefficiency of much of British industry in the war period. (On this history see Tiratsoo and Tomlinson 1993*a*: ch. 1, and Ch. 8, below.)

Concern with industrial efficiency linked both goals. The balance of payments emerged as crucial to stability, and was responded to by the campaigns to raise output. Equally the

desire to put Britain's economic future on a more secure basis
led to policies related to industrial modernization which looked
beyond the immediate need to raise output to a longer-term
problem of efficiency and competitiveness (Robinson 1986).

MARKETS

Policy in the early post-war years was focused on expanding
exports, but strict controls over imports, especially dollar imports, were also retained to deal with the current account
problem. Towards the end of the war it had been calculated that
an export expansion of 75 per cent over 1938 levels would be
necessary to pay for the 1938 level of imports in the face of
wartime losses of invisible earnings and returns on foreign
investment. In the event, this aim was more than met, as exports
absorbed nearly three-quarters of the growth in GDP over the
1945–52 period (Cairncross 1985: 25–8). This export success was
effective in dealing with the immediate balance of payments
problem, though highly misleading about Britain's long-term
competitive strength. Total world trade was expanding fast,
whilst competitors like Germany and Japan were only slowly
recovering from wartime devastation. The late 1940s were thus a
typical, in that export expansion was largely limited by Britain's
capacity to produce, not by the efficiency with which that
production was carried out.

TABLE 7.1. *British trade and payments 1946–52* (£m.)

	1946	1947	1948	1949	1950	1951	1952
Exports and re-exports	960	1,180	1,639	1,863	2,261	2,735	2,769
Imports	1,063	1,541	1,790	2,000	2,312	3,424	3,048
Balance on visible trade	−103	−361	−151	−137	−51	−689	−279
Balance on invisibles	−127	−20	177	−136	358	320	442
Balance on current account	−230	−381	26	− 1	307	−369	163

Source: Cairncross (1985), p. 201.

Given the existence of easy markets at home, British producers had to be persuaded to expand their exports by government action. This included tying the allocation of raw materials to production for export and putting limits on what could be sold in the home market. The most striking (and successful) example was the car industry, which is discussed further in Chapter 14. The government publicized export targets in 1947, though how much impact these had is debatable, as they had been prepared basically as a propaganda measure in the Board of Trade, without consultation with the firms actually involved in producing the goods.

Whilst controls played their part in shifting output into export markets, they were much less effective in determining the destination of exports. A Dollar Export Board was created to try to steer British goods to secure supplies of scarce dollars, but seemingly without much success. The major export expansion was into Sterling Area markets, where demand was high and access to dollars limited. By 1950 almost 48 per cent of all British exports went to the Sterling Area, compared with 45 per cent in 1946 (Cairncross 1985: 66).

The level of protectionism in this period was governed by two contrary forces. On the one hand, there was the British government's broad acceptance of the American grand design for a liberal world economic order as the long-term goal. On the other hand the historic legacy of protectionism and the current balance of payments difficulties meant this ideal could not be realized in the years of the Labour government. In particular, discrimination against dollar goods was an inescapable policy given the degree of dollar shortage at the prevailing exchange rate. After the brief period in 1947, when exchange control had been lifted and then re-imposed as a capital flight ensued, controls were maintained with American agreement, not to disappear for current account transactions until the mid-1950s.

Britain's pattern of Imperial protectionism inherited from the 1930s was a source of contention in the post-war debates with the United States. Britain resisted an early end to this preferential system, arguing that it did not have a significant impact in reducing US exports to the Empire, because the constraint on such exports was dollar earnings of countries in the Empire (or, strictly, the Sterling Area, with which it was roughly, but not exactly, coterminious). The point was that, at this time, all the countries in the Sterling Area pooled their dollar reserves in London, Britain acting to try to maximize the receipts and minimize the disbursements of dollars for the area as a whole. This discriminating system was reluctantly accepted by the United States *pro tem*, and was slowly eroded as the dollar shortage eased.[1] Some have argued that these Commonwealth linkages damaged Britain both by allowing an excessive scale of capital export within the Sterling Area (some of which leaked out into dollars through weak exchange controls) and by focusing trade on the relatively slow-growing Commonwealth markets (Cairncross 1985: 277).

The long-run commitment to a liberal world economy was not without its opponents, but progress on that road, whilst slow in this period, was encouraged not only by US leverage over British policy, but also by a strong shift in much informed opinion against the restrictionism which was said to have characterized the 1930s, and which many argued would need to be resisted, especially as immediate post-war problems were solved. Whilst on both Left (e.g. Balogh 1948) and Right (Amery 1946, esp. ch. 9) this conclusion was challenged, increasingly the great bulk of central opinion, embracing most in the government, accepted that trade liberalization was the best long-term aim.

PROFITS

A socialist government, intent on nationalizing a significant proportion but by no means all sectors of industry faces a dilemma over profits. How far is it to try to control profits in the remaining private sector in an attempt to redistribute income and/or control the activities of private firms? The 1945 government gave no clear answer to that question. On the one hand it made profits tax for the first time a standard part of the peace-time tax regime, replacing the wartime Excess Profits Tax with a Profits Tax in 1947. On the other hand, there was implicit recognition that whilst the majority of the economy remained in private hands profits had to be accepted for their economic

---

[1] This is discussed further in Tomlinson (1991*a*).

effects. This latter was spelt out in an unusually explicit manner by Gaitskell when Chancellor of the Exchequer in 1951: 'There are some who disapprove of profits in principle. I do not share their view. In an economy three-quarters of which is run by private enterprise, it is foolish to ignore the function of profit as an incentive' (cited Rogow and Shore 1955: 129).

The compromise position between regarding profits as an illegitimate source of income, but realizing that they were unavoidable under private ownership, was to differentiate between distributed and undistributed profits. The latter were subject to a 10 per cent tax, whilst the former faced the higher rates varying from 25 per cent in 1947 up to 50 per cent in 1951. In addition, distributed profits were further liable to the standard rate of income tax at 9s. 6d. (47.5 p) in the pound.

In this way Labour aimed to encourage profit retention and reinvestment and succeeded in doing so. This had a number of effects. On the income distribution aspect, it meant profits could be capitalized by share appreciation, which in the absence of a capital gains tax offered a route for tax-free benefits. For political reasons the government pretended these undistributed profits were not a source of personal income but accrued only to corporations (Seers 1950). Secondly, it had the effect of reinforcing the traditional reliance of British firms on ploughed-back profits for their investment funds. In consequence, it reduced the leverage government had over firms that would result from being able to control their access to investment funds. Thus encouraging plough-back unintentionally but significantly undermined the idea that the government would plan investment, as its rhetoric of 1945 suggested it would (see the section on Investment, below). Rogow and Shore (1955: 28–9) cite figures which suggest that in large companies in this period only 20–30 per cent of investment expenditure was financed from external sources.

This policy of encouraging investment from internal sources also led to a policy of investment allowances, accelerating the speed at which investment could be written off against tax liabilities. These allowances were also seen as an attempt to be realistic about the effects of the rise in prices in reducing the real value of depreciation funds. For this reason the allowances were doubled in 1949 (Dow 1965: 205–9). These allowances, whilst small in terms of overall effects on company income, acted to reduce a little the impact of profits taxation, and symbolized a desire to encourage private investment, even if that investment was not planned by government.

The general behaviour of profits in this period reflected more the impact of the buoyant state of demand than the intentions of a socialist government. In a speech to the House of Commons in 1949 Cripps spoke of the 'frightfully high' profits being earnt, and how they could be reduced as part of the current anti-inflationary policy. Contemporary academic analysis bears out Cripps's suggestion that profits were high. By comparison with 1938 they had risen in money terms by 250 per cent by 1948, whilst money wages had risen by 200 per cent. Barna (1949: 223) calculated that prices could fall by around 9 per cent if the profit increase was only the same scale as that of wages. Equally rates of return were 'handsome' at around 14 per cent.[2] However, because of the policy on profit distribution noted above, distributed profits may have halved over this period (Seers 1950: 279, 1949).

High taxation of distributed profits in this period may have encouraged the high level of export of capital already noted in this period (Rogow and Shore 1955: 120–3). They also meant that firms' investment behaviour was largely unaffected by financial constraints. Rather, the limits on such investment were almost entirely from the physical controls which the government inherited from the war, most especially the building licensing system which was the most important of these controls throughout the government's period in office.

THE EFFICIENCY OF LABOUR

Labour's approach to industrial relations was extremely conservative in so far as the legal framework was concerned. Apart from repealing the 1927 Trade Disputes Act, it reasserted (with some opposition) its traditional belief in free collective bargaining as central to British trade unionism and labourism. There was much discussion of 'wage planning' as a logical component

---

[2] Barna (1949: 221) suggests that profits were especially high in distribution and amongst small industrial firms.

of economic planning more generally, but the majority of the leadership of the Party supported the view that this would fundamentally disrupt the traditional division between union and political roles and would politicize every wage bargain. The lines of disagreement on this were not, as is often suggested, between trade unions and politicians (e.g. Roberts 1958: 62–4; Beer 1982, 200–8; Brooke 1991). Rather it was more of a Left/Right division, with the Left favouring wage planning as part of a thoroughgoing planned economy, the Right resisting. This political line-up was then inverted, when wage planning was pursued at the macroeconomic level in the form of incomes policy, in the period 1948–50 (Panitch 1976: ch. 1; Tomlinson 1991*c*; on the incomes policy see Jones 1987: ch. 4).

The link between industrial relations and efficiency in this period was seen by the government and the union leaderships largely through the perception of a new relationship between workers and managers on the basis of the existence of full employment. This condition was argued to render anachronistic traditional worries about and opposition to technical change on the part of workers, and to make better treatment and co-operation with their work-force mandatory for management. The change in the balance of supply and demand in the labour-market was then to underpin a new co-operative relationship at work which would be functional for enhanced output and productivity. In this way full employment would complement not contradict industrial efficiency.

This approach was embodied in the range of 'peak association' tripartite bodies previously noted, but more particularly in the attempt to revive the wartime system of Joint Production Committees, whose prevalance seems to have been greatly reduced at the war's end by the redistribution of the labour-force and the focus of much working-class political energy on preparing for a Labour general election victory (Tomlinson 1987*b*).

The attempt to revive the JPCs from 1946 met with some success as far as can be told from unpublished estimates, though what exactly they contributed to the drive for output and efficiency is much less clear. Some JPCs clearly focused entirely on 'tea and toilets' not on production issues, but others were claimed to have made a significant contribution both in improving the general factory climate and bringing forward specific ideas for improvements in working methods (Tiratsoo and Tomlinson 1993*a*: chs. 5, 8). Employers generally conceded the political strength of the case for such attempts at co-operation, though they were insistent that the JPCs should be entirely domestic in orientation, and should not establish links with other firms. It is also clear that formal agreement of employers' organizations did not guarantee a warm support for such arrangements in all factories.

JPCs symbolized what the government hoped would be a new relationship in factories, based on management appreciation of the human factor in production. 'Human relations' became a catchphrase of the period, grounded on the perceived shift in the balance of forces on the shopfloor resulting from full employment, the desire to prevent any return to the conflictual industrial relations of the inter-war period, and, to a limited extent, academic inquiry which suggested that psychological and sociological relationships were indeed a key factor in determining productivity (Tiratsoo and Tomlinson 1993*a*: ch. 5).

One of Labour's legacies from the coalition government was the 1944 Education Act. This had established the principle of free secondary education for all, and the '11 plus' as a stepping-stone into a tripartite system of secondary schools—grammar, secondary modern, and technical. The principles of the 1944 Act were not widely challenged in Labour circles. A case was made for 'multilateral' (comprehensive) schools, but for many in the Labour Party the Act provided the basis for a desired social mobility, a meritocratic system providing entry to the prized grammar school for the bright working-class child (Barker 1972).

The emphasis on the grammar school as the jewel in the crown of secondary education has been widely seen as bad for industrial efficiency, by its emphasis on the academic, public-school curriculum at the expense of technical education. Certainly the option of technical high schools included in the 1944 Act was little taken up by local education authorities, for most of whom the grammar school/secondary modern divide was the appropriate structure.

The rather limited role given to technical education in the whole debate around the 1944 Act was criticized at the time, and led to the setting up of the Percy Committee on Higher Technical Education and the Barlow Committee on Scientific Manpower.

Both of these focused on the need to expand post-school technical education. Something was done in this field, most notably the creation of new specialized colleges such as that in aeronautics at Cranfield. However, the more general expansion of higher level technical education was bedevilled by the politics of higher education (Sanderson 1972*b*: ch. 7; Price 1978).

Lower-level part-time technical education continued its rapid wartime expansion, the numbers involved rising from about 40,000 pre-war to 200,000 by 1948/9. This emphasis on non-school technical education is manifest in the Ministry of Education pressing strongly for more building resources for this area of provision, ironically being resisted by the Treasury on the grounds that education spending was part of social services, which had to be restrained to divert resources into fuel, transport, and industry (PEP 1953; Tomlinson 1993*a*).

In this period a big effort was also put into expanding Training Within Industry (TWI), a programme of training primarily for foremen, at the workplace and based on an American model originally followed in wartime. This was a programme not so much about training in technical skills as part of that emphasis on human relations already noted. Foremen were seen as crucial to that improvement in labour relations so much desired by the government. By the late 1940s TWI had grown to cover 270,000 workers and 2,724 firms (PEP 1951: 20–5).

THE EFFICIENCY OF CAPITAL

In the 1930s the control of investment by a National Investment Board had been central to Labour's programme.[3] Such a body had been seen as vital to determine the macroeconomic aspect of investment, that is to maintain a level appropriate for full employment. It had also been seen as having a microeconomic function, determining priorities between different investment projects. This commitment to control of investment was strongly reiterated when Labour came to power in 1945, but in the event

[3] A National Investment Board was by no means an idea exclusive to the Labour Party. It was part of the progressive consensus of the 1920s and 1930s, and was advocated, for example, in the famous Liberal Party 'Yellow Book' entitled Britain's Industrial Future in 1928.

control was always patchy. It relied largely on the controls inherited from the war, and as these were relaxed Labour found no new institutions to continue this job. A National Investment Council was created, but this had minimal powers, and faded away after a few meetings (Rogow and Shore 1955: 27–9: 61–2; Cairncross 1985: 455–62).

The reasons for this failure to pursue one of Labour's key policy devices remains obscure. When taxed on the issue the Chancellor, Dalton, mouthed evasions about keeping key planning decisions in Cabinet hands, but this hardly addressed the issue, as no one had assumed the NIB would have complete autonomy to make decisions. More plausible is the suggestion that with around 50 per cent of investment in the hands of nationalized industry, the government believed that this would provide a sufficient basis for investment planning (Davenport 1974: 154; see also Ch. 8). Rollings (1990) has stressed Treasury opposition to such an overarching planning mechanism as an NIB, being content with the sharp distinction between the physical controls inherited from war and financial controls, on the assumption that the former would be temporary and the latter in the Treasury's domain. Overall, Labour seems to have been notably pusillanimous in its approach to financial institutions, satisfying itself in the end with the largely symbolic nationalization of the Bank of England.[4]

The NIB had been seen as a multi-purpose body whose relationship to existing financial institutions was unclear (Mayhew 1939: 31–48). But the long-standing critique of the poor level of industrial finance provided by those institutions was addressed at the beginning of the Labour government's period in office by the creation of the Industrial and Commercial Finance Corporation (ICFC) and the Finance Corporation for Industry (FCI). Their creation flowed partly from the wartime discussions of the inefficiencies of British industry, but also from a pre-emptive move by the wartime Bank of England. As in the period of the second Labour government (1929–31), the Bank was keen to discourage possible radical moves by Labour on the financial sectors, by being seen to be doing something itself. This was the

---

[4] Nationalization of the clearing banks was not on Labour's agenda by the late 1930s—see Pollard (1978).

origin of the ICFC and FCI which played some role in filling the 'Macmillan gap', though they hardly represented a major break with the general pattern of finance–industry relations in Britain.[5]

THE EFFICIENCY OF TECHNICAL CHANGE

The Labour government spent a great deal of money on R & D. Expenditure on civil R & D probably rose around 5 times between 1945/6 and 1950/1, to a total of about £30m. This included a doubling of the DSIR budget and a much larger expansion of subventions to universities and learned societies, though the former did not play the role in British R & D that they had assumed in the United States (Vig 1968: 14–15).

However this civilian-oriented expenditure was dwarfed by expenditure on defence and other strategic (e.g. nuclear power) areas. By 1950 the Ministry of Supply was spending £89m. on R & D, by far the largest single element of government spending in this area, and far larger than the money spent by private industry, estimated at £24m. for the same year (Edgerton 1992: 102–3). So, under Labour, 'the national R & D output remained overwhelmingly warlike' (Edgerton: 102).

This scale of commitment to defence R & D reflected the broader level of expenditure in this area. Whilst as a share of GDP the level of defence spending was cut from 16.7 per cent in 1946/7 to 5.8 per cent by 1950/1, it still remained high by peacetime standards or in comparison with other major industrial powers (Chalmers 1985: ch. 2). And with the onset of the Korean war the figure rose sharply again, to peak at 8.7 per cent in 1952/3 (Chalmers 1985: 50–1).

Whilst the weight of R & D spending strongly reflected the continued British commitment to a world political and military role, it would be wrong to see that spending entirely in that light. As already noted, civil expenditure did increase rapidly in this period even if the absolute amounts spent were small in comparison with defence-related areas. A greatly enhanced belief in the importance of R & D (and science generally) was an important

---

[5] On the foundation of ICFC see its first chairman's evidence to the Radcliffe Committee, Piercy (1959).

feature of the 1940s. It reflected partly the 'technocratic' ideas prevalent in the 1930s, and strongly evident in both the scientific and political community, and partly the wartime experience, and the belief that 'big science' had played a major role in the war, from areas ranging from code-breaking (a major stimulus to computer development) to radar, jet engines, and of course nuclear fission[6] (Price 1978).

Perhaps the most interesting development in government's efforts on civilian R & D in this period was the creation of the National Research and Development Corporation. This seems to have had three major factors in its creation. First was the general pre-disposition to expand civil R & D as noted above. Second was the widespread belief on the Left that capitalist firms had and were operating to suppress inventions and slow technical development to maintain profits. Third was the long-held view that Britain was good at basic inventions, but much less competent at turning these into commercially successful projects, penicillin being commonly cited as an example of this (Keith 1981; Hendry 1989: ch. 1).

The aim of the NRDC was to aid the development of inventions through to the production stage, especially inventions made in the public sector. The idea was supported by the FBI, though they wanted it to be autonomous of government and self-financing as soon as possible (Keith 1981: 102–3). However its efforts were hindered by its total reliance on the private sector to take up the ideas it wanted to disseminate. Its biggest effort was in trying to encourage the development of a computer industry, but it faced grave obstacles in doing this. Its first head, Halsbury,

felt, with some reason, that the NRDC had done all it could to stimulate the British computer industry, but that it had no answer to the chronic indecision and conservatism of British industry as a whole when it came to ordering equipment. Even the computer manufacturers had often been slow to become computer users (Hendry 1989: 152).

Expenditure on military-related R & D was arguably more successful in obtaining its objectives (Edgerton 1992), but the

---

[6] The decision to go ahead with a large-scale nuclear programme was a source of considerable dispute in the Cabinet under Labour, but despite economic arguments against the proposal the (ill-fated) economic benefits and military linkage secured the programme (PRO 1946).

spin-offs from this to the civilian sector seem to have been very limited. Overall, therefore, the greatly expanded government R & D effort of the early post-war years cannot be said to have made the impact on Britain's commercial competitiveness that many of its promoters desired.

THE EFFICIENCY OF COMPANY STRUCTURE AND ORGANIZATION

Labour of course legislated a major change in corporate organization, in the sense of taking roughly 20 per cent of British industry from private into public hands. How far these changes in ownership involved other changes is discussed in the general context of nationalization in the next chapter.

As regards the private sector, as already indicated this had tended to be treated as a residual category in Labour Party discussion, with rather little detailed policy development: 'The Labour Party had concentrated on the problems of nationalization and had not given due consideration to those of the private sector' (Diamond 1948: 58). But this point should not be exaggerated. Labour did have some ideas in this area at its accession to office, and developed more on the hoof as the issue became more important over the next six years.

Labour's most distinctive policy for the private sector was the idea of Development Councils (Henderson 1952; Brady 1950: 531–68; Mercer 1991*a*). These were to be councils for a wide range of industries composed of employers, workers, and experts. To some extent the idea came from the rationalization movement of the 1920s and 1930s, though they were mainly concerned with consumer industries. They had also been proposed in the wartime Board of Trade as part of its General Support of Trade proposals for post-war economic change. The idea was that such bodies would be able to create a consensual framework for economic change allowing for the provision of common services to fragmented industrial sectors, such as Research and Development, marketing and labour-force issues and possibly a framework for 'rationalization' of the industries.

Undoubtedly these Councils were seen as the spearhead of a major reform of the private sector, especially by their most important advocate, Stafford Cripps. He had originally proposed that they be composed entirely of employers and workers, but the Cabinet forced an expert element into the idea on the basis of the threat of consumers losing out from a cosy producers' alliance if no third party were involved (Tomlinson 1993*c*).

Proposals for such Commissions arose from a series of tripartite (i.e. employer–worker–expert) working parties which investigated a range of consumer industries between 1945 and 1947. In the event such proposals were bitterly resisted by most employers, orchestrated by the FBI, whose role was much less amenable to government policy than its historian has suggested (Blank 1972). The grounds of opposition were a combination of a belief that DCs represented 'backdoor nationalization', hostility to union involvement in running industry, but above all perhaps hostility to the threat to 'self-government in industry' and especially the role of trade associations, which had been strengthened by wartime control mechanisms and which were the foundation of the FBI's strength (Mercer 1991*a*: 82–3).

Against such hostility the government proved almost powerless. The wartime Cotton Board was reconstructed as a Development Council in 1948, largely because of agreement in the industry that the Board had worked well. The other DCs were all in minor industries, such as furniture, jewellery, and silver. In 1950 Harold Wilson used the Development Council episode to emphasize the difficulties of Labour's relation with the private sector, and the need to develop new policy ideas in this area (PRO 1950*b*).

Perhaps Labour's best-known initiative in the area of industrial efficiency and raising major issues of corporate organization was the Anglo-American Council on Productivity. This was established in 1948 in response to an American initiative under the auspices of Marshall Aid. The AACP involved employers' organizations and unions from both the UK and the USA, and its main activity was the sending of 'productivity teams' of managers and workers from Britain to tour US production facilities and report back to Britain on the explanations for differences in productivity. Sixty-six reports were finally issued mostly concerning specific industrial sectors, but with some on general topics such as management education and cost accounting (Tomlinson 1991*d*).

The whole episode can be viewed from a number of viewpoints. Carew (1987) sees the teams as bridgeheads for the infiltration of American managerialism, with a focus on restrictive labour practices as the key efficiency issue. Certainly many of the reports were taken up with facile exhortations for the (alleged) advantages of US attitudes to industry, and indeed uncritical praise for the American way of life. This approach comes across strongly in the semi-official history of the AACP (Hutton 1953). Other commentators (e.g. Broadberry and Crafts 1990) have seen the AACP reports as focusing on a wider range of failures of management as well as unions, whilst others (e.g. Tomlinson 1993*c*) have argued that, whilst it is difficult to generalize about such a multitude and diversity of reports, in many cases the criticism was more of management than of unions. Certainly most of the reports suggested that even without massive new capital expenditure there was much to be learnt from many aspects of US factory organization such as costing methods, production scheduling, maintenance systems, and a host of issues under the broad heading of production engineering and more broadly scientific management.

The reports of the AACP achieved a wide circulation, and considerable publicity in both official and private media. What effect they had is difficult to say. Some objected to the whole idea of Anglo-American comparisons, a view based either on economic arguments about the different factor-bases of the two economies (Jewkes 1946), on more specific arguments about the structure of Britain's export trade, more crudely, on hostility to the idea that the British had anything to learn from the Americans. But there is some evidence that at least in some industries the AACP message got through, and encouraged, for example, the organized spread of know-how between firms (Tiratsoo and Tomlinson 1993*a*: ch. 7). The AACP was an important part of the attempt to raise productivity consciousness in this period, though these attempts seem to have encountered a considerable degree of public misunderstanding and opposition, whilst not being without their successes (Crofts 1989).

One of the major themes of those who pressed the case for the American model of productive efficiency was standardization. This was not just a theme of the AACP, but, for example, was pressed by the Ministry of Supply on the engineering industry, and by some of the Ministries on their client nationalized industries. The Ministry of Supply set up a major committee on standardization in engineering, and this advocated, amongst other measures, a substantial expansion of the British Standards Institute, and this expansion did take place in the late 1940s (Lemon 1949). As with the American model more generally, there were substantial debates about the relevance of the emphasis on standardization. Many in Britain saw, or claimed to see, a trade-off between quantity and quality, and believed Britain had succeeded and could continue to succeed by exporting short runs of high quality products (e.g. Friedlander 1946).

But the wartime discussions of post-war trade had included a strong view that Britain was falling substantially behind the United States in the quality of products, and called for much more attention to what, thirty years later, would be called non-price factors in competitiveness (Maguire 1991). To respond to this challenge a Council of Industrial Design was established before the end of the war, but like other initiatives of the 1940s it had difficulty gaining industrial support, not least because of the easy export markets for existing products that most industries faced.

More specific attempts to raise labour productivity were made through the metamorphosis of the wartime Ministry of Aircraft Production's Production Efficiency Service into a Board of Trade Production Efficiency Board. This was another idea due largely to Stafford Cripps, who was especially keen on wanting the PEB to promulgate method study as a way of decreasing worker effort whilst expanding output. Another Board of Trade body was the Special Research Unit, with a remit focusing on encouraging standardization, which was another popular notion at this time amongst the advocates of increased productivity (Tiratsoo and Tomlinson 1993*a*; Tomlinson 1992).

The issue of general managerial competence had been discussed during the war and led to the proposals for a British Institute of Management, charged with improving managerial education and managerial standards generally. During the war period the idea of state support for such a body was resisted by Conservative members of the Coalition, but once again it was Cripps (along with Dalton: Chancellor of the Exchequer during 1945–7) who pursued the matter and saw the establishment of the BIM in 1946 (Tiratsoo and Tomlinson 1993*a*: ch. 6).

Labour's 1945 election manifesto had placed a great deal of emphasis on the need for anti-monopoly action to open the way for industrial expansion and full employment. This rhetorical emphasis led to the birth of a mouse, in the form of the 1948 Monopolies and Mergers Act. Because of the screening of referrals to the Monopolies Commission by the Board of Trade, and its role as initiator of any action proposed by the Commission, there were many opportunities for pressure on the government to minimize intervention in industry in the name of anti-monopoly policy. As with DCs, the FBI seems to have mobilized employers effectively to blunt the Act, so few Monopoly Commission reports were published before Labour lost office, and little action was taken on those that did appear (Mercer 1991*a*, 1993).

STATE CAPACITY AND STATE ACHIEVEMENTS

Much of the running on issues of industrial efficiency in wartime was made by the supply ministries, the Ministries of Aircraft Production and Supply, rather than the Board of Trade. In the post-war years this was also true, but whilst Cripps was President of the Board (1945–47) he attempted to turn the Board into the 'Ministry of Industry' (Edgerton 1992: 95–6). But this activity in the sense of producing reports, creating bodies like the PEB and SRU could not disguise the fact that in key ways the Board was a weak Ministry. Its direct industrial responsibilities were largely limited to consumer industries, and its role was largely advisory over many of the key issues. In particular it had little role in the key area of engineering, which was the responsibility of the Ministry of Supply. This Ministry seems to have developed much cosier relations with industries in its areas of responsibility, and to have been publicly much less of a dynamic force for raising efficiency than the Board of Trade under Cripps. However, it has been argued that at least in the area of military procurement and efficiency and technical progress in the production of military goods, the Ministry was an effective force for higher standards (Edgerton 1992).

It may be noted that the Ministry of Supply successfully resisted the pressures for tripartism, so that, for example, there was never any likelihood of a Development Council in the car industry, but only an Advisory Council with a very limited union role (see also Ch. 14). The absence of such tripartism may have facilitated a more discriminatory industrial policy in the sectors overseen by the Ministry of Supply, as arguably such tripartism (or corporatism) may inhibit governments from undermining the consensus on which such arrangements rely by favouring some firms or sectors over others (Kenworthy 1990). On the other hand, the key factor was probably the much greater dependence of most Ministry of Supply industries on government purchasing than was common across most of British industry. Indeed economists like Balogh (1949) called for the expansion of such purchasing precisely to use as a means of imposing greater standardization and efficiency on private-sector firms.

Certainly, for all Cripps's efforts the Board of Trade did not establish itself as the Ministry of Industry, as a focus for all the forces trying to raise industrial efficiency, and advance industry's claims against other departments. Thus Labour's efforts to raise industrial efficiency were numerous but rather lacking in co-ordination and focus. Labour did not change the structure of government in a way to prevent the eventual reassertion of the Treasury as the primary economic Ministry with its particular concerns and procedures.

The state's capacity to organize change was also restricted by the extent to which its main levers of control over the private sector—the inherited, wartime physical controls—were in the hands of the private sector. So these levers were ambiguous in their implications. The powers of trade associations and employers' organizations were generally enhanced by this system of control, and this put limits on how far government can be said to have had control over the private sector. Certainly the government seemed susceptible to pressure from the private sector—not only in the cases of DCs and monopoly policy, but also in such areas as the speed with which controls would be removed (Rollings 1992).

This problem relates to a larger one. Labour was strongly committed to tripartism and co-operation between government, unions, and the private sector. This led to the creation of a myriad of tripartite bodies, some already noted above. Yet the evidence of these bodies' deliberations would seem to be that they were seen by the government as sounding-boards and channels of information, rather than as places where government significantly shared its decision-making with others. At the same time the desire for co-operation made the government unwilling to put strong pressure on the private sector, at least outside areas where it felt it had a clear electoral mandate. So tripartism in some ways blocked action as much as it facilitated it (Tomlinson 1993*c*).

CONCLUSIONS

The changes seen as brought about by the 1945 Labour government were obviously many, and much attention has been focused on the programme of nationalization and the major extension of the welfare state. Historians have also emphasized the growth of macroeconomic management in the period, and the erosion of Labour's idea of the planned economy (Morgan 1986; Cairncross 1985; Brooke 1991). All these were important, if controversial, features of Labour's period in office. But focus on them has tended to obscure the extent to which Labour in this period was a government of industrial modernization, the first in peace-time Britain to put raising industrial efficiency close to the centre of its economic policy agenda. How far this translated into actual improvements is unclear, though a moderately positive view is possible (Tiratsoo and Tomlinson 1993*a*: ch. 8; compare Barnett 1986). Rostas (1952: 20–2) suggested an increase in industrial output per head between 1946 and 1950 of about 5 per cent per annum, with manufacturing productivity rising at 6 per cent.[7] This was despite a fall in working hours, the rise in paid holidays, and the fall in direct production workers in the total work-force. These favourable trends were, however, greatly disrupted by the impact of the massive (and unsustainable) diversion of resources

[7] Cairncross (1985: 18–19), basing himself on Feinstein (1972), gives a manufacturing labour productivity increase of 2.5 per cent for 1945–51, and 3.5 per cent for 1948–51. Reddaway and Smith (1960), in a pioneering study of total factor productivity, suggested an increase of 3.3 per cent per annum for this measure over the period 1948–51. They regarded this figure as 'exceptional', and a reflection of recovery from wartime disorganization, not to be expected in the longer term. Indeed, their figure for 1951–4 is only 1.1 per cent per annum. They do not assess the impact of rearmament on the trend.

into military spending sparked by the Korean war (Mitchell 1963, esp. ch. 10).

But whatever its impact on industry on the ground, the modernizing aspect of Labour's approach needs to be emphasized against a historiographical tradition which has too easily accepted the adage that Labour is 'a party of distribution not production'. The Party which produced *Production: The Bridge to Socialism* in 1948 (Labour Party 1948*a*), or a government which had Stafford Cripps as a senior figure throughout its life hardly matches this stereotype.

Further Reading

Brady, R. (1950), *Crisis in Britain*, esp. ch. 12, London.

Cairncross, A. (1985), *Years of Recovery: British Economic Policy 1945–51*, London.

Mercer, H. (1993), *Constructing a Competitive Order: The Hidden History of Anti-Trust*, Cambridge.

Mercer, H., Rollings, N., and Tomlinson, J. (1992), *Labour Governments and the Private Sector: The Experience of 1945–51*, Edinburgh.

Robinson, E. A. G. (1986), 'The Economic Problem of the Transition from War to Peace', *Cambridge Journal of Economics*, 10: 165–85.

Rogow, A. A. and Shore, P. (1955), *The Labour Government and British Industry*, 1945–51, Oxford.

Tiratsoo, N. (1991) (ed.), *The Attlee Years*, London.

Tiratsoo, N., and Tomlinson, J. (1993), *Industrial Efficiency and State Intervention: Labour, 1939–51*, London.

Tomlinson, J. (1993), 'Mr. Attlee's Supply-Side Socialism', *Economic History Review*, 46: 1–22.

Worswick, G. D. N., and Ady, P. H. (1952) (eds.), *The British Economy 1945–50*, Oxford.

8

Nationalization: Ownership and Organization

INTRODUCTION

The question of who should own industry has been a major issue of British politics in the twentieth century. In 1918 the Labour Party made nationalization a key part of its political programme. Between 1945 and 1951 the Labour government nationalized a significant proportion, about 20 per cent, of British industry. In the 1980s a Conservative government reversed much of this nationalization in its programme of privatization.

This history may be seen in a number of lights. Obviously it can be seen as a significant part of British political history (e.g. Barry 1965; Morgan 1987); it can be seen as a fundamentally administrative phenomenon (e.g. Gordon 1938; Chester 1975); it can be seen in relation to economic theory (e.g. Brech 1985; Vickers and Yarrow 1988); or it can be seen in the light of the development of the individual industries concerned (e.g. Supple 1986). This diversity of approaches reflects an obvious but important truth about nationalization—that its objectives and its implications have been extremely diverse and complex. Without denying this diversity and complexity this chapter, in line with the concerns of the book, focuses upon nationalization as an efficiency issue. Part of the argument for and against nationalization always related to the perceived impact on industrial efficiency, though this was, as always, efficiency perceived in a particular sense which needs to be understood in context.

Most attention in this chapter is given to the years 1945–51, with the previous period treated as a prologue to that period of major extension of public ownership, and the period since then as a period of working through the implications of that extension. The privatization programme after 1979 is treated not so much as an entirely new departure in policy but rather as a

particular way of resolving problems thrown up by the nationalizations of the 1940s.

NATIONALIZATION AND BRITISH SOCIALISM BEFORE 1945

Nationalization has been part of British socialism ever since that
doctrine achieved a significant foothold in the late nineteenth
century. Socialists of this epoch in turn drew on an older lineage
of Radical proposals for nationalization of specific sectors such
as land, railways, and coal-mining royalties stretching well back
into the nineteenth century. The elements which came to dominate British socialism regarded these nationalization proposals
as integral to their programme for a wholesale reconstruction of
the social order, though before the First World War actual
nationalization proposals tended to focus on the same narrow
range of sectors (Barry 1965: chs. 1–4).

In 1918, reflecting the radical impact of the First World War,
Labour's constitution and policies were reconstructed. Before the
war Labour had paid little attention to policy-making, the focus
of attention being on delivering working-class representatives
into parliament, rather than falling out over what exactly the
Party stood for. But in 1918 the wartime strengthening of
Labour and the desire to differentiate the Party from its pre-war
Liberal ally led to a new emphasis on doctrine and policy. Hence
the 1918 constitution embodied the famous Clause 4, committing
the party to 'common ownership of the means of production,
distribution and exchange'. At the time this change was not
regarded as earth-shaking, though later it became a key symbol of
Labour's socialist commitment. In the context of 1918 it may be
seen as a consolidation and extension of Labour's pre-war stance,
coupled to an invigorated desire to give Labour a distinct
political stance (McKibbin 1974: 91–106; Winter 1974).

What was perhaps the most important change in Labour's
nationalization policy in 1918 in the context of the concerns of
this book was the new emphasis on, and new meaning given to,
efficiency. Broadly speaking, before the First World War, advocacy of nationalization had been seen, at least by most Labour
theoreticians, as grounded on both equity and efficiency con-

siderations. Fabian socialists had developed a distinctive economic theory which applied the Ricardian idea of an unearned increment accruing to landowners as a consequence of land development to other monopoly sectors like the railways and land used for coal-mining. In the Fabian view, such an unearned increment caused both inequity, by generating high incomes for unproductive owners, and inefficiency, by throwing a burden on the productive enterprise (MacBriar 1962; Barry 1965: chs. 2–6).

Nationalization in this account was about efficiency, but not in the sense of efficiency of industrial organization. The nationalization of the land, railways, and mines was seen as a way of removing an inefficiency imposed on other sectors by the extraction of monopoly rents. Secondly, the maldistribution of incomes which resulted from such monopolies was seen as lowering the incomes of workers, and making them inefficient (a similar notion of inefficiency to that discussed in Ch. 2).

Post-war, the concept of inefficiency and its relation to nationalization was reshaped. In the *Constitution for a Socialist Commonwealth of Great Britain* (1920: 324), the Webbs (of whom Sidney had been the author of the 1918 Constitution) argued that 'it was one of the unexpected discoveries of government during the Great War that the system of capitalist profit-making as a method of producing commodities and services, habitually fell so enormously short of the maximum efficiency of which it was capable'. Prior to the war most socialists had assumed competitive private enterprise was at least efficient in its own terms, however unjustly its rewards were distributed. Not the least interesting of the war's effects on Labour was the loss of that faith.

This shift of emphasis is carried over into the discussion of particular costs of nationalization by Webb in *Labour and the New Social Order* (1918: 17). For example the advocacy of railway and electricity nationalization was based on the centrality of efficiency in these industries to the efficiency of the economy as a whole, and the obstacle provided by private ownership to the realization of the economies of scale available in these two cases.

Much of Labour's whole approach to industry from 1918 onwards can be seen as based on this idea of unexploited economies of scale. As Crosland (1956: 469) was to argue many years later 'Before the war, it was treated as axiomatic that, in the words of a typical and well-known judgement "large scale production, especially when conducted in large-size firms and plants, results in maximum efficiency" '.[1] This judgement led to considerable Labour support for the inter-war rationalization movement (see Ch. 4) as well as underpinning its case for nationalization. Nationalization became, in part, a means of realizing such scale economies where the private sector had proved incapable of grasping the opportunity.

Labour was only briefly in power in the inter-war years (1924, 1929–31), and never with an overall majority. Its capacity to enact nationalization was severely restricted, though it did support nationalization of electricity distribution (the Central Electricity Board), the BBC, and the London Passenger Transport Board, the latter on a model largely based on legislation drawn up by Labour before they lost office in 1931. (These cases will be returned to in the next section).

After the election defeat of 1931 Labour underwent a major reorientation. Amongst other changes, it slowly built up a much more systematic policy-making apparatus, and this led to the emergence of a much more solidly based policy programme. In 1934 the Party published *For Socialism and Peace*, which set out an agenda of economic reorganization, focused on economic planning and public ownership. Nationalization was to extend to banking, transport, coal and power, water supply, iron and steel, and other key industries.

This was a nationalization agenda already close to that carried out by Labour after 1945, with the exception of the clearing banks and water supply.[2] It was largely reaffirmed in *Labour's Immediate Programme* in 1937, the last major policy statement before the war (though iron and steel were excluded). The proposals for nationalization did not remain simply at the level of a shopping list. At least in some industries, quite detailed schemes were drawn up for how nationalization was to be organized—notably in iron and steel and cotton (Barry 1965: 333–40). Nationalization was also discussed in some detail at this time by the new breed of Labour Party economists who were increasingly active in Labour Party circles. They discussed na-

[1] The quote is from Sargant Florence (1933): p. 11.
[2] On Labour and the nationalization of the banks, see Pollard (1978).

tionalization in great detail, ranging over most of the economic issues such as pricing policy, investment criteria, and the use of financial surpluses (Durbin 1985: 121–5, 214–18). These policy discussions suggest that the oft-repeated claim that, when Labour came to power in 1945 there had been no detailed preparation for nationalization, is exaggerated (e.g. Morgan 1984: 97). Many of the issues discussed in the 1940s had been thoroughly debated, though not resolved, in the 1930s.

Discussions of nationalization in the 1930s tended to see public ownership as having three main goals. First, it was part of the process of planning, which became the key (if ambiguous) word in most Left discussions of the economy in this decade: 'Planning was the lingua franca of socialists in the nineteen thirties' (Brooke 1989: 159). Nationalization would be aimed at the 'commanding heights' of the economy, and would give government enormous leverage to control the overall pattern of economic activity. Second, nationalization would be about raising the efficiency of specific industries, especially where rationalization had not occurred and economies of scale were deemed available if only private ownership's obstructiveness could be removed. Third, nationalization was about eliminating the monopoly profits gained by privately owned utilities or natural monopolies, and fitted with the growing political suspicion of big business, coupled to a rather limited faith in competition as an alternative anti-monopoly stance.

This approach to nationalization provided a broad-based consensus in the Labour Party of the 1930s. By and large, all sections of the Party embraced the central role of nationalization in Labour's programme, 'revisionists' like Durbin and Crosland, as much as the Left. But this consensus was rendered both stronger and weaker by the war. Stronger, in the sense that Labour's political strength was greatly enhanced, and a majority of the Party saw nationalization as central to its distinctive claim to political power. On the other hand, the seeming efficacy of other forms of physical economic control, and to a lesser extent financial policy, during the war, weakened the status of nationalization as a combination of panacea and goal in its own right that it had come to be in many Labour Party eyes in the 1930s. Increasingly, nationalization was seen, at least by the Party's leadership and much of its intelligentsia, as one means amongst several of achieving socialist goals rather than the defining element of socialism (Brooke 1989).

The 1945–51 nationalizations did represent a consensus view in the Labour Party, but this consensus was based on different views as to what those nationalizations represented. Were they simply the first steps on a road which led to more or less complete nationalization of the whole economy? Or were they rather the culmination of a process which assumed that nationalization had an important but limited part in Labour's repertoire of policy? This issue was only to come to the fore as the programme of nationalization began to be enacted after 1945.

ORGANIZING NATIONALIZATION: THE DEBATE TO 1945

Of itself, public ownership says nothing about how the industries are to be organized. But by 1945 this issue, or at least some aspects of it, had been widely debated for a number of years, and the form of nationalization was settled. The Morrisonian public corporation, named after Herbert Morrison, had come to be the widely if not unanimously accepted form of organization. This embodied the idea of the control of nationalized industries being vested in public boards whose members were to be appointed by a Minister on the basis of expertise, not as representatives of any interests. These boards would be charged with the day-to-day running of the industries, with only broad policy guidance from the Minister.

This organizational form evolved over a long period. In the six nationalization proposals (unsuccessfully) put before Parliament before First World War, Labour had advocated the 'Post Office model', of direct control of the industry concerned by a government department. However this model came under challenge in Labour ranks both because it was deemed bureaucratic and inefficient in more commercial areas of the economy, and also because it allowed an inadequate role for workers in the industry (Ostergaard 1954: 194, 204). Until the 1920s Labour was torn two ways on the issue: on the one hand, it wanted a greater role for the workers than direct subordination to a Ministry would allow; on the other hand, it was keen to see Parliament have effective control over the industry—or else what would become of parliamentary sovereignty?

These contradictory impulses are shown in Labour's response to the creation of public corporations in the early twentieth century. The first of these was the Port of London Authority, usually seen as the first public corporation of the modern type, and created in 1909 (Gordon 1938: ch. 2). Labour attacked this type of public ownership (where control was largely vested in the port users) as being inappropriate because of lack of parliamentary control. A similar line was taken by Labour's Clement Attlee in the parliamentary debate over the Central Electricity Board in 1926, but by this time much Labour opinion was tending to view the idea much more sympathetically, and by the time of the 1929–31 Labour government the public corporation was fast becoming the preferred form of public ownership in Labour circles (Ostergaard 1954: 196, 206–11).

During the Labour government's period in office a bill was put forward by Herbert Morrison for public ownership of London Transport via a public corporation (the London Passenger Transport Board). In making his case for this form of organization in the House of Commons, Morrison made three main points: first, that in the context of socialist debates this was the best form of nationalization; second, that it was common ground with the Liberals, most importantly in their 1928 'Yellow Book'; and finally, that it reflected the perceived success of the Central Electricity Board (Hansard, Commons 1930, vol. 250, col. 56).

These three points would seem to cover the main components of Labour's conversion to the public corporation, developed at length by Morrison in a later book (1933). In this he argued that what Labour wanted from nationalization was 'a combination of public ownership, public accountability, and business management for public ends' (149). Thus the LPTB would combine the traditional socialist emphasis on parliamentary accountability with management free from day-to-day ministerial control on the Post Office model. This version of public ownership had become part of the progressive consensus of the period covering both Liberals and advanced Conservatives, so that the public corporation was not just a Labour Party idea. The Conservatives had introduced the Central Electricity Board, widely seen as successful in expanding the industry and lowering prices significantly

(Gordon 1938: ch. 3). However, initially there were some differences in the reasons for this support. Labour, Liberals, and
Tories wanted to take nationalization out of politics in a day-to-
day sense, but whilst the Tories especially saw this as providing
a space for business management of the industries Labour saw it
as making 'industry more, not less, democratic and, in particular,
more responsive to the wishes of the workers in industry'
(Ostergaard 1954: 206). But this desire raised the issue of how far
workers were to have a direct role in the management of
nationalized industries.

Morrison, in his discussion of the LPTB, was quite clear in his
opposition to any notion of workers' control. This is opposed
partly on the basis that workers are not interested in high policy
in industry. They are 'more interested in the organization,
conditions, and life of their own immediate workshop than in
those finer balances of financial, industrial, and commercial
policy which are discussed in the Board room' (1933: 225). This
is supported on the basis of Soviet experience, where it is pointed
out how 'crude' notions of workers control in the early Soviet
period have given way to a sharp separation of management and
trade-union functions in the enterprise (213–23). But perhaps
most important for Morrison was the argument that the boards
should not be representatives of interests at all, but as in the
LPTB case composed of 'persons who have had wide experience
and have shown capacity in transport, industrial, commercial, or
financial matters or in the conduct of public affairs' (212). This
position involved two key propositions: that such people would
be better equipped to manage the corporation than those appointed by interest groups, but even more fundamentally, that
any Board nominated on the basis of interests 'would be destruct-
ive of the Ministers' accountability' (191).

The Labour position on public corporations as put forward at
the time of the LPTB proposals was far from unanimous in
support of Morrison. In the early 1930s at both Labour and
Trade Union Conferences a lively debate raged on whether this
should become the model. Assessed in terms of the coherence of
the arguments this debate was highly unsatisfactory (Tomlinson
1982: 70–9). On the one hand proponents of direct trade-union
representation on boards tended just to assert the need for
workers to have their interests represented, without spelling out

what those interests were. On the other hand Morrison stressed the importance of the general interest against sectional interests, without being clear what this meant. In addition he assumed that this general interest would be secured by Ministerial parliamentary responsibility for the industries, though it was far from clear how this responsibility was to be exercised.

Obviously the case was not settled by these rather underdeveloped arguments about interests and their representation. More important in determining the outcome of the dispute in favour of the Morrisonian corporation was the trade-union ambivalence on the issue. Whilst some trade unionists were avid supporters of some forms of workers' control, many were worried about the split responsibilities of trade unionists on boards of public corporations: on the one hand the responsibility to the union members, on the other hand the responsibility for the corporation as a whole (e.g. TUC 1931: 395; 1932: 436).

Ultimately though, the key reason for the general Labour support for the public corporation was political:

Two features of the Fabian conception of the state and government led inevitably to the rejection of workers' control. The first was the acceptance of parliamentary supremacy as an expression of the majority will. . . . all attempts to impinge on the supremacy of Parliament or to weaken Parliament as a majoritarian institution were consistently opposed by the Fabians . . . To have any public official ultimately responsible to some agency other than Parliament was a denial of the whole meaning of the British constitution . . . The other determining feature of the Fabian conception of government was an uncommon respect for the expert' (Dahl 1947: 877–8).

Related to the idea of the central role of the expert manager was the growing belief at this time that private-sector managers were increasingly to be seen as experts, rather than as representatives of the capitalist interest. This in turn was linked to the idea of the alleged divorce between ownership and control in the large private corporation, consequent on the dispersion of shareholding. This view of the private sector developed alongside support for the public corporation. It was strongly present in the Yellow Book and propounded in the progressive Conservative manifesto, Macmillan's *The Middle Way* of 1938. It was taken on board more slowly by Labour thinkers, but was evident in debates in the 1930s, and by the early 1940s seems to have been quite widely supported, especially following the publication of James Burnham's *The Managerial Revolution* in 1940.

This analysis of the private sector was very important for the debate on nationalization, because it suggested a convergence between large companies, public or private, towards managerial control divorced from questions of ownership. The line was to be consummated by Crosland in 1956 with his *Future of Socialism* (chs. 1, 3) when he used this alleged convergence to suggest that capitalism in the traditional sense had ceased to exist.

This alleged parallel between private and public corporations was emphasized by those who stressed the administrative aspects of the public corporation. 'In essence the public corporation represents an attempt to apply the public administration when extended to commercial enterprise to the type of organization evolved for large-scale private administration by the joint stock company' (Gordon 1938: 3). More politically, this idea of a parallel that was developed brings out both the extent to which the public corporation was not a peculiarly Labour idea, but rather part of the progressive consensus of the 1930s (Marwick 1964), and also the extent to which this consensus was built on the idea that in certain circumstances the public corporation could be the most efficient way of organizing production. This attitude is, as usual, well summarized by Morrison: 'As I have said, socialisation is not an end in itself. The object is to make possible organization of a more efficient industry, rendering more public service, and because of its efficiency and increased productivity enable to do progressively more for its workers' (Hansard, 30 January 1946, col. 969).

NATIONALIZATION, 1945–51

Labour's election manifesto of 1945 *Let Us Face the Future* laid out a programme of nationalization closely akin to that in *Labour's Immediate Programme* of 1937. The manifesto itemized the Bank of England, the coal-mines, electricity, gas, railways and other transport services, and iron and steel. Joint-stock bank nationalization had been dropped since 1937 (Pollard 1978), whilst iron and steel had been added. The Labour leadership had attempted to put a much more limited programme to the 1944

Labour Party Conference, but had been overruled from the Conference floor. For many in the Labour Party nationalization was its key policy, crucial in distinguishing it from the capitalist parties (Brooke 1989: 172–3).

But the particular political debates of 1944/5 may serve to exaggerate the ideological as opposed to the pragmatic bases of Labour's nationalization programme. First, as already noted there was quite a strong consensus emerging in the 1920s and 1930s about the need for rationalization in British industry and how in some industries this could be met best by nationalization. Second, there was the consensus around the public corporation as an entity which could combine business management and public responsibility. Third, some of the nationalized industries (notably coal and the railways) had long histories of state involvement, increased during the Second World War, so that nationalization was in many ways just a further step down a long-trodden road. Finally, the war had left some industries (again, notably coal and railways) with extremely rundown capital equipment, and this made their revival and reconstruction under private ownership extremely problematic.

Recently, scholarly histories of the nationalized industries (Supple 1986, 1987; Ashworth 1986; Hannah 1979, 1982; Gourvish 1986) have placed nationalizations firmly in a context of industrial history rather than political history, and in that light the nationalizations of 1945–51 appear more of a particular administrative solution to long-existing problems rather than instalments of socialism. For Supple (on coal), 'To optimists on 1st January 1946 nationalization may have appeared the "End of History" and the "Beginning of Nowadays". It was neither. It was the continuation of industrial politics by other means' (1986: 250; see also Gourvish 1991: 114–18).

Of course this approach to nationalization and its significance should not be exaggerated. In large part it was undoubtedly about reorganizing and trying to make more efficient industries where the state had long been involved and/or where there were major problems in the industry. But this argument would not strongly apply to iron and steel, which perhaps best illustrates the major objective of nationalization other than the efficiency of particular sectors—to gain control of the commanding heights of the economy. Whether or not nationalization was the first instalment of socialism might be disputed in the Labour Party, but it was common ground that planning the economy was both desirable and legitimized by the experiences of the Second World War, and that part of the planning involved public ownership of key sectors in the economy. Together these two motives largely account for the extent and character of the nationalization (Table 8.1).

TABLE 8.1. *State-owned enterprise in 1951*

	Turnover (£m.)	Employment (00s)
Inland Transport	617	888
(of which, railways)	385	600
Coal	541	780
Iron and steel	502	292
Electricity	269	182
Gas	261	148
Airways	44	25
TOTAL	2235	2315

Source: Gourvish (1991), p. 113.

The first and obvious thing about the nationalization was that overwhelmingly it was whole sectors or activities rather than individual enterprises that were nationalized. This reflected both the utility or natural monopoly character of much of the programme, or, as in the case of iron and steel, the belief that the sector was a 'commanding height' which should be planned as a unit. Another way of putting the point is to say that whilst nationalization had important efficiency aims, efficiency was seen largely in terms of scale economies not competition (Chick 1991). Indeed, it would be broadly right to say that Labour saw nationalization as a superior alternative to trying to enhance competition as a route to efficiency (this issue is returned to below).

As noted above, the extent to which Labour lacked blueprints for nationalization has been exaggerated in much of the literature. The economic debates of the 1930s had been quite detailed about at least some of the problem of running public corporations. This was supplemented by plenty of wartime work on individual industries by civil servants and technocrats who anticipated radical changes in the industries post-war, if not necessarily nationalization (Gourvish 1991: 118–19). On the other hand, the scale (around 17 per cent of GDP, 19 per cent of investment, 10 per cent of the work-force) and the speed (all this done in five years 1946–51) of the nationalizations certainly meant that the pre-planning was far from perfect, and major issues remained to be resolved after nationalization had taken place.

One of the striking characteristics of the nationalization process was the very limited discussion of the objectives of the industries, something that was the case in other countries whose extensive nationalitization took place in this period. The British Transport Commission (covering all the nationalized inland transport industries) had a characteristic statutory duty to provide an 'efficient, adequate economic and properly integrated system of public transport', but without any clear guidelines on how this Nirvana might be achieved. Equally, the financial remit of the industries was usually limited to the need to break even 'taking one year with another'. Pricing policy was left equally vague.

Organizationally, the degree of centralization was a very key issue, with the National Coal Board being set up on a highly centralized basis; this was later widely thought to have been an error, and subsequent nationalizations had a more decentralized framework (Chester 1975: 1025–34). Indeed, much discussion of the organization of nationalized industries rose little above debates over the degree of decentralization that was appropriate, the decentralizers often making heroic assumptions about how a more decentralized framework would improve those human relations seen as so important to industrial morale and efficiency (Ch. 7).

One of the plain problems with the 1945–51 nationalizations was that they were overburdened with objectives. Apart from what seem to be the overarching aims—to increase the efficiency of particular sectors, especially by achievement of economies of scale, and to provide the basis for a planned economy—they were seen by some as a route to better industrial relations and a way of redistributing income (Ashworth 1991: ch. 2). Inevitably all these aims could not be achieved. Discontent followed, and this discontent is apparent in the late 1940s even as the process of nationalization continues.

Discontent was partly the result of the exaggerated hopes entertained about the impact of nationalization on workers' attitudes and hence output. This was most apparent in coal, suffering in the late 1940s from a major problem of meeting demand at prevailing prices, and where nationalization was widely seen as a panacea for its poor history of industrial relations. But no revolutionary change in those relations occurred and neither did any productivity miracle (Ashworth 1986: ch. 4).

More generally, the government soon became concerned with the lack of ministerial control over the nationalized industries. This issue had been debated in wartime, and there had been a shift compared with the 1920s and 1930s towards more emphasis on ministerial control. But this control seemed in practice to be much weaker than those discussions had assumed.

The problem arose in a number of areas. Politically important was the area of worker consultation. Whilst the government stuck firmly to the pre-war rejection of appointment of worker representatives to boards of the nationalized industries (though they could be and were appointed on a personal basis), they were very keen to have workers consulted. This was aimed both at conciliating workers who otherwise felt little had changed with nationalization, and also as a means of improving human relations in order to improve productivity. All the nationalization statutes (except that of the Bank of England) obliged the industries to set up consultative frameworks. But the new Boards' enthusiasm for this offer seems to have been limited despite government prodding (PRO 1949a, 1951a). Equally met by resistance from the Boards was the government's idea of an 'efficiency unit' to scrutinize the industries' efficiency (PRO 1950a; Chester 1975: 956–80).

More important economically was the problem of the industries being used to plan the economy. Government control over their investment was far from achieved. For example, the NCB resisted the Ministry of Fuel and Power's plans for a big increase in investment in coke ovens (Chester 1975: 981–90). Several industries resisted the idea that they should establish a 'shelf' of investment projects against the possibility of a future slump (Tomlinson 1987a: ch. 5).

Whilst neither in investment nor other issues was the story one of an unremitting conflict between the government and the

nationalized boards, it was certainly not quite how the relationship had been assumed by many proponents of nationalization.
On this it is most appropriate to quote Herbert Morrison who in
1949 wrote that:

We ought to take a fairly early opportunity to review the powers of the
government to control socialised industries. It is of great advantage to
have brought the public utility services and certain basic industries
under the control of public boards which can administer those services
and industries in the private interest; but the government has a wider
viewpoint of the public interest than the Boards, and I am far from
happy that we are in a position to exercise the control on wide issues of
policy which the national economy requires (PRO 1949*b*).

As early as 1946 the Labour Party NEC called for a review of
nationalization policy. A Research Department document of that
year laid down the criteria against which further proposals,
beyond those of *Let Us Face the Future*, should be assessed. The
two key criteria were said to be aiding full employment, especially by regulating public investment, and raising production,
which was seen to be achieved by a range of features of the
nationalized bodies, from 'securing benefits of large-scale organization' to improving management (Labour Party 1946).

But as Brooke (1989) points out, once the issue was posed in
terms of the nationalization as a means to an end, rather than
itself an end as embodying progress towards socialism, the way
was open for revisionists to question the utility of nationalization
to achieve Labour's goals. This debate did indeed begin soon
after the paper noted above was circulated. This line is very
explicit in a paper from the Labour Party's research director,
Michael Young in 1947 (Labour Party 1947). But more striking
is a paper by Douglas Jay published in 1948. Jay had written a
major revisionist work in 1937, where nationalization was present, but seen as clearly secondary to financial policy in Labour's
policy armoury. Like most revisionists, Jay accepted the nationalizations of 1945–51, but wanted to set a different kind of agenda
for the policy thereafter. In his paper of 1948 (Labour Party,
1948*b*) Jay put forward what seems to be the first proposal from
a significant Labour figure for what later came to be called
'competitive public enterprise':

We should move in the direction of establishing efficient public enterprise, competing, if necessary, with private enterprise, rather than the old pattern—to which we have perhaps given rather dogmatic adherence—of 100 per cent compulsory purchase by legislation, together with a ban on all outside competition with the public monopoly thus set up. It might assist thought if we stopped talking of 'nationalization' of an 'industry', and thought in terms of public enterprise for higher production instead.

This view was quickly taken up in public by the Labour Party. At the Labour Party Conference of 1949 Herbert Morrison was proclaiming competitive public enterprise as 'a new application of socialism and socialist doctrine. . . . We shall push into new fields and revitalise private enterprise with its own techniques of competition' (cited Labour Party 1949*a*). This view was also embodied in Labour's major statement of policy of 1949 *Labour Believes in Britain* (Labour Party 1949*b*), which set up the criteria of private enterprise 'failing the nation' as when competitive public enterprise would be appropriate.[4]

Whilst the extent of nationalization was to remain a contentious issue for the Labour Party for many years to come, in practice most of the Party came to accept that the nationalizations of 1945–51 completed a phase of public ownership, and that, at a minimum, in future the pattern of such ownership would be different from what had occurred in that 'heroic' period. By 1951 that pattern was widely regarded as at least not having yielded all the expected benefits hoped for, a view expressed across the spectrum of Labour opinion (Crosland 1956: 474–82).

This disillusion seems to have led to an acceptance that nationalization should be seen as having a restricted number of aims. In 1950 (Labour Party 1950*a*: 20) these were stated to be threefold: 'a means of controlling the basic industries and services' . . . 'a way of dealing with industries in which inefficiency persists' . . . 'a means of ensuring that monopolies do not exploit the public'. Thus the debate over public ownership had narrowed—the criteria now were predominantly economic, and within these efficiency increasingly took pride of place.

[4] A term repeated in Labour Party (1950*a*), p. 3 and the 1950 Election Manifesto (Labour Party 1950*b*). The latter restricted its nationalization proposals to sugar, cement, and (possibly) chemicals.

In the 1940s 'competitive public enterprise' was commonly seen as an idea coming from the revisionist wing of the Labour Party (e.g. Crosland 1956: ch. 13; Gaitskell 1956; see also Weiner 1960: 82–95). But in later years it was taken up by the Left, and was the centrepiece of Labour's industrial policy in the 1970s (Ch. 11). 1945-style sectoral nationalization was pursued in later years—steel in 1967 (which had been denationalized by the Conservatives in the 1950s), shipbuilding and aerospace in the 1970s. But taken in the long view, the nationalizations of the 1940s look like the culmination of developments in an analysis of industry deriving largely from the 1920s and 1930s rather than the beginning of a new phase.

FROM 1945 TO 1979

The broad scope of nationalization did not alter a great deal over the next twenty-five years. The Conservatives after 1951 denationalized steel (Burk 1988), which was in turn renationalized in 1967, and parts of road transport. But the rest of the nationalizations remained untouched—part of the broad consensus on economic policy of the 'long-boom years'. The boundaries of nationalization started to change in the 1970s when that long boom turned to stagflation. Notable casualties of the more troubled economic climate like Rolls Royce (engines) and British Leyland were nationalized by Conservative and Labour governments respectively in that decade. Labour also extended public ownership into shipbuilding and aerospace. But the predominant issue for most of the period down to 1979 was not the scope of nationalization, but how public corporations were to be run.

In the first ten years of Conservative rule after 1951 most of the attention was on administrative structures, rather than questions of objectives or criteria for management in the industries. As Gourvish (1991: 121) notes 'decentralisation was the contemporary watchword'. This was strongly pursued in railways and electricity, though in coal excessive decentralisation was diagnosed and its central authority was strengthened. Problems diagnosed in the 1940s were not addressed. Coal and electricity continued to be underpriced into the 1950s, which meant both constant shortages of supply and poor financial performance by the industries. The nationalized industries generally continued to lack clear objectives, and management often seemed unsure what its aims and objectives should be.

However from the late 1950s the situation began to change. A Select Committee on Nationalised Industries was set up (despite the opposition of figures like Morrison[5]) to improve parliamentary scrutiny of the industries. Changing politics in the Treasury led to an attempt to provide a more elaborated framework within which the industries should operate. A landmark in this development was the publication in 1961 of a White Paper on *The Financial and Economic Obligations of the Nationalised Industries* (Cmnd. 1337). This may be seen as the first step in imposing clearer economic goals on the industries, moving the debate away from the organizational issues which had predominated over the previous decade and a half.

Up to 1961 the industries had only the broad duty to meet the demand for their products in an efficient way, and financially to break even, after making a contribution to reserves (Cmnd. 1337: 4). The 1961 White Paper focused not on what precisely was meant by that ambiguous word efficiency in this context, but on financial behaviour. In the new framework, the requirement to break even over a 'period of years' would be specifically over 5 years, after providing for interest and depreciation at historic cost. Provision should be made for the difference between historic and the replacement cost of assets, and some contribution made towards the industry's future capital requirements (7).

Part of the purpose was to reduce the dependence of the nationalized industries on Exchequer finance. Up to 1956 investment in coal had been entirely funded by the Exchequer, but other industries could raise money directly from the markets. After 1956 all money came from the Exchequer, creating a tension between government's desires to control public borrowing and spending and the investment needs of the public corporations which was to be extremely important in the 1970s and beyond, especially in opening the way to privatization.

The second important stage in the regulation of the nationalized industries in the 1960s was a further White Paper, *Nationalised Industries: A Review of Economic and Financial Objectives* (Cmnd.

---

[5] Select Committee (1952/3) Qs. 381–507.

3437). Under this framework, the financial regime of the industries was much more clearly specified. All investment projects were to be subjected to discounted cash flow calculation, whereby all projects were supposed to yield at least the test discount rate of 8 per cent. This was supposed to equate returns in the nationalized industries to the average rate of return on low-risk projects in the private sector over the preceding few years (Cmnd. 3437: para. 64).

This subjection of the corporations to greater financial discipline may be seen in two contexts. On the one hand, as already indicated, it was related to the public finance implications of the nationalized corporations' decision-making. On the other, it was related to the whole focus of public policy on growth in the 1960s (Ch. 10), and the belief that one way higher growth could be delivered was through better scientific forms of investment appraisal. DCF was the calculative technology of the time, to be applied in both private and public sectors to raise the productivity of investment (Miller 1991).

The 1967 White Paper also encouraged a particular kind of pricing policy for the industries. This was part of a debate which went back to the 1930s and 1940s (e.g. Wilson 1945). Economists had argued from that time onwards that a Pareto optimum allocation of resources required the industries to price at marginal-cost, the basic idea being that in this way the benefit to society (registered by the price) would be equated to the cost to society of using extra resources (the marginal-cost). The problem with this principal had long been recognized as its creation of a potential conflict between economic and financial objectives for public corporations. If the corporation's activities did show long-run declines in average costs, then marginal-costs would always be below average costs and marginal-cost pricing would always yield a loss to the corporation (the loss being the result of prices being below average costs). Even economists who in principal accepted the appropriateness of the marginal-cost pricing rule, had argued that in practice it would be undesirable, because by sanctioning financial losses, it would remove all incentives to efficiency for the managers of the corporations. The debate had continued in more practical vein in the 1940s, especially around the issue of how far consumers should be charged different prices reflecting different marginal costs, for example, where producing electricity at peak times cost more than a similar unit produced at another time of day. By and large the issue had been resolved in favour of uniform (average cost) pricing (Chick 1990).

The 1967 advocacy of long-run marginal-cost pricing alongside a strong emphasis on investment appraisal created a tension in the direction of the industries. Marginal-cost pricing might well conflict with the rates of return deemed desirable on financial grounds. The picture is further complicated where the industries were deemed to have social responsibilities which justify deviating from these performance criteria. The difficulty is that if these responsibilities are implicit rather than explicit they make both the incentives for the corporations' managers and assessment of the industries' performances more complicated. The 1967 White Paper recommended that such responsibilities or 'obligations' be explicitly priced and allowed for in the industries' operating framework, but this was only done in the case of British Rail (Vickers and Yarrow 1988: 131).

Whatever the potentials of this programme for changing the behaviour of the nationalized industries, it was increasingly overshadowed by the macroeconomic concerns of government. As noted above, one of the major motives for nationalization was the idea of using the industries to plan the economy. As planning gave way to management of the economy from the end of the 1940s this idea was not given up—indeed given the weight of the industries in the national economy it was implausible that it would ever be given up. *Ad hoc* intervention in the industries' pricing and investment policies was common in the 1950s and 1960s, but intensified in the 1970s with the general deterioration in economic performance. This led to frequent arm-twisting of the industries by government to hold prices down in the name of counter-inflation policy. But most importantly it led to an increasing concern with the industries' financial position, as the 1970s deterioration in Britain's fiscal position took place. The Public Sector Borrowing Requirement emerged as a key indicator of fiscal responsibility, and up to 1976 all public corporation investment was included in the PSBR (i.e. even if financed from ploughed-back profit). In 1976 this was changed to bring Britain in line with international conventions, so that only finance provided by the government appeared in the PSBR. But despite this change, the climate of financial stringency led to the creation of External Financial Limits (EFLs)—cash limits on the total funding from government of individual public corporations (Heald 1983: 17–18, 193–6, 126–7).

This emphasis on finance, in the narrow sense of minimizing the industries' dependence on government finance, is strongly embedded in the 1978 White Paper *The Nationalised Industries* (Cmnd. 7131). As Heald (1980) argues, this paper re-emphasized the financial criteria embodied in the 1961 White Paper, played down the economic criteria such as marginal-cost pricing of the 1967 Paper, and essentially dealt with any conflict between the two by subordinating the economic issues to financial limits.

It is worth emphasizing that this new governmental posture on the nationalized industries pre-dated the privatization programme of the 1980s, and reflects the fiscal crisis of the 1970s.[6] But it did to a significant extent pave the way to those privatizations, by basing the assessment of the performance of nationalized industry almost entirely on financial results, rather than any of the other criteria which had been previously essayed.

PRIVATIZATION AND PUBLIC INDUSTRY PERFORMANCE

Just like nationalization, privatization was a policy with many objectives. At least eight such objectives have been officially pronounced (Cmnd. 9734). These are (i) a general commitment to reducing involvement in industrial decisions; (ii) the separation of industrial investment decisions from government financial policy; (iii) reducing the PSBR; (iv) promoting wider share ownership; (v) promoting worker/manager ownership of companies they work in; (vi) encouraging an enterprise culture; (vii) increasing competition and efficiency; (viii) replacing ownership and financial controls by the government with other forms of more efficient regulation, where competition is not possible.

---

[6] Though the Labour government did sell £500m. of shares in BP as part of its response to the fiscal crisis.

Of course this prospectus for privatization contained a good deal of the neo-liberal rhetoric of the 1980s. But arguably what made the privatization programme so appealing to the government was the possibility it offered of decoupling public finances from the industries' investment decisions. Pressure to do this in the early 1980s arose in three particular ways. First the problem of underinvestment in one nationalized industry in particular, telecommunications. In this case, the public-finance constraint was widely seen to have contained desirable investment in an area of fast-changing technology and rapidly expanding demand. Privatization offered a way of expanding such investment without posing fiscal problems for the government. Second, the slump of the early 1980s drove most of the nationalized industries deep into deficit, thus exacerbating the fiscal problem of a government committed to cutting borrowing, taxation, and public spending. Third, privatization offered a way of reducing public borrowing, as by Treasury convention, public asset sales counted as 'negative public expenditure' in the public financial accounts. Also, by low-pricing of the assets wider share-ownership could be encouraged by offering a substantial 'bribe' to new share purchasers. Driven by these various calculations, by the end of the 1980s privatization had covered most of the nationalized industries likely to yield significant revenues to the government, with the only large industries left being coal and railways, where the fiscal benefits of sales are likely to be very limited (Table 8.2).

The privatization programme was driven by a combination of fiscal pressure, ideological zeal, and electoral calculation. It has been analysed in great detail by economists (e.g. Vickers and Yarrow 1988). One of the issues they have highlighted is the conflict between the different objectives of privatization—most obviously between the desire to maximize the revenue from sales (allowing for the desire to encourage new participants into the equity market) and the desire to encourage competition in the privatized industries. More generally the economists have emphasized the extent to which traditional economic analysis has played down the importance of ownership in understanding the economic behaviour of enterprises, as opposed to the central role of competition. Privatization, as a change in ownership, has opened up quite new areas of discussion about whether ownership matters.

TABLE 8.2. *Privatization 1979–89*

	Company	Revenue (£bn. 1988)
1979	BP	0.7
1980	Ferranti	0.6
1981	British Aerospace BP Cable and Wireless	0.7
1982	Britoil National Freight	0.6
1983	BP Cable and Wireless	1.4
1984	British Telecom Jaguar Enterprise Oil	2.5
1985	British Aerospace Britoil Cable and Wireless	2.9
1986	British Gas National Bus	4.7
1987	British Airports British Airways BP Rolls Royce	5.1
1988	British Steel Rover Group	6.5
1989	Water Supply	4.7

Source: Begg *et al.* (1991), p. 328

The most obvious way in which the changed pattern of ownership brought about by privatization has altered in the industries is that they are now subject to the disciplines of private ownership—the threat of take-over and the displacement of one set of managers by another. The consequences of this depend on the view taken of the efficacy of such financial market discipline in encouraging efficiency. This issue is addressed in Chapter 12, in the context of discussion of the overall neo-liberal policy agenda of the 1980s. But it is worth noting here that much talk of the benefits of privatization assumes that performance will be enhanced irrespective of the actual regime operative in private financial markets—a rather implausible view.

The case for privatization has been made in a negative fashion by emphasizing the poor performance of the nationalized industries. Clearly the financial performance of the public corporations in the early 1980s was poor, and thus provided a major impetus to the privatization programme. But there is need for at least some discussion of the wider problems of measuring the performance of the nationalized industries.

The first and obvious point to be made is that the benchmarks against which they are to be judged are far from clear or uncontroversial. The problem in part is the conflict between economic objectives embodied in the nationalized statutes and in subsequent government policies. But the issue goes deeper than this. As emphasized already, nationalization had a number of different objectives, but clearly the assumption of the major increase in public ownership of 1945–51 was that publicly owned firms would be qualitatively different from private-sector firms. Yes, they would achieve economies of scale inhibited by the structure of private ownership, but beyond this they would be managed in a way which would improve social relations at the enterprise level, which in turn would also help their efficiency. This idea of nationalized industries as potentially qualitatively different from the private sector has generated little subsequent commentary, though such commentary does exist for the French public sector (e.g. Frost 1991). By and large it has been the economists, with their narrow range of concerns, who have dominated the discussion of the performance of the nationalized industries.

Equally, there has been rather little discussion of the role of the industries in the management of the national economy. Most treatments simply decry this interference in the corporations'

TABLE 8.3. *Profitability of public corporations compared with industrial and commercial companies* (%)

	Public corporations	Industrial and commercial companies
1970–4	5.9	17.6
1975–9	5.6	16.7
1980–5	5.9	18.3

Source: Vickers and Yarrow (1988), p. 143.

activities. In fact, a simple economics case can be made for such intervention e.g. where private-sector investment causes cycles in the economy which can be smoothed by variations in public investment (a policy pursued with some success in Sweden, for example). Again, however, there has been little discussion of this issue in the British literature.

Most assessments of the nationalized industries' performance has focused on a narrow range of divergent measure of such performance, especially financial performance and productivity (Ashworth 1991: ch. 5; Gourvish 1991: 125–30; Vickers and Yarrow 1988: ch. 5; Millward 1991). In aggregate the financial performance of the nationalized industries has usually been poor in the sense of not yielding a consistent surplus over labour costs and interest payments and yielding profit rates inferior to those of the private sector, especially since the 1970s (Table 8.3). Of course these results must been seen in context. The various ways in which governments have intervened in the industries in pursuit of macroeconomic goals has worsened their profitability, as too has the (usually implicit) belief that the industries should pursue social rather than economic goals. The figures are also affected by the degree of monopoly in the industry concerned.

TABLE 8.4. *Productivity in British manufacturing and public enterprise 1951–1985* (% change p.a.)

	1951–64	1964–73	1973–85	1951–85
Manufacturing				
Labour productivity	+2.5	+4.0	+2.3	+2.8
Capital productivity	−0.8	−0.7	−2.2	−1.3
Total factor productivity	+1.9	+2.4	+1.1	+1.6
Public enterprise				
Labour productivity	+3.3	+5.0	+2.1	+3.2
Capital productivity	+0.4	+0.1	+0.2	+0.1
Total factor productivity	+2.4	+2.9	+1.4	+2.2

Source: Millward (1991), p. 144.

On the other hand, productivity performance, at least in some periods, and perhaps overall, has been quite good. Whilst this is an area of quite vigorous debate (e.g. Pryke 1971, 1981; Molyneaux and Thompson 1987) the calculations of Millward (1991) suggest that almost throughout their existence the nationalized industries turned in a better productivity performance than manufacturing, however that performance is measured (Table 8.4).

Millward uses the above data to attack the myths of the 1970s which led up to privatization: 'The proposition that their performance is poor in terms of productive efficiency, that their record is worse than other parts of the British economy, and that this manifested itself in the 1970s in the form of huge increases in prices, is actually lacking substantive support' (Millward 1991: 138). But he argues that the productivity peformance was quite respectable not only in the 1970s but over the whole post-war period. Of course, as always, there were particular reasons which might be advanced for this performance.

The good performance of the nationalized industries in the 1950s was partly due to labour-shedding on a massive scale, notably in coal and the railways. As so often in Britain, fast rises in labour productivity are most readily secured when output is falling but employment falls even faster. We might say that with reference to this period, a paradoxical benefit of nationalization is that it allowed the rapid rundown of these industries without much strife, albeit greatly helped by the prevailing climate of full employment. Productivity has also been affected by the change in financial regime—for example in the case of steel the improvements of the 1980s are closely linked not only to labour-shedding but also to the tight financial controls, though the overall financial performance is complicated by the very large debt write-offs which the industry has been allowed.

There is clearly a conflict between financial and productive performance in the nationalized industries. As Millward (152–3) remarks 'there is really no convincing evidence that the general trends in the nationalized industries prices and finances in the post-war period were reflecting an underlying managerial incompetence'. Unfortunately for the industries, by the 1970s financial criteria had come to have overwhelming weight in the assessment of public (and, indeed, private) companies whatever the productive realities. Their failure to develop clear alternative measures of performance left them highly vulnerable to a government driven by ideological fervour to 'roll back the state', coupled with the strong desire to improve public finances and convey in a very material way to the voter the benefits of share ownership.

CONCLUSIONS

In general terms the nationalization programme of 1945–51 arose from two broad contexts. On the one hand it arose from an industrial policy context, where significant numbers of basic industries were seen to have failed the nation, by their inability to reorganize and re-equip. This context arose initially in the 1920s and 1930s, but was reinforced by the seemingly successful extension of state control in the 1940s, and the parallel decline in the condition of several of the industries. This agenda could be supported intellectually from the economist's tool-kit of natural monopolies and externalities. By the 1940s there was a progressive consensus on the broad shape of nationalization.

The other context was socialism, interpreted both in a narrow sense to involve an enhanced power of government to control the economy, and more widely as a qualitative change in the functioning of industry, most especially in the place of workers within it. At its most optimistic, this agenda implied that nationalization was a first step towards the transformation of social relations at both the enterprise and a wider societal level.

In post-war Britain nationalization has been discussed predominantly in terms of the first of these contexts. Increasingly solely financial criteria were used to assess the industries, but even where efficiency criteria, in the broadest economic sense, have been used, this has tended to expose the rather limited basis on which the industrial policy agenda for nationalization was developed. Much of it depended on a rather crude notion of economies of scale, defined in a largely technological sense. This tended to ignore the severe limits to realizing such economies in complex, multi-product enterprises dependent on high levels of managerial competence (Williams *et al.* 1986). So whilst their productive record may be respectable, it has been marred by some notable failures. Equally the belief that different human relations in the public corporations would transform efficiency appears in retrospect a pious hope rather than something which significantly set the agenda for the industries.

Public ownership failed in post-war Britain, but that failure was above all a political failure. As Michael Shanks argued in 1963 concerning the poor reputation of the nationalized industries 'Labour is to blame because it has failed to provide a coherent philosophy or code of conduct for nationalised industries, or think out what they should be expected to do in the present state of our society' (19). From the beginning nationalization was saddled with an excessive number of competing objectives. As a policy instrument it was both underdeveloped and overdetermined. It declined in the face of post-war pressures into a panacea for the socialist few and a vulnerable residue of the past for the majority. After 1979 it was ripe for the picking.

Further Reading

Ashworth, W. (1991), *The State in Business: 1945 to the mid-1980s*, London.

Barry, E. E. (1965), *Nationalisation in British Politics*, London.

Chester, D. N. (1975), *The Nationalisation of British Industry 1945–51*, London.

Dahl, R. (1947), 'Workers Control and the British Labour Party', *American Political Science Review*, 41: 875–900.

Gourvish, T. (1991), 'The Rise (and Fall?) of State-Owned Enterprises', in T. Gourvish and A. O'Day (eds.), *Britain Since 1945*, London: 111–34.

Hannah, L. (1993), 'The Socialist Experiment: The Economic Consequences of the State Ownership of Industry in the U.K., 1945–1990', in R. Floud and D. McCloskey (eds.), *The Economic History of Britain Since 1700*, 2nd edn., vol. iii, Cambridge.

Morgan, K. (1987), 'The Rise and Fall of Public Ownership in Britain', in J. M. W. Bean (ed.), *The Political Culture of Modern Britain*, London: 277–98.

Morrison, H. (1933), *Socialism and Transport*, London.

Ostergaard, G. N. (1954), 'Labour and the Development of the Public Corporation', *Manchester School*, 22: 192–216.

9

1951–1961: Consumption and Competition

INTRODUCTION

The return of a Conservative government in 1951 carried no simple implication for future economic policy. On the one hand, the Conservatives had based much of their election appeal on 'setting the people free' from the austerity and rationing of the 1940s, and this suggested a much more liberal economic regime would follow their victory (Zweiniger-Bargielowska 1993). On the other hand, Labour actually secured more votes than the Tories in 1951, and Tory leaders were conscious that they did not have a mandate to reverse the major shifts in economic (or social) policy of the 1940s. The key post-war statement of policy, the Industrial Charter (Conservative Party 1947) had signalled a broad acceptance of the 'post-war settlement', especially if the focus was on actual policy proposals rather than the more liberal rhetoric of the document (Ramsden 1980: 110–11).

Industrial efficiency was not as central to the economic policy agenda in the 1950s as in the 1940s. Once the strains of the Korean war had been overcome the balance of payments, whilst periodically in crisis, did not have the appearance of fundamental imbalance which had impelled so much of the supply-side socialism of 1945–51. Equally, growth consciousness, whilst apparent from the mid-1950s, did not bring any significant policy changes before 1961. Output grew at a similar rate in this period as under the Attlee governments, but the distribution of this output was much more towards consumption, rather than the exports and investment priorities of the late 1940s. The growth of a consumer society went along with a renewed emphasis on the economic benefits of competition, both domestic and international, and in so far as policy was aimed at increasing efficiency it was this emphasis on reviving and encouraging competition that was pre-eminent. However Shonfield's (1965: 99) claim that 'the outstanding feature of the period was a kind of rigorous spiritual back-pedalling, the expression of a nostalgia for some bygone age when market forces produced the important economic decisions' was becoming less true towards the end of the decade when a growing realization of the deficiencies of the economy started to undermine previous self-confidence.

THE CONTEXT

Macroeconomically the 1950s were characterized by a boom which provided a much more congenial set of circumstances for economic policy than at any time since at least the late 1920s. Once the Korean war was over, the terms of trade moved sharply in Britain's favour, easing the balance of payments constraint and adding significantly to the rise in living standards brought about by the growth of domestic output (Ady 1962). Most symbolic of the changes in the policy climate was not only the achievement of full employment, but the ease with which this was achieved. How far the Conservatives would have maintained that policy objective if threatened with a severe slump remains open to debate, but in the event the problem did not arise (Tomlinson 1987a: ch. 8; Rollings 1990). The surge in private investment and the buoyancy of international trade, coupled to the generally expansionary emphasis of economic ideas, meant that full employment was secured largely without strain, and without the kind of fiscal deficits Keynesians thought might be necessary to maintain demand (Matthews 1968).

This does not mean macroeconomic policy was passive. These were years of highly active macro-policy, when governments discovered the pleasures and pains of manipulating aggregate demand and economic activity to try to gain political advantage. But the stop–go character of policy operated within narrow parameters. Stops were usually inaugurated by runs on sterling which mainly reflected Britain's continued attempt to keep the pound a top currency and maintain heavy overseas commitments, rather than problems in maintaining a full-employment level of current imports (Strange 1971; Scott 1962). The go phase was inaugurated when unemployment threatened to rise above the 250,000–300,000 level deemed politically acceptable. In terms of substantive impact on the macro-economy, stop–go was largely much ado about nothing.

Increasingly macro-policy focused on the issue of inflation. By later standards this was quite low, averaging around 3 per cent after the sharp increases brought about by the Korean war. But politically inflation was important as it was deemed to represent a consequence of, but also a threat to, full employment. In an important White Paper of 1956 (Cmd. 9725) inflation was presented as a broad consequence of full employment of resources, especially labour, without spelling out how exactly the problem arose or how it might be addressed. The paper stressed that post-war wages had risen much faster than dividends, without quite saying that inflation derived from this wage pressure (a theme to come to prominence later in the 1950s). Inflation was also linked to growth. Whilst holding out the prospects of a rise in living standards from the harnessing of technical change, it was argued that 'Quite apart therefore from the serious economic and social strains they create, rising prices endanger the full realisation of the possibilities of economic progress' (para. 6).

But quite how the problem was to be combated was less clear. Much debate, especially in the later 1950s, polarized between those who emphasized cost-(mainly wage) push, and those who saw the main culprit as excessive levels of demand. Whilst economically this distinction may be dubious, as the elements of inflationary pressure are very hard to disentangle, it suggested two different policy approaches. Believers in 'cost-push' explanations saw incomes policies as an appropriate response. The government approached the TUC about such a policy in 1956, and the General Council of the TUC might have agreed but for their probably correct perception that such a posture would be repudiated by the union rank-and-file (Fishbein 1984: 32–3). After that the government did intervene in wage bargaining in the later 1950s, but in an *ad hoc* and indeed arbitrary way, without arriving at anything which deserves the name of a policy.

A similar point may be made about policy on nationalized industries. These industries were subject to frequent intervention to hold their prices down, which not only caused some of the financial problems for the industries discussed in Chapter 8, but also favoured domestic consumers at the expense of industrial consumers. Thus in the name of anti-inflationary policy quite major and macroeconomically arbitrary effects were produced in the public industries (PEP 1960: ch. 4).

On the demand side, the government was willing to deploy monetary as well as fiscal policy, ending two decades of cheap money (Cairncross 1992: 95–9; Kennedy 1962). But in the 1950s monetary instruments were generally used sparingly and subordinated to fiscal policy. The big problem here was that any strong action on the demand side to restrain inflation would threaten full employment, and politically this was unacceptable to the majority of Conservative leaders. A very hostile response followed the proposals of the Council for Prices, Productivity and Incomes in 1958 for a greater margin of unemployment to reduce inflationary pressure. When the Chancellor of the Exchequer tried to press for similar policies in the Cabinet in 1958, opposition forced his resignation, along with a couple of his supporters.[1]

In the 1950s the unemployment record was very good by any standards, and likewise the inflation record, certainly by the standards of later rather than earlier decades. But in other ways the period was less satisfactory.

Taking the decade as a whole, economic performance was disappointing in comparison with the early post-war years, when major adjustments were successfully carried out; or with the 1960s, when growth was perceptibly faster and exports much higher; or with foreign competitors who gained more ground on the United Kingdom in the 1950s than in any other post-war decade (Cairncross 1992: 92).

But as Worswick long ago pointed out (1962: 68) such a critical assessment is more likely to come from the economist than from the 1950s 'man in the street', who, unlike the economist, would have regarded the 1950s as far superior to the late 1940s. This contrast in perceptions is best understood by looking at the distribution of economic resources, contrasting the Attlee Years with the 1950s (Table 9.1). As the Table makes clear, the Conservatives' rhetorical commitments to ending austerity and

---

[1] The actual resignation issue was the scale of cuts in public expenditure, but this was part of a broader dispute about how anti-inflationary policy should be conducted (Brittan 1964: 185–96).

raising personal consumption were matched by the way resources were allocated in the 1950s. Whilst personal consumption took the lion's share of the increase in output in the 1950s, exports and investment actually rose less, despite the period being twice as long.

TABLE 9.1. *The fruits of economic growth, 1945–50, 1950–60*
(£bn. at 1985 prices)

	Change 1945–50	Change 1950–60
Consumer expenditure	+16.0	+26.8
Public consumption	−34.8[a]	+ 6.0
Investment (Gross Domestic Fixed Capital Formation)	+13.2	+12.8
Exports	+18.1	+ 8.1
Gross Domestic Product (at factor cost)	13.6	+40.3

Source: Cairncross (1992), pp. 58, 93.
[a] This figure reflects the reduction in the public expenditure on armaments as a result of demobilization from war.

On the investment side, this meant that by the end of the period Britain had a considerably weaker capital stock position than major competitors. On the export side, there was a failure to take much advantage of the boom in world trade. The most striking consequence of this was the fall in Britain's share of world trade in manufactures, from 25.4 per cent in 1950 to 16.3 per cent in 1960. This was accompanied by only small shifts in the geographical distribution of exports; the Sterling Area remained pre-eminent, its share falling only from 47 to 39 per cent, whilst that of Western Europe rose only slowly from 26 to 29 per cent. Britain was not therefore gaining much benefit from the rapid growth of the Western European economies which characterized this period.

But for the man in the street and for most politicians these harbingers of problems to come were little recognized. Rather it was the rise in consumption that many saw as the most important economic feature of the decade: 'You've never had it so good' was in an important sense a fair assessment. In 1954 prices consumers' expenditure more than doubled between 1950 and 1960 (from £553m. to £1269m.) but much more striking was the rise in the consumption of consumer durables (Table 9.2). Other indicators of the growth of the consumer society would be the rise in the number of workers with two weeks' paid annual holiday, which rose from 3m. in 1948 to 12.3m. by 1955, about 95 per cent of all manual workers (Hall 1962: 433).

TABLE 9.2. *Home sales of consumer durables 1950–60* (monthly averages)

	1950	1960
Car registrations	11,117	67,218
Motor-cycles	11,085	22,821
Domestic refrigerators	445	2,550
Television sets	42,400	151,400

Source: Hall (1962), p. 432.

This rise in consumption was accompanied by other changes— a reduction in some of the more conspicuous differences in the standards of life of the working and middle classes, a rapid rise of hire purchase to finance the new durable acquisitions, and a greater political salience for consumer interests. This latter factor links consumption to the other great theme of the 1950s, increasing competition, for one of the causes of the passing of the 1956 Restrictive Practices Act was as an appeal to the newly important consumer against producer interests. (Competition is returned to in the section on the Efficiency of Company Structure and Organization, below.)

MARKETS

The highly protectionist trade regime of the war and the early post-war years was already being significantly liberalized by the time the Attlee government lost office. The most important initiative in this area was the European Payments Union (EPU). As Kaplan and Schleiminger (1989: 1) summarize its role and importance,

A creation and component of the Organisation for European Economic Co-operation, the EPU was both an instrument of Europe's economic integration and a half-way house in its transition from bilateralism to currency convertibility. It made all of the currencies of Western Europe transferable into one another, making it possible to free Intra-European trade from quantitative restrictions and discriminatory regulations.

Britain under Labour was reluctant to pursue the idea of the EPU, largely for fears of its impact on the role of sterling as an international currency. But with some concessions on the role of the Sterling Area in the Union, the government eventually supported the idea. The EPU came into being on the basis of payments between its members being settled at the level of the Union as a whole. This achieved a multilateralism in trade, coupled to the settling of overall deficits to the Union by a combination of credits and gold, with gold playing a larger role as the size of deficits expanded. Within this framework trade was liberalized within Western Europe to the extent of 60 per cent of all imports initially, 75 per cent by 1951, and soon afterwards 90 per cent (Kaplan and Schleiminger 1989: 94; Hemming *et al* 1958).

This, of course, still left controls over trade with the United States and the dollar area. These were eventually abandoned following the restoration of dollar convertibility achieved, *de facto* largely by 1954 and *de jure* in 1958. By the latter date the proportion of imports subject to government purchase or control had fallen to 10 per cent, from 96 per cent in 1948 and 54 per cent in 1951, with a slight blip in the Korean war (1952) to 65 per cent (Dow 1965: 174).

By the end of the 1950s the British market had not been restored to its pristine nineteenth-century free-trade position, but was some way down that road. Import controls on goods from the Soviet bloc and Japan remained, and some specific items continued to be protected, mainly by tariffs rather than physical controls. Tariffs were still higher than in competitive countries such as Germany, but were on a clear downward trend (Streeten 1962; Ray 1960).

In later decades the opening up of the British market to foreign competition has had a major impact on economic activity, mainly by raising the degree of import penetration in manufactured goods. This process of change was proceeding but only relatively slowly in the 1950s. Imports of manufactures, whilst expanding rapidly, made up only 14 per cent of total visible imports in 1950, rising to almost 20 per cent in 1959 (Scott 1962:

134). But this still represented only 7–9 per cent of total home demand for manufactures and with no clear trend in this ratio (Williams *et al.* 1983: 118).[2] In this period, at least, the opening up of the British market to imported manufactures had, in aggregate, rather limited affects. Britain remained a major net exporter of manufactures, with these exports still being largely used to finance imports of food, raw materials, and fuels. Within manufacturing imports, machinery, accounting for around 40 per cent of the total, remained much more important than the consumer durables later to cause so much difficulty for British producers (Ray 1960: 19).

This reduction in controls over imports was intertwined with a reduction in other, domestic, physical controls. Both began to be reduced significantly under Labour from 1948, and by the end of the 1950s consumer, price, investment, and material controls had largely disappeared, after brief revivals in some commodities during the Korean and Suez crises (Dow 1965: ch. 6). De-control was not complete, and some continued, e.g. the control over jute as an indirect means of restricting imports of jute manufactures, or the control over the export of iron and steel scrap—but these were very much exceptions to the rule by 1960 (Henderson 1962). This general policy, it should be noted, neither began with the Conservatives nor was it usually resisted by the Labour opposition, though in the early 1950s they had seen some role for a few controls abolished by the Conservatives (Rollings 1992). As Henderson (1962: 336) emphasizes 'over the main features of policy in the nineteen fifties—the virtual abandonment of controls over the period as whole, and the gradual and uneven fashion in which the process of abandonment was carried through—there was substantial continuity and agreement' between the two Parties. Nevertheless, the Conservatives could with some credibility point to themselves as the party of liberalization (much as Labour was to argue with the notion of planning in the 1960s), and certainly this was a key element in their propaganda on the economy in this period. For example, in 1958, noting their commitment to raising the standard of living, they went on to say that 'we believe that this promise can become

---

[2] In 1960 the volume of imported manufactures grew to equal the 1929 level (Ray 1960: 12).

achievement only if the fresh winds of freedom and opportunity are allowed to blow vigorously through the economy' and any return to 'socialist bureaucracy and controls' resisted (Conservative Party 1958: 18). It is also probably right to say that the Conservatives were more comfortable as champions of consumption than Labour. High mass consumption was not something which Labour easily incorporated into its often rather ascetic, non–conformist attitudes to life's pleasures. New Jerusalem was not usually thought of as a home for hedonists (Tiratsoo 1990).[3]

PROFITS

Profits were a significant issue in political debate in the 1950s. Much of this debate focused on the appropriate tax regime for profits. As noted in Chapter 7, Labour had introduced a sharp differentiation of taxes, with much higher rates on distributed than undistributed profits. The aims of this had been to encourage investment and also to maintain at least the appearance of greater equality of economic rewards by holding down dividend growth.

In the 1950s this regime came under considerable criticism (Thomas 1978: 233–7). Doubts were raised about whether either of its purported aims was being achieved. As the Majority Report of the Royal Commission on the Taxation of Profits and Income (Cmd. 9474) emphasized, retention of profits did not necessarily lead to investment, and where it did this investment might be less desirable than if the money were distributed and then borrowed by other firms with better projects to finance. Equally, while dividends had been held down by the tax rules, this had not prevented some rise in distribution since 1953. Moreover, the Commission argued, in so far as dividends were kept low, this depressed share prices and thus obstructed the raising of capital by equity issues.

The more Left-leaning minority report of the Royal Commission (including Woodcock of the TUC and the economist

---

[3] It was against this socialist attitude that Crosland (1956: 524) wrote 'Now the time has come for a reaction: for a greater emphasis on private life, on freedom and dissent, on culture, beauty, leisure and even frivolity. Total abstinence and a good filing system are not now the right sign-posts to the socialist Utopia.'

Nicholas Kaldor) accepted the efficiency case against the differential profits tax, but argued that it shouldn't be abolished unless accompanied by the imposition of a capital gains tax intended to lessen the impact on the income distribution of higher share prices, and to take the political sting out of the inegalitarian consequences of this rise.

This recommendation for an end to differentiation was followed by the government in the budget of 1958, when the two rates of 30 and 3 per cent were combined into a standard rate of 10 per cent. This change was not combined with the introduction of a capital gains tax, and dividends did rise noticeably after 1958, though this rise was also linked to the take-over boom which characterized the late 1950s (Thomas 1978: 220; see below on this boom).

Probably the effects of this change on investment were small. Investigators were able to find little relationship between earnings retention by companies and investment, and some evidence that companies 'which retain a relatively high proportion of profits select relatively unprofitable investments' (Little 1962a: 413). On the other hand, the 'recycling' of profits through distribution may have increased consumption levels as individuals had higher propensities to consume than companies, and may have disfavoured small companies who continued to have problems of access to formal capital markets (Balogh 1958; see further below).

Probably more important for investment than these tax changes was the combination in the 1950s of a fall in overall levels of pre-tax profits and the stemming of the impact of this tide by reductions in total company taxation. Profit rates are very uncertain in this period because of uncertainties about the size of the capital stock, but the pre-tax profits share of national income certainly fell—from perhaps 38 per cent in 1950 to 33 per cent in 1960 (King 1975: 42).[4] On the other hand, the tax burden on companies was also reduced, the effective tax rate falling from around 37 per cent in 1950/3 to about 25 per cent in 1960 (King 1975: 45). This meant that the post-tax share of profits was roughly constant through the decade.

[4] The relationship between the profit share in national income and the profit rate depends upon the capital–output ratio: if this ratio is rising a lower profit share indicates a significant fall in the rate of profit.

Other aid to companies was given by the introduction of investment allowances in place of the previous depreciation allowances. These allowed for more than 100 per cent of asset values to be written-off against tax, and therefore helped company cash flows. These were introduced in 1954, but withdrawn in 1956, and then reintroduced in 1959 (Thomas 1978: 149, 224–5). Their impact was thus lessened by being tied to macroeconomic concerns to regulate overall aggregate demand in the economy, though their impact in this regard was probably small (Dow 1965: 372–3).

So, the picture of the 1950s is one of full employment tending to squeeze company profits, though from a high starting-point. This fits in with the fast rise in consumption based on an increased share of output going to employment incomes (wages and salaries), although the personal savings ratio also shows a substantial increase over the period. Company profits were significantly aided by the government's easing of the tax burden, in line with its general policy of reducing direct taxes, though the overall changes in the burden of taxation were small, and after 1954 negligible (Little 1962*b*: 278–85).

THE EFFICIENCY OF LABOUR

The marginal nature of the victory of 1951, combined with the shift in political attitudes signalled by the *Industrial Charter*, led the Conservatives for much of the 1950s to adopt a strongly conciliatory attitude to labour. As noted already, in the later 1950s there was growing concern with labour costs as a macroeconomic problem, but initially this led to a search for agreement with the TUC, and only when this failed was a more aggressive but *ad hoc* policy pursued. There was no significant attempt in this decade to change the legal framework of industrial relations or the system of voluntary collective bargaining over wages.

The issue of wage inflation in the domain of macroeconomic policy can usefully be separated from the issue of labour costs and other aspects of labour in the context of concerns with growth and efficiency. An undercurrent in Conservative thinking had always regarded labour, the unions, and especially their alleged restrictive practices as a major problem in industrial efficiency.

But this theme was muted for most of the 1950s. This was partly due to the generally conciliatory attitude towards labour and the unions, but it also reflected the lack of desire on the part of the government to get involved in company-level issues. Thus for example in the productivity field, the British Productivity Council succeeded the Anglo-American Council on Productivity in 1952, but the government seems to have taken much less interest in the BPC's activities than the Labour Government had in the AACP.

This approach altered somewhat in the late 1950s, partly reflecting a new political confidence after the 1955 election victory, and partly the growing if largely unfocused concern with economic growth. In addition concern with labour's restrictive practices could be presented as an even-handed parallel to producer restrictive practices, dealt with by the 1956 Restrictive Practices Act. Thus in a policy statement of 1958, the Conservative Party proclaimed 'To rid private enterprise of restrictive trade practices that militate against progress and the public interest we have enacted new comprehensive legislation; at the same time, an industry-by-industry examination is being undertaken of labour practices which restrict the production of goods and services' (Conservative Party 1958: 19).

This enquiry was launched by the Ministry of Labour via the National Joint Advisory Council, but seems to have led to inconclusive results and rather little in the way of action. Above all, it did not establish the thesis that labour restrictive practices were a major cause of Britain's slow growth in the core areas of manufacturing (Ministry of Labour 1959). This conclusion was also borne out by major private investigations:

We have no doubt that isolated cases of labour restrictive practices can be found in many firms in many industries, and that occasionally they obstruct technical progress; but we still see no evidence that industry is so universally weighed down by labour restrictive practices that these must be regarded as a major obstacle to technical change (Carter and Williams 1959: 168).

The government was notably more active in the training and education of labour than on industrial relations and work-practice issues, though the approach was a partial one. Most policy activity was focused on the area of technical education provided by technical colleges, especially for part-time and evening students. Up to the mid-1950s the government continued the policy of encouraging the growth of technical-college provision begun under Labour, and by 1954/5 the number of students had risen to 64,000 full-timers (45,000 in 1946/7), 402,000 part-timers (200,000 in 1946/7), and 1.6m. evening students (1.2m. in 1946/7) (Cmd. 9703: para. 27). But this still left the overall participation rate low, and in 1956 the government announced plans for the doubling of the number of places on most technical college courses over five years.

In the introduction to the White Paper announcing this policy Anthony Eden, the Prime Minister, employed a rhetoric becoming typical of the decade:

The prizes will not go the countries with the largest population. Those with the best systems of education will win. Science and technological skill give a dozen men the power to do as thousands did fifty years ago. Our scientists are doing brilliant work. But if we are to make full use of what we are learning, we shall need many more scientists, engineers and technicians. I am determined that this shortage shall be made good (Cmd. 9703: para. 1).

But this determination did not stretch very far. Whilst technical-college expansion went ahead, other key parts of education and training remained little changed. At the school level the Conservative Party was very much the champion of the grammar school, and did nothing to encourage any local initiatives on technical high schools, which remained a tiny proportion of schools.

Probably more important was the failure to do anything significant on industrial training beyond the encouragement of day release. In this area the main Ministry was the Ministry of Labour, which, as in labour issues generally in this period, pursued a largely hands-off approach. Apprenticeship was still the main form of industry-based training, and this remained largely regulated by joint agreement between unions and employers, with a focus on the form of the apprenticeship rather than its skill content. For most of the 1950s, the relative health of the economy provided a context in which government, employers, and unions were highly complacent about this system. In particular, 'Beyond a watching brief on apprenticeship schemes, the scope of training policy in the Ministry of Labour receded to the margins of the labour-market—the young, the disabled, the hard to place—training policy fulfilled social welfare rather than economic aims or functions' (Sheldrake and Vickerstaff 1987: 28).

This complacency came under some challenge at the end of the 1950s with a Ministry of Labour review of apprenticeship (led by Robert Carr) called *Training for Skills* (Ministry of Labour 1958). This recognized most of the problems of existing apprenticeship arrangements—the low numbers involved, the tendency to 'poaching' of skilled workers between employers, the narrow syllabuses, excessive length, and lack of formal qualifications usually involved. But an accurate diagnosis did not lead to proposals for radical treatment, 'the existing division of responsibility between government and industry should be maintained' (para. 18) it concluded, with proposals limited to an anodyne tripartite Industrial Training Council to review the system (or lack of it). 'The ITC did not herald a new phase of government action or reform, it did, however, mark a recognition that lack of training was a problem for the economy as a whole' (Sheldrake and Vickerstaff 1987: 30).

At the higher level of graduate scientific and technical education the 1950s saw only limited progress. The number of undergraduates in these areas fell back in the 1950s from the 1950/1 peak based on the ending of the 'bulge' of demobilized servicemen. Here the government also wanted to see expansion, but the scale of this was inhibited by opposition from the Universities, and the whole issue of how the expansion was to fit into the traditional patterns of higher education, plus the jealousy of the professional bodies of any extended governmental role (Davis 1990). Undergraduate numbers rose only slowly over the decade, from 78,000 in 1949/50 to 90,000 in 1960/61, the number of pure and applied scientists rising from 32.6 per cent to 40.6 per cent, largely at the expense of medicine and dentistry. For most of the period this slow expansion led to a clear excess demand for scientific and technical graduates (Sanderson 1972*a*: ch. 12).

By the end of the 1950s government departments, notably the Ministries of Labour and Education, recognized serious deficiencies in the education and training of the work-force in science and technology. But this recognition was not readily turned into action to remedy the situation. This partly reflected the government's general unwillingness to disturb the institutional status quo—whether it be the institutions of higher education, the unions, or the employers. This unwillingness was also, of course, a parallel to the belief in competition, which obviously implied a lack of need for government to get involved. As yet the counter political pressure to do something to rectify Britain's industrial inefficiencies was insufficient to outweigh this fundamental predisposition.

THE EFFICIENCY OF CAPITAL

The provision of capital to industry was not a major policy issue in the 1950s. At the end of the period the Radcliffe Committee (Cmnd. 827: paras. 932–52) reaffirmed the existence of the 'Macmillan gap' in financial provision for small firms, despite the role of bodies like the Industrial and Commercial Finance Corporation set up to fill the gap. It recommended one particular remedy for this, an expansion of term loans by the banks to replace the predominance of overdrafts. This was aimed at securing funds which could be more safely used by small firms for financing fixed assets. It also called for an Industrial Guarantee Corporation to guarantee loans from existing institutions to help finance innovations.

This narrow focus and limited proposal for change reflected the substantial degree of complacency in policy-making circles on the issue of industrial finance. This complacency reflected the peculiarities of company finance in this period, when companies financed the great bulk of their investment from ploughed-back profit (Table 9.3). High levels of plough-back have been common in Britain over a long period, but they were at a particularly high level in this period. This was due to the combination of physical controls over investment and comfortable profits of the late 1940s, which left companies very liquid and able easily to finance investment projects without recourse to outside funds, and the high (post-tax) profits of the 1950s, and the low level of distribution of those profits, at least until late in the decade. Overall, Tew and Henderson's (1959: ch. 16) conclusion for 1949–53 would seem to apply to most of the 1950s: they found little evidence of companies facing financial stringency, and especially for the big and expanding companies, if external finance was required this was readily available. Their detailed study of a large sample of quoted companies found that new issues of equity financed around 28 per cent of investment, though again this source of funds was especially concentrated amongst the large and fast-growing businesses. On the other hand bank credit was extremely unimportant—financing only about 4 per cent of net assets (chs. 5, 6).

TABLE 9.3. *Sources of investment funds from 1948/51 to 1956/60* (%)

	Gross trading profits	Other current income[a]	Total internal	External
1948–51	65	23	88	12
1952–5	72	22	94	6
1956–60	69	21	90	10

Source: Thomas (1978), p. 218.
[a] includes rent, non-trading income, and income from abroad.

It has always been difficult to establish a finance problem for large (though not for small) industrial companies. This may be partly because these companies have come to 'love their chains'— have learnt to accept the terms and conditions on which banks and the stock market have made external funds available as appropriate and left them unchallenged (Williams *et al.* 1983: 58–76). But possibly in the 1950s this problem was minor (again, except for small firms) because of the highly favourable conditions firms found themselves in (Burn 1958: 455–60).

Also largely absent in the 1950s was the problem of the kind of calculation (emphasizing short-term profitability) forced on companies by the stock market, acting as a market for take-overs. The hostile take-over (as opposed to voluntary amalgamation) was largely invented in the 1950s. This followed the much tighter rules on company disclosure of the 1948 Companies Act, which facilitated external assessment of potential gains from take-over. High post-war profits leading to high levels of liquid assets also made some companies extremely attractive to predators, especially when share prices were depressed by dividend restraint (Hannah 1983: ch. 10; Roberts 1992).

Whilst in practice only a minority of mergers in this period were hostile take-overs, they did provide a new and important impetus to corporate changes. Between 1948 and 1963 one quarter of the companies quoted on the London Stock Exchange were acquired by other quoted companies, the pace of acquisition being particularly rapid from 1957 onwards: 'The impact of the divorce of ownership and control on creating a more fluid market in corporate control was thus belatedly, but forcefully, established as a major pressure on the directors of industrial firms' (Hannah 1983: 150).

The authorities' (Treasury and Bank of England) response to this new phenomenon was at first strongly hostile, especially when the Prime Minister's favourite watering-hole, the Savoy, was threatened in 1953. Take-overs were regarded as speculations, and the government put pressure on financial institutions not to finance such ventures. But by the time of the much more intense take-over boom in the late 1950s the authorities had radically changed their attitude, believing that take-overs in fact enhance efficiency through the displacement of less efficient managements by more efficient ones (though there seems no contemporary evidence on the truth or otherwise of this belief). The government contented itself with encouraging the self-regulation by the City of take-overs—rather than following the example of the state-organized regulation of such activity by the Securities and Exchange Commission in the USA (Roberts 1992).

Formal government intervention in the capital market was largely restricted to two types of control—over new issues and bank advances. The government inherited the former control, embodied in the Capital Issues Committee, from the Labour government and continued to employ it for domestic issues until 1959. The CIC operated with very broad guidelines, embodying some loose notion of priority for issues to finance projects in export industries, areas of rapid technical change, or where they would add 'to the general health of the economy'. Controls were slackened from 1952 in line with the trend of macro-policy, and likewise tightened from 1956. The CIC's overall impact on the level of investment or on its distribution was probably small (Henderson 1962: 332–4; Wright 1962: 476–8).

Similarly, government control over bank lending was probably very limited in its direct impact on company finance. As noted above, in aggregate bank credit was marginal for most companies. And like the control over share issues, the allocative effect was limited as banks were left to make their own judgements within extremely broad guidelines laid down by the Bank of England.

Finally, a financial control which indirectly affected some companies was hire-purchase control. Part of the stop–go armoury were changes in the deposit levels and repayment periods of hire-purchase contracts. These changes obviously impacted on demand for the durable goods that were so popular in the 1950s. They made little obvious impact on the long-run trend in consumption of these goods, though they may have caused at least short-run problems for some durable producers, notably in the car industry (Ch. 14).

THE EFFICIENCY OF TECHNICAL CHANGE

The rhetoric of technological revolution cited above in discussion of educational change also implied a significant government interest in technical change, and especially the issue of R & D. As has been true ever since the Second World War, the main expenditure by government in this area was on defence-related concerns. It was calculated that in 1955/6 such money paid for two-thirds of all R & D in private industry (Carter and Williams 1959: 110). This overwhelming weight of government-funded military R & D would seem to be the crucial problem of the government's role in this field, certainly in the 1940s and 1950s. Given that there is little evidence of significant spin-off from defence R & D to civilian processes or products, in economic terms this pattern was a major hindrance to enhancing British efficiency in non-defence sectors, especially in a context of short supply of trained researchers, who were thus crowded-out of the civilian sector.

Alongside the explicitly military R & D effort was a large amount of spending on prestige projects such as nuclear power and aircraft which also added little to Britain's competitiveness.[5] In both cases the industries had strategic aspects, but the money spent on them was also enhanced by the bias towards big project,

[5] On nuclear power see Buckley and Day (1980), on aircraft, Gardner (1976).

basic research in the UK in comparison with other countries. The problem was not that the British government was spending too little on R & D, but that it was overcommitted to projects whose benefits for growth and efficiency were very limited (Peck 1968).

The main directly civilian role for the government in the area of R & D was funding of Industrial Research Associations via the DSIR, though the department did also carry out research in its own establishments. The number of such Associations rose from 27 in 1945 to 46 in 1955, and whilst government spending on them rose from £356,000 to £1.4m, as a share of total IRA spending, it remained stable, at around 28 per cent (Edwards and Townsend 1956: 364). The DSIR was substantially reformed in 1956 and the budget expanded (Grove 1962: 272–6).

But this government subvention was a tiny amount in comparison with either government spending on defence R & D or total industrial spending—the latter estimated at £325m. in 1955. But this sum in turn was dwarfed by the spending levels in the United States, calculated as perhaps three times as high (Edwards and Townsend 1956: 540).

Data on R & D was extremely sparse until the mid-1950s, and this reflected the low priority accorded in practice to the area, despite the rhetoric of scientific advance. Government spending in the area grew, mainly in the defence area, but also in an *ad hoc* way elsewhere, not subject to any clear strategy: 'The Government's contributions to the finance of industrial research in general and the particular branches have tended to grow like topsy' (Edwards and Townsend 1956: 374).

A major research programme into R & D in this period could find little logic in the pattern of government intervention in this area. It regarded the government's role as positive, but requiring revamping. Its main conclusion was that the problem of low R & D activity levels lay at the firm level, and, in particular, with the absence of integration of R & D into the firms' functioning (Carter and Williams 1957: ch. 17; Carter and Williams 1959: pt. II). But they also emphasized the absence of enough highly skilled scientists and technologists and the low scientific content of general school education, where, as noted above, the government, despite the best of intentions, was making at best only slow headway.

TABLE 9.4. *Government spending on research
and development 1960/1 (£m.)*

	Government spending
Government departments	
(a) Defence departments (including Ministry of Aviation)	242
(b) Civil departments (including DSIR)	27
Research Councils	
(a) Agricultural Research Council	6.4
(b) Medical Research Council	4.3
(c) Nature Conservancy	0.5
National Institute for Research in Nuclear Science	6
TOTAL	286

Source: Grove (1962), p. 268

Indeed there were quite strong parallels between the obviously related areas of R & D and technical education. In both areas, by the end of the 1950s governments were alert to the possibilities, and believed Britain was lagging behind other industrial countries. But in neither area could it be said that much had been done to get a closer fit between policy and the requirements for enhanced industrial efficiency. In the case of education the vested interests remained largely unchallenged. In R & D the government's own concern with Britain's supposed status as a world power, with its consequences of excessive resources being deployed in defence and prestige projects, militated against any major switch of attention to the commercially oriented civilian sector.

THE EFFICIENCY OF COMPANY STRUCTURE AND ORGANIZATION

By the Restrictive Practices Act of 1956 the Government launched the first very significant attack on restrictionism in British industry. Before looking at this legislation in greater detail it is worth saying a little about why such policies were so late in entering the armoury of British governments.

As discussed in earlier chapters, fears of trusts had been a feature of early twentieth-century Britain, and came closest to forcing a legislative response at the end of the First World War, in the context of opposition to profiteering. In the event the moment passed, and the law retained a benign attitude to any form of industrial combination. There was a common-law presumption against combinations 'in restraint of trade' but in practice this was impotent, as it required proof of injury to the public interest, which was very difficult to achieve (Hunter 1966: 68–72; Swann *et al.* 1974: 49–51).

The absence of legislative intervention in this area in the inter-war period was linked to the way in which that period of depression and unemployment was usually interpreted. In the 1920s, as discussed in Chapter 4, much attention came to focus on rationalization as the solution to Britain's industrial problems, and this usually involved active co-operation between companies, rather than the belief that competition would be effective in forcing out the inefficient and concentrating production on the efficient. This attitude received governmental support in the 1930s, and this approach was reinforced by the belief that the key to Britain's problems was too low prices, which cut profits and investment (Ch. 5). The overall result was that 'Between the two world wars belief in Britain in the merits of competition had almost entirely disappeared' (Jewkes 1958: 1).

Some shift in policy perceptions was evident by the end of the war. The predicate of wartime industrial and economic discussion was post-war full employment and economic expansion. This meant that pre-war restrictionism would no longer be appropriate, indeed would be a threat to such expansion (Mercer 1993: chs. 4, 5). This cast of thinking is evident in the 1944 White Paper on *Employment Policy* (Cmd. 6527), where the fear is expressed that if restrictionism persists, higher demand will not lead to higher output and employment, but only to higher prices. This view fitted closely with the ideas of many economists, of different ideological persuasions, who played some part in shaping policy in this period (Hannah 1990: 356–8). Of course, there was some conflict between these attitudes and the war's effect of reinforcing and expanding the role of trade associations, however the majority of these seemed to have concentrated on their representational role rather than acting as agents of price and output fixing (Turner 1988).

The employment concern, plus a political concern with the power of big business, led the Labour Party to put a great deal of emphasis on anti-monopoly policy in its 1945 manifesto (Mercer 1991*b*, 1992). This eventually led to the enactment of the 1948 Monopolies and Restrictive Practices (Inquiry and Control) Act, the first legislative intervention in this area. However in practice this Act had only an extremely limited effect. Mercer (1991*b*) has persuasively argued that this resulted from the way in which both referrals to the Monopolies Commission, and actions arising from its Reports, were initiated by the Board of Trade. That Ministry remained sceptical of the benefits of competition, especially in the context of conducting policies which required the consent and support of private firms, who lobbied strongly against a strong anti-monopoly policy. The result was a low rate of referral to the Commission, a very slow process of reporting, and little action by the Board of Trade once the Reports were made.

This was not, then, a policy which matched the rhetoric of anti-monopoly. In her defence of the early Monopoly Commission, its secretary from 1949–52 emphasized the absence of an American-style presumption that monopoly is against the public interest, and the historical legacy within which the policy had to be conducted

Consequently the experience which formed and informs many of our old heads in industry—they were young heads in the 1920s and 1930s—is not of consumers having to pay too much for what they bought, but of industry receiving too little for what it sold, with the consequence of unemployment and low wages (Kilroy 1954: 39–40).

This unpropitious atmosphere for stringent pro-competition policy was altered by a number of forces in the early 1950s. One force was disappointment with the workings of the 1948 Act felt by some Ministers who were strongly pro-competition, such as Peter Thorneycroft; this attitude was supported by the Labour Party (e.g. Douglas Jay in Hansard 1955/6). Also important was one of the Monopolies Commission Reports, on Collective Discrimination (Cmd. 9504), which investigated the extent of collective agreements in the British economy, and after showing them to be extremely extensive reported 'We do not say that in every individual case this restriction is necessarily against the public interest, but we are satisfied that all types of agreement which we have examined do adversely affect the public interest, some to a considerably greater extent than others' (para. 233). The majority of the Commission concluded in favour of a general prohibition of all such agreements, though a dissenting minority reported that the majority offered 'too sweeping a condemnation' (para. 255) and favoured a registration procedure rather than prohibition (para. 209).

Mercer (1991*a*: 85–6) argues that the crucial element in the genesis of the 1956 Act was the desire of certain Ministers to respond to the unpopularity of the Monopolies Commission with industry, by changing the shape of the policy to put it into the hands of the courts, thus allowing the government to distance itself from the whole process. But what seems to have been the common assumption amongst businessmen, that the new framework would be easier on anti-competitive practices than the old, was soon belied. The Act re-established and effectively downgraded the Monopolies Commission, declared collective resale price maintenance illegal, and declared all restrictive agreements illegal unless deemed to pass through seven 'gateways', such as having a clear benefit to consumers, or serving some macroeconomic objective like improving the balance of payments or the level of employment (Swann *et al.* 1974: ch. 2; Hunter 1966: ch. 5; Guenault and Jackson 1960: ch. 10).

These gateways were generally stringently interpreted. For example, in a landmark case in 1957, the Court declared the Yarn Spinners Agreement unlawful, even though it accepted its ending would have some effects in raising unemployment. In consequence of this toughness, most agreements were terminated rather than being brought to court. Hunter (1966: 161–2) calculates that by mid-1963 1,610 or about 66 per cent of all agreements registered had disappeared.

While other actions mitigated the effects of the Act, for example forms of 'price-leadership', it probably did make a significant difference to the amount of competition in Britain in the late 1950s and early 1960s. Certainly economists tended to welcome the legislation: 'the Act seems to have assisted at the birth of a healthy "loosening-up" process for British industry and a greater receptivity to new ideas both technological and commercial' (Hunter 1966: 187). On the other hand, the response to the legislation of many companies was to look to merger as an alternative way of trying to control the market (Swann *et al.* 1974: 172–3). So the 1956 Act played some part in encouraging the merger boom which began in the late 1950s (Hannah 1983: 148–9).

The strengthening of competition by the 1956 Restrictive Practices Act was probably greater than intended by the government, although it did fit in with the general rhetoric of competition so prevalent in this decade. But in taking up such rhetoric the Conservatives faced substantial opposition from many industrialists, who were by no means all convinced of the benefits of free competition. This resistance can be treated as simply the defensive response of a group whose cosy arrangements were being disrupted by the winds of competition, and who defended themselves with a range of implausible rationales (e.g. Jewkes 1958: 8–11). On the other hand businessmen were right to point to the divergent if not contradictory public-policy pressures they were subject to. On the one hand was the new emphasis on competition; on the other, as the CBI later stressed, 'Industry is urged to rationalise, to specialise, to standardise, to form itself into larger, more efficient units to meet the challenge of foreign competition. All involve an element of agreement and co-operation between firms. Yet to do so runs the constant risk of coming up against existing legislation' (cited Swann *et al.* 1974: 82).

This dilemma was to become much more acute in the 1960s, though it was emerging by the late 1950s. But in that earlier decade the main emphasis was on greater competition—at the macro level via the freeing of trade, in capital markets via increased threats of take-over, in product markets by the restrictive practices legislation. This trend was in part offset by increased mergers. The usual measure of the effects of mergers on market power, concentration ratios, suggest that these rose quite substantially in the 1950s. Hannah (1983: 180) put the share of the top 100 firms in manufacturing net output as rising from 22 per cent in 1948, to 26 per cent in 1953, and 38 per cent in 1963. Of course, these figures would overestimate the market power of the companies concerned in so far as the reduction of tariff barriers created effective competition for domestic producers in British markets.

There is no obvious evidence from the 1950s that this enhancement of competition increased the efficiency of British industry.

This must be a controversial area, but data on the rate of growth of industrial production and on productivity do not show a speed-up in the 1950s as liberalization was pursued. This is not an argument against competition, but merely to note the absence of any evidence from this period that competition was a sufficient condition for the achievement of greater industrial efficiency.

Governmental interest in the encouragement of industrial efficiency by the improvement of management seems to have waned in comparison with the 1940s. The British Institute of Management was deprived of its grant by a Ministerial decision in 1956, and had to greatly reduce its operations in consequence (PRO 1956). Similarly, the creation of the Cohen Council on Productivity Prices and Incomes did not lead to significant initiatives on productivity in the manner of the 1940s. The focus was on prices and incomes.

STATE CAPACITY AND STATE ACHIEVEMENTS

As emphasized in Chapter 1, *laissez-faire* is best seen as a particular kind of state policy rather than an absence of policy. Though the British economy in the 1950s was a long way from *laissez-faire*, there was a great deal of emphasis on liberalization and increased competition, and this was also a definite policy stance rather than an absence of policy. This is most apparent in the area of competition policy, which was pursued in a highly specific way and with particular consequences. Above all the legislation focused on collusion between separate firms, whilst doing almost nothing to inhibit mergers and increased industrial concentration.

This emphasis on competition and liberalization did not prevent government from becoming heavily involved in specific interventions in industry. For example, regional policy, initially run down in the early 1950s, was strongly revived at the end of the decade when significant regional unemployment reappeared. Government pressure led to highly publicized location decisions by several private companies in 1960 to locate new car-production facilities in areas of high unemployment. Two years earlier the government had passed a Distribution of Industry (Industrial Finances) Act, which significantly extended the Treasury's ability to grant financial aid for industrial buildings in Development Areas. Under the Local Employment Act of 1960 the restriction on industrial development in prosperous areas by Industrial Development Certificates was tightened (Henderson 1962: 337–45).

Other important specific interventions were in cotton (see Ch. 13), shipbuilding, and aircraft. The former involved government aid for replacement 'Queen' liners to be built by Cunard for the North Atlantic route—though in the end the scheme did not go ahead when Cunard recognized the shrinking market for such forms of transport. More important was intervention in the aircraft industry, where the government by its purchasing policies forced a concentration of the industry, mainly to secure a better procurement of military aircraft (Henderson 1962: 351–3, 361–2). These actions by no means complete the list of government interventions in this period, though they convey the *ad hoc* flavour of response to short-term pressures or, in the case of aircraft, the compelling need to maintain an efficient defence sector.

As far as the civilian sector is concerned, industrial policy in the 1950s has to be seen as formed largely by two conflicting trends. On the one hand a growing recognition of failure, which tempted government to intervention, although before 1961 that sense of failure was never sufficient to do much more than raise worries in the minds of policy-makers. On the other, and in line with the emphasis on freeing industry from control, except where failure manifested itself in unemployment (e.g. cotton) or threats to defence capacity (e.g. aircraft), there was little in the way of action, though quite a lot in the way of diagnosis. In that sense the 1950s forms a prelude to the greater activism of the 1960s, when the diagnoses of the 1950s were turned into changes in substantive policy.

The lack of activism in the 1950s went along with a highly stable institutional framework for the state. The dominance of the Treasury in economic policy-making was if anything reinforced, and in symbolic recognition of this the Economic Section, previously in the Cabinet Office, transferred into the Treasury in 1953. The Bank of England became more important as monetary policy was revived, though its subordination to government policy was asked for by the Radcliffe Committee in 1959. The one new institution in the industrial area was the Restrictive Practices Court, and its judicial status emphasized the government's desire for an arm's-length relationship with industry—however much this aim might be compromised by such *ad hoc* intervention as noted above. Certainly no question of a Ministry for Industry appeared in this period, the Board of Trade retaining its industrial role alongside its other functions.

One governmental innovation was the creation of a Ministry for Science in 1959. This arose partly from the growing consciousness of Britain's slow growth, and the idea that this stemmed from technological backwardness which meant that 'science policy became increasingly "resonant" as a political issue in the latter half of the fifties' (Vig 1968: 30). But more important in the short run in the creation of this Ministry was the reappraisal of defence policy begun in 1957, which led to proposals for a Ministry of Technology to preserve civilian research from cuts in defence spending. The Ministry for Science was essentially a watered down version of this idea, but nevertheless gives some idea that scientific research was moving up the government agenda (Vig 1968: 31).

One area where a questioning of policy priorities emerged in the late 1950s was in defence. At the onset of the Korean war the Labour Government embarked on a huge rearmament programme which, under the Conservatives, proved unsustainable. After a 50 per cent increase in real spending between 1950/1 and 1952/3, there were small cut-backs in the mid-1950s, but these still left Britain spending a larger proportion of GDP on defence than any other Western country except the United States (Table 9.5).

By 1957 this scale of expenditure was worrying the government. A White Paper (Cmnd. 124) emphasized the primacy of a healthy economy for Britain's place in the world. It underlined the scale of Britain's defence commitment, noting not only the share of defence spending in GDP but also the scale of its manpower use and in particular its impact on qualified manpower, asserting that an 'undue proportion of qualified scientists and engineers are engaged in military work' (para. 7).

TABLE 9.5. *Military spending as a percentage of GDP 1950–60*

	1950	1955	1960
USA	5.1	10.2	9.2
UK	6.6	8.2	6.5
France	5.5	6.4	6.5
Germany	4.4	4.1	4.0
Italy	4.3	3.7	3.3
Japan	—	1.8	1.1

Source: Chalmers (1985), p. 113.

It proposed not only very big cuts in total military manpower but in particular the need to restrict military R & D to the 'absolutely essential' on manpower grounds (para. 58).

What is striking about this document is its dominance by manpower criteria. Whilst there was a military logic to the exercise, especially a replacement of manpower by nuclear weapons, a primary concern was clearly economic. The change 'will further appreciably reduce the burden on the economy. Above all, it will release skilled men, including many badly needed scientists and technicians, for employment in civilian industry. Both exports and capital investment will gain' (para. 72).

This White Paper did indeed herald significant cuts in expenditure, which fell in real terms by over 10 per cent between 1957/8 and 1959/60 (Chalmers 1985: 68). However, thereafter it began to increase again, indicating above all that whilst the government recognized the strains put on the economy by such a scale of military effort, it was unwilling to give up major defence commitments such as the 'East of Suez' posture, despite the trauma of the Suez crisis of 1956.[6]

A long tradition in writing about the British economy has seen the 1950s as epitomizing the dominance in economic policy of macroeconomic issues, to the neglect of industrial policy aimed at increasing efficiency and growth. Such a view can be traced back at least to Shanks (1961) with the evocative title of his book *The Stagnant Society*. This story may be in need of some revision. Schenk (1991) has argued that Britain's determination

---

[6] There was also the military change of heart away from a purely nuclear deterrent in Europe ('massive retaliation') towards a graduated response requiring significant conventional forces in NATO.

to maintain the international role of sterling may have been less damaging than is commonly alleged (e.g. Strange 1971), while stop–go may have been less harmful to industry than is often suggested (e.g. Whiting 1976).

Nevertheless, it must be emphasized that the orientation of policy in this period was undoubtedly largely macroeconomic. The predominant policy objectives were full employment, inflation, and the balance of payments, and these were seen as largely macroeconomic issues. Growth was well established as a desire in the political rhetoric of the period, but led to little in the way of direct policy action. The apparatus of policy-making was largely geared to that emphasis, with the budget and fiscal manipulation the key elements in the repertoire of policy-making.

CONCLUSIONS

The phrase 'consumption and competition' summarizes the ethos of policy-making in the 1950s. Higher living standards measured above all by consumption levels were central to the Conservatives' claims to power. The major means to this end was not an active, interventionist search for growth, but creating the appropriate competitive environment in which the traditional forces of free enterprise could prove their worth. Government was also drawn into other areas where its role could be seen as compatible with that competitive framework. Most notably, perhaps, to those who think of the 1960s as the period of rhetoric about the scientific and technological revolution, is the emphasis on technical education and technological development in the previous decade, with some limited action flowing from this concern. But in practice to seriously change British practices in these areas would have required a scale and scope of intervention which would have severely cut across the rhetoric of free enterprise and competition.

Further Reading

Cairncross, A. (1992), *The British Economy Since 1945*, Oxford: ch. 3.

Cairncross, A., and Watts, N. (1989), *The Economic Section 1939–1961: A Study in Economic Advising*, London.

Dow, J. C. R. (1965), *The Management of the British Economy 1945–1960*, Cambridge: chs. 3, 6.

Grove, J. W. (1962), *Government and Industry in Britain*, London.

Harris, N. (1972), *Competition and the Corporate Society: British Conservatives, The State and Industry 1945–64*, London.

Hunter, A. (1966), *Competition and the Law*, London.

Mercer, H. (1991), 'The Monopolies and Restrictive Practices Commission 1949–56: A Study in Regulatory Failure', in G. Jones and M. Kirby (eds.) *Competitiveness and the State*, Manchester: 78–99.

Worswick, G. D. N. and Ady, P. H. (1962) (eds.), *The British Economy in the Nineteen-Fifties*, Oxford.

10

1961–1970 New Frontiers and National Champions

INTRODUCTION

The election of the Labour Government in 1964 marked a significant shift in British economic policy, and in the succeeding six years industrial policy probably had its highest political profile in post-war Britain. But this new departure had at least some of its origins in an earlier shift in policy perceptions which need to be taken into account in looking at Labour's policies.

In his assessment of policy from 1951 to 1964 Brittan (1964) called his chapter on the early 1960s 'The Great Reappraisal', and argued that this reappraisal began in 1960, 'The year in which everything really happened but which no one really remembers' and that 'It was about this time that the first papers were written on the conditions of long-term growth and that interest blossomed in French planning methods, and in the Common Market' (204, 207). As the quotations indicate, 1960 began the process by which the rhetoric of growth was to frame discussion of the economy, and the related theme that planning was to be the route to faster growth.

Of course growth was not a new policy objective in 1960. As the Radcliffe Committee noted in 1959, 'During recent years there has been an increasing mention, both in public discussion and in Government pronouncements, of the need to foster economic growth and the general raising of standards of living' (Cmnd. 827: para. 58). But before 1960 the perceived route to higher growth was unclear, and it remained more a happy aspiration than the central issue of economic policy. From 1960 that began to change, with the Conservatives' increasing movement away from the belief that the market left to itself could deliver higher growth. In this broad sense Labour after 1964 was to build on a shift in the national mood, a shift in the parameters of policy debate, though its policies were to go far beyond those envisaged by the Conservatives in the early 1960s.

CONTEXT

The increased attention to economic growth had no one source. Partly it represented a simple logical corollary of the achievement of full employment; with all resources fully employed increased living standards could only come from using these resources more productively. Partly it related to inter-party electoral competition—growth could deliver more of everything—private consumption, investment, exports, public expenditure, obviating the need for painful choices. In addition growth was seen as part of the competition between the Communist and capitalist systems, growth being the criteria by which it was thought the systems would be judged. More prosaically, the growth argument in Britain arose from a recognition that her performance in the 1950s had put her close to the bottom of the emergent league tables of growth, these tables being an unintended product of the war-driven revolution in national-income accounting (Arndt 1978; Tomlinson 1985, ch. 4).

This new enthusiasm for growth was commonly counterpointed to a critique of the existing stop–go policy regime. Commentaries like those of Shanks (1961), Shonfield (1959), and Brittan (1964) attacked the preoccupation with the balance of payments and the value of sterling, which were alleged to underlie the stop–go cycle, and argued that this cycle was a key cause of the low investment and low growth in the economy. Subsequent work suggests this critique was exaggerated, Britain's fluctuations in output under stop–go being no greater than those in faster-growing countries (Wilson 1966; Whiting 1976). But the important point is that the debate about economic growth commonly focused on the need for a major reorientation of British policy, not just a marginal shift to achieve the new goal.

'Planning' was the catchword of much of the critique of stop–go. The meaning of this term was and is extremely problematic. Advocacy of planning often meant little more than an attempt to suggest a new purposiveness, a new determination to 'get things moving' without any particular policy mechanisms being involved. For the Conservatives to attach themselves to planning is surprising, given their rhetoric and practice of liberalization in the 1950s. But the planning they came to advocate was a long way from the 1940s controls, against which they had successfully propagandized at the beginning of the 1950s. First, the new planning was not negative in the sense of controls, but positive and aimed at encouraging expansion. Second, it relied largely on the exchange of information and ideas between government and industry, not enforceable government policies. Third, it could draw on the perceived success of French 'indicative planning' which came into vogue in Britain in 1960–1. How far in fact French planning deserves the credit for the French economic miracle remains much disputed, and how far such success as it achieved depended upon rather more active intervention than the British version also remains contentious (e.g. Estrin and Holmes 1983). But to the Conservative government the French model appeared to offer an ideologically congenial version of planning, which was not too difficult to square with existing predilections.

This conversion to planning was aided by the unexpected enthusiasm of the Federation of British Industry, which at a conference in November 1960 embraced much of the critique of existing policy and called on the government to put new emphasis on policies for expansion (Harris 1972: 240–2). Another stimulus was the Plowden Report on public expenditure, which called for the planning of that expenditure over five years, rather than the largely year-by-year current pattern (Meadows 1978). Two other strands of thinking were also interwoven into policy debate. The counterpoint of planning versus stop–go was reinforced by the sterling crisis of 1961, which once again seemed to suggest that defence of the pound remained both pre-eminent in policy-making and a major obstacle to expansion. Finally, the Treasury, whilst commonly seen as part of the problem, precisely because of its key role in stop–go, saw planning as a way of getting its long-desired incomes policy in by the back door (Brittan 1964: 219).

The main result of all this was the creation of the National Economic Development Council in 1961/2. This was a tripartite body, aimed at planning for higher growth, in the sense of setting out plausible targets for such growth, and analysing the obstacles to their achievement. The creation of NEDC encapsulates much of the spirit of the 'great reappraisal'. 'Its inception came as a response to a pervasive sense of failure and an accelerating awareness that the instruments of demand management lacked strength when confronted by mass expectations of rising living standards, stable prices and full employment' (Middlemas 1983: 19).

The short-run, substantive impact of NEDC is much less clear than its symbolism of the new mood. It did successfully engage the commitment of employers and the TUC, and it did useful investigative work, especially in the sector-based 'Little Neddies'. It produced a plan for growth, which embodied the idea of a 4 per cent growth in GDP, and a subsequent analysis of the constraints (NEDO 1962, 1963). The broad thrust of the latter was on the problem of market failure, especially in the area of the labour-market and training (Middlemas 1983: ch. 2). But its solutions remained rather general, and in particular did not engage with the key problem of how this new growth was to be made compatible with the old bugbear of the balance of payments.

Parallel to the NEDC the Conservatives also created a National Incomes Commission (Nicky). But unlike NEDC this was not tripartite, the government failing to get the support of the trade unions for anything which suggested an incomes policy. Issues of growth were then discussed largely separately from those of wages and incomes, a separation strictly at odds with Neddy's emphasis on the labour-market as crucial to faster growth.

Under the 1964 Wilson government NEDC survived, but was marginalized by the creation of the Department of Economic Affairs. The creation of this new Ministry also reflected the critique of stop–go, and the belief that an effective growth strategy required a counterweight to the Treasury, a Ministry of Industry to offset the Treasury's concerns with the balance of payments and the exchange rate. Like NEDC, the DEA produced a growth strategy, embodied in a National Plan (Cmnd. 2764). This restated the objective of a 3.8 per cent per annum growth rate, and drew on information from the Little Neddies. But its scope was substantially enlarged from the previous NEDC positions.

At the centre of the plan was the idea of channelling both more and better trained workers and higher investment into manufacturing, and using these resources more efficiently, especially by a greater and redirected research effort and rationalization of production. All this was to be achieved by an extension of planning, though it was accepted that,

most manufacturing industry is, and will continue to be, largely governed by the market economy. But this does not necessarily, and without active Government influence, bring about the results which the nation needs . . . positive Government action is required to supplement market forces. Each case must be judged on its merits. Care will be taken not to destroy the complex mechanisms on which the market economy is based. The end product of both co-operative planning and the market economy is an internationally competitive industry; and in securing this aim they complement each other (Cmnd. 2764: paras. 11, 12).

The National Plan was no Soviet-style central plan, but it did involve a very wide range of changes in government policy. These embraced everything from stopping the increase in defence spending and reducing outflows of overseas investment to encouraging a range of changes in industrial organization and training. Much of this programme will be looked at in more detail below, but it is important at this stage to note one of the central difficulties of the Plan.

The opening paragraph of the Plan stated 'This is a plan to provide the basis for greater economic growth. An essential part of the Plan is a solution to Britain's balance of payments problem; for growth cannot be maintained unless we pay our way in the world'. The relation between the plan and the balance of payments was ambiguous. On the one hand, the Plan aimed at easing the balance of payments constraint. On the other, its pursuit was predicated above all on a steadily rising level of demand which would be impossible unless that constraint was first eased.

One way of viewing the plan is as a proposed 'third way' solution to Britain's balance of payments problems. The alternatives debated in the 1950s had largely been devaluation and deflation. The former was ruled out by Labour largely on political grounds. Wilson did not want Labour to be the 'party of devaluation'. Such a decision would also strongly offend both the City of London and American opinion (Ponting 1990). The economic case for devaluation was never unambiguous, resting on the proposition that the current account deficits of the mid-1960s were long-term, trend problems, rather than the results of the pre-election boom (Cairncross and Eichengreen 1983: ch. 5). But the key decision was a political one, and once made in the immediate aftermath of the 1964 election it was only to be rescinded in the face of unremitting pressure on the exchanges in November 1967.

With deflation also ruled out, as incompatible with Labour's commitment to full employment, the Labour Government relied on industrial change in its broadest sense to achieve an improvement in the payments position. But the obvious problem was that whatever the efficacy of its policies for such change, they would have their results over a longer time period than required by the compelling short-term pressures of the balance of payments. Hence, much of the economic historiography of the Labour Government tells a story of conflict between short-run balance of payments goals and the desire for long-run growth, resolved in favour of the former. The aptness of this verdict is returned to in the conclusion to this chapter.

MARKETS

As noted in Chapter 9, by the end of the 1950s Britain was substantially free of direct controls and quotas in manufactured trade, but still had a significant level of tariffs, above the levels of other major Western European economies (Ray 1960). Through the 1960s this liberalizing trend continued, though in an uneven and complex manner. This liberalization was partly secured by the mechanism of GATT, notably the Kennedy Round of 1964–7. This brought a substantial reduction in tariffs with all of Britain's major trading partners (Cmnd. 3347).

Alongside this broad process of world-wide trade liberalization were the bargains struck with other European countries. In 1960, following a Swedish initiative, the European Free Trade Association was created. Britain became an enthusiastic member on being rejected for EC membership in 1963. EFTA, as its name suggests, was very much a trade bloc, with few of the supra-national ambitions of the EC, and without even a common external tariff. In successive stages between 1960 and 1966 it led to complete free trade between its seven members (Britain, Denmark, Sweden, Norway, Switzerland, Austria, and Iceland). But in some respects this was clearly a second best to EC membership. Whilst between 1958 and 1965 the share of Britain's trade with EFTA increased, it grew more slowly than Britain's trade with the EC (Wells 1966). This reflected in part the fact that the EC's common external tariff on manufactures was quite small, and therefore did relatively little to deflect the trend towards greater trade relations between Britain and her near neighbours, which has been such a striking feature of the post-war period.

TABLE 10.1. *The pattern of British trade in the 1960s* (% of total)

	Imports			Exports		
	1955	1965	1971	1955	1965	1971
Sterling Area	39.4	30.1	25.9	45.0	33.6	28.7
Developed	16.6	13.7	12.8	23.4	17.7	15.5
Developing	22.8	16.3	13.0	21.6	15.9	13.2
Western Europe	25.7	33.0	39.3	28.9	37.4	39.8
EEC	12.6	17.3	21.4	15.0	20.0	21.0
EFTA	11.4	13.6	15.9	11.6	14.0	15.0
North America	19.5	19.7	17.6	12.0	14.9	15.7

Source: Prest and Coppock (1972), p. 119.

The early 1960s also saw a significant shift in Britain's trade pattern away from the Overseas Sterling Area (OSA), predomin-antly the 'White Commonwealth'. Whilst Britain's share of non-OSA markets fell by 14 per cent between 1959/60 and 1965/6, its share of OSA imports fell by 46 per cent. A significant part of this was due to the ending of dollar discrimination, which along with increased US aid and inflows of investment led to a big loss in Britain's exports to these countries and off-setting gains for the United States. This process was probably exacer-bated by the erosion of Imperial trade preference, though this was quite stable in this period and should not be given an exaggerated role (Krause 1968: 215–18).

Overall, by the end of the 1960s Britain was very much a free-trade country as far as manufactured goods were concerned, and this was reflected in the level of import penetration, which rose from 9 to 15 per cent over the decade (imports as a percentage of home demand; Williams *et al.* 1983: 118–19). This was paralleled by a continued downward shift in Britain's share of world trade in manufactured exports, from 16.5 per cent to 10.8 per cent (Williams *et al.*: 116–17). More serious however, given the rapid growth in total world exports, was the slow growth of exports compared to total manufacturing sales, which rose from 18 to 21 per cent (Williams *et al.*: 118–19). Britain was increasingly feeling the competitive pressures arising from the liberalizing of world trade, especially in the previously favoured markets of the Commonwealth.

The major interruption of the liberalizing trend in the 1960s was the import surcharge scheme of 1964–5. This imposed a 15 per cent surcharge on imports from November 1964 (reduced to 10 per cent in April 1965), despite being in clear breach of both GATT and EFTA treaties. The importance of this move should not be exaggerated. It was not part of a general rejection by Labour of the case for trade liberalization. Maudling, the previous Conservative Chancellor, had suggested the possible use of such a scheme in 1963 (Brittan 1964: 252–3), and it should be seen as a short-term attempt to escape both devaluation and deflation as solutions to the balance of payments problems, rather than anything more profound.

Labour's main response to the enhanced international competitive pressures was to look for greater competitiveness on the part of British industry. These pressures were a central foundation in particular for the government's emphasis on the scale of industry:

British industry faces the problem of the small size of many of its production units compared with those in the United States and other competing countries. The lowering of international tariffs through GATT negotiations such as the Kennedy Round and through economic groupings such as EEC and EFTA means the intensification of international competition. British industry must be organised so that it cannot only face but take positive advantage of this competitive situation. The scale of operations is very important to competitive survival and this seems likely to involve a considerable reorganisation of the size of the units of which British industry is comprised' (Cmnd. 2764: para. 37).

Labour's answer to competition in home and export markets was not to be protection, but the promotion of 'national champions'.

PROFITS

The squeeze on profits evident in the 1950s continued in the next decade. The share of pre-tax profits in incomes fell in every year in the 1960s except 1965, though as in the previous period the post-tax trend was much flatter (King 1975; Glyn and Sutcliffe 1971). This suggested a substantial fall in both pre- and post-tax profit rates.

Like the 1940s Labour government, that in the 1960s was mostly concerned with the issue of profit distribution, seeing the encouragement of profit retention as both an encouragement to investment and, by limiting dividends, a help for incomes policy. Profit retention by companies was encouraged by the new Corporation Tax of 1965. This for the first time made a clear separation between the tax on companies and income tax. Corporation tax was levied on all profits, but the recipients of distributed profits were then subject to the normal income tax regime.[1] The new rules also aimed to discourage foreign investment by companies, as the tax exemption of profits earned abroad by overseas trading corporations was lost (Graham 1972: 185–7).

The other major reform affecting profits directly was the abolition of investment allowances in favour of investment grants. The logic of this change was to provide a quicker stimulus to investment, to focus attention on investment in manufacturing and the extractive industries (where the balance of payments problem was believed to be best tackled), and to help small growing firms who might gain little from the allowance system which helped most those earning substantial profits (Cmnd. 2874).

The incomes policy aspect of policy on profits is a feature of the whole of the 1960s . When the Conservatives created the

---

[1] The recipients of investment income faced an increase in tax rates under the Labour government, the actual rates depending on the level of income. The top rate rose from 72 to 79 per cent from 1964/5 to 1970/1 (Stewart 1972: 93).

National Income Commission, one of its remits 'was to have regard to the Government pledge that if any undue growth in the aggregate of profits should result from restraint in earned incomes, that growth would itself be restrained by fiscal or other appropriate means' (Cmnd. 1844: para. 8).

Under Labour the equity aspect of profits was also important in the context of the pursuit of incomes policy. But the government was also concerned with the investment consequences of any excessively tight control on profits. The National Board for Prices and Incomes encompassed profits in its remit to prevent unnecessary price increases, and in that context profits could only be increased if that was necessary to raise capital (Fels 1972: ch. 12). On the other hand it was clear that incomes policy was not to be a means of redistributing incomes away from profits, and the 1969 White Paper (Cmnd. 4237: para. 113) was quite explicit that 'the Government does not believe that any general reduction in the level of return on capital invested in British industry . . . would be helpful in the context of the essential modernisation of the economy'.

The Labour government, then, was sensitive to the potential impact of profit levels on investment, which it wanted to encourage. However, its attempt to maintain retained profits by discouraging dividends seems to have failed, as dividend levels were static in this period. Equally, whilst on balance reducing the tax burden on companies, it did pursue policies of encouraging trade liberalization, which are presumably a major explanation of the long-run pre-tax profit squeeze. However, investment seems to have held up well in the later 1960s, allowing for the quite severe stop in aggregate demand for much of the period (Graham 1972: 206–9).

THE EFFICIENCY OF LABOUR

Labour in its broadest sense was at the centre of the 1964 Government's policies for industry. In his famous speech at Scarborough in 1963 announcing Labour's commitment to the 'white heat of the scientific revolution', Harold Wilson announced four key policy proposals. These were (i) to produce more scientists; (ii) to keep more of them in the country; (iii) to make better use of them; and (iv) to organize industry better to make use of scientific research.

The theme of industrial modernization being hampered by a shortage of adequately trained people was not of course a new one, and a similar rhetoric to Wilson's is apparent both in Conservative proposals for educational reform in the 1950s (Ch. 9), and in more serious analysis, such as the report by the NEDC in 1963 (Elliott 1978: 597).[2] But as in so many other areas, Labour placed a much stronger policy emphasis on tackling this problem. The National Plan's argument was organized around the thesis that a key constraint on output expansion would be shortages of skilled labour. In a manner reminiscent of the *Economic Surveys* of the late 1940s, it produced a manpower budget and projected a manpower shortage which could arise if output expanded as hoped, unless remedial action was taken. Such action included an increase in labour-saving investment, improvements in the efficiency of labour usage, and an all-round improvement in the quality of the labour-force (Cmnd. 2764: 29).

Labour was thus committed to a form of manpower planning with a number of components, but which may be summarized as, first, measures to increase the supply of skilled labour; second, measures to increase (labour) productivity; and, finally, measures to encourage more mobility of labour. In addition to these there was a major attempt to reform the whole system of industrial relations, for both macroeconomic and efficiency reasons. Each of these can be looked at in turn (Elliott 1978: 597–617).

On the supply of skilled labour, the Government's focus was on technical education, at both craft and graduate level. Two particular policies for the latter were the expansion of higher education to provide larger numbers of graduates, and a redeployment of such people from defence-oriented to more commercially useful tasks.

The Wilson government inherited the previous government's endorsement of the Robbins Report (Cmnd. 2154), which had advocated a major expansion of higher education to provide a place for every suitably qualified student who wanted one. This policy was continued under Labour: the total number of university students rose from 143,000 in 1964–5 to 226,000 in 1969–70.

---

[2] Academic analysis in support of such arguments may be found in Peck (1968).

However, a demand-led system obviously meant that the subjects studied by undergraduates were not determined by government, and the biggest expansions came in arts and social sciences, rather than in engineering and science, though the numbers in these subjects did expand.

As regards the redeployment of technologically qualified graduates, a central part of the efforts of the Ministry of Technology was aimed at diverting British R & D workers from defence into the civilian sector. This was attempted by making efforts to reduce the share of defence in total R & D (see the section on Technological Change, below), and by using existing groups of researchers, e.g. at the Atomic Energy Authority, for civilian purposes.

On industrial training, Labour inherited a major shift of emphasis under the Conservatives. At the time of the Carr Committee on apprenticeship in 1958, it was quite clear that growing worries about that system's ability to deliver adequate craft training still had not led to any notion of a greater role for government. But after 1958 the government slowly shifted its ground. In a White Paper in 1962 (Cmnd. 1892) it was accepted that there was a case for an enhanced government role, based on an argument for market failure in this area. The problem, it was argued, was the poaching of trained workers by firms who did not themselves train their workers: 'While the benefits of training are shared by all, the cost is borne only by those firms which decide to undertake training themselves' (para. 5). The solution was a levy system, whereby all firms in an industry would have to pay a training levy, which could then be reclaimed by those providing schemes of training approved by a tripartite training board (Perry 1976: chs. 9–12). This was a major intervention in the area of industrial training, and one embraced and expanded by Labour. By 1970 28 boards had been set up under the 1964 Act, with 90 per cent of the work-force in the industries covered affected by the new training scheme. Workers in training expanded by 15 per cent 1964–9, the number of staff involved in training rose even faster—for example, in engineering from 6,430 in 1965 to 10,582 in 1968. And even liberal critics of the Act thought the quality of the training improved (Lees and Chiplin 1970; see also Perry 1976: chs. 17–23).

Up to a point the training board system was an example of successful corporatist forms of industrial intervention. It engaged the support of the TUC and CBI, and to some degree delivered a consensus on training. However it came under increasing pressure from small business, which felt itself excluded from the benefits of the system. Nor did it lead to a radical change in the apprenticeship system as many had hoped (Vickerstaff 1985: 53–5).

Labour productivity, as we have seen in Chapter 7, was the critical concern of industrial policy under the Attlee government. Whilst never having the same centrality in the 1960s, it did still form an important part of the repertoire of concerns implicated in the desire to raise growth. In part this flowed from the same simple logic of trying to raise output in a fully employed economy. But, as in the 1940s, whilst labour productivity could in principle be raised by a vast range of measures, concern with this measure easily slipped into a focus on labour practices as the problem. Above all what came to be called productivity bargaining came close to centre stage.

Of course, systems of linking pay to output and productivity were hardly new in the 1960s; forms of piece-work and payment by results had been around for generations. But what was new was the emphasis on plant-level bargaining about productivity. The trend-setting example was the agreement at the Esso refinery at Fawley in 1960, an agreement 'without precedent or even proximate parallel in the history of collective bargaining in Great Britain' (Flanders 1964: 13). Under these agreements large increases in pay were exchanged for major changes in labour practices, coupled with a movement towards the almost total elimination of overtime, which as in much of British industry had come to form a major part of the total wage (Flanders 1964: chs. 5, 6) Analysis of this agreement suggested, albeit with qualifications, that it had indeed delivered a significant upward shift in productivity, whilst maintaining good labour relations.

Productivity bargaining in the 1960s, however, owed its popularity at least as much to the desire to escape the effects of incomes policies as it did to a positive desire to follow the lead of Fawley. Incomes policies themselves are an important part of the economic policy story of the 1960s. They can be interpreted as part of macroeconomic policy—as an attempt to improve the perceived trade-off between inflation and unemployment in the Phillips Curve framework then fashionable (e.g. Jones 1987: chs.

5, 6). They can be seen in a broader framework as part of the post-war search for a consensual or corporatist agreement on wage bargaining (e.g. Fishbein 1984*a*: ch. 2). But they can also be seen as closely linked with the issue of productivity. The first major government document on incomes policies in the 1960s was called a 'Joint Statement of Intent on Productivity, Prices and Incomes' and this set the tone for all the subsequent policy development. The National Board for Prices and Incomes (NBPI) set up by Labour to administer its policy had a twofold aim: 'One part of the NBPI's strategy was to break the hold of traditional factors in income determination: the other was to introduce different factors, such as the incomes norm, and, most notably, productivity' (Fels 1972: 133). Productivity agreements were not the only way this aim was pursued, and the Board also, for example, encouraged payment-by-results schemes. But productivity agreements were central to its positive strategy. The attractiveness of such agreements to unions (and employers) was that they were a means of avoiding restrictions on pay increases otherwise imposed by incomes policy. Genuine increases in productivity could usually be the grounds for above-the-norm increases. Fels (1972: 134–41) suggests that in many cases the rapid spread of productivity agreements was a façade: 'it is likely that the majority of productivity agreements during this period were simply devices to raise wages in the only way permitted by the incomes policy' (138). However, it is also likely that 'some useful changes may have been brought about in the field of reforming industrial relations institutions and in bringing productivity into the wage bargaining process' (152).

The third aspect of Labour's focus on manpower was the issue of its distribution. The National Plan's projected growth rates implied a significant worsening of labour shortages, but the Plan also suggested that there was much under-utilization of labour. The solution was more efficient utilization, a shake-out of labour and its redeployment elsewhere. Such labour mobility was to be encouraged by a range of measures. Redundancy payments, income-related unemployment pay, the easier transfer of occupational pension rights, and better allowances for mobile workers were all proposed in the National Plan and later implemented (Cmnd. 2764: 39).

This manpower policy received a further twist in the explicit attempt to shift labour from service employment to manufacturing. This derived in significant part from the work of the economist Nicholas Kaldor, an adviser to the Labour Government. He argued that Britain's slow growth problem was fundamentally the result of too small a manufacturing sector, which he saw as the productivity-enhancing, dynamic part of the economy. In his view this sector in Britain was being held back by the absence of a ready pool of agricultural workers, wanting to migrate into industry, as in the fast growing Western European economies (Kaldor 1966). The solution to the problem was to apply a differential employment tax, thereby raising the relative cost of employing someone in the service sector. This was the Selective Employment Tax (SET), introduced in 1966. The logic of the Tax (apart from raising revenue) was that it would raise productivity in both services and manufacturing. Kaldor saw the service sector as having diminishing returns to scale, whilst manufacturing had increasing returns. The movement of labour from one to another would therefore raise productivity in both (Thirlwall 1987: 241–5). The Tax was later given a further twist by the Regional Employment Premium which gave added incentives to manufacturing employment in the Development Areas.

Certainly there was a substantial labour shake-out in the late 1960s, and retrospectively we can see 1967/8 as the beginning of the end of the very low unemployment rates previously characteristic of the post-war period. But it is not apparent that the policies pursued achieved the aim of increasing workers' willingness to move jobs: whilst most of the unemployment was short term and could be deemed 'frictional' (i.e. job changing), there was an upward shift in the overall level of unemployment which was likely to discourage workers from taking redundancy. Equally there is no evidence that SET had a significant impact on the trend in manufacturing employment, which peaked in 1966 and then began a much more rapid decline than in most industrialized countries (Thatcher 1979; Cutler *et al.* 1986). Kaldor's argument that high growth in Western Europe was aided by the contraction of low productivity agriculture seems plausible, but the idea that British manufacturing was constrained by general labour shortages seems much less persuasive, though there were undoubtedly specific skills in short supply.

Much of what the Wilson Government attempted to do in the area of manpower impinged on industrial relations in the sense of wage bargaining. But initially it did not see its task as a wholesale reform of those relations. Rather it looked to a co-operation with the unions which would improve the industrial climate, and right at the beginning of its period in office it reversed the *Rookes* v. *Barnard* court judgment of 1964, in which the judges tried to nibble away at the unions immunities from claims for damages in industrial disputes.

But over Labour's period in office union–government relations deteriorated. This was due in part to the disagreements about incomes policy, especially when these were made statutory, and it also related to particular industrial disputes which government saw as damaging to its attempts to maintain foreign confidence in its economic management. But perhaps most important was the emergence of an argument which located a key problem of British industrial efficiency and wage inflation in the structure of British unions. This analysis received its major representation in the Donovan Commission, which reported in 1968 (Cmnd. 3623).

In the Donovan view, British industrial relations were characterized by two systems—a national, official, and formal system of collective bargaining, and a local, unofficial, informal system largely operated by shop stewards, the latter increasingly predominating over the former. In Donovan's analysis the 'central defect [is] . . . the disorder in factory and workshop relations and pay structures promoted by the conflict between the formal and informal system' (Cmnd. 3623: para. 1019). The solution offered did not involve, at least in the first instance, changes in the legal framework of collective bargaining, but the encouragement of formal plant-level agreements preferably embracing productivity, reducing both the role of shop stewards and national bargaining.

Whilst Donovan's analysis picked up on some important trends in parts of British industry, its general characterization of the system seems highly dubious. As Turner (1969) pointed out the Commission had extrapolated wildly from the engineering industry to the whole of British industry, ignoring the continued prevalence of national agreements in most sectors. Moreover the Report's 'extraordinary absence' was the lack of any serious discussion of how plant-level bargaining could be more compatible with incomes policies, when most serious discussions of the latter accepted that it would require more effective national bargaining if there was any hope of it working.

Whatever the merits or otherwise of Donovan's analysis it encouraged the government in an attempt to reform the legal framework of industrial relations, proposed in a document, called with unintended irony, *In Place of Strife* (Cmnd. 3888). This attempted to secure by law the following of the proper disputes procedure before a strike (official or unofficial) was called. It also allowed for the requirement of a ballot to be imposed by the government prior to a strike in certain circumstances. As Tolliday (1987a: 138–9) rightly emphasizes, this measure was not wholly anti-union. It extended union rights to organize and negotiate and proposed that the *status quo ante* should prevail during a dispute. But it involved the unions acting constitutionally and controlling their members during disputes.

These proposals generated enormous opposition and 'the traditional alliance of trade unions and politically-based socialists in the Labour Party was threatened as perhaps never before' (Robinson 1972: 325). Eventually the proposals were dropped, leaving a legacy of bad feeling between the unions and the Labour Party. More important in the current context, the whole episode added greatly to the trend towards seeing unions as crucial to Britain's poor industrial performance, a trend which was to continue in the 1970s and culminate, of course, in the Thatcher Government's trade-union policies after 1979. This retrospective lens of the 'problem of trade unions' has distorted much discussion of the 1960s, when the most serious and interesting attempts were made to reform the labour-market *in collaboration with* the unions. These policies, as suggested above, were not without success, though it would be an exaggeration to say that they fundamentally changed all the workings of the labour-market.

THE EFFICIENCY OF CAPITAL

Unlike the supply of labour, issues relating to the supply of capital were not prominent in the 1960s. Whilst bodies like the Industrial Reorganization Corporation did supply government funds to industry, this can best be seen in the context of government attempts to reorganize industry, rather than as aimed at correcting deficiencies in the capital market. Similarly, the government did tighten exchange control, especially aimed at restricting the outflow of capital. But the main aim of this was to aid the balance of payments, rather than to try to redirect investment funds towards domestic industry (Cmnd. 2764: 71–2).

Whilst the National Plan saw investment as 'at the heart of the Plan' (55), the policies to raise investment did not include changes to the financial system.[3] Rather the emphasis was on aggregate demand, and it was integral to the whole idea of indicative planning in the 1960s that if industry could be enabled to assume adequate demand for its products then investment would be forthcoming. Active policy outside the management of demand was largely restricted to the action on investment allowances already noted. It is a curious feature of the reformism of the 1960s that it had so little to say on the long-standing issue of the character of financial institutions and their suitability for the process of industrial modernization. This is perhaps particularly odd given the enthusiasm for French-style planning, a form of planning which in its early days at least, seems to have relied crucially on state control of investment funds (e.g. Lynch 1991).

THE EFFICIENCY OF TECHNICAL CHANGE

A programme of accelerating technical change was at the heart of Labour's policies in the 1960s. Doubts about Britain's ability to produce and adapt to such change was, of course, hardly new in the 1960s. As noted in Chapter 9, the Conservatives in the 1950s had at times produced a rhetoric of the challenge of technology not unlike that of Wilson. But after 1964 this rhetoric was translated into a number of important practical proposals.

Of course, the 'white heat of technology' rhetoric was in part a purely electoral ploy. It attempted to contrast the white-coated,

---

[3] The emphasis on investment as the key to economic growth reflected the traditional view of economists, represented by such bench-mark works as that by Solow (1956). But by the 1960s work was appearing that challenged this emphasis (e.g. Denison 1967) and the trend since then has been increasingly to emphasize not the quantity of factor inputs (capital and labour) but their quality, as well as managerial and organizational factors. For discussion of theories and evidence on growth in the post-war period, see e.g. Crafts (1992*a*).

scientifically trained technocrats of Labour with the befuddled, dilettante aristocrats of the Conservative Party. It drew on the Kennedy 'new frontiers' ideas, promising a new world of abundance vouchsafed by the knowledgeable management of ever-accelerating scientific and technological progress. Wilson's speech at the 1963 Labour Party conference attempted to give the new frontier a socialist hue:

Since technological progress left to the mechanism of private industry and private property can lead only to high profits for a few, and to mass redundancies for the many, if there had never been a case for socialism before, automation would have created it. Because only if technical progress becomes part of our national planning can that progress be directed to national ends (Labour Party 1963: 135).

But what did this rhetoric of planned industrial modernization actually imply for policy? In his 1963 speech Wilson was quite explicit about one facet of this—the need to redirect Britain's R & D effort from defence to civilian uses 'Until recently over half of our trained scientists were engaged in defence projects or so called defence projects. Real defence, of course, is essential. But so many of our scientists were employed on purely prestige projects that never left the drawing board'. And later he went on

What we need is new industries and it will be the job of the next government to see that we get them. This means mobilising scientific resources in this country in producing a new technological breakthrough. We have spent thousands of millions in the past few years on misdirected research and development contracts in the field of defence. If we are now to use the technologies of R & D contracts in civil industry, I believe we could within a measurable period of time establish new industries which would make us once again one of the foremost industrial nations in the world (Labour Party 1963: 137, 138).

This idea of switching the R & D effort away from defence into civilian uses was linked to an emerging analysis of Britain's peculiarities in the R & D field. In the 1950s and 1960s the evidence suggested that Britain's total spending on R & D was not a problem. Though it fell below that of the United States, it compared well with other major industrial countries. For example, one calculation at the end of the 1960s put Britain's expenditure on R & D at 2.3 per cent of GNP, compared with 1.4 per cent in Germany, 1.6 per cent in France, and 0.6 per cent in Italy (Johnson 1969: 36). The problem, it was argued, was not the volume but the direction of this effort.

Freeman and Young (1965) pointed out that in comparison with other major OECD countries Britain stood out as having a very high proportion of its R & D effort financed by government and directed to a few areas of high technology—especially nuclear technology, aerospace, and military electronics. The converse of this was a very low proportion devoted to machinery and engineering. This pattern was not dissimilar to that of the United States, but the USA's total effort was much greater, so making Britain's position in these favoured sectors relatively weak. And in any event the United States was being overtaken in key high-technology markets by countries like Germany and Japan. In sum 'In product groups which were decisive for world trade in the 1950s and 1960s British technical effort was relatively poor in comparison with Germany and several other countries' (Freeman 1979: 70).

To try to redirect Britain's research effort away from defence made a lot of sense in the 1960s, and went along with the reining back and then reduction of total defence expenditure. The figures suggest that this policy met a degree of success. Between 1966 and 1969 defence R & D spending fell by about 10 per cent, whilst civil expenditure rose by 20 per cent, so that for the first time since the war the government spent more on civil than defence research.

One of the more interesting features of this strategy was the use of existing research facilities for civilian rather than defence projects. These included the movement of some of the resources of the Atomic Energy Authority, Royal Radar, and Aircraft Establishments into such areas as non-destructive testing, desalination, kidney dialysis, computer languages, and numerically-controlled machine tools (Coopey *et al.* 1992).

However, whilst there were extremely interesting developments, they did raise an important issue about the government's R & D strategy. By and large MinTech (the Ministry of Technology) tried to hold the existing research apparatus together and to reorient its activity, rather than to reorganize that apparatus.

In part this was because the government did not want to abandon areas like nuclear power entirely—they wanted to keep teams and capacities together in case of later expansion. This stance was also linked to the belief in substantial economies of scale in research. In R & D as in other areas of industrial organization, 'big is beautiful' tended to hold sway in government circles in the 1960s.

This view of R & D is not lightly to be dismissed. In some areas very substantial economies of scale did exist, such as in research into aircraft and computers (Freeman 1979: 68). On the other hand, the evidence does not endorse any universal pattern in this regard. Whilst research effort in Britain was (and is) highly concentrated in a small number of big firms, the pattern of innovation suggests that small firms remained important (Jewkes *et al.* 1958). Even with the movement from defence to civilian R & D, it may have been that the government's own R & D effort was still tied too much to 'big science' and big prestige projects.

Whilst changing the pattern of their own R & D spending, the Wilson governments of the 1960s were also concerned to encourage private R & D. A range of advisory and service functions was built up, notably for example in the computer industry (Campbell-Kelly 1989: 246–8), but also in more traditional ideas like the Production Engineering Advisory Service. Government funding of private R & D expanded both via the traditional Industrial Research Associations, and in new ways such as grants given in return for a governmental right to publicize results obtained. Public procurement, long used to guide R & D in the defence sector, was expanded into civilian sectors. Wilson's picture of increased civilian contracting of R & D by government was to some extent achieved. By 1969, whilst still financing about half of all R & D, the government was directly conducting about 22 per cent, almost two-thirds being carried out by private industry (Johnson 1969: 39).

In sum, MinTech presided over a major policy shift in R & D which is now emerging as a central part of the Labour Government's industrial policy. Recent work (Coopey *et al.* 1992), gives a much more rounded and on the whole positive picture of this policy than previously common. This work does not suggest the MinTech strategy was an unqualified success. It encountered significant inertia and resistance, and some of the technologies supported were over-complex or remained military-related. Some elements of higher bureaucracy, for example in the Ministry of Aviation, were incapable or unwilling to support the restructuring.

Also, MinTech was undoubtedly set up to provide a quick fix or rapid technical change and hence economic growth to ease the pressing constraints on economic policy in the period. This political context explains why it was substantially expanded in 1968 and 1969 to become a Ministry of Industry, which tended to submerge the original, more focused, MinTech approach. Nevertheless the sectors targeted by the strategy—machine tools, electronics, telecommunications, and computers appear in retrospect to have been a pretty good selection of winners to pick.

THE EFFICIENCY OF COMPANY ORGANIZATION

If the Labour Government's R & D policy has been rather neglected, the same cannot be said of its approach to industrial organization. The most discussed institutional initiative of the Labour Government is probably the Industrial Reorganization Corporation (Hague and Wilkinson 1983; Young and Lowe 1978: pt. II). The founding document of this body (Cmnd. 2889) clearly spelt out the logic behind it: 'Our future prosperity depends on our ability to bring about a fundamental improvement in the balance of payments. If we are to succeed in this, new initiatives are required to enable British industry to meet more effectively the growing competition it will face in world markets' (para. 1). The key to meeting this competition was seen as scale.

Many of the production units in this country are small by comparison with the most successful countries in international trade, whose operations are often based on a much larger market. In some sectors the typical company in Britain is too small to achieve long production runs; to take advantage of economies of scale; to undertake effective research and development; to support specialist departments for design and marketing; to install the most modern equipment or to attract the best qualified management (para. 3).

This paragraph summarizes much of the 'big is beautiful' rhetoric of the 1960s. Given this set of assumptions, the purpose of the IRC was 'to search for rationalisation schemes which could yield substantial benefits to the national economy' (para. 5). Note that the IRC was not intended to expand the public sector, unlike the NEB in the 1970s (Ch. 11).[4] Rather, its aim was to find potential mergers, encourage them and possibly put up money to facilitate them, but not to maintain a continuing financial interest.

The IRC was involved in some highly publicized mergers in 1967–70 period when it was effectively operating. These included the creation of the British Motor Corporation (BMC), the only British-owned volume car producer from British Motor Holdings. and the Leyland truck producer; GEC and AEI in the electrical and electronics industry; and ICL (in co-operation with MinTech) in the computer industry.

It is important to note, however, that these mergers might well have happened without a government role (excepting ICL), and that the whole exercise needs to be seen in the context of the general merger boom of the period (Table 10.2). This was a boom driven in part by the same forces as had emerged in the 1950s, such as the company law changes facilitating hostile take-overs, and the tougher government stance against restrictive practices. But in the 1960s this was added to by the stock market boom. Kuehn (1975) has shown the great extent to which so much of the boom was financed by issuing paper rather than cash bids. Between 1957 and 1969, he suggests, almost two-thirds of take-overs were financed partly or entirely with company paper. Low profitability therefore did not restrain take-over, but we should not see this as a process of the more profitable taking over the less profitable. The merger boom, though encouraged by government, was basically privately driven. British companies, in the context of growing international competition, increasingly saw merger as a way of combating that competition by strategies which the financial system very actively encouraged.

---

[4] Though some of the background discussion to the IRC did envisage something rather closer to the NEB than the IRC as it actually turned out (e.g. Posner and Pryke 1965).

TABLE 10.2. *Mergers in the 1960s*

	No. of firms disappearing by merger	Value of firms disappearing (£m.;1961 prices)	Mergers as % of total investment expenditure
1960	513[a]	324[a]	22[a]
1961	486	479	26
1962	479	322	20
1963	583	271	20
1964	700	378	24
1965	668	410	22
1966	572	409	21
1967	525	653	32
1968	631[a]	1020[a]	49[a]
1969	478[a]	443[a]	26[a]

[a] major break in series.
Source: Hannah (1983), app. 1.

The governmental enthusiasm for actively encouraging this process of merger may be questioned on a number of counts. First
the evidence does not suggest that, even at the beginning of the
1960s, the British economy was characterized by small firms by
comparison with other major European countries. The evidence
on plant size is more equivocal, but does suggest that the general
idea that British factories were normally well below the size of
those in Germany, France, or Italy was mistaken (Prais 1976).

The merger boom of the 1960s was a merger of companies,
with much less effect on plants. Prais (1976: 4, 51) makes clear
that the typical merger produced substantially larger firms, but
these new firms normally owned a large number of often small
plants. Taking just the 100 top manufacturing firms, whilst their
share of manufacturing output rose from 32 per cent in 1958 to
41 per cent by 1968, by 1972 the average plant owned by these
firms employed only 430 workers, compared with an average of
750 in 1958.

These figures suggest the extent to which the mergers of the
1960s were finance-driven, or defensive, rather than based on a
clear productive logic implied by standard notions of economies
of scale. The financial evidence suggests that many of these
mergers failed in productive terms, however much they have

boosted short-run stock market prices (Meeks 1977). This is backed up by evidence of the very limited extent to which the mergers of the 1960s involved significant rationalization and closure of plant (Newbould 1970).

Thus it may be argued that the 'big is beautiful' merger policy embodied in the IRC was both based on a mistaken analysis of the shape of British industry, and in so far as it was part of the merger boom, did not result in a substantial improvement in company performance. This point can be pushed too far. In some sectors there undoubtedly were potential economies of scale—but the problem was that they remained potential rather than realized. See, for example, the discussion of cars in Chapter 14. The role of the IRC should not be exaggerated—it was only involved in about 2 per cent of the mergers of the period. The Corporation was very sensitive to the need to ensure that the newly merged firms were properly managed, but one of its problems was that its limited financial role gave it little say in the post-merger firms (Hague and Wilkinson 1983: 131). The evidence would suggest that British management in general was much better at spotting a financial opportunity than it was at managing complex issues of rationalization and development of industrial activity in newly expanded firms.

A central theme in the encouragement of mergers, as already noted, was the idea that only new national champions could stand up to international competition, and hence help the balance of payments. This approach is clear in the support for British Leyland—with results discussed below (Ch. 14). The GEC/AEI merger is commonly seen as a much more successful venture, though as more sceptical work has suggested, the downside of GEC's good financial performance has been a rather modest success in manufacturing output; short-term profitability at the expense of long-run productive success (Thomas 1983).

ICL is also an interesting case. Here the rhetoric of national champion was strongest, and the role of government (both IRC, and, more importantly, MinTech), largest. ICL was formed from a merger of International Computers and Tabulators and the computer interests of English Electric, with MinTech initially owning 10.5 per cent of the shares. This was an area where economies of scale, especially in research, were available, and the attempt to maintain British presence in this fast-expanding area was a reasonable idea, especially given the relatively small public financial stake in the business. Whether ICL then followed an appropriate strategy is another matter (Campbell-Kelly 1989: chs. 12, 13).

This enthusiasm for mergers went along with new law on monopolies and mergers, under the 1965 Monopolies and Mergers Act. This Act largely followed proposed reforms suggested at the end of the previous Conservative government (Cmnd. 2299). Some of these followed experience of the workings of the 1956 Restrictive Practices Act, such as the amendment to make 'information agreements' (i.e. price-leadership arrangements) registerable with the Restrictive Practices Court (Allen 1968: ch. 9). Paradoxically perhaps, in the context of the discussion above, mergers and not just monopolies were potential targets of Monopolies Commission investigation. Encouraging some mergers and discouraging others is not necessarily incoherent (Mottershead 1978). But there was no clear policy developed in the 1960s, and the general trend was for only a few merger ideas to pass through the filter of the Board of Trade to the Commission for investigation, and in the few cases that did so, the investigation usually led to a favourable report. The Wilson Government was extremely concerned with the issue of competitiveness, but its attitude to competition was predominantly focused on the international aspect, and in this context mergers were largely seen as favouring rather than undermining competition.

STATE CAPACITY AND STATE ACHIEVEMENTS

The critique of stop–go at the beginning of the 1960s had in significant part involved a critique of the British state, above all in the area of economic policy, with its orientation towards external issues of sterling and overseas influence, rather than towards domestic industry. This involved a critical attitude to the Treasury, and the belief in the need for an alternative Ministry which would effectively represent the needs of industry.

Usually this story is developed in terms of the Department of Economic Affairs. It is pointed out how this body effectively lived and died with the National Plan. When the Plan was aborted by the deflations pursued to defend the pound the *raison d'être* of the Department also disappeared. This story is not wholly inaccurate. The DEA and the National Plan did represent a symbolic and, to a degree, substantive effort to break out of the old stop–go cycle. Many of the policies outlined in the National Plan, e.g. on the labour-market, were pursued, despite the restrictive macroeconomic context.

But what this story neglects is the emergence and development of MinTech as, effectively, a Ministry of Industry by the end of the 1960s. Founded in 1964, the Ministry initially took control of most of the DSIR's functions, had responsibility for NRDC and the Atomic Energy Authority, and acted as sponsoring Ministry for the computer, electronics, telecommunications, and machine-tool industries. In 1967 this was added to by the Ministry of Aviation and associated research establishments, and added to again two years later by the taking over of the Ministry of Power, and of responsibility for most of the remaining manufacturing industries. Finally, administration of investment grants and regional policy was taken over from the Board of Trade, and of the IRC from the now defunct DEA. By the end of the Wilson government MinTech was a 'super ministry', before that term came into common use in the early 1970s.

TABLE 10.3. *The balance of payments in the 1960s*

	Current account balance	Capital flows	Total currency flow (including balancing item)
1960	−255	+ 286	+ 325
1961	+ 6	− 316	− 339
1962	+122	− 3	+ 192
1963	+124	− 99	− 58
1964	−382	− 301	− 695
1965	− 49	− 326	− 353
1966	+ 84	− 578	− 591
1967	−313	− 600	− 671
1968	−280	−1007	−1410
1969	+449	− 109	+ 743
1970	+707	+ 459	+1420

Source: Tomlinson (1990*a*), p. 242.

For all its powers, MinTech did not establish the unambiguous primacy of industrial policy as traditional proponents of such a Ministry had hoped, hopes mainly embodied in the DEA, though arguably more appropriately in MinTech. The Treasury remained the dominant economic Ministry, and many of the traditional Treasury concerns—defence of the pound, the balance of payments, constraining public borrowing—were even more manifest in the 1960s than in the 1950s. Such an emphasis in macro-policy clearly aborted the National Plan, in the sense of a mechanism of indicative planning predicated upon a kind of virtuous circle, in which if everyone could be persuaded growth would accelerate, it would indeed do so. Even by the time the Plan was published in September 1965 it was recognized that 'The need to protect the balance of payments and the position of sterling in the intervening period will involve some slowing down in the rate of expansion in the next year or so' (Cmnd. 2764: 13). Doubts may, however, be entertained on whether even in the absence of such macroeconomic policies purely indicative planning would deliver as much growth as envisaged in the plan. Many authors are sceptical, and regard the deflationary policy as more as an alibi than the fundamental reason for the failure of planning (e.g. Hare 1985).

But this chapter has tried to indicate that whilst some features of the enhancement of state capacity under French planning were not followed in Britain, notably powerful government control over bank lending, in other ways state capacity in this period was both substantially reorganized and enhanced. If defeat for Labour had been avoided in 1970 and its policies continued it is possible that the flawed but often sensible initiatives of the late 1960s would have been continued and improved upon.

CONCLUSIONS

In macroeconomic terms the story of the Wilson Government might be told as one of quite good levels of achievement of standard British macroeconomic goals by the end of its period in office. By 1969 the effects of the 1967 devaluation and subsequent deflation were being felt, and the balance of payments moved strongly into surplus (Table 10.3). At the same time the public finances moved sharply into surplus, a negative Public Sector Borrowing Requirement being recorded in 1968/9 and 1969/70. But most commentaries have seen the price of these achievements as very high, above all in terms of slow growth. Rather than the 3.8 per cent rate of growth of GDP in the National Plan, the actual rate between 1964 and 1970 was 2.6 per cent, slower than the 2.9 per cent of 1950–64 (Cairncross 1992: 155). In these figures may be seen the effect not of an end to stop–go, but an almost continuous stop.

On the other hand, the productivity data show a rather more interesting picture. Labour productivity in manufacturing in Britain was on a clear upward trend in the 1960s, rising from 2.2 per cent p.a. in 1955–60 to 4.5 per cent p.a. by 1969–73. By the latter period it was almost equivalent to the average rate in the EC countries (4.63 per cent), a marked improvement in relative performance (Jones 1976). This is a quite striking performance given the macroeconomic difficulties of most of the 1960s. It is at least possible that this reflected in part some of Labour's industrial policies, which allowed at least a partial offset to the effects of deflation. Perhaps Wilson's 'white heat of technology' deserves rather less condescension than it is traditionally accorded? Equally, the oft-cited remark of Silberston (1981: 49) that industrial policy in this period was 'directed at helping old industries to survive rather than encouraging new products and new technology' seems to need, at least, substantial qualification.

Further Reading

Beckerman, W. (1974) (ed.), *The Labour Government's Economic Record*, London.

Blackaby, F.T. (1978) (ed.), *British Economic Policy 1960–74*, Cambridge: chs. 8–14.

Cmnd. 2764 (1965), *The National Plan*, PP 1965/6, vol. 13.

Hague, D., and Wilkinson, G. (1983), *The I.R.C.: An Experiment in Industrial Organisation*, London.

Young, S., and Lowe, S. V. (1978), *Intervention in the Mixed Economy: The Evolution of British Industrial Policy 1964–72*, London.

11

1970–1979: Stagflation and Surrender

INTRODUCTION

The adage that history is written by the victors applies very strongly to the economic history of the 1970s. In the immediate aftermath of the sharp reversal of economic policy after 1979 accounts appeared which tried to present events in the previous years as so dire as both requiring and justifying a radical new departure (e.g. Holmes 1985). Plainly, in terms of most policy objectives, the 1970s represented a clear deterioration compared with the experience of the previous twenty-five years. Inflation rose to its post-war peak of 25 per cent in 1975; unemployment grew sharply, especially in the period 1974–6, when it passed the one million mark; output growth slowed to under 1 per cent per annum, and the visible account of the balance of payments saw the worst post-war deficit in 1974. These were not years of high achievement.

But most accounts of the period go beyond a recital of deterioration in economic outcomes, and suggest that this failure can be traced back to major flaws in policy design and execution. Much attention has focused on macro-policy, notably on the U-turn under the Conservative Heath government in 1972, and the succeeding Labour government's corporatist policies, which gave a key role in economic management to an agreement with the trade unions. This latter aimed, from the Government side, at reducing inflation without massive increases in unemployment, by trading policy goals desired by the unions for an agreement on wage constraint.

These policies have found their defenders. The 'Barber boom' of 1972–3, whilst clearly based on an excessively rapid expansion of demand, did not demonstrate that Keynesian policies could never work, as later critics alleged (e.g. Joseph 1975). Rather, they showed that to try to expand demand rapidly, in a period of fast inflation of commodity prices and without due attention to the conditions of supply, is to court danger (Blackaby 1978). But even so, growth was at a rate of 5 per cent in the year to the middle of 1973.

Even more contentiously, the macro-policies of the 1974 Labour government have received a measured defence (Artis and Cobham 1991: ch. 16; Artis *et al.* 1992). They argue that the government did have a coherent strategy, albeit one of high risk, pursued in almost uniquely unfavourable circumstances. The government moved 'pragmatically to adapt policy to the new environment of higher inflation and slower growth. Given this achievement it seems fair to claim that the Labour governments left the economy and the policy-making machinery in better condition in 1979 than they found them in 1974' (Artis *et al.* 1992: 58).

Elements of these macroeconomic controversies will be touched on further below, but what is striking is the extent to which condemnation of industrial policy in this period remains almost universal whatever might be said about macroeconomic policy. Whilst Sawyer (1991*a*) can find mitigating factors, Artis *et al.* (1992: 54) summarize a common view: 'On industrial policy, by contrast, the judgement has to be harsher. More than other areas, industrial policy was the scene of the Labour Party's own civil war (equalled perhaps by the EEC referendum), resulting in vacillations between extremes in policy statements and an essentially sterile and unproductive policy period'.

This chapter is not concerned to defend industrial policy in the 1970s, but to offer a context for and discussion of that policy which will enable the reader to see why the very high hopes entertained for such policies in the early 1970s were so difficult to realize. Most of the discussion focuses on Labour's industrial policies, because whilst, as we shall see, the Conservatives between 1970 and 1974 made major changes in this area, these were largely by way of *ad hoc* adjustment to circumstance, whilst for Labour industrial policy was at the heart of their policy agenda when they were elected to government in 1974.

CONTEXT

Two contextual elements are particularly important to industrial policies in the 1970s. First, the deteriorating international and

macroeconomic environment in which such policies had to operate, and secondly the context of ideas from which these policies
developed.

Central to the external economic context of the 1970s is of
course the quadrupling of oil prices at the end of 1974 ('OPEC
I'). This was in fact the culmination of a trend apparent from at
least 1972, whereby the parallel booms in the advanced industrial
countries drove up demand for primary commodities and therefore their prices. This deterioration in the terms of trade became
insupportable after OPEC I, which imposed both a sharp upward
lurch on the overall price level, because of the inelasticity of
demand and generality of use of oil, and a pressure for deflation
to finance the new more expensive oil imports.

Initially, there was a widely held hope that the deflationary
impact of OPEC I could be at least mitigated by national
governments maintaining domestic demand, and financing the
impact of oil by 'recycling' OPEC oil receipts into capital
inflows. This approach was aborted very quickly in most countries because of the inflationary pressures of the period, which
drove all OECD countries to their highest inflation levels since
at least the 1940s. Britain tried to stick with this approach longer
than most, but plainly such a policy requires international
agreement and this was not forthcoming, despite support from
international bodies like the IMF (Britton 1991). British policy
became more restrictionist, culminating in a combination of high
inflation and high unemployment—stagflation, though the rise in
both was arrested after 1975 (Table 11.1).

Deflationary policies did eventually improve the balance of
payments, the current account deficit peaking in 1974 and
realizing a substantial surplus in 1978. But the cost was felt not
only in unemployment but also in growth, which was negative in
1974/5, recovered thereafter, but peak to peak (1974 to 1979) was
significantly below previous levels. Productivity showed a similar
cyclical pattern, falling in 1973–5 and then showing a healthy
recovery in the upswing (Table 11.1).

These macroeconomic figures show quite clearly that the worst
period of the 1970s was 1974/5, which may be seen as the delayed
and painful adjustment to OPEC I. But probably the single
best-remembered macroeconomic event of the 1970s is the sterling crisis of 1976, the visit to negotiate a loan to the British

TABLE 11.1. *Main economic indicators 1970–79*

	Inflation (% change in RPI)	Unemployment (000s)	Balance of payments current account (£m.)	Growth (% GDP)	Index of manufacturing productivity (1975 = 100)
1970	6.5	532	+ 821	+1.99	88.6
1971	9.2	746	+1114	+1.58	90.6
1972	7.5	668	+ 203	+2.74	95.9
1973	9.1	445	− 996	+7.69	104.2
1974	15.9	554	−3186	−1.62	102.7
1975	24.0	978	−1526	−0.84	100.0
1976	16.7	1116	− 963	+2.74	105.3
1977	15.9	1199	− 175	+2.56	107.0
1978	8.2	1110	+ 936	+3.04	108.1
1978	13.4	1052	− 550	+2.69	109.8

Source: Artis and Cobham (1991), app. B.

Government by the IMF, and the toughening of policy which seemed to follow from this. Thus there appears to be a disparity between economic indicators, showing an improvement after 1975, and the crisis of 1976.

As Artis and Cobham (1991) argue, the whole 1976 IMF crisis appears in retrospect difficult to explain, given that the fundamentals of the economy seem to have been improving, albeit from a low level of performance. This is even true if one looks at what the IMF focused so much attention on, public expenditure and the fiscal balance. Although not publicly clear in the summer of 1976, it was already the case that the government had cut public expenditure and public borrowing significantly. Public expenditure reached a peak of 45.4 per cent of GDP in 1975/6 and fell sharply thereafter, by 2.4 and 6.9 per cent respectively over the next two fiscal years. Similarly, the nominal PSBR peaked at the same time, at 9.6 per cent of GDP, falling to 6.6 and then 3.8 per cent in the next two fiscal years (Tomlinson 1990*a*: 285–8). Given this background, much of the Cabinet argument over what expenditure cuts should be agreed with the IMF was based on a mistaken premiss about Britain's public finances (Cairncross and Burk 1992).

But the crisis was real enough in the sense of flowing from the collapse of sterling, with its nominal value against the dollar falling from over \$2 to 1.55. The causes of this fall seem to have been an initial desire by the authorities to see the rate fall to reflect Britain's recent inflation, this policy exacerbating a general shortage of confidence in Britain's economic policy stance, which, whilst having changed significantly in 1975, was still beset by disagreement and uncertainty (Artis and Cobham 1991: 31–4).

More broadly the sterling crisis of 1976 illustrated how, once floated in 1972, the exchange rate could be extremely unstable, constraining governments to pursue policies congenial to the foreign exchange markets or suffer very serious pressures. In the long view this might be seen as one of the major changes in the economic environment of the period, with national governments, especially of weak economies like that of the United Kingdom, finding the scope for national economic management narrowing significantly. This would be especially so if financial markets found the government's objectives politically uncongenial, as was certainly the case in the mid-1970s.

These serious macroeconomic difficulties of the 1970s came, of course, at the end of a long period of relative economic decline. This trend deterioration in relative performance exacerbated the impact of OPEC I on the British economy. Almost all economies performed less well in the 1970s than the 1960s, but in Britain, starting from a low level of performance, the deterioration was felt that much harder. This long period of decline was also the background to the other major contextual element of the period for industrial policy—the particular analysis of that decline offered by those who came to dominate Labour's official policy-making machinery.

Labour's post-mortem into the 1964–70 government and its defeat in 1970 can be divided schematically into two strands of conclusions, only the second of which bore directly on issues of Britain's decline and industrial policy to respond to that decline. The first conclusion, and the one adopted by most of the Labour leadership, was that the problem of 1964–70 and the defeat of 1970 were fundamentally to do with the relationship between unions and government. The statutory incomes policy and the later attempt to reform industrial relations with *In Place of Strife* were regarded as having undermined this relationship, and so undermined a major part of Labour's claim to government. The prime task in opposition after 1970 was, in this view, to establish union–party links on a firmer basis. This led to intensive discussions in the early 1970s, and though the Party leadership failed to secure union support for an incomes policy, these negotiations laid the foundations of what became after 1974 the Social Contract (Hatfield 1978: ch. 5; Brown 1991).

This corporatist strategy was profoundly important for the overall thrust of Labour's policy after 1974, and the Party–union deal included, amongst other things, the Party agreeing to pursue a highly interventionist industrial policy. But the roots of the industrial policy which was to become official policy in 1973/4 lay in rather different conclusions being drawn from the failure of the 1964–70 government's policies than those which underlay the Social Contract.

A major starting-point for this second strand of Labour thinking were changes in industrial structure. It became widely recognized in the late 1960s and early 1970s that, largely driven by the merger boom, British industry had become highly concentrated.

The most popular way of measuring this was by the share of the top 100 manufacturing firms in total manufacturing output, which rose from around 22 per cent in 1948 to 33 per cent by 1958, and 40 per cent by 1970 (Hannah 1983: 180). Many of the Left projected this increase into the future and saw the figure rising to two-thirds by 1980 (e.g. Labour 1973a: 13). This growth in concentration was seen as fundamentally undermining the capacity of government to control the private sector, and therefore to achieve its policy goals without a major extension of public ownership and public regulation. In this view the attempt by the 1964 government to plan the economy had been undermined by this shift in power:

The experience of the last 10 years has shown very clearly that economic planning in the national interest has been continually frustrated by the inability to exercise effective control over those vital economic processes which determine our national well-being. In particular, the level of investment in industry has shown itself to be highly resistant to incentives, exhortations and the limited measures of control over private industry which are at the disposal of governments (Labour 1973b: 10).

The proposals relied on the belief that investment was the key to Britain's relative decline, and that the private sector could not be relied on to undertake the necessary level of investment. It logically flowed from this that public ownership needed to be expanded into the major firms in the manufacturing sector, to give a decisive role for the state in the strategies pursued in that sector.

Whilst commonly identified with the Left of the Labour Party, such a strategy in some ways drew on the long-standing revisionist critique of existing forms of nationalization and proposals for competitive public enterprise, which dated back to the 1940s (Ch. 8). Another element in the policy's genesis was the Italian Instituto Recostruziane Italiano, a state-holding company dating from the 1930s, but which post-war had played a major role in the industrial development of the Italian South.

A central figure in drawing these various strands of thought together was the economist Stuart Holland, whose arguments are most fully developed in his *The Socialist Challenge* (1975). This centred on the argument that in modern industrial economies the key actors were no longer national governments (macro-actors) or competitive firms (micro-actors) but 'meso-economic' firms which in large measure escaped both government control and the pressures of competition. The basic socialist challenge was to subject these firms to effective public policy measures.

These arguments captured the Labour Party's official policy-making machinery, and received conference backing in 1973, though the leadership was always sceptical (Hatfield 1978). *Labour's Programme 1973* (Labour Party 1973a), which embodied most of these ideas, saw three key policy implications. The first was the creation of a state holding company, designated the National Enterprise Board, with a major and continuing equity stake in large manufacturing companies. The second would be a system of planning agreements whereby large companies would exchange information and strategies with government in return for public money. Third would be a new Industry Act which would give the government wide-ranging and discretionary powers to intervene in the public sector.

The major political flashpoints in this policy menu were the NEB's role in taking over a significant number of major profitable manufacturing companies and the idea of compulsory planning agreements. In the event the Labour leadership was able to water the proposals down to exclude these two elements, after a long battle which focused on the role of Tony Benn, who became Industry Minister in 1974, but was switched to Energy Minister after the EEC referendum in the summer of 1975.[1]

The link between industrial policy and the EEC debate was seen by Benn and his allies as straightforward. For them the EEC's founding Treaty of Rome embodied a commitment to the market economy which was wholly incompatible with the interventionism of the industrial strategy. Hence the anti-EEC posture was closely interwoven with the industrial policy, and proponents of that policy rejected the view that the renegotiations over Britain's terms of EEC membership had secured Britain's right to pursue that policy, as the official White Paper argued (Cmnd. 6003: paras. 54–67). The decision of the electorate to stay in the EEC was thus turned into a defeat for

---

[1] This battle, as seen from Benn's viewpoint, is told in great detail in his diaries (Benn 1989).

proposals of the radical industrial strategy.[2] Nevertheless though in a modified form, the NEB was created, and its role will be looked at in some detail in appropriate sections below.[3]

MARKETS

Whilst the broad tendency to higher industrial concentration was undisputed in this period its implications were much more contentious. Above all, its implications for market dominance by large companies was contested, especially given the growing competition from imports. For example, an official report calculated that looking at individual product groups in 1972, the five-firm concentration ratio (i.e. the share of the top five firms in total output) was greater than half in 47 per cent of such groups if imports were ignored, but fell to 37 per cent if imports were included (Cmnd. 7198: para. 3.9). However, this calculation raises the problem of how far imports were within multinational companies, and therefore could not be unambiguously regarded as an index of a competitive environment for domestic producers (Cowling and Sugden 1987: ch. 6).

TABLE 11.2. *Import penetration in manufactures in the 1970s* (Imports as % of home demand)

1970	15
1971	16
1972	18
1973	21
1974	22
1975	22
1976	24
1977	26
1978	28
1979	29

Source: Williams *et al.* (1983), p. 118.

[2] This postulated link between EEC membership and industrial strategy was odd given that proponents of the NEB drew on the experience of other member states, notably Italy, to argue for such policies.
[3] Planning agreements deserve no more than a footnote. Only two were ever negotiated, one with Chrysler, with no perceptible effects on the company's behaviour, and one with the National Coal Board, which just restated policies already agreed.

The precise implications of import penetration for the level of market power may be disputed, but the growth of import penetration is undisputable (Table 11.2). This was an acceleration of trends apparent in the 1960s. Part of this acceleration was due to a further instalment of tariff reductions, the final results of the Kennedy Round of GATT reductions coming in 1972. Also the long-run upward shift in the propensity to purchase imported manufactures was exacerbated by the 'Barber boom', with the demand expansion unmatched by domestic output growth (Morgan 1978: 558–63).

Most controversial are the effects of EEC membership on Britain's level of import penetration (and balance of payments). This issue is complicated by the long-run shift in Britain's trade away from the Commonwealth towards European markets and sources of supply which dates back to the 1950s (Table 11.3). This in turn was linked to the changing composition of British imports, with foodstuffs and raw materials being displaced in importance by semi- and finished manufactures (Table 11.4). Entry into the EEC therefore intensified existing trends rather than creating a new pattern for British trade.

TABLE 11.3. *Sources and destinations of British trade 1955–79* (%)

	Imports				Exports			
	1955	1965	1975	1979	1955	1965	1975	1979
EEC 9	12.6	23.6	36.3	43.1	15.0	26.3	32.2	41.8
Developed countries	59.4	67.4	72.2	78.7	61.4	71.4	70.3	75.3

Source: Prest and Coppock (1980), p. 129.

TABLE 11.4. *Composition of British trade 1955–79* (%)

	1955	1965	1975	1979
Food, drink, and tobacco	36.2	29.7	17.7	13.4
Fuel	10.4	10.6	17.7	11.9
Materials and semi-manufactures	47.9	43.0	34.1	36.8
Finished manufactures	5.2	15.3	28.3	36.2

Source: Prest and Coppock (1980), p. 130.-

Some analysts suggested a very serious deterioration of Britain's balance of payments resulting from EEC membership, with its ending of tariffs on imported EEC manufactures—especially those from Germany. Fetherstone *et al.* (1979) suggested that the balance of payments constraint thus imposed on Britain by EEC membership led to National Income 15 per cent below its potential in 1977/8, though they accept this is an upper-band estimate. The difficulty is that their own graphs show clearly a sharp turning-point in EEC imports into Britain in 1970/1, before Britain's membership, and they do not satisfactorily disentangle the seeming 'ratchet' effect of the 1970–3 demand expansion on Britain's imports from the impact of EEC membership.

Whatever the precise causes, British industry in the 1970s faced import competition on an unprecedented scale. Coupled to the deterioration in the balance of payments and the rise in unemployment, there were, perhaps unsurprisingly, strong calls for protectionism, which became a live political issue for the first time since the 1940s.

The most systematic case for protection came from the Cambridge Economic Policy Group. They argued that Britain's slow growth and unemployment was the consequence of a vicious circle of uncompetitive industry leading to balance of payments difficulties and hence slower growth of demand, lower levels of investment, and the reinforcement of uncompetitiveness. The way to break out of this, they argued, was a general control of manufactured imports which would ease the balance of payments constraint, encourage higher investment, and allow a break-out of the vicious circle.

The Cambridge Group were extremely sensitive to the economists' standard arguments against such protectionism. First of all they accepted that in many ways devaluation would have the same economic effects as import controls, but argued that devaluation would not work in Britain because of 'real wage resistance'—workers would not allow their wages to be eroded by higher import prices consequent on devaluation. If the revenues from import controls (e.g. from auctioning quota rights) were used to cut taxes, the higher import prices from such controls would not translate into a fall in real wages.

Secondly, sensitive to the problem of retaliation, they argued that Britain's absolute level of imports would not be reduced because the aim was to allow faster growth in Britain, so that a lower import ratio would be compatible with maintaining total imports. Finally, sensitive to the potential political pressures and distortions to economic policy which commonly arise from piecemeal protectionism, the Cambridge Group emphasized they were proposing general controls on manufactured imports, not the privileging of particular industrial sectors.

The CEPG made a powerful economic case, though one which can be challenged, especially on how far their policy, like devaluation, required a fall in real wages to be effective (Hare 1980). But the defeat of the CEPG view was more on political grounds than through weaknesses in economic argument. The argument crystallized at the time of the IMF visit in 1976, when proponents of the radical industrial strategy, led by Benn, also embraced the Alternative Economic Strategy and import controls. (Other Cabinet members, such as Crosland, suggested using the threat of protectionism as a bargaining-counter with the IMF—Artis and Cobham 1991: 13). But the policy never looked like gaining a Cabinet majority.

One reason was the quite contingent association of protectionism with the Left, which probably undermined any chance of substantial business support for the policy. Also, this was a time when most business and mainstream opinion had become strongly attached to EEC membership, with which protectionism was clearly incompatible. Finally and more generally, free consumer access to imported finished manufactures had become an implicit political datum, whatever the balance of economic advantage for the national economy.

All this meant that in the 1970s Britain moved quite close to free trade in manufactured goods, which meant that industrial policy had to be pursued in a highly competitive environment. Government policy was not used to trying to secure markets for British manufacturers in general.[4]

PROFITS

A key slogan of Labour in 1974 was that its policies were aimed to secure 'an irreversible shift in the balance of power of wealth

[4] This notably did not apply to imports from Japan, subject to voluntary export restraints, nor textile goods covered by the Multi-Fibre Agreement.

towards working people and their families'. The industrial policy proposals involved shifting power by the NEB and planning agreements and shifting wealth by reducing the role of profit as a source of income as well as a guide to investment decisions. In this view 'the only acceptable role for profits at present is that they provide a large part of the finance needed for investment' (Labour 1973*a*: 23–4).

But this role for profits was a problem for Labour in two respects. First, it assumed profits would be sufficient to finance most of the desired increase in the level of investment without undermining the agreements, such as they were, on the growth of wages. Secondly, the implicit assumption on profits was that their level would not be subject to strong downward pressure.

TABLE 11.5. *Profitability in the 1970s* (%)

	Pre-tax profits on historic cost base	Pre-tax profits, historic cost, net of stock appreciation	Pre-tax real	Post-tax real
1970	14.4	12.2	8.6	5.2
1971	15.1	13.1	8.8	6.1
1972	16.8	14.5	9.3	6.5
1973	19.8	15.3	9.1	8.1
1974	18.7	10.7	5.2	6.0
1975	18.5	12.1	5.3	3.9
1976	20.1	13.1	5.4	5.4
1977	19.4	15.0	6.2	6.8
1978	19.0	15.6	6.2	6.3
1979	18.5	12.4	4.3	6.1

Source: Bank of England (1981), p. 228.

The first problem raised the old issue about retained and distributed profits—investment finance obviously relying on the level of the former, discussion of the Social Contract on the level of the latter. To encourage the retention of profits the government did impose very high taxes on distributed profits via taxes on unearned income and the Capital Gains Tax. Nevertheless, the rise in profits after the slump 1973/4 (Table 11.5) did not help to secure union support for the later stages of the Social Contract. Profits were also crucial to the operations of the price controls, another important feature of the Social Contract. The aim here was to secure political support for wage restraint by taking a tough line on price increases. To this end the Price Commission was continued. The Price Code which the Commission operated explicitly accepted the need for prices to be sufficient to finance investment, and the Code was eased as the problem of the profit squeeze became apparent. Because of this pressure to ease the profits situation, the impact of the Price Commission on prices was probably small, though it may have favourably affected inflationary expectations (Sawyer 1991*b*). After 1977 the Commission was more important as a kind of state auditor and management consultancy than as an effective controller of prices (Tomlinson 1983).

More important in this period than the distributed/undistributed aspect was the overall volume of profits. The figures in Table 11.5 show differing estimates of that volume. Broadly speaking two forces were at work in determining the pattern. Most importantly, the sharp cycle in output 1973–5, had, as usual, a disproportionate impact on profits, almost halving pre-tax real rates of return between 1973 and 1974. This typical cyclical movement was probably exacerbated by the accompanying combination of strong cost pressure from both wages and materials. The picture was also affected by stock appreciation. The rapid inflation raised the values of stocks and hence nominal profits, obscuring the fact that this was a purely nominal shift. As the difference between columns 1 and 2 in Table 11.5 makes clear, adjustment for this factor makes a substantial difference to declared profits. As columns 3 and 4 suggest, the government reacted strongly to the decline in pre-tax profits by easing the tax burden on companies substantially, so that overall the company sector ceased to contribute to tax revenues in the late 1970s. This process began as early as November 1974, when in the Budget of that month tax relief was given on the nominal gains of stock appreciation.

Ormerod (1991) sees the honouring of the Heath Government's threshold agreements on wages as crucial in squeezing profits in 1974, and in turn sees this squeeze as a major contribution to the low level of investment and consequent unemployment of the later 1970s. As he accepts, a close link between profits and investment is difficult to establish, but it is not easy to reject the view that the profit squeeze, however caused, contributed to the low level of investment of the period (Table 11.6). And this is especially important when, as already suggested, the whole of the radical industrial strategy was predicated on reversing the low level of investment as the major cause of Britain's poor industrial performance.

TABLE 11.6. *Fixed investment in manufacturing industry in the 1970s* (£m. at 1975 prices)

1970	4,177
1971	3,898
1972	3,370
1973	3,440
1974	3,782
1975	3,522
1976	3,326
1977	3,476
1978	3,769
1979	3,969

Source: *Economic Trends, Annual Supplement* (1983).

THE EFFICIENCY OF LABOUR

After the 1970 general election the Conservatives pursued the policy abandoned by Labour in 1969 of legal reform of industrial relations. The 1971 Industrial Relations Act aimed to move away from the voluntarist system by imposing a system of registration and a range of legal restraints on unions in pursuit of their aims. The core of the Act was successfully turned into a dead-letter by the trade unions, with an effective policy of non-registration. Other parts of the Act proved ill-fitted to deal with disputes that arose, and the emphasis on legal remedies to industrial-relations issues was commonly regarded, even by those unsympathetic to the unions, as having been mistaken (R. Elliott 1978: 580–95).

Part of the Social Contract between the Labour Government and the TUC was the repeal of the Industrial Relations Act and the strengthening of trade-union rights within a still essentially voluntarist framework. This was perhaps the only part of the Social Contract to have been unambiguously carried out, and in legal as well as political terms the 1970s was the peak period for union strength.

One of the most interesting might-have-beens of the 1970s was the attempt to change Labour's whole relation to the company sector by a system of union participation on company boards of directors. This was proposed in the Bullock Committee in 1976 (Cmnd. 6706), which in turn flowed from the vague commitments of the Social Contract to extend industrial democracy. Bullock proposed that in each company with over 2000 employees the Board be established on a '$2x + y$' basis, the xs representing shareholders and trade union, the y an independent element. The arguments made in support of this arrangement were not entirely consistent. At one point the emphasis is on industrial democracy as the next stage in the long progress of democracy broadening down 'from precedent to precedent', but this is difficult to reconcile with the key emphasis on a 'single channel' of representation via trade-union selection of worker directors, rather than universal suffrage. Equally the Bullock majority saw its proposals as creating a 'new legitimacy' for management, an approach which suggested British management's legitimacy needed to be reinforced rather than challenged.

Whatever the intellectual merits of the Bullock proposals, they never came close to realization for two major political reasons. On the one hand, whilst gaining TUC support, it is clear that the Bullock proposals were anathema to many trade unionists, who believed any such responsibility for company management to be incompatible with the adversarial, free collective-bargaining system. This opposition was to be found on both the Left and Right of the union movement. Even more important the Government, eager to conciliate the private sector, was resistant to any such proposals so vehemently disliked by the employers (J. Elliott 1978).

In some ways parallel to the debate on industrial democracy was the support by Benn whilst Industry Secretary for three worker co-operatives—Kirby Machinery and Engineering, the Scottish Daily News, and the Meriden motor-cycle firm. Each of these was a 'lame duck', driven to attempt the transition to a co-operative more by the lack of an alternative than by widespread positive conviction. Government support for these ventures, which all failed eventually, was highly controversial, though in public-expenditure terms the amounts involved were trivial.

The failure of the Bullock proposals and the very limited support for the idea of co-operatives suggest how limited the rhetoric of industrial democracy was as a component of the Social Contract. That Contract was seen by most people in both unions and government as something necessitated by crisis, but on the assumption that normal practices would be restored as soon as possible. In that context attempts to use the cry of democratization as an opening to a fundamental reform of social relations at the factory level were bound to prove abortive.

As Brown (1991) has persuasively argued, the unions in the 1970s were being asked to play a political role which was beyond their capacities. They could not deliver on centrally struck deals, and so exposed themselves to tensions which were then thoroughly exploited by the succeeding Conservative government. Equally the Labour government vested too much influence in an ill-prepared union movement by making wage restraint so central to its strategy, an approach which brought nemesis even faster.

On the question of the quality of labour supply the whole context of discussion of this shifted in the 1970s with the rise in unemployment. In the 1960s, as noted in Chapter 10, there was much talk of manpower planning and measures to increase the mobility of labour in the context of tight labour-markets. But the rise in unemployment tipped the emphasis of policy towards employment provision rather than training as central to manpower policy.

In 1972 the Conservative government proposed to phase out the levy/grant system under the Industrial Training Boards, and to offer a broader set of courses less geared to manual skills under a civil service National Training Agency. However such policies were resisted by the TUC, who wanted the continuation of levy grants and more emphasis on employment opportunities. To try to gain support for its incomes policy the Conservatives made some concessions to the TUC, agreeing to a slimming-down rather than gradual abolition of levy/grants and the creation of a tripartite Manpower Services Commission with some limited powers to create jobs. The MSC came into being at the beginning of 1974 (R. Elliott 1978: 607–11).

The MSC secured a substantial degree of bi-partisan political support, and became the key agency in labour-market policy under the Labour government. The major initiatives under the aegis of the MSC related to employment creation or 'special employment measures', of which the most important was the Temporary Employment Subsidy, which over the period 1975 to 1979 supported over half a million jobs, though the net effects would be significantly smaller (Bowen 1991: 194–8).

On the training front the most important initiative was the Training Opportunities Scheme (TOPS), begun in 1972 and expanded to almost 100,000 completions in 1977. The state also increased its financial support for ITB's, that support rising from one-twentieth of ITB income in 1974/5 to one-third in 1977/8. Effectively the state was filling the gap as private-sector training contracted in the face of the squeeze on company profits and the slack labour-markets.

Another initiative from the MSC was the Youth Opportunities Programme (YOPS) begun in 1978 to offer work experience to 16–18-year-olds. This expanded rapidly to 216,400 starts in 1979/80, though the quality of experience offered was often poor, partly because supervision of the scheme was inadequate. There were also union worries about big 'displacement' effects, whereby young workers on YOPS replaced other older, more expensive workers (Ryan 1989).

As Bowen (1991: 205) notes, under the Labour government schemes for employment creation tended to crowd out the ambitious aims for the expansion of training put forward in 1974. Change in the broader educational system was also limited. Much energy went into the completion of the trend towards comprehensive schools, while overall rates of participation in further and higher education hardly changed, that of 16–19-year-olds overall actually fell, and the proportion of school leavers with no qualifications fell very slightly to 48 per cent in 1978/9. In 1976 Jim Callaghan began a 'Great Debate' on education, but this had borne almost no fruit before the government fell in 1979 (Bowen 1991: 204).

THE EFFICIENCY OF CAPITAL

In some ways the issue of the provision of capital to industry was central to industrial policy in the later 1970s. As already suggested, the policy under Labour was predicated on the belief that higher investment was the key to Britain's industrial renewal. The assumption usually made was that this higher investment would continue to come largely from ploughed-back profits, and this ran into difficulties when these profits sagged heavily after 1973.

But alongside this went a revival of discussion of nationalization of the banking system, along with other parts of the financial system (Pollard 1978: 181–4). The aims of such policies were numerous, but included the idea that this would enable more savings to be channelled into industry to supplement ploughed-back profits (Labour Party 1975: 8–10). But all this talk produced no new policy initiatives, partly because the leadership of the Labour Party was always extremely sensitive to the idea that any such proposal would be presented by political opponents as the 'nationalization of savings'. The only result was a Committee on Financial Institutions chaired by Harold Wilson, which in 1980 produced a largely anodyne majority report, with most of its criticisms of the financial system limited to the traditional area of provision of funds to the small-firm sector (Wilson 1980).

Labour's major impact on finance for industry lay elsewhere than nationalization or even reform of the financial system. An important role was played by the NEB: whilst the centrepiece of the NEB proposal was always the taking over of a significant number of large manufacturing companies, its important roles actually lay in two other areas. First, the NEB became the home of large lame ducks like Rolls Royce (nationalized under the Conservatives) and British Leyland (nationalized in 1975). Both of these became recipients of substantial funds, indeed the majority of NEB funds went into such companies. Sawyer (1991*a*: 160) calculates that together they accounted for £664m. of the £777m. received by the NEB to the end of March 1979. Other lame ducks were also acquired with varying degrees of success—Alfred Herbert, the machine-tool company, which could not ultimately be saved from bankruptcy, and Ferranti, which was successfully turned around whilst in NEB hands and sold back to the private sector at a profit.

Much smaller sums went into what may be called the 'venture capital' aspect of the NEB's activities. This had been mooted in early discussions of the NEB (Labour Party 1973*b*: ch. 2), though not regarded by many of its proponents as central to its activities. Kramer (1988) has stressed how this role became increasingly important to the NEB. This role meant acquiring stakes in high-tech, small companies, but without getting much involved in their management. He argues that in this role the NEB was quite successful. There were losers as well as winners, but this is to be expected in the high-tech, venture-capital area. Overall he suggests, judging by orthodox criteria of rate of return, the NEB did as well as venture capital organizations in the United States. This conclusion is borne out, albeit in more guarded fashion, by a report from the National Audit Office (1987).

A final area where the government had a significant impact on investment decisions was in the nationalized industries. The very special case of BL and cars is returned to in Chapter 14, but as a general point it is notable how in industries such as coal and steel as well as cars the government underwrote extremely expensive and ambitious investment projects. With the benefits of hindsight we may see these decisions as the last burst of giantism in policies for industry—the belief that large-scale and capital-intensive projects are the way to competitive success (Williams *et al.* 1986). In each of these cases the government was sold a dodgy prospectus, was sucked into writing off huge debts, and left a legacy of financial problems for the industries which provided a major excuse, reason, and occasion for the drive to privatization under the Thatcher government (Ch. 8).

THE EFFICIENCY OF TECHNICAL CHANGE

The encouragement of technical change did not have the central role in either Labour's rhetoric or practice of the 1970s that it had had in the 1960s. The Conservative government in 1970 had committed itself to a lower level of intervention, and used the newly established 'Think-Tank' (Central Policy Review Staff) to investigate the whole issue of government support for R & D. Its Rothschild Report (Cmnd. 4814) argued for a clear contractor–customer relationship in the area of applied research 'applied R & D, that is R & D with a practical application as its objective, must be done on a customer–contractor basis. The customer says what he wants; the contractor does it (if he can); and the customer pays' (para. 6). Whilst this fitted with the government's business ethic, it did not solve the issue of the government's role in fundamental research where the concept of the customer was very difficult to apply.

1972 saw a significant U-turn in Conservative industrial policies with the passing of the Industry Act. This ended the idea of substantial government disengagement from industry in technology and other areas, and for the rest of their period in office the Conservatives showed a willingness to put money into high-tech areas like computers and machine tools and Concorde not significantly different from its predecessor (Mottershead 1978: 447–9).

After 1974 there is no evidence of a major shift in R & D policy. In aggregate most government R & D support still went into areas of dubious commercial value like aerospace, nuclear power and weapons, and military electronics. There was no reordering of priorities parallel to that of the 1960s. On the other hand, as noted in the previous section, there was more government-based support for small high-tech companies via the NEB. This produced mixed results, but in some cases gave Britain a stake in sectors otherwise likely to have gone by default, such as INMOS in silicon-chip production.

THE EFFICIENCY OF COMPANY STRUCTURE AND ORGANIZATION

As already noted, the centrepiece of Labour's industrial policy and what underlay the call for a highly interventionist NEB and planning agreements system, was the idea of a long-term and ineluctable trend towards greater industrial concentration. This was not usually or primarily seen as undesirable in traditional microeconomic terms, i.e. as bringing excessive monopoly power, but as undesirable because it brought a shift in power to large companies whose priorities were at variance with those of national governments like that of the UK.

The broad posture raised a number of issues about industrial organization and government policies to change it. First, the question of the attitude to mergers. As we have seen in the previous chapter, a key part of the 1960s Labour government's policies was the encouragement of mergers through the Industrial Reorganization Corporation (IRC). In the debates of the early 1970s much more scepticism was evinced about the benefits of such mergers (e.g. Labour Party 1973*a*: 19–20). This was in line with the trend of empirical economic debate, which increasingly questioned the production and profitability benefits accruing from merger activity (e.g. Newbould 1970; Kuehn 1975; Meeks 1977). However in Labour circles this did not lead to a strong emphasis on controls of mergers and competition policy. Whilst the 1973 *Programme* (20) suggested the desirability of a new law on monopolies and mergers, this was never central to Labour's approach. No new legislation on monopolies and mergers was forthcoming, though there was a review of policy in this area in 1978 (Cmnd. 7198).[5] This accepted the academic evidence that 'the results of many mergers have been disappointing' (para. 1.4).[6] It recommended in the face of such evidence that policy should shift from a benign to a more neutral attitude to mergers (para. 1.10).

The report also looked more generally at the issue of the effects of increased industrial concentration. In particular, it drew on the important work of Prais (1976) to note how the trend towards higher industrial concentration at enterprise level was not linked to growth in concentration at plant level, where Prais's work suggested concentration had been much more stable over a long period. The implication of this argument was that increasing industrial concentration was not significantly based on the realization of economies of scale at plant level where their existence might seem most obvious. Prais himself, partly for this reason, was sceptical of the benefits of higher industrial concentration, though the Monopolies and Mergers Review was more neutral.

This debate about the benefits of concentration (largely caused by merger) tended to proceed on the assumption that the trend to such concentration was proceeding apace. But retrospective evidence shows that the process was already tailing off in the early to mid-1970s. Calculations in Hannah (1983: 152–3, 180)

---

[5] The Conservatives had passed the Fair Trading Act in 1973, reforming monopolies and mergers law and establishing the Office of Fair Trading, but this did not signify an important immediate change in the direction of policy, though it presaged the shift to more emphasis on anti-competitive practices in assessing mergers, which came to the fore in the 1980s (Sawyer 1985: 296–7).
[6] Annex D of the Report is devoted to a discussion of the effects of mergers.

suggest that the share of the top 100 manufacturing firms peaked at 42 per cent in the mid-1970s before falling back slightly in the late 1970s. This change in trend was closely linked to the end of the merger boom which, having peaked in 1968, continued strongly into the early 1970s but then fell away very sharply with only a minor revival at the end of the decade. Measured by the value of firms disappearing by merger, the peak of 1968 was £1,666m., with a lower peak of £1,292m. in 1972, but then falling to only £168m. in 1975 (in current prices; Hannah 1983: 177). These figures are for manufacturing only, and ignore the boom in service-sector mergers which also seems to have arisen in the late 1960s.

Thus the idea of an ineluctable movement towards increased concentration was being reversed at the time when the policy predicated upon it was being so hotly disputed. However this reversal of trend was not apparent at the time; opponents of the radical industrial policy seem to have largely shared its proponents' views about what was happening to the industrial structure, the argument was about the appropriate governmental response. In any event the reversal of trend did not of itself contradict the view that Britain by the early 1970s had got an unusually concentrated and therefore, other things equal, very powerful corporate sector.

One other feature of the industrial structure was the cause of debate in the 1970s. One of the last acts of Anthony Crosland as a Minister in the 1964–70 government had been to set up an inquiry into small firms, which was published as the Bolton Report in 1972 (Cmnd. 4811). This outlined the decline of the small-firm sector in manufacturing, with firms in this sector with less than 200 employees falling from 44 per cent of employment in 1924 to 29 per cent by 1968, and stressed how this put Britain out of line with major competitor countries in the small size of this sector (Chs. 5, 6). It also pointed out that, adjusted for differences in labour intensity, the efficiency of small firms was not demonstrably inferior to those of large firms. In the early 1970s there was some revival of the small-firm sector (Stanworth and Gray 1991: ch. 1), but this was only slowly recognized (e.g. Cmnd. 7198: para. 3.3), and the attitude of government at the time of Bolton was largely one of indifference. The Bolton Committee had come out strongly against any discrimination in favour of small firms, but called for the end of 'unintended discrimination' and the creation of a section of the Department of Trade and Industry with special responsibility for small firms (Cmnd. 4811: ch. 19).

Most Labour thinking remained hostile to small firms, rightly noting that many of them were the sites of poor pay and bad conditions. However this attitude led to a rather crude reinforcement of 'big is beautiful' attitudes, which were not only problematic in efficiency terms, but also matched rather poorly with attitudes to industrial democracy, where smallness could arguably be an important element in generating effective democratic structures (Tomlinson 1980).

Very crudely summarized, Labour's industrial policies in the 1960s may be said to have had a clear rationale, being dominated by a belief that firms should be bigger, to realize economies of scale, and more oriented to technological change. In the 1970s there was much less clarity in Labour ideology about how firms should change in order to increase their efficiency. It was still assumed that they should invest more (especially in the regions) but the key argument was now not so much about what they should do, but who should have a say in what they did. In that sense the arguments of the 1970s were more directly about the locus of power in industry and the economy than how industry should change. This was quite explicit, because proponents of the 1970s policies argued that the 1960s policies had been unsuccessful precisely because they assumed much greater power for the government over corporate activities than actually existed (e.g. Labour 1973*b*: 24). This analysis of the shift of power was not necessarily wrong, but it did leave a rather large hole in arguments about what governments (and unions) would actually want companies to do if subjected to more effective regulation.

The main answer was to get the companies to invest more. It was a long-standing view on the Left in Britain that the key to Britain's poor industrial performance was low levels of investment in comparison with major competing countries. The evidence gives some support to this thesis Brown and Sheriff (1978: 247–8), for example, suggest that in 1973 British manufacturing investment per head was at best under 50 per cent of the level of major competitors (Blackaby 1978; Stout 1979). But in the 1970s economists increasingly questioned whether the low level of investment could be seen as the key causal factor in Britain's problems. In particular, there were a number of studies which suggested that the problem might more helpfully be seen as the poor productivity of much of the investment which was undertaken. A difficulty with this line of argument was that it often went along with a moralistic and evidentially dubious argument that the real problem of British industry was labour and union restrictive practices (a discussion returned to in Ch. 12). Obviously such a position was hardly congenial to Labour. But this ideological dispute tended to distract attention from the fact that to focus attention on investment *per se* is to encourage a very limited view of corporate behaviour and possible reforms. Investment decisions are, after all, the result of a whole range of forms of corporate calculation, calculations embedded in a range of organizational features. A simple injunction to invest more was hardly likely to get to grips with Britain's corporate deficiencies.

In its own way the radical industrial strategy, especially the NEB, reinforced the naïve belief that competition is both a necessary and sufficient condition for efficient company operations. The new publicly owned manufacturing companies would compete with those that remained in private hands, for whom 'fear of losing their share of the market can be a more effective stimulus than the wise words of the government' (Labour 1973*b*: 12). It is not an argument against competition to say that the evidence of post-war Britain is not likely to convince the sceptic that competition by itself is a guarantee of efficiency.

The industrial policy proposals of Labour in the early 1970s were radical. If fully carried out they would have entailed a major shift in power to government bodies, with large if incalculable consequences. At another level, however, the policies were less than radical—they did not get to grips with the relative institutional inefficiency of the British manufacturing company. Indeed they had strikingly little to say about how those companies should change in any organizational sense, beyond an injunction to democratization and consultation with government and workers.[7] However desirable this might be, it failed to say

---

[7] The British Productivity Council, successor to the Anglo-American Council of Productivity, and therefore symbol of an earlier age of industrial intervention, was deprived of its government grant in 1973, blocking one potential avenue for more activity on efficiency within the firm (BPC 1972/3).

what changes in company behaviour could or should result. The company in these proposals remained largely a black box, with governments and unions adding their inputs to its governance, but with little idea about what went on inside or how that should be reformed.

STATE CAPACITY AND STATE ACHIEVEMENTS

The 1970 Conservative government came to power committed to a less interventionist attitude to industry than its predecessor. However, influenced by the emergence of lame ducks such as Rolls Royce, which it was politically impossible to avoid saving, and more generally by the apparent lack of response of private industry to the government's policy approach, a U-turn was performed, crucially in the passing of the 1972 Industry Act (Cmnd. 4942). This Act gave very wide-ranging powers to the government: and a Minister for Industrial Development was appointed and a new Industrial Development Executive was set up to carry out policy. Under this arrangement the Conservatives gave support to a wide-ranging group of industries under three broad headings: high-risk investment which might be in the nation's long-run interest; adjustment assistance; and cases where social considerations might warrant support. This was a wide remit, which gave more or less *carte blanche* for crisis-driven intervention, although it lacked much in a way of a strategic orientation. Mottershead's (1978: 483) conclusions seem particularly apt for this period: 'industrial policies seem limited to a peripheral role of tidying up at the edges of the economy, rather than providing any central thrust to alter and improve industry's performance and that of the economy as a whole'.

In principle Labour's industrial policy could not have been more different. It, too, was supposed to avoid the development of lame-ducks, not in the name of celebration of market forces, but in the name of government achieving a wholesale reversal of industrial trends by a decisive stage in key, profitable manufacturing in firms. In practice things were much different. As we have already noted, the NEB in fact spent the vast bulk of its money on lame ducks, and no money at all on acquiring controlling stakes in large profitable companies. The strategy, in short, came to nothing in terms of its original intentions.

This result followed directly from political calculations at Cabinet and Prime Ministerial level. Wilson, the PM, had never accepted either the take-over of major profitable manufacturing companies by the NEB nor the idea of compulsory planning agreements. The first sign of this resistance was the February 1974 election manifesto which, unlike the previous year's *Programme*, made no mention of any number of private companies to be taken over. The White Paper of August 1974 *The Regeneration of British Industry* (Cmnd. 5710) was also vague on the precise scope of the NEB's role and made clear that any planning agreements would be voluntary. The White Paper issued in November 1975 (Cmnd. 6315), after Benn's removal from the Industry Ministry, was even vaguer, and strongly signalled the change in the rhetoric of policy, declaiming that 'The Government emphasises the importance of sustaining a private sector of industry which is vigorous, alert, responsible and profitable' (para. 3), warning of the danger of 'pre-emption of resources by the public sector and by personal consumption to the detriment of industry's investment and export performance' (para. 5). Much emphasis was put on the role of the National Economic Development Council and the various sector development councils (paras. 16–28).

This development in attitude to industrial intervention was seemingly driven by a lack of faith in the capacity of state bodies like the NEB to achieve their original aims, but above all a calculation that such policies would be a powerful blow to the private sector's confidence in the government, with major harmful affects for co-operation between government and employers and a likely serious undermining of investment. The majority of the Cabinet seem to have taken Denis Healey's view that 'the whole of our future depends on the confidence of businessmen' (Benn 1989: 327; also Healey 1990: 404–9). Such a view plainly gained credence from the strong hostility of the CBI to the NEB, and the collapse of investment taking place at this time. Whether the radical industrial policy's rather coercive attitude to the private sector could have worked remains a moot point, but it was plainly unpropitious to attempt such a policy during the first serious recession since the Second World War and with a government which had either no overall majority (February–October 1974), or a majority of only three, (after the General Election of that November).

Alongside the much-altered NEB the government did put some emphasis on building up the NEDC and the sector development councils, expanded in number and renamed sector working parties. This 'was not a strategy but a methodology' mainly aiming 'to ensure that the practices of the most efficient firms in each sector were followed by the rest' (Healey 1990: 407). This was a cautious, long-term approach, and it is difficult to believe that the SWP's made a major impact (Stout 1978: 189–96). They may have had some impact on slowing down the rise in import penetration, one of their major tasks, but the evidence is not overwhelming (Driver 1983).

Despite all the political flurry over the NEB it would be a mistake to see that as the central feature of government indus-trial intervention under Labour, certainly as measured by public expenditure on that area. As Table 11.7 shows only in 1977/8 did the NEB absorb a significant proportion of that total expend-iture, and even then it accounted for only 30 per cent of the total (these figures exclude subsidies to nationalized industries, except those financed by the NEB). Most of the money was still being spent in a traditional, *ad hoc* way which cannot be described in any helpful sense as strategic.

As an institution the NEB was the major innovation of industrial policy in the 1970s. Apart from the account already given of its priorities, it is useful to look at its precise role in the companies, lame ducks and high-tech, which it became involved with. In the case of the lame ducks the general policy seems to have been to search for new senior managers and then let them get on with managing the companies—as was largely the case with Michael Edwards, who the NEB found for British Leyland (Kramer 1988: ch. 14). Relations with Rolls Royce were in some ways more complex, with the company resistant to the NEB playing any significant role, which led eventually to it going back to Department of Industry control and the resignation of import-ant members of the NEB (Kramer 1988: ch. 13). In the small high-tech companies, the role was more unambiguously hands-off once capital had been supplied (Kramer 1988: ch. 7). In sum, the degree of intervention in company affairs involved in the NEB was very limited. It was not a significant source of any shift in the capacity of government to change the decisions of the private sector.

TABLE 11.7. *Government expenditure on industrial intervention 1973/4 to 1978/9 (£m. at 1978 prices)*

	1973/4	1974/5	1975/6	1976/7	1977/8	1978/9
General support	762	520	771	466	427	396
(of which, NEB)	—	—	12	158	368	70
Industrial innovation	465	482	459	348	275	358
(of which:						
aerospace	288	313	260	135	103	164
nuclear)	126	115	139	157	114	120
Shipbuilding	282	294	231	157	−35	66
Selective assistance	32	30	423	105	59	225
Selective assistance in development areas	50	58	74	35	34	92
Other (mainly investment grants)	448	196	105	46	35	35
TOTAL	2,039	1,580	2,063	1,157	793	1,172

Source: Cmnd. 7439 (1979), pp. 48–9.

Outside the ambit of the NEB there were other major interventions in the private sector. Shipbuilding, a long-term declining industry with many separate companies, was nationalized along with aerospace, an oligopoly heavily dependent on government contracts. Both of these were more notable for their break with the natural monopoly pattern of the 1945–51 nationalizations than for any transformation wrought in the fortunes of the two sectors. Also important was the creation of the British National Oil Corporation as a major player in the exploitation of North Sea Oil.

CONCLUSIONS

Industrial policy was important in the 1970s. Much effort went into Labour Party policy in this area, and this in turn produced a major political battle in the government after 1974. An interventionist industrial strategy was supposed to be part of the Social Contract, but this was one of the areas, other than industrial relations law, where the government did not deliver on its side of the Contract.

Whilst the NEB was not ultimately a major institutional change, and the DTI remained a Ministry largely subordinate to the Treasury, the importance of industrial policy to government rose. This partly reflected the serious situation of the recession and the slow down in an already slow rate of industrial growth, but it also reflected the growing disillusion with macroeconomic policy. Whilst the overall Labour government strategy revolved around the incomes policy, supported by demand management (e.g. Allsopp 1991), there was a growing belief that industrial policy of some sort should be given greater weight in the policy mix. This was due to the problem of profits, and the perceived need to shift resources from consumption, public and private, into industrial investment. To some extent this happened in the later 1970s, after the very fast rises in private consumption in 1972 and 1973, and the fast rise in public consumption up to 1975 (Cairncross 1992: 186). As we have already noted, the government took the profits crisis seriously and did eventually see a profit revival.

But whilst emphasis on the needs of industry gained official support from private-sector unions like the Amalgamated Union of Engineering Workers, it meant a squeeze on private consumption and public expenditure, which, however necessary in macroeconomic terms, was politically a major problem. It meant that consumers' expenditure fell in three of the four years 1974 to 1977, although it expanded rapidly in 1978 and 1979. The curbs on public expenditure were also directly related to the squeeze on public-sector pay which led to the 'winter of discontent' in 1978/9 (Dean 1981).

The need to shift resources into investment, whilst clearly recognized by proponents of a radical NEB, had never been followed through in terms of its macroeconomic implications. In particular, the need for consumption to be reined back in such circumstances had not been properly faced. This same dilemma was faced by the government after 1974, but in a context of sharply declining profits, which made the possibility of financing higher investment from profits even less likely. Thus in many ways the government was faced with the classic social democratic dilemma—wanting to privilege industrial investment in the belief, right or wrong, that this was the key to industrial success, but finding that the political possibility of doing so, whilst trying to maintain good relations with the trade unions, was ultimately absent.

The Social Contract strategy of the Labour leadership and the radical industrial policy of the Labour Left were united by their corporatism, or more exactly by their desire to give unions a major role in policy-making. In the event that corporatism ultimately failed—in the industrial sector it was never seriously tried outside the sector working parties, and in macroeconomic policy it broke down as the TUC was unable to deliver on a wage policy which overreached itself in 1978/9. The 1970s may well have been the last occasion when such corporatism was attempted in Britain, above all because it is difficult to see the trade unions regaining such a primary political role. What should be clear though is that, whilst corporatism in its macro sense may reasonably be said to have been tried and failed (though differences can well exist on the degree of failure), it was never tried in the context of industrial policy. Whether a larger union role via planning agreements and industrial democracy could have improved industrial policy must remain an open question.

Finally, the corporatist industrial policy proposals of the early 1970s were not only predicated on a major managerial-cum-political role for unions, but also on the belief that large private-sector companies were growing in power and influence and escaped effective public regulation. Whilst the weight of such large companies in manufacturing may not have followed the path projected for them in the 1970s, the fundamental issue of how far and in what ways such private concentrations of power could and should be subordinated to public policy concerns remains a central issue for any industrial policy, which the debates of the 1970s at least highlighted, even if they led to no resolution either in doctrine or practice.

Further Reading

Artis, M. and Cobham, D. (1991) (eds.), *Labour's Economic Policies 1974–79*, Manchester.

Blackaby, F. T. (1978) (ed.), *De-Industrialisation*, London.

Elliott, J. (1978), *Conflict or Co-operation?*, London.

Holland, S. (1975), *The Socialist Challenge*, London.

Kramer, D. (1978), *State Capital and Private Enterprise: The Case of the U.K. National Enterprise Board*, London.

Labour Party (1973), *Labour's Programme 1973*, London.

Prais, S. (1976), *The Evolution of Giant Firms in Great Britain*, Cambridge.

Williams, K., Williams, J., and Thomas, D. (1983), *Why Are the British Bad at Manufacturing?*, London: ch. 1.

12

1979–1990: Enterprise and Economic Liberalism

INTRODUCTION

The Conservative government elected in 1979 was committed to a reversal of most of the norms of economic policy of the post-war period. Rather than using demand management to control output and employment, the centrepiece of policy was to be the control of the money supply to beat inflation. This was to be accompanied by a 'rolling back' of the state, measured both by the level of public expenditure, borrowing, and taxation and the extent of state regulation of the economy. The defeat of inflation and the reduction in the role of the state were aimed to provide the conditions for sustained economic growth. This aim was also seen as requiring a major shift in the balance of power in the labour-market, away from trade unions towards employers. This reduction of union power was aimed not only at freeing the labour-market to operate more like the competitive model of economics textbooks, but also at ending the corporatism of the 1970s, with its extension of the unions' political role.

As far as the rhetoric of economic policy is concerned, the change offered in 1979 was not to be limited to a narrow switch in objectives and instruments—from a Keynesian focus on unemployment to a monetarist focus on inflation. Rather the thrust of policy was increasingly argued to require a cultural revolution, the creation of an enterprise culture within which the dynamic force of a reborn entrepreneurialism was to be unleashed. In principle such a stance would mean a sharp break with all post-war industrial policy, whose concerns, although variegated, had never embraced such a radical reconstruction not only of institutions but also of social and cultural norms. This purported change in direction is aptly summarized at the end of a document produced by the Department of Trade and Industry (DTI) in 1988 outlining the enterprise policy:

Is this an 'industrial policy'? The phrase itself is unfortunate because it appears to concentrate on industry rather than to consider all the factors which affect the ability of industry and commerce to create wealth; it also carries the flavour of DTI taking responsibility for the fortunes of individual industries and companies. It will be obvious that neither is consistent with the philosophy of this paper. But the government have a coherent set of policies towards industry and commerce. That set of policies is better described as an enterprise strategy than an industrial strategy (CM. 278: paras. 10.2, 10.3).

The main purpose of this chapter is to assess the meaning of that enterprise strategy over the period from 1979 to 1990. This end date is chosen not only because of the departure of Mrs Thatcher in that year, but also because 1989/90 marked the peak of the economic cycle, and therefore allows our assessment of the period to be based on peak to peak data. This is especially important in this period, both because of the violence of economic fluctuations which characterized these years, and the way in which debate on the economy was often conducted without proper regard to the need to disentangle these cycles from the trends.

CONTEXT

At the beginning the focus of attention of the Thatcher Government was the reduction of inflation by means of control of the money supply. This policy was embodied in the Medium Term Financial Strategy (MTFS) which targeted the growth of the £M3 measure of the money supply and the Public Sector Borrowing Requirement (PSBR) for reduction over a period of four years. This, as has been widely recognized, was a very peculiar form of monetarism, which relied on reducing the demand for money largely by reducing government borrowing and raising interest rates, rather than trying directly to control the supply of money (Johnson 1991: ch. 2; Cairncross 1992: ch. 6; Tomlinson 1990a: ch. 10).

In the short run the main effects of this policy operated through the exchange rate. This was already on an upward path from 1977/8 under the influence of North Sea oil, but the high interest rates and generally deflationary stance of the Conservative government greatly accelerated this rise. Combined with an initial high inflation rate, this rise in the nominal international value of the pound led to the sharpest rise in the real exchange rate (a measure of price competitiveness) ever recorded in a major country. The result was a sharp fall in GDP, by 2 per cent in 1980 and 1.2 per cent in 1981, but a much sharper fall in manufacturing output, by almost 15 per cent from the peak of 1979 to the low in 1981.

TABLE 12.1. *Manufacturing production 1979–89* (1985 = 100)

1979	106
1980	96.8
1981	91.0
1982	91.2
1983	93.8
1984	97.4
1985	100
1986	101.3
1987	106.6
1988	114.1
1989	118.9

Source: Economic Trends.

From this low point in 1981 GDP expanded continuously until 1989, growth peaking at 4.7 per cent in 1988, before the brakes were put on once again and Britain entered the next recession. Manufacturing output also expanded in the upswing, though only reaching the 1979 level in 1987 (which was still below the 1973 peak). This performance meant that for the whole period 1979–89 British GDP rose at 2.2 per cent per annum, the same as the average of the EC, though slower than for the OECD area which included the faster-growing United States and Japan. This rate of growth was exactly the same as that of the much decried 1970s (Johnson 1991: 12–14). The manufacturing growth record was the second poorest in the OECD 'big six' (United States, Japan, Germany, France, Italy, United Kingdom), the British average being 1.4 per cent per annum for the period 1979–89 (OECD 1991: 89).

These violent fluctuations in output were matched by those in other economic variables. Inflation (measured by the Retail Price Index) averaged 7.4 per cent 1979–89 compared with 12.5 per cent 1969–79, falling to a low of 3.3 per cent in 1986 and then rising to 9.5 per cent in 1990. The average was very close to that of the EC, but above that of the 'big six' (Johnson 1991: 72, 281). The balance of payments swung into current account surplus in the recession of the early 1980s, but by the end of the boom had deteriorated to a far worse state (a deficit of $29.8bn.) than any EC country, and the deficit was larger than that of the United States in relation to the size of GDP (OECD 1991: 119).

Finally, unemployment also fluctuated, though here the effects of the boom of the 1980s were longer delayed and more short-lived. The figures have been subject to much manipulation and controversy, but if we use OECD figures the picture is one where unemployment was about 6 percentage points higher on average in the 1980s than in the 1970s, with Britain above the EC average in all years except at the peak of the boom in 1987–9. On these figures unemployment peaked at 12.4 per cent in 1983, falling to 6.9 per cent in 1989 (Johnson 1991: 245–9, 315).

Overall, at the macroeconomic level we have a picture of an economy subject to a very sharp deflationary shock which eventually produced a fall in inflation (helped by a sharp fall in the price of imported commodities) but at the cost of a fall in output and employment concentrated on the tradable and especially manufacturing sector. This was followed by a revival and boom led by a consumption expansion, and which proved unsustainable as demand rose much faster than supply and resulted in a renewal of inflation and a sharp deterioration in the current account of the balance of payments. Whatever else might be said of the 1980s, it was not the period of steady, non-inflationary growth promised in 1979.

Much of the assessment of the Thatcher period has focused not on these macroeconomic aggregates but on productivity, usually productivity in manufacturing. Walters (1986: ch. 10) in his defence of the government's policies (on which he was an adviser) accepts the behaviour of productivity as a 'litmus test' of the success of Thatcher's policies. Walters emphasizes that in this area comparisons should be made with OECD countries, and these are given in Table 12.2. These figures only cover manufacturing, the record for whole-economy productivity in Britain is much poorer—averaging under 2 per cent per annum. These figures are for labour productivity only, partly because estimates of capital inputs into production are much more difficult to make, especially in a period of such major economic change. In manufacturing, capital productivity was probably much more variable than that of labour, falling in each year 1980 to 1982, but then rising in the boom to a peak of 6.2 per cent in 1988. Total Factor Productivity (output increases relative to both capital and labour inputs) in manufacturing possibly peaked in 1983 but ran at around 6 per cent in 1987 and 1988 (Johnson 1991: 267).

TABLE 12.2. *Labour productivity in manufacturing 1979–89*
(% growth p.a.)

	1979–84	1984–9
USA	3.4	4.1
Japan	6.3	5.3
France	1.9	3.2
Germany	1.5	0.2
Italy	4.4	4.2
UK	4.0	4.5
Weighted average for OECD	3.7	3.4

Source: OECD (1991), p. 116.

Overall it is clear that the manufacturing productivity perform-ance of the 1980s was an improvement over the 1970s, an improvement common to most OECD countries. For Britain there was also some relative improvement, mainly in relation to France and especially Germany. Indeed the impression from Table 12.2 is that it was Germany's poor performance which was exceptional in this period rather than the good performance of the United Kingdom (see also Crafts 1992*b*). The causes and implications of this productivity performance are returned to in more detail below, but two macroeconomic points should be made here.

First, with the slow growth of output (Table 12.1), the manu-facturing productivity figures of the 1980s reflect above all a process of labour-shedding. Employment in manufacturing fell by approximately 25 per cent during 1979–89, with the loss of about 2 million jobs. Thus the productivity increase was not accompanied by a major expansion of capacity, and this position is reflected in the current account deficits and inflation of the late 1980s, as the boom quickly hit capacity constraints.

Second, the productivity performance did not translate directly into a major gain in manufacturing competitiveness because of the parallel increase in wage costs. The manufacturing deficit on the balance of payments continued to increase (from £5bn. in 1983, the first year of deficit, to £16bn. in 1990), and this despite a fall in the exchange rate, which from its peak of 127 in the first quarter of 1981 fell to 94.1 by the end of 1990 (1985 = 100).

The intellectual context of the government's policies after 1979 is complex. At the macroeconomic level the impact of monetarist economics has been much debated, especially given the gap between the policy proposals stemming from advocates of such economics and the highly particular form of the MTFS in its various guises. Whilst monetarism in the narrow sense only suggested a relationship between monetary growth and inflation, most monetarists in practice tied their arguments to free-market ideas and the belief that governments should focus their attention on supply-side policies. Even from believers in free markets, supply-side policies can embrace a very wide range of options. In the United States, for example, such policies tended to focus on tax cuts and deregulation, and whilst in Britain these have not been absent, the centre-piece of Conservative policy most of the time was the labour-market in general and the trade unions in particular.

Hostility to trade unions has always been a bench-mark of economic liberalism, but British Conservatism has usually had a more ambivalent attitude. Certainly for most of the post-war period the Conservatives accepted the unions as an estate of the realm, to be criticized but usually to be negotiated with, rather than subjected to full-scale denunciation and attack. But by 1979 this was changing rapidly. This new strength of hostility was based in part on enthusiasm for the works of New Right writers like Friedman and Hayek. Hayek in particular constructed a demonology of trade unions arguing that the powers of the unions

have become the biggest obstacle to raising the living standards of the working class as a whole. They are the chief cause of the unnecessarily big differences between the best and the worst-paid workers. They are the prime source of unemployment. They are the main reason for the decline of the British economy in general (Hayek 1980: 52).[1]

Such attitudes to trade unionism gained a great deal more credibility from the Labour government's period in office from 1974 to 1979. This government, as discussed in Chapter 11, put co-operation with the unions at the centre of its strategy, greatly enhancing their political as well as their economic role. For whatever reasons that strategy must be considered a failure, and of course collapsed into the ignominious 'winter of discontent' of 1978/9. Ideological predisposition thus nicely dovetailed with political opportunity for the Conservatives, and the destruction of union power became a key theme of the period after 1979.

However, this policy was conducted in a careful, step-by-step fashion, by a series of pieces of legislation which gradually narrowed the immunity from claims of damages which has been the traditional legal framework of trade-union activity in Britain. The economic impact of this legal attack on unions is much disputed, and is returned to in the section on 'Labour' below, but perhaps just as important was the political attack on the unions. Whilst Labour in the 1970s had sought to make the various trade-union leaders privileged partners in government, in the 1980s they were ejected from most bodies with any policy-influencing role. For Mrs Thatcher unions were the problem, rarely part of the solution.[2]

Whilst the trade unions were the Conservatives' prime political enemy, the analysis of the unions' economic role was tied to a broader theme, which can be summarized by saying that the Conservative government saw a key part of supply-side reform as the restoration of 'flexibility' in the labour-market. Flexibility became one of the fashionable words of the 1980s, applied to all aspects of the labour-market (e.g. CM. 540). This emphasis reflected the Conservative belief in simple textbook models of how labour-markets could and should work, in which wage

[1] On Hayek and the unions see Wedderburn (1989), Tomlinson (1990*b*): ch. 4.
[2] Unions retained a reduced role in NEDO (abolished in 1992), and a still considerable role in the Health and Safety Executive and bodies such as industrial tribunals.

flexibility was crucial to their operation. Partly it arose from the belief that inflexibility in the use of labour was a key problem for productivity. It was also part of the demonology of trade unions that they obstructed such flexibility and hence caused unemployment, a theme of particular importance with the re-emergence of mass unemployment in the early 1980s, and about which the Conservatives, initially at least, felt extremely politically sensitive.

This attention to an inflexible labour-market was in turn often broadened out to link to a theme of lack of enterprise in the British economy, a lack of willingness to change, to take risks in order to better oneself. This theme, like others in the Conservatives' rhetoric, had both broad ideological and more specific policy connotations. The idea of the key role of enterprise and the entrepreneur in the capitalist economy has always been a key point of neo-Austrians like Hayek and Schumpeter. But the ideological congeniality of such ideas to the Conservative government was accompanied by a more specific tactical deployment. Concerned to raise growth and in particular to reduce unemployment, the government focused on the obstacles to job growth arising from entrepreneurial deficiency. This linkage was made very clear in the publications of government departments: 'The prime aim of the Department of Employment is to encourage the development of an enterprise economy' (Cmnd. 9474: foreword). 'There are two key elements in the Government's economic policy: to keep down inflation and offer real incentives for enterprise, in order to generate jobs' (Cmnd. 9571: para. 1.1).

Encouraging the development of an enterprise economy was in large part similar to the project for 'rolling back the state'. At the macroeconomic level this project was much more difficult to achieve than had been hoped. The original aim of cutting public expenditure in absolute terms was abandoned in 1982, and the aim of a reduction in the share of public spending in GNP was not clearly achieved until the late 1980s (Johnson 1991: 282–3). Public borrowing was more successfully controlled (at least until the recession of 1991/2) but only at the cost of a level of taxation which rose from 1979 until 1982, and then fell back, but remained significantly above its 1979 level in 1989 (Johnson 1991: 292). These changes in the aggregate level of taxation were accompanied by a significant shift in tax composition, away from direct to indirect taxes. In particular cuts in income tax rates for the higher paid were very substantial. Tax and social security changes together brought about a major inegalitarian shift in income distribution, and an absolute decline in the living standards of the poorest groups (Hills 1989). These consequences of tax and welfare policy can be seen as linked to the focus on the labour-market, as the aim was explicitly made to 'price people into jobs'. In particular this was the first time the welfare system had been deliberately used for that purpose (Waine 1991: 147–51).

Microeconomically rolling back the state had a number of facets—reducing planning controls, reducing employment protection, ending most minimum wage laws, and raising the threshold for VAT. Whilst some positive encouragement was given to entrepreneurship and the enterprise culture, the logic of such a strategy was to focus on the negative aspect of reducing the state's role rather than redirecting that role. Hence deregulation was central to the strategy. Deregulation found a logical counterpart in denationalization and the government undertook a major privatization programme (Ch. 8 above). However, this programme also involved a major extension of regulation, as many of the newly privatized industries were natural monopolies where effective competition or its threat were difficult to envisage. In its absence government found it impossible to avoid erecting a whole new regulatory apparatus.

This point linked to a final general theme in the Thatcher government's policies. Whilst putting a lot of emphasis in their rhetoric on competition the government was notably different from, say, the Conservative governments of the 1950s with in some sense a similar rhetoric. Whilst anxious to encourage small business, and to attack union restrictive practices, company-level monopoly, mergers, and restrictive practices were little attended to. One can look at this in two lights. In terms of economic doctrine, it can be seen as a concern with productive rather than allocative efficiency, for example with the enhanced efficiency of privatized industries being seen as arising from competition for their ownership in the capital market rather than competition in the product market. Alternatively, this unwillingness to attack private-sector circumvention of competition may be put down to a continuing attention to the consequences for Conservative

Party finances of any direct break with big business (Johnson 1991: 193–5).

MARKETS

Unqualified enthusiasm for free trade was part of the *laissez-faire* rhetoric of the Conservative government. In some areas there was little tension between rhetoric and policy. For example, whilst sceptical of many of the activities of the EC, Mrs Thatcher and her government, after initial caution and suspicion, enthusiastically endorsed the '1992 programme' of completion of the single market in the EC, grounded as it largely was on traditional liberal economic arguments about the benefits of free trade and competition.[3] Although certain parts of the creation of a level playing-field in Europe posed serious political problems for the Conservatives—for example, the harmonization of the coverage of VAT—in this area the government was a Euro-enthusiast. This enthusiasm was encouraged by the belief that in the financial services area, which was likely to be most strongly affected by the 1992 programme, Britain had a strong competitive position and was therefore likely to be a gainer from freer trade.[4]

In other areas there was more tension between free-trade rhetoric and policy. Voluntary export restraints with Japan, restricting Japanese penetration of UK markets, were continued, and similarly the Multi-Fibre Agreement restricting the entry of textiles from low-wage countries stayed in force. In these cases the political costs of defending domestic employment appeared small, and the benefits probably larger. In addition, restricting Japanese imports fitted with a policy of encouraging inward Japanese investment, though despite well-publicized examples the scale of this remained trivial.

Overall there was no serious break in policy in the area of international trade under the Conservatives. Import penetration continued to rise, as it had done in the previous decade, and it rose especially fast in the boom of the late 1980s.

---

[3] For a sceptical assessment of these arguments see e.g. Cutler *et al.* (1989).

[4] For an analysis of British competitiveness in services, see Smith (1992). Note that in the mid-1980s financial services contributed only around 5 per cent of British exports, so their role should not be exaggerated.

TABLE 12.3. *Changes in manufacturing 1979–89*
(1979 = 100)

Real profits	143.9
Real profits per unit of capital	127.7
Investment	112.8
Real dividends	173.2
Real share prices	224.8

Source: Glyn (1992), p. 80.

PROFITS

The 1980s (eventually) saw some reversal of the profit squeeze of the 1970s. Over the whole period 1979–89 profits shared an even sharper cycle than most other economic variables. The real appreciation of the pound in the early 1980s threatened to squeeze out profits between rising costs and price cuts in order to try to stay competitive. For industrial and commercial companies as a whole the rate of return on capital fell to its lowest recorded level of 4.8 per cent. In manufacturing the figure fell to below 4 per cent. There then followed a strong revival, especially in the broader category, which in 1988 reached 9.1 per cent, back to the previous peak of 1972, before falling again.[5] In manufacturing the peak was lower at around 7 per cent, only slightly above the late 1970s level.

The general revival of profits in the later 1980s was then in large part a cyclical phenomenon, but with some suggestion that the long downward trend might have been at least temporarily interrupted. The government welcomed this profit revival, seeing it as a basis for the expansion of investment. However, the link between profits and investment is always an indirect one, and this was particularly so in the 1980s. As the figures in Table 12.3 suggest, in manufacturing the profit revival was largely distributed in dividends rather than being used to finance investment. Table 12.4 gives the value of investment in manufacturing for 1979–89, showing how sharp the cycle was. This cyclical pattern is typical for investment, and is true for all sectors.

---

[5] On a different basis of calculation OECD figures suggest a rate of return of 8.8 per cent in the UK business sector for 1989, compared with an OECD average of 16.2 per cent (OECD 1991: 117).

However, the overall level of investment expansion in the boom was higher in non-manufacturing sectors, especially financial services, which grew at an average rate of 13.4 per cent during 1979–89 (Johnson 1991: 307).

TABLE 12.4. *Gross fixed investment in manufacturing 1979–89* (£bn., 1985 prices)

1979	10.99
1980	9.78
1981	7.67
1982	7.48
1983	8.82
1984	10.12
1986	9.42
1987	10.05
1988	11.20
1989	12.39

Source: Economic Trends: Annual Supplement.

For manufacturing it is most striking that the rise in productivity and profits of the 1980s did not lead to an investment-led recovery. The rate of investment was the lowest of the OECD 'big six' over the period 1979–87 (OECD 1991: 89). This, of course, again fits in with our picture of a highly capacity-constrained economy by the late 1980s.

The government's most specific impact on profits was via changes to profit tax. Whilst milking North Sea oil and banking profits hard, the main thrust of policy in this area was to remove investment allowances whilst reducing the rate of corporation tax (from 52 to 35 per cent). The case for such a change was to move company's returns on investment closer to pre-tax levels and discourage uneconomic investment in capital-intensive industries. These changes in themselves were intended to be neutral in their impact on tax revenue. But the effects were changed by the simultaneous abolition of stock relief, introduced in the 1970s to stop companies paying tax on the paper profits resulting from inflation. The abolition of this relief came in 1984 at the bottom of the inflation cycle, but was not reintroduced when inflation once again took off in the late 1980s (Johnson 1991: 131–4).

THE EFFICIENCY OF LABOUR

The Conservative government was strongly committed to the view that trade unions were crucial to Britain's low level of efficiency. A White Paper of 1988 was typical in asserting that

trade unions have used their powers in ways which adversely affected labour costs, productivity and jobs. Managers who recognised and negotiated with trade unions were less likely to experience job gains and more likely to suffer job losses than managers who did not. In general, trade unions tended to push up earnings of people they represented while blocking the improvements in productivity which are needed to pay for those higher earnings (CM. 540: para. 2.4).

This, of course, was not a new refrain. The British worker question and the related belief that trade unions were crucial to slow economic growth were as old as the perception of Britain's lagging growth itself. But such an analysis did reach new levels of prominence and support in the 1970s, supported by seemingly plausible academic studies on the causes of Britain's productivity shortfall behind continental European competitors (Pratten 1976; CPRS 1975). But Nichols (1986) has shown the great extent to which these studies were flawed in both conception and execution. The material was drawn almost entirely from management opinion, with trade unionists almost ignored. The comparisons made related only to specific processes not to whole products. Differences in capital equipment were glossed over, and the effects of such differences assumed away in favour of an emphasis on labour practices. As Cutler (1992: 167) has further pointed out, the studies ignored issues such as the impact of poor model range and poor distribution networks on labour productivity via their effects on output levels. (A similar sceptical view of the alleged impact of labour restrictive practices on productivity in the 1940s is given in Tiratsoo and Tomlinson 1993a; see also Fogarty and Brooks 1989: ch. 2).

Despite the poor basis in the historic record for the emphasis given to the British worker question in explaining Britain's poor economic performance, this approach moved centre-stage in the 1980s. The government and its supporters saw the productivity improvement in manufacturing in the 1980s as vindicating their attack on the trade unions. This linkage has provoked a lively debate. Certainly there is something to be explained in those productivity figures, even if, in context, they appear somewhat less startling than government rhetoric would suggest. In the earlier phases it was common to explain this productivity change as a 'batting average' effect, whereby the recession of 1980/81 knocked the lower productivity plants out of action, and thereby increased the average attainment of those that continued to produce. However, like many economists' plausible stories, this one seems to have been empirically ill-founded. Oulton (1987) found that the recession hit hard at the companies with poor liquidity or poor profits, neither of which had a clear relationship to productivity—indeed closures seem to have been concentrated on larger plants with higher than average productivity.

Another view would be that the increase in labour productivity was not a genuine productivity increase at all, but reflected an increase in (unmeasured) labour input, an increase in labour effort. This has been measured by the Percentage Utilisation of Labour (PUL) index since 1979, and shows a rise from 100.5 in that year to 104.1 in 1983, followed by stability (Bennett and Smith-Gavine 1987). This doesn't suggest a huge shift in effort, and these figures have been subject to criticism, for example because of their basis in work-study standards rather than actual practices and the problems of changing composition of the workers involved (Guest 1990). Whilst in some industries such as coal extra effort may have played a significant part in the productivity shift (Glyn 1988), its general importance is less clear (Nolan 1989).

Metcalf (cited by the Government in support of their case) has argued that unlike previous efforts to raise productivity, 'the methods pursued in the 1980s—legislation to control union power, high unemployment, heightened product market competition and emphasis on numerical and functional flexibility in the labour-market—seem to have done the trick' (1989: 27). But the precise role of the first of these is not clearly identified. Metcalf himself (1990: 250) accepts that in principle the impact of trade unions on productivity is equivocal. He accepts that the level of unionization was not related to the big changes in productivity in the early 1980s (1989: 18), and that the adoption of new technology was not related to levels of unionization (1989: 22).

This latter point is borne out by Daniels's large-scale survey, which showed how strongly trade unions (and workers) supported technical change (Daniels 1987: chs. 6, 8, 11). For Metcalf, in fact, despite the emphasis on unions in the above quotation, the key change in the 1980s which lay behind the productivity increase was unemployment, and the effects of that unemployment on worker attitudes: 'fear must be what matters here' (1989: 19).

Some other investigations have suggested that levels of unionization did affect productivity performance in the early 1980s (Oulton 1990), but others have shown this is not a consistent relationship over longer periods (Wadhwani 1990). Trying to identify the effects of the anti-union legislation of the 1980s is another way of approaching the issue. As far as the effects of this legislation on productivity are concerned there is the obvious difficulty that the first significant legislation was that of 1982, which post-dates the beginnings of the productivity improvement. More general studies of the impact of the legislation have highlighted its strikingly limited impact on wage behaviour, with the real wages of those remaining in unionized manufacturing plants rising very sharply in the 1980s, which is hard to reconcile with a general weakening of union power (Wadhwani and Brown 1990).

Overall, it is difficult to find much evidence that unionization *per se* was a crucial issue in the rise in productivity in the 1980s. Metcalf's invocation of the fear factor associated with the sharp rise in unemployment in 1980/1 seems plausible in shifting the willingness of some workers and unions to trade changes in working practices against higher wages. Mass unemployment shifted the balance of power towards management, though the effects (for example, on wages) were less than many would have anticipated. Organizational change may have been facilitated, though the evidence of big change is very limited (New and Myers 1987). Certainly the productivity increase was not the result of a big increase in investment, as our previous discussion has shown. In conclusion, the causes of the productivity rise of the 1980s remain controversial, but the Conservative case that the attack on trade unions was crucial remains unproven.

Like many others, Metcalf saw changes in the level of flexibility as an important feature of the 1980s. This fad word of the period needs to be carefully defined. Hakim (1987: 550) suggests four types of flexibility which might be used to analyse labour. These relate to wages, to labour mobility, to functional flexibility, and to patterns and organization of work. Many economists have focused their attention on the first of these, and especially the seeming ineffectiveness of both mass unemployment and the weakening of trade unions to make much difference to wage flexibility. In particular, attention has been given to the issue of why the Non-Accelerating Inflation Rate of Unemployment has seemingly not shifted, so that the inflation/unemployment trade-off has not improved (Layard 1987; Wadhwani and Brown 1990).

The government has strongly encouraged the decentralization of wage-bargaining and linkages between performance and pay. The evidence does suggest that industry-wide bargaining declined significantly in the 1980s with the main gainer being single-firm bargaining. How far this was due to government policy and how much to changing industrial structures (and managerial fashions) remains obscure. The government's aim was to link wages more closely to company performance for incentive reasons, though one effect of the growth of company-level bargaining was probably to intensify 'insider / outsider' effects and reduce the impact of unemployment on wage bargains, as employers ceased to regard the unemployed as plausible replacements for the currently employed.

The government's most direct influence was in the public sector, where both local bargaining and performance-related pay were encouraged, though by the end of the decade national bargaining remained in place for most major groups of public-sector workers. The government's biggest impact on labour in the public sector was perhaps to unleash a massive wave of bureaucratic managerialism, purveying every faddish managerial nostrum in usually quite inappropriate contexts.

Labour mobility raises questions of both the regional and occupational distribution of workers in comparison with job vacancies. Apparent regional mismatch is evident in the disparity in regional unemployment figures. The government in this period was sceptical of traditional regional policy with its aim of attenuating market forces, though it continued to spend significant sums in this area. In fact, as Thompson (1990: ch. 5) argues, policy in this area became more interventionist rather than less as assistance generally available in broad zones became available only on a more discriminatory basis to more restricted districts. Commentators lavished much attention on the effects of council housing on labour mobility, though as a solution to this problem the sale of council houses (1.3 million were sold during 1979–89) ignored the immobilizing effects of high transaction costs in the privately owned sector. Occupational and industrial mismatch raises much broader issues concerned with training, and is returned to below.

Functional flexibility was a major issue in the 1980s. This reflected the Government's concern with (alleged) trade-union restrictive practices such as job demarcation, but equally the government believed that modern competitive conditions required more of such task flexibility. Trends in this type of flexibility have been the subject of impassioned debate by academics. This arises in part because of the debate about the long-term trend in capitalist economies with regard to skill levels and deployment. Much social science work had taken up Braverman's (1974) argument that modern capitalism systematically deskilled the work-force in order to facilitate mass production at lowest cost (e.g. Wood 1989). In the 1980s this debate was given a new twist by the invention of the concept of 'flexible specialization'. The originators of this concept argued that with the growing differentiation of markets in the major industrial countries, the old world of mass production of homogeneous goods by unskilled workers on dedicated machines was, at least potentially, giving way to a world of short production runs for niche markets, produced by skilled workers using flexible machines. In this view the skill degradation of mass production could be reversed by small firms, but small firms provided with common services by public authorities, thus recreating industrial districts like the cotton towns in nineteenth-century Lancashire in a new, high-tech guise (Piore and Sabel 1984; Sabel and Zeitlin 1985; for the debate Pollert 1991; Williams *et al.* 1987*a*).

Whatever the merits of the paradigm of flexible specialization, it has undoubtedly stimulated much research on flexibility in Britain, especially related to skill. Elger (1991) provides a survey of some of this material. He concludes that 'during the 1980s much of U.K. manufacturing has experienced a significant, though uneven and incremental, change in aspects of task flexibility, of a sort which may be best characterized in terms of increased managerial control over "manning", modest task enlargement and an intensification of work' (63). The pattern has undoubtedly been uneven between sectors—for example in cars more radical changes in skill deployment seem to have taken place (e.g. Starkey and McKinlay 1989)—but overall the evidence supports neither a thesis of deskilling nor one of widespread multi-skilling, though some traditional barriers, e.g. between craftsmen and maintenance workers, have tended to be eroded (Daniel 1987: 275–7).

Hakim's final category of flexibility relates to patterns of working hours, work contracts, etc. Her own research focuses on this area. She suggests that there are longstanding tendencies to greater flexibility in the sense of a growth of part-time work, temporary work, and self-employment; all of these have significantly expanded in the 1980s. For example, part-timers as a proportion of the labour-force have expanded from 3 per cent in 1951 to 23 per cent by 1987, most of this expansion taking place in the 1970s and 1980s (Hakim 1987: 555). Self-employment increased from 1.9 to 2.8 million between 1979 and 1987 (Rubery 1989: 159). Hakim regards the spread of such forms of work as largely benign, emphasizing that in the 1960s and 1970s it was workers and unions rather than employers who pressed for flexibility. She also points to survey evidence that most flexible workers prefer those patterns to full-time, permanent employee status.

Others see this growth in flexibility in a less positive light, either in terms of its impact on the individuals involved or its implications for economic efficiency. For example, self-employment, whilst seeming to offer advantages of greater control over work, has grown in part because of the unavailability of employment and often offers poor economic rewards (Rainbird 1991). Similarly, whilst no doubt many workers like part-time work, for others it is attractive only because of the absence of childcare facilities which would make full-time work possible (Rubery 1989). The idea of a core work-force of skilled, full-time, and permanent workers and a periphery of unskilled, part-time, and impermanent workers or sub-contractors (predominantly women) may be too crude a notion to capture the complexity of the 1980s labour-market, but it does serve to emphasize the potential welfare costs of flexibility.

The government's impact on all this development of flexibility has largely been via macro-policy (i.e. creating unemployment and the shift in bargaining power) and propaganda. Government pronouncements celebrated and encouraged all forms of flexibility (e.g. CM. 540), but the implications of flexibility for economic efficiency seem to be more ambiguous than such simple-minded enthusiasm would suggest. Proponents of flexibility operate with a notion of production in which continual adjustment of labour inputs is best able to secure the right pattern and level of output in response to market conditions. This ignores all the evidence that productive efficiency is not just a matter of the optimum combination of quantities of inputs, but is also about the motivation and attitudes of labour. The implications of this for flexibility are brought out by Dore's *Flexible Rigidities* (1986), which, in discussing Japanese industry, stresses how the rigidity of life-long employment (for some workers) creates a spirit of confidence and co-operation in which workers are willing to be very flexible in day-to-day tasks. Such co-operation would not be secured if flexibility applied to all aspects of labour.

The point is not to idealize the Japanese system, but to stress that flexibility may be a mixed blessing from the point of view of economic efficiency. Rubery (1989: 172–3) goes further and argues that in so far as companies in Britain in the 1980s achieved more flexibility with respect to hours, training, and pay, this trend undermined the capacity to control real wage growth and the development of a large skilled work-force mobile between firms. 'In general, Conservative labour-market policy has not been designed to provide a framework which would foster the type of co-operation both between firms and between capital and labour which is necessary to achieve long-term and significant change in the productivity potential of the British economy.' (172).

Alongside flexibility, calls for more training became one of the great cries of the 1980s, so that by the end of the period all political forces seem to have argued that training was the key to Britain's industrial future. But this return to a very old theme of linking Britain's slow growth to the deficiencies of the training and education system (see Ch. 2) only emerged in the late 1980s. Training did not figure highly in initial Conservative policies, and emerged as an issue not in the context of analyses of long-run decline, but in the face of the rather more politically compelling problem of emergent mass unemployment (CM. 316).

When the Conservatives came to power in 1979 the major government role in training was via the Industrial Training Boards and the Manpower Services Commission, the latter established in the 1970s by the Labour government to co-ordinate training and engage in manpower planning. The Conservatives were hostile to the bureaucracy and alleged rigidity of ITBs and their perceived failure to deal with cross-sectoral skills and moved quickly to abolish many of them (Cmnd. 8455: paras. 59–60). They were also hostile to the MSC with its interventionist and corporatist stance (Finn 1987: 131–42). However rather than abolish the Commission, from late 1980 the government acted to reshape it to a new role, essentially one of 'managing unemployment' (Benn and Fairley 1986: 1–2). The initial focus here was on the young unemployed. The Labour government had created the Youth Opportunities Programme (YOP) in 1978 at the request of the TUC to provide subsidies for firms to take on some of the growing number of young unemployed. Initially the Conservatives just expanded the YOP, but made clear that the agenda was not just to provide training but explicitly to drive down the wages of young people and equip them with attitudes desired by employers in order to improve their chances of employment (Cmnd. 8455). By 1982 1 in 2 school-leavers were on YOPs; as trainees they were denied employee status and were exempt from, for example, health and safety regulations.

In 1983 YOPs was replaced by the Youth Training Scheme (1 year initially, later expanded to 2 years). YTS essentially aimed to abolish the possibility of official unemployment amongst school-leavers by offering all of them training and refusing benefit to those who did not take up the offer. (YTS trainees received only travel and other expenses). The Community Programme offered something similar to the adult unemployed.

During the worst of the unemployment in the early and mid-1980s YTS and related programmes became very big operations. By the end of 1988 2 million young people had been through YTS, 1 million after it became a two-year programme in

1986 (CM. 540: para. 6.9). The impact of all this training is highly controversial. Critics of the scheme have emphasized the extent to which by subsidizing young people they displaced other workers and gave firms an incentive to rely on a stream of YTS recruits rather than create long-term jobs (Finn 1987: 143–5). As to the training content of YTS, being employer-based, it gave an incentive for training to be very limited and/or very specific (Sheldrake and Vickerstaff 1987: 59). Much emphasis was put on attitudes rather than broad applicable skills: 'far too much of the new vocationalism and the new training seem to involve the writing in of context and process for commerce, whilst writing out the general skills of critical analysis and conceptual understanding' (Benn and Fairley 1986: 14).

On the other hand YTS did something, if only a little, to remedy the 1979 situation where 40 per cent of the school-leavers who went into jobs got no training at all (Cmnd. 8455: para. 18; Deakin and Pratten 1987). Also the government could point to the fact that by the late 1980s three-quarters of people leaving YTS went to jobs, further education, or training (CM. 540: para. 6.9). This outcome reflected the big improvement in the unemployment rate amongst young people in the late 1980s, and in that period the government's attention turned away from the short-run problem of getting people off the dole to a longer-term view of skill deficiency and policies to address that deficiency.

This realignment of policy invoked the need for a cultural revolution of which more training would only be a part. Also involved would be a reorientation of the education system towards encouraging enterprise and entrepreneurial values: 'Bridging the historical divide between business and education is vital to encourage the enterprise culture, to encourage young people to work in industry and commerce, to bring greater relevance to their education and to prepare them better for working life' (CM. 278: para. 4.2; CM. 540: ch. 6). Hence what the government proposed was not so much a reform of education and training as one of the greatest pieces of social engineering ever attempted in Britain—a programme to change the hearts and minds of the population. How much of this change actually occurred is very difficult to assess. Certainly the late 1980s were full of initiatives to try to reform education in the name of enterprise—the Training and Vocational Education Initiative

(TVEI), Enterprise in Education Initiative, Enterprise in Higher Education, Work-Related Further Education, etc. Significant impacts have been recorded in some areas, notably TVEI on the secondary school curriculum (Chitty 1986). Whether this general programme will have much impact on British economic perform-ance seems doubtful. The programme drew support from some fashionable historical writing of the 1980s which described Brit-ish decline in culturalist terms, notably Wiener (1985) and Barnett (1986). However such accounts have been shown to be highly dubious, not least because they tend implicitly or explicitly to compare Britain with the German model of success, whilst either ignoring or misrepresenting German education and its cultural context (e.g. Collins and Robbins 1990).

More specifically, in the late 1980s the government embarked on a major restructuring of the training system. Most of the remaining ITBs (excepting that in construction) were abolished and the new key institutions were to be Training and Enterprise Councils (TECs). These drew explicitly on an American model of locally based, employer-dominated bodies acting as agents for training and small business support services. The Government's stated aim in establishing TECs was to 'place "ownership" of the training and enterprise system where it belongs—with employers' (CM. 540: para. 5.7). TECs were not only to have at least two-thirds of their members from top management, but quite clearly it would be those managers who would determine the skill needs in their locality: 'The government believe that the most effective incentive for companies to train is knowledge and understanding of their skill needs, not centralised regulation based on statutory powers' (CM. 540: para. 4.24).

TECs thus seemed to be based on the rejection of the tradi-tional notion of market failure in training, whereby individual employers would tend to undertrain because of the likelihood of the poaching of workers with transferable skills by firms who did not undertake the expense of training themselves. ITBs had been based explicitly on such analysis, but TECs seem to assume that local employers would not be subject to such disincentives.

The idea of a wholly employer-led training system raises the wider issue of how far such an approach would tend to reinforce the low-skill strategies adopted by many British firms. In a general context of short-termism firms usually take the skill composition of the available labour as a given, and adopt a production strategy to fit. Some have suggested that this is common in Britain (Green and Ashton 1992), and TECs seem an unlikely way of breaking out of such a circle.[6]

The final general point about training is the broad issue of how far at the beginning of the 1990s this was indeed the major problem facing Britain in trying to improve its industrial efficiency. Much of the near unanimity in support of this proposition was reinforced by a series of studies from the National Institute of Economic Research (e.g. Prais and Steedman 1986; Steedman 1988; Steedman and Wagner 1989). These studies convincingly demonstrated the great deficiencies in skill levels in Britain compared with France and Germany, especially in the craft skills area. This is an area where apprenticeship collapsed in the 1980s without being replaced by alternative schemes. However, as Cutler (1992) argues, these studies like those on restrictive practices in the 1970s, fail to demonstrate that skill levels are the crucial determinant of the relative inefficiency of British industry. As in the earlier work, the National Institute studies do not offer broad comparisons of the production of similar goods, but focus on a very small number of processes, which in fact are quite dissimilar in the countries compared. Equally the context in which products are sold and the overall management of the enterprise is played down in describing differences in output and productivity. The new emphasis on vocational training appears, like the British worker question, in new but no more convincing guise.

This, of course, is not an argument against training, which potentially has all sorts of social as well as economic benefits. But it is an argument against reducing British industrial inefficiency to one cause, rather than seeing that inefficiency as the product of a whole set of enterprise practices themselves embedded in broader features of the economy. History can at least teach us that too much emphasis on training, like most remedies proposed in the past, is likely to lead to as much disappointment as previous panaceas.

---

[6] For a highly critical review of TECs, especially of their voluntarist basis, see Centre for Local Economic Strategies (1992).

TABLE 12.5. *UK acquisition activity 1980–8*

Years (annual average)	No. of acquisitions	Expenditure on acquisitions (£m. current prices)
1974–81	509	1,289
1982–5	561	5,005
1986	1054	22,105
1987	1809	22,511
1988	1943	28,383
1989	1865	37,196

Source: Hughes (1992), p. 310.

THE EFFICIENCY OF CAPITAL

Historically, public and governmental concern with the provision of capital to industry has been linked to the desire to encourage investment-led growth. This was not the attitude of the Conservatives in the 1980s: 'The thrust of policy was to attack restrictive practices rather than to aim for investment-led growth' (Crafts 1991: 90). This led logically to an emphasis on deregulation and liberalization of the financial system as much as other sectors. This liberalization may have had some effects in lowering borrowing costs for the industrial sector. Equity issues expanded rapidly in the mid-1980s boom up until the stock-market crash of 1987. However, as in other recent stock-market booms, these issues were most significant not as a source of company investment in new equipment, but to finance acquisitions in a merger boom. This merger boom reawakened a debate about short-termism in the British economy. According to this argument the financial system, by judging company performance on a short-term basis, biased company decisions towards behaviour likely to lead to short-term profits, rather than investments, particularly in R & D, requiring a long-term perspective. This was linked to high dividend pay-out rates. Companies which did not conform to this perspective were likely to be subject to take-over. In turn, company acquisition was likely to be a better route to a good stock-market performance than organic, long-term growth. A common comparison was with the role of the German banks in German industry. The point was not that they provided more lending to industry than British banks, but that they shielded companies from hostile take-overs and short-termism (Mayer and Alexander 1990).

Coupled to evidence that mergers were not in general creating more profitable and efficient companies, concern with short-termism and the scale of take-over activity spread across the political spectrum, to include Ministers (House of Lords 1991; Cosh *et al.* 1990; Peacock and Bannock 1991). However this concern did not translate into government action, the government being unwilling to reregulate a financial system so recently deregulated. Indeed the government encouraged the export of take-overs and hence short-termism to other EC countries via changes to EC regulations. The government's role in company structure was largely confined to cases where monopolies threatened to arise from merger activity—and even here action was limited. (A point returned to in the section on Company Organization, below).

The partial exception to this attitude, and the government's main intervention in company finance was in the area of small business. As part of its desire to encourage an enterprise culture the government pursued a number of policies to aid the birth and growth of small businesses. Policies in this area were set out in a number of government documents with titles which summarize the approach: *Lifting the Burden* (Cmnd. 9571), *Build Businesses—Not Barriers* (Cmnd. 9794), *Releasing Enterprise* (CM. 512). As these titles suggest the main emphasis in policy for encouraging small business was on deregulation and generally reducing government impositions on small business. But in addition there was positive help such as subsidized consultancy services, lower corporation tax, programmes for technological transfer, and various schemes to encourage investment in small business (Bannock and Albach 1991). These latter included the Business Expansion Scheme, with tax breaks for investors in small business. However the latter was widely believed to have been exploited as a tax loophole and was ended in 1988.

THE EFFICIENCY OF TECHNICAL CHANGE

One of the often noted tensions in Conservative policy after 1979 was between a neo-classical economics emphasis on static, allocative efficiency and an Austrian economics emphasis on dynamic efficiency (e.g. King 1987). In the area of technical change the Austrian approach would seem to be the relevant one: technical change is obviously not about creating perfect competition and optimum resource allocation, but creating new processes and products and faster growth. But in practice government policy in this area tended to work against the logic of this approach. Whilst extolling the virtues of the free-wheeling entrepreneur and innovator, with the implication of the importance of autonomy and diversity in research activity, the government attempted to centralize control over science and research policy and hence reduce the diversity of publicly supported activity (Edgerton and Hughes 1989).

Alongside this drive for centralization went an overall reduction in the money spent on R & D: 'The U.K. was the only country in which Gross Domestic Expenditure on R & D (GERD) declined as a percentage of G.D.P. over the period 1981 to 1988. The proportions of GERD financed by government and industry, respectively, reveal that this decline was largely the result of the reduction in government support for R & D' (House of Lords 1991: para. 1.17).[7]

This fall in the overall spend was accompanied by a shift in its pattern. The basic idea behind this seems to have been a notion of 'market failure' whereby the private returns to R & D activity fell (or became less certain) the further from the final marketing of the product. Consequently, the government argued, support for near market activity should be curtailed and the focus should be more on basic research (CM. 278: ch. 8). However this approach was widely criticized as ignoring the fact that many of the problems of R & D in Britain seemed to relate to turning inventions into viable products. As an economist told a House of Lords Committee, this was particularly a problem for small firms: 'current Government innovation support policy, with its emphasis on collaboration and "far from market" scientific development is contrary to the needs of smaller firms. This policy fails to address the risk factor in innovation which is a major consideration limiting the ability of smaller firms to

---

[7] The British government financed a larger proportion of total R & D (almost 40 per cent) than governments in other OECD countries, basically because of high spending on defence-oriented R & D (CM. 185).

innovate'. A similar view seems to have been taken by representatives of large firms (House of Lords 1991: paras. 7.20, 7.22).

The Thatcher government (led by the first British Prime
Minister with a scientific training) remained heavily involved in
Research and Development spending. Whilst recognizing the
need to restrain the proportion of this spending going on defence
(CM. 185: para. 4) in practice it did little to reorientate that
spending towards more commercially viable products. In addition, its rather *simpliste* market-failure approach ignored the
extent to which it is not just basic science whose pay-off is
uncertain, but also the process of innovation very close to the
market.

THE EFFICIENCY OF COMPANY STRUCTURE AND ORGANIZATION

As already noted, as part of its enthusiasm for the enterprise
culture the government took a keen interest in one aspect of
company structure, the role of small business. Most policy here
was seen as 'barrier removal' rather than positive encouragement: 'the philosophy of the present British government is that
if both direct taxation and regulation are minimised, then the
small business sector will be able to look after itself, although
some interventions to correct market imperfections are justified'
(Bannock and Albach 1991: 68). Intensive government intervention to aid small firms in the name of the enterprise culture
would obviously be a contradictory policy. In practice the British
government does spend considerable sums encouraging small
business—estimated at around £1bn. in 1988/9, roughly equally
divided between direct expenditure and tax relief (a lower rate of
corporation tax). Whilst this sum is hardly trivial, direct expenditure was little more than 25 per cent of the level of that in
Germany at the same date, where it has been a long-standing
public policy objective to encourage social and political stability
by encouraging small firms (Bannock and Albach 1991).

The climate of encouragement has been accompanied by an
expansion of small firms in the economy. In fact the share of
small firms in manufacturing seems to have bottomed out in the
early 1970s and then risen (Hughes 1989: 142–3). Over the period

1979–89 the share of firms of 1–99 employees in total manufacturing employment went from 17.5 to 24.3 per cent, and of output from 14.6 to 18.6 per cent (Hughes 1992: 306). Most small businesses are not in manufacturing, and the total number of businesses registered for VAT rose by 400,000 between 1979 and 1989. This net figure was made up of 1.9 million new registrations and 1.4 million deregistrations—as Hughes notes (1992: 302) 'the world of enterprise is an extremely turbulent one'.

This picture of revival of small firms in the 1980s may be qualified in a number of ways. First, the role of small firms still seems to be significantly less in Britain than in other major industrial countries. Second, a considerable part of the change in the small firm share of the manufacturing sector reflected the collapse in employment in that sector which was concentrated at the top end of the size range, rather than a massive expansion of small firms (Hughes 1992: 308–9). There is also the question, parallel to that which may be asked about self-employment, about how far the small business revival is a consequence of a lack of employment alternatives, rather than a positive embracing of the enterprise culture.

The growth of smaller firms from the 1970s contributed to the stagnation in the level of industrial concentration, measured by the share of the hundred largest companies in manufacturing output. This figure seems to have fluctuated in the 1980s, with some tendency to fall in the middle of the decade, but then, under the impact of the merger boom, rising in 1988 and 1989 (Bannock and Albach 1991: 24). Whilst committed to the encouragement of small business and to competition generally, the Thatcher government was not very active in regulating mergers and take-overs which favoured the growth of large firms and concentrated industries. (Though they did make high-profile attacks on a small number of markets for services, especially those provided by professional groups, such as opticians, barristers and solicitors, and members of the stock exchange).

Some ambivalence in merger and monopoly policy may again be traced back to a tension between an Austrian/Hayekian emphasis on dynamic efficiency and a neo-classical focus on static allocative efficiency, with quite different implications for attitudes to competition. For the neo-classicals, competition is the driving force behind economic efficiency and the benevolent operation of the invisible hand. Monopoly is a distortion and cause of economic failure. A key function of governments, in this view, is to prevent the emergence of monopolies. From the Austrian point of view, however, excess profits are a reward for endeavour and enterprise and it is only through the creation of monopolies that entrepreneurs enjoy the fruits of their efforts. The market provides the carrots to entice risk-taking, the stick of competition is a deterrence. For Austrians like Hayek, perfect competition is not the ideal but a state in which competition has ceased to exist (Helm *et al.* 1991: 3). In this view the main issue of competition policy should be barriers to entry, whilst recognizing that governments are usually the worst offenders in creating such barriers (Littlechild 1989).

This tension partly explains the weakness of government action on mergers and monopolies in the 1980s. The advisory body in monopolies and mergers, the Office of Fair Trading, examined between 150 and 350 mergers per annum which fell within the legislative remit per annum in the 1980s, but never recommended investigation by the Monopolies and Mergers Commission of more than 14 in any one year. This represents only about 1 per cent of all mergers. Even then investigation only follows if the Department of Trade and Industry agrees. So overall the impact of the MMC is very small in relation to the total number of mergers.

The MMC had traditionally been able to look at the wider range of public interest issues when assessing mergers and monopolies, but in the 1980s the government argued that competition should be the sole criteron—issues of employment, the balance of payments, regional impacts, etc. should be excluded (Fairburn 1989). This is consistent with a hard-nosed neo-classical view, but its impact depends on the notion of competition employed. The evidence of the 1980s is that the threat to competition had to be very overt and significant before even the investigatory powers of the MMC would be invoked.

Direct intervention in internal company matters would have been quite at variance with 1980s economic liberalism. By and large the Thatcher government seemed to regard private-sector management as close to perfection, as it attempted to spread private-sector approaches to management to the public sector, without asking whether such practices had served industry well (let alone whether they could sensibly be transferred to quite different activities in the public sector). Similarly, in line with the idea of the enterprise culture, the government was keen to change popular attitudes to industry and commerce, and to encourage the brightest and the best not to spurn its opportunities, but again this was not linked to a critical assessment of what private-sector management could or should do.

The one very partial exception to this generalization was the government's enthusiasm for flexibility, already discussed. This again was largely based on an approach of removing barriers to what managers would want to do anyway, rather than trying to institute new kinds of managerial practice. A similar point could be made about employee consultation. The government assumed good managers would see the benefits of this, and fought hard against any imposition of such consultation by law, for example, as threatened by the proposed European Company Law proposal from the EC Commission.

In short, in this area at least, the government's actions were consistent with their liberal economics rhetoric. The aim of government should be to allow owners and managers the maximum possibile freedom, it being assumed that from the competition that followed the best possible practices would evolve. What this allowed, amongst other things, was a period of striking fads and fashions in management discourse (though probably less in practice) as various notions—quality circles, total quality control, human-resource management—came and went. These fashion-driven discourses also infected the public sector, with incalculable affects on efficiency.

STATE CAPACITY AND STATE ACHIEVEMENTS

The core of industrial policy after 1979 was to replace policy for industry with a policy which would maximize the freedom of industry to do so as it wished. How far was this policy pursued in practice? We know from the behaviour of aggregate public expenditure that the general aim of rolling back the state was far more difficult to achieve than the government envisaged in 1979. Public spending rose from 42.5 per cent of GDP in 1979, then fell back after 1984 to 41 per cent in 1989. In the area of spending on industrial support a similar cycle is evident (Table 12.6). Expenditure on such areas as nationalized industries rose in the recession, but was then cut back with the progress of privatization. Increasingly, the Department of Employment became a key agency of the enterprise policy whilst the Department of Trade and Industry cut back some of its traditional spending. But even if we take DTI spending as the core of industrial policy, the 36 per cent fall in spending still left it a significant player in the field, and these figures cover only expenditure, not the tax breaks, which for small business at least, cost the exchequer nearly as much as expenditure.

Defining industrial support narrowly, and restricting it to direct expenditure, would suggest by the late 1980s that Britain was a relatively small spender by EC standards. Hughes (1992: 300) suggests that in 1986 Britain spent 4.6 per cent of GDP on such efforts, compared with 7.8 per cent in France, 6.2 per cent in Germany, and an EC average of 7.5 per cent.

TABLE 12.6. *Public expenditure on industrial support 1979/80 to 1988/9* (1979/80 prices)

	% Change 1979 to 1983/4	% Change 1979/80 to 1988/9
Department of Trade and Industry	+ 1	−36
Department of Energy	+70	−98
Department of Employment	+60	+38
Other departments	+58	+ 0.5
TOTAL	+41	−12

Source: Thompson (1990), p. 97.

Of course public spending is at best an imperfect proxy of the impact of government. Thompson (1990: ch. 5) persuasively suggests that a corollary of the shrinkage of public expenditure on industrial intervention in the late 1980s was a more discriminatory set of policies, as broadly available grants and allowances were replaced by more specific aid. This had the perhaps paradoxical effect of increasing the degree of scrutiny of individual firms in order to justify receipt of government money. An Audit Commission study agreed this process was going on, but suggested the DTI was poorly equipped to carry out such close scrutiny of company behaviour (Public Money 1987).

Encouragement of the enterprise culture did not then unambiguously lead to a reduction in government intervention. Deregulation on a significant scale did take place in the 1980s (especially in areas which shifted the balance of power in the enterprise from workers to enterprises). But this was accompanied by some greater centralization of power, for example in science and research policy, and greater scrutiny of company activity in the case of disbursement of grants and allowances. Perhaps most strikingly, policy on the labour-market was highly interventionist, ranging from reforms of social security to the creation of new institutions for training, with the basic aim of cheapening labour and making the labour-market more flexible (Waine 1991: 144–51). There was no straightforward and unambiguous freeing of the economy.

Did the (qualified) movement towards an enterprise economy deliver the goods? As already noticed industrial productivity did recover from its poor 1970 levels in the 1980s, to a level on a par with other OECD countries, though still inferior to the 1960s (Crafts 1991: 83), when Britain was allegedly a highly unenterprising economy. And if we look at the economy as a whole, dominated by the service sector where most small business and self-employed enterprise is active, productivity performance is far poorer. Whatever caused the improvement in productivity in the 1980s was largely confined to manufacturing and therefore seems difficult to relate to the growth of an enterprise culture.

The relative growth of small business should not be exaggerated. Most employment in manufacturing remains in large firms, with four-fifths of all employees working in firms of over 100 people, half in firms of over 500. Equally the contribution of small firms in general to employment growth in the 1980s was no faster than that of larger firms (Hart 1987). In manufacturing the contribution of small firms to total exports is disproportionately small, though this varies greatly from sector to sector (Pratten 1991: 46–8, 232–4). Conditions of work in small firms are almost invariably worse than in larger firms (e.g. Rainnie 1989). On the other hand small firms may be a particularly good source of invention and innovation relative to the resources they devote to R & D (Freeman 1982: ch. 6).

But the point is not to set up an argument on whether small firms are good or bad but to emphasize that their role in the British economy, especially in high-productivity sectors and in the production of tradables, remains quite limited, and that, whatever expansion has taken place has not altered that basic position. Even advocates of small firms in the context of flexible specialization accept that there is little evidence of them playing a major dynamic role in the British economy by the end of the 1980s (Hirst and Zeitlin 1989, 1991).[8]

CONCLUSIONS

The aim of the Conservatives in 1979 was to lay the foundations of a period of non-inflationary sustained growth. What followed was a very severe recession and an unsustainable boom. Whilst in the late 1980s it could be argued with some plausibility that the early 1980s slump was a 'one-off shake-up' (Crafts 1991: 94), the severe recession of 1990–2 suggested that the old problems of inflation and balance of trade problems were now to be encountered even with high levels of unemployment. Even the respectable growth rate of the 1980s seems tarnished when put alongside the combination of low savings and current account deficits which accompanied it.

This is not to argue that nothing changed in the 1980s. The balance of power in the labour-market has shifted dramatically, though this was more apparent in the pay and conditions of work of those at the bottom of the job hierarchy, than those in highly unionized sectors such as manufacturing, where the weakening of unions at the political level had not translated into an obvious shift in wage-bargaining behaviour, though with probably some effect on the effort-bargain.

How far there has been the creation of an enterprise culture is inherently difficult to judge, though surveys of public opinion suggested that the attitudes usually linked to such a culture were not more prevalent in 1990 than in 1979. The cultural diagnosis of British decline had at the same time been powerfully attacked

---

[8] For an up-to-date survey of the place of small firms in the British economy, see Stanworth and Gray (1991).

by historians, and the idea that a particular set of attitudes is the key to economic success seems difficult to square with the major cultural differences between successful countries such as Japan, Germany, and the Asian newly industrializing countries.

Finally the physical infrastructure for sustained economic growth seems to have been neglected in the 1980s. As we have seen, manufacturing investment stagnated. At the same time the infrastructure (roads, railways, etc.) also suffered from the fiscal pressure on public investment expenditure. In 1990 the economy looked considerably different from 1979, but not obviously better equipped for sustained growth. Talk of miracles certainly looks inappropriate. If we take the bench-mark miracle to be turning water into wine, this was not even turning tap water into Perrier.

Further Reading

Crafts, N. (1992), *Was the Thatcher Experiment Worth It?: British Economic Growth in a European Context*, Centre for Economic Policy Research, discussion paper no. 710.

Green, F. (1989) (ed.), *The Restructuring of the U.K. Economy*, London.

Johnson, C. (1991), *The Economy Under Mrs. Thatcher*, Harmondsworth.

Maynard, G. (1988), *The Economy Under Mrs. Thatcher*, Oxford.

Michie, J. (1992) (ed.), *The Economic Legacy 1979–1992*, London.

Minford, P. (1991), *The Supply-Side Revolution in Britain*, London.

Thompson, G. (1990), *The Political Economy of the New Right*, London.

Walters, A. (1986), *Britain's Economic Renaissance*, Oxford.

13

A Case-Study: Cotton

INTRODUCTION

A small number of sectors dominated the industrial landscape of
Britain at the beginning of the twentieth century. The first census
of production in 1907 showed that four such sectors—shipbuilding, iron and steel, coal-mining, and cotton—provided 60 per
cent of manufacturing output and together formed a bloc of
staple industries on which the industrial development of Britain
in the half century before the Great War depended. None of these
was so redolent of Britain's pioneering role in industrialization
as cotton. The key industry of the Industrial Revolution by many
accounts, cotton remained a major industry by any standard up
to 1914. Whilst smaller in employment and output than coal, it
still employed over 600,000 workers. Above all, cotton represented British pre-eminence in international trade in manufactures (Tyson 1968). It was Britain's largest export industry from
the Napoleonic almost to the Second World War. At its peak in
the 1880s, the Lancashire industry supplied 82 per cent of all the
world's trade in cotton-piece goods, the major export product of
the industry (Table 13.1).

By the late 1930s the industry had collapsed, its output was
under half of the 1913 level, its exports little more than 20 per
cent. By the late 1950s, after a brief revival in the late 1940s, the
industry was on the verge of extinction and 'ceased to be an
independently functioning industry during the mid-1960s' (Singleton 1990a: 142) as it was absorbed into the man-made fibre
business. Nothing perhaps symbolizes that demise more than
Britain's reversion to a net cotton-cloth importer from the end
of the 1950s.

This chapter is concerned with the response by government to
the collapse of this old staple industry in the period after 1913.
How did government respond, why did the response take the
form it did, and could the government have done more? In

looking at these issues the focus is on the attempts to secure markets for the industry and attempts to reorganize its structure, the two main types of response to competitive pressure, but other features of the industry's development are also discussed.

MARKETS

The condition of the Lancashire cotton industry in 1913 has been described as 'highly developed, technologically stagnant, competitively fragile' (Kindleberger 1964: 296). That competitive fragility is apparent from the development of the industry's exports in the half-century or so before 1913. The industry was above all an export industry. It exported two-thirds of its total output in 1913, accounting for 70 per cent of world exports of cotton-pieces (Table 13.1). These figures suggest that Britain still held a significant comparative advantage in the industry up to the First World War, though new entrants to world trade such as the USA and Japan (and also Italy) were making some headway. The fragility of this position arose from the fact that the range of markets in which Britain was selling its exports were narrowing sharply even as the total quantities sold abroad expanded.

TABLE 13.1. *Shares of world exports of cotton pieces 1882/4–1955* (%)

	UK	USA	India	Japan
1882–4	82.0	2.8	0.9	—
1910–13	70.0	4.2	1.0	2.1
1926–8	46.1	6.3	2.0	16.3
1936–8	26.9	3.9	3.1	38.9
1949	19.7	19.3	10.1	16.2
1955	11.8	11.5	16.3	24.2

Source: Robson (1957), p. 359.

As Sandberg (1974: ch. 8) shows, the rate of growth of British cotton-piece exports in the period before 1913 was slow in all major markets except that of India. For example, in 1905 the biggest markets apart from India were the Middle East, Latin America, and China, which showed growth of only 3.8 per cent, 1.1 per cent, and minus 10.4 per cent in the period to 1913 (Sandberg 1974: 145–6). Growth was rapid only in the smaller markets of Europe, the White Colonies, and the colonies in Africa. The rate of increase of exports to India over the same period (26.7 per cent) was relatively modest, but the absolute increase was huge. In 1905 that market was already taking 2.5 bn. yards out of 6bn. yards of exports, and by 1913 3.2bn. out of a 7bn. total. Indeed for the whole period 1887 to 1913 three-quarters of all the increase in exports went to India (Sandberg 1974: 142–3).

The fragility of such a dependence on one market is not only evident retrospectively. Cotton is the classic case of an industry easily entered by newly industrializing countries because of its relatively low skill and capital requirements. The nineteenth-century pattern was for country after country to build up its own cotton textile industry, usually behind tariff barriers. This meant that import substitution led to a continuous fall in the proportion of total cotton-goods output entering international trade. According to Robson (1957: 359) this share fell from 45 per cent in 1882–4 to 31 per cent by 1910–13, and continued to fall to 12 per cent by 1953–5. Before the First World War most new entrants to the cotton industry concentrated on conquering home rather than export markets, but in doing so they forced Britain into a dependence on countries which had not yet been able to respond to the strong incentives to create their own modern cotton industry.[1] Lancashire's position, then, 'depended mainly, not on the winning of markets in competition with other modern industries, but on using our industrial lead to sell factory products to non-industrialized countries in which British political influence was used to maintain the British creed of free trade' (Working Party 1946: 4).

In looking at the government's relation to the industry in its period of decline a large part of the story is how far the government was able to keep open foreign markets on which Lancashire was so dependent—though by the 1950s the issue shifted to the extent to which the government would protect the British producers against foreign imports. As already noted the most important such overseas market was India, and this chapter focuses on developments relating to that country.

---

[1] 'Modern' here is taken to exclude handspinning and handloom industries which were very extensive in some countries in the nineteenth century, notably India and China.

From their peak of 3.2bn. yards in 1913, British cotton-piece exports fell to around a quarter of that figure in 1919, before reviving to about half the 1913 level for most of the 1920s (Sandberg 1974: 27). The war was thus a major watershed in sales to this largest export market. The collapse of sales in the war period came in a number of a stages. Initially the fall seems to have reflected a rebound from the overstocking of the market in 1913 and the impact of a poor monsoon in that year on demand. This was followed in 1917 by a further large drop, largely as a result of the shipping shortage in Britain and its effect in driving up export prices. In 1918 these effects on the supply side were added to on the demand side by another monsoon failure and a catastrophic influenza epidemic (Tomlinson 1979: 503–4).

The cutting-off of traditional sources of supply gave a fillip to the factory industry of India (though not to the handloom sector). The share of the market from Indian factories rose from 20 to 40 per cent. Japanese imports into India multiplied by 30–40 times over the war period, but still in 1918/19 accounted for a small proportion of the total market—perhaps 7 per cent. The war had provided a degree of protection for the domestic industry to expand, most of this protection coming not from tariffs or quotas but the inflated prices of the British product (Tomlinson 1979: 497–501). Nevertheless, the war began a major shift in the political capacity of India which increasingly saw her following the example of so many other countries, and building up her cotton industry behind tariff barriers.

Prior to the First World War Britain had successfully imposed on India an almost entirely free-trade regime. This regime posed problems for Indian public finance, given the general difficulties of collecting taxes and their inelasticity in the face of rising public expenditure. This dilemma was resolved in the case of cotton by imposing a 3.5 per cent revenue tariff coupled, from the mid-1890s, to an equivalent duty on cotton goods produced in Indian factories[2] (Harnetty 1962). This remained the tariff position for cottons down to the First World War.

---

[2] This obviously gave a small advantage to the non-factory industry in India, though the amount of direct competition between either Lancashire or Bombay mills and that industry was probably quite small; see Tomlinson (1977).

During that war the public finance position deteriorated as tax revenues declined whilst there was pressure on the Indian Government to spend more on the war effort. This was resolved by raising tariffs to provide backing for a £100m. loan from the Indian to the British Government. The new 7.5 per cent tariff raised a storm of indignation in Lancashire, but the British government gave its support, believing Lancashire's discontent was a price worth paying for the support of articulate India, which saw this tariff as a significant step towards fiscal autonomy (Tomlinson 1979: 502–3).

The tariff was increased in 1921 and the excise duty on Indian factory goods removed in 1925. But the really sharp increase in protectionism came with the slump of the 1930s. In March 1930 the Indian tariff was raised to 15 per cent on British cotton cloth and 20 per cent from other countries. By October 1931 the rates were 25 per cent and 31.25 per cent respectively. Largely in consequence of these changes total Indian imports fell to less than a third of their pre-war level by 1930–1 (Sandberg 1974: 185). But in addition to the shrinkage of the total Indian import market, Britain was losing share to Japan. Despite the discriminating tariff Britain's share of the market was 50 per cent in 1931/2 (97 per cent in 1913) while Japan's was 45 per cent (0.1 per cent in 1913).

The significance of this collapse of Indian demand for British imports is stressed by Sandberg (184): 'In 1938, India imported cotton cloth from Great Britain equal to 3 per cent of the cotton cloth produced in 1912/13. In 1912/13 India had imported 36 per cent of all the cotton cloth produced in Great Britain. The shrinkage of Indian demand alone thus equalled one-third of the British industry's total demand from all sources in 1912/13'.

This loss of Britain's primary market could have been slowed, though certainly not prevented, if Britain had been able to resist growing pressure for Indian fiscal autonomy as part of the wider call for political freedom. But viewed in retrospect any such sustained resistance appears implausible. Indian nationalism was a growing force in the inter-war period, and fiscal policy represented a central symbol of that nationalist struggle.

This is not to say that there was no political pressure on the Indian Government. Whilst the response of Lancashire to the changes of the 1920s was muted, there was renewed disquiet with the tariff increases from 1930. However both the Labour government of 1929–31 and its successor were clearly informed by the Viceroy of India that any attempt to question tariff autonomy would be politically disastrous, and would be likely amongst other things to strengthen the boycotts of British cotton goods which were a feature of the Nationalist struggle in the period. By the time of the Imperial Economic Conference at Ottawa in 1932, India was recognized as on a par with other Dominions in respect of fiscal policy (Tomlinson 1975: 18–21).

However some recent research has suggested that Lancashire retained some influence on British Policy on India through the 1930s (Chatterji 1981; Dupree 1990). Lancashire was certainly active in trying to modify Indian tariffs in the 1930s. Raymond Streat, Secretary of the Manchester Chamber of Commerce (MCC) in this period, acted as an ambassador for the industry in the tariff discussions which characterized this period following the breakdown of free trade in the face of the slump. He journeyed to India three times in this period, acting as part of a delegation from the industry but with government help. These efforts did yield some small fruit in 1936, with some tariff reductions on British imports, but by then the expansion of domestic production and Japanese import penetration had gone too far to be reversed by small tariff changes (Dupree 1987: i: xxiv–xxvi; Dupree 1990: 106–9).

In India governmental or private pressure on tariffs was complicated by the delicate political situation. In the case of exports to other Colonial countries without significant indigenous industries no such political inhibitions existed. In particular, when negotiations with Japan to limit her exports to such markets broke down in 1934, the British government imposed tariffs, which gave a boost to British cotton exports in the 1930s. Help also came from the independent Empire countries, Canada, Australia, and New Zealand, who had no domestic industries to protect and were willing to make some concessions to British goods in the Ottawa negotiations. But all these countries together were taking less than 0.5bn. sq. yds of British cloth in the peak year of 1937, so it was little compensation for the loss in India (Sandberg 1974: 200–2). By 1936–8 Lancashire's export position was heavily dependent on government action, three-quarters of all exports were being given some protection (Robson 1957: 10).

TABLE 13.2. *British cotton-piece exports 1900–60* (bn. yds.)

1900	5.0
1905	6.2
1913	7.1
1919	3.5
1929	3.8
1931	1.8
1939	1.5
1945	0.5
1948	0.9
1955	0.5
1960	0.2

Sources: 1900–55, Robson (1957), p.333; 1960, Singleton (1991a), p. 118.

The MCC worked closely with the Board of Trade in the 1930s to try to maintain Lancashire's export markets. But even apart from the obvious broader political issues involved in such tariff negotiations, especially in India, the Board was not by any means simply an agent of Lancashire's wishes. In particular it stuck firmly to the policy of most-favoured-nation trade treaties, whereby a trade concession granted to one country was granted to all. This ran against the MCC's desire for more unambiguous discrimination where this was perceived to be to Britain's advantage (Dupree 1990: 113–14).

During the Second World War the climate in which the industry operated was subject to sharp reversal. As in the First World War the constraint on the industry's level of activity shifted from the demand to the supply side, as shipping availability reduced both raw cotton supplies and export availability, whilst total output was reduced by a 40 per cent reduction in the work-force. By the end of the war capacity had been reduced by one-third compared with 1939 and exports fell from 1.5bn. yds. in 1939 to 0.5bn. in 1945 (Table 13.2).

However the war had had a much more devastating effect on the Japanese industry, and in general the early post-war years were characterized by a sellers' market as consumers restocked in a context of constrained supply capacity. Exports expanded, almost doubling between 1945 and 1948, but never getting close to their pre-war level. From 1951 and more sharply from 1953 decline set in, until by the end of the decade exports had become almost negligible and Britain was a net importer of cotton goods.

On Independence in 1947 India and Pakistan raised tariffs against British goods, which meant that imports of British cottons were negligible by 1950. In addition, India now emerged as a significant exporter of cotton goods, successfully replacing many British and Japanese exports especially in low-income Commonwealth markets, and gaining a larger share of total world exports by the early 1950s.

Japan's industry was also reviving in the late 1940s. Lancashire made efforts to use the power of the Occupation authorities in Japan to block the expansion of the industry, but there was never any chance that Britain and the United States would cripple the chances of Japan being restored to economic health by inhibiting the production of a non-warlike commodity. But the Japanese threat to export markets was quickly surpassed by Indian and Hong Kong incursions into the UK market.

TABLE 13.3. *Imports of cotton cloth into the UK 1938–65* (m. yds.)

Source	1938	1950	1955	1960	1965
Hong Kong	—	5	51	123	123
India	1	76	137	231	157
Japan	19	91	64	52	28
Pakistan	—	—	—	40	43
TOTAL	52	287	300	728	529

Source: Singleton (1986), p. 100.

Unsurprisingly, Lancashire reacted with alarm to this import growth, but 'Despite protests and deputations including one to Churchill at 10 Downing Street in 1955, Raymond Streat and the Cotton Board were unable to alter the government policy, which refused to risk the tariff preferences in India for other UK exports' (Dupree 1987: ii: xxiv). However, voluntary export quota agreements were made with the three biggest suppliers of imports in 1959, although these were not very restrictive. Hong Kong, for example, acquired a quota ceiling of 164m. sq. yds. per annum, over 40m. more than its exports to Britain in 1958. Further, more widespread and somewhat more stringent restrictions were agreed in the 1960s, but by then the damage had been done (Singleton 1986: 100–1).

In retrospect it is plain that exports could not provide a permanent basis for an industry on the scale of Lancashire cotton in 1913. The already well-established trend was for import-substitution behind tariff barriers. By 1913 this pattern left Britain extraordinarily dependent on one market, India, where the political pressures for that country to follow suit and erect tariff barriers to protect its own factory industry would soon prove irresistible. Similarly in the 1950s Britain's claims to an enlightened relationship with its poor Commonwealth partners meant there was little scope for keeping out cheap textile imports. In the general protectionist climate of the 1930s controls on Japanese exports were politically possible, but the movement in a more liberal direction in the 1950s made that kind of protectionism increasingly unfashionable.

Lying behind this interplay of economic and political calculation was the basic problem of Britain's eroding comparative advantage in basic cotton textiles. The precise basis of this comparative advantage may be disputed (e.g. Mass and Lazonick 1990, and below) but given the low skill, low capital requirements for the production of basic cotton textiles, loss of competitiveness appears largely inevitable. Thus cotton can be seen in the context of product-cycle approaches to industry, in which sectors develop first in the most advanced countries (in Britain around 1800) but then spread to, eventually, the poorer countries able to compete with relatively unsophisticated technology on the basis of lower labour costs (Singleton 1991a: 21–2). This approach suggests that any government attempt to restrict competition would only delay the inevitable, and certainly it would be difficult to imagine how Britain could have hung on to its dominance in the world cotton trade of the early twentieth century. On the other hand protective policies might have been used to facilitate and/or encourage changes in products and production processes which might have slowed the decline of the industry. This issue will be returned to below.

PROFITS

The cotton export boom of 1900–13 was accompanied by healthy rates of profit in Lancashire. Whilst no figures are available on rates of return in the industry, Robson's (1957: 338) figures suggest sharp cycles in profitability but no trend decline, and some evidence of improving returns (and dividend payments) from 1905. Sandberg (1974: chs. 4, 5) argues that these buoyant profits reflected significant efficiency gains in this period, despite the industry's much-lamented and much-debated failure to adopt ring-spinning and automatic looms which represented technological best practice.[3]

In the First World War profits were squeezed hard in 1915 as output was restricted, but thereafter recovered in a smaller market, reaching unprecedented levels in 1918 and 1919. 'Whilst it must be borne in mind that profits in excess of the immediate pre-war average were taxed at a rate of 50 per cent from 1915 and 80 per cent from 1917, it is clear that the owners of the cotton industry did not have to go hungry between 1914 and 1918' (Singleton 1992: 4).

This boom in profitability was prolonged into 1919/20 and was to have serious long-term consequences for the industry. On the back of the boom and the profits it generated, many cotton companies were refloated at highly inflated prices. The usual method was for syndicates to finance purchases of mills with bank loans repayable from the proceeds of the reflotation. But when the boom broke this left many banks heavily committed with unrepayable loans to the industry. This process of reflotation, amongst other implications, had a debilitating effect on the financial position of the reconstituted companies by burdening them with large fixed-interest debt (Daniel and Jewkes 1928; Bamberg 1988: 84–7).

The underlying profitability of the industry was hit hard by the export collapse after 1920. No continuous series is available for the inter-war period, but Robson's (1957: 338) figures suggest

---

[3] These claims about efficiency gains are controversial, and disputed by, for example, Mass and Lazonick (1990): 28–31. They argue that Britain maintained its competitiveness in some low-income markets in the decades before 1913 by using lower quality inputs and higher labour effort rather than real efficiency gains.

that profits were negative from 1927 to 1933, before staging a recovery from 1935. Some of this recovery of the late 1930s no doubt reflected the bankruptcy of some of the least profitable and most heavily indebted companies, helped by the provisions of the Cotton Spinning Industry Act of 1936 and its encouragement of the scrapping of capacity (discussed further in the section on the Efficiency of Company Structure and Organization). Nevertheless, with continuing excess capacity in the industry it is unsurprising that aggregate profitability remained low.

The profitability revival of the late 1930s seems to have peaked in 1940, but to have been quite well maintained during the Second World War (Robson 1957: 338). The strong demand and cuts in supply favoured profitability despite price controls, and this situation continued into the post-war period. Singleton (1991*a*: 101–4) compares these profits with machinery prices, and shows that the former increased faster than the latter from the mid-1930s until the mid-1940s. Hence, despite employers' moans about the impact of tax on the industry's finances (which ignored the general investment allowance introduced in 1945), 'profits were not the obstacle to re-equipment after 1945 that they had been before World War Two' (Singleton 1991*a*: 104). Specific investment subsidies for the cotton industry, effectively raising the rate of profit on investment also failed to secure much of a response, for reasons which will be returned to below.

This renaissance of profit levels was relatively short-lived, and from 1951 profits seem to have fallen sharply. Dividends, which had risen to over 20 per cent in 1951, fell back much less, so that the internal funds for re-equipment were extremely low and the industry did not respond to the new market conditions by trying to modernize its plant and equipment (Singleton 1991*a*: 147–8). A further government scheme to finance re-equipment (as well as scrapping) was introduced in 1959, but like the 1948 Act the implied increased level of profits had little but a short-term impact on investment (Miles 1968: chs. 4, 5).

In sum, for most of the period from 1913 to the 1960s profits in the cotton industry were depressed. The government attempted to offset the direct impact of this on investment by the acts of 1948 and 1959, but in neither case with much success. The failure of the high profits of the late 1940s to stimulate significant investment suggests that short-run profits, either as an incentive or a source of funds, were not the crucial limitation on investment in the industry in the years of long-run decline.

THE EFFICIENCY OF LABOUR

Until the First World War the state's role in the supply of labour, the skills of labour, or the systems of labour use in the cotton industry was more or less zero. The industry drew on highly localized labour-markets where competition for workers, especially for the women workers who made up over half its work-force, was extremely limited. These workers were almost all trained by informal on-the-job methods which fell well short of the apprenticeship arrangements common in other craft trades. The workers were highly unionized, and whilst local agreements remained important, by the late nineteenth century there had evolved 'lists' in both spinning and weaving sectors which regulated wages on a basically piece-rate system. Before the War this system provided an adequate inflow of labour into the industry and with a largely stable industrial-relations system provided no reason for such state intervention as occurred in the pre-1913 coal industry (Penn 1983).

The government's impact on labour in the cotton industry in any of its aspects was only significant in the two World Wars and in the Attlee Government period, and only in the last of these periods was the government trying to pursue a policy aimed at expanding the output and increasing the efficiency of the industry.

In the First World War the demands for manpower led to a loss of manpower in the industry, though the major constraint on output was the supply of raw cotton. Total numbers in the industry fell by about 20 per cent, but by 1917 this was an insufficient decline to allow for the employment of the remainder. Under the aegis of the Cotton Control Board, set up to allocate supplies of raw cotton, a system of rotating unemployment was established, so that considerable reserves of labour were maintained in the industry rather than being drawn into munitions work or the army. This occurred despite wages in cotton lagging behind both price rises and wages in other sectors (Singleton 1992).

In contrast to the Second World War, the First did not see the creation of a problem of labour shortage—rather, of course, after the post-war boom of 1919/20, mass unemployment came to characterize the industry in the 1920s and 1930s. Between 1926 and 1939 the rate of unemployment of cotton operatives never fell below 10 per cent, and reached a maximum of 43.2 per cent in 1931, a figure comparable to that in the other old staples: coal, steel, and shipbuilding. As Singleton (1991*a*: 12) remarks 'It was during these years that the seeds were sown for the later reluctance of Lancastrians to enter the mills'.

In the employers' attempts to respond to the inter-war crisis industrial relations became a major flashpoint on one occasion. This was the 'more looms movement' initiated by the employers and given support by the Committee set up by the Labour government to investigate the industry (Cmd. 3615). The issue came to crisis when the employers, in attempting to reduce weavers' wages, provoked a strike, which they won in 1932. As a result the number of looms worked by a weaver rose from 4 to 6 or 8, with very little increase in pay (Hilton *et al.* 1935). In 1935 the government intervened to give statutory backing to wage levels to try to prevent competitive undercutting by firms.

Overall government involvement in labour issues was limited and *ad hoc* in this period. In part this reflected the predisposition of governments not to get involved in such issues, but it also reflected a lack of a clear plan by the employers on such matters, as true on labour as it was in other areas.

The Second World War, like the First, led to a loss of labour from the industry. In 1941 production in the industry was concentrated as part of the general policy of freeing resources from inessential industries for the war effort. This led to the closure (but not scrapping) of almost 40 per cent of spinning and weaving capacity. The total numbers (employed and unemployed) attached to the industry fell from 393,000 in 1938 to 209,000 by 1945 (Working Party 1946: 7). Faced with booming demand, and physical capacity little different from before the war, the key problem for the industry at the end of the war was to recruit more labour, and to raise the output of those employed. The Working Party (54) estimated that the industry had the capacity to employ 390,000, but was 42 per cent in deficit on this figure in January 1946. They proposed a major campaign of recruitment to overcome this deficit. The industry had also seen a major ageing of its work-force—in 1939 half the male work-force was between the ages of 20 and 40, but less than a quarter was in this age-group in 1945 (Lacey 1947: 34).

The Attlee Government was initially strongly committed to the idea of 'manpower planning'—drawing up budgets of manpower, and trying to move labour into undermanned industries (Cairncross 1985: 385–99). One such industry was cotton, especially because of its potential to help with the crying need for export expansion. The government took a number of measures to try to encourage labour recruitment into cotton. They established a Ministry of Labour Training Centre in Lancashire and they encouraged the American-style 'Training Within Industry' for foremen and junior managers. They also set up the Evershed Commission to try to reform the wage system in the industry and make employment in it more attractive by narrowing the unskilled/skilled wage differential (Ministry of Labour 1945).

The government also encouraged the improvement of working conditions and amenities in the industry. However the government resisted more radical expedients of compulsion, urged on them by many authorities. This was in line with their general reluctance to reimpose wartime controls over labour (see Ch. 7). In the absence of coercion, a great effort was put into persuasion (Crofts 1989, esp. chs. 8–10). Their efforts together achieved limited success. Singleton (1991*a*: ch. 3) stresses the failure of policy to restore employment to pre-war levels. Dupree (1992: 31) on the other hand emphasizes that between 1945 and 1952 the labour-force did rise by more than 100,000, well in excess of the Working Party's expectations (Working Party 1946: 61).

The second major strand of government policy was to try to improve labour productivity, especially through what came to be known as redeployment. This focus arose partly from the problems encountered in labour recruitment, partly from widely publicized accounts of the low labour productivity in cotton in comparison with the United States. The government took the lead on this issue, reflecting Ministers', and especially Stafford Cripps's enthusiasm for such managerial techniques as time study (Tiratsoo and Tomlinson 1993*a*). Trials and experiments in this particular area were pursued in both spinning and weaving in the late 1940s. However progress was slow. Employers were making handsome profits with existing methods and were reluctant to force the pace. Most of the union leaderships were in favour of the new techniques, though there was more reluctance in some local centres (Singleton 1991*a*: ch. 4). Certainly the government's hopes of reforms to work practices as part of a wholesale re-equipment of the industry were not realized.

The government's attempt at a comprehensive modernization of the industry, including changes in work practices, is shown in the design of the 1948 Cotton Spinning (Re-equipment) Subsidy Act. This offered investment subsidies on condition that mills combined into groups of approximately 500,000 spindles, while the unions would have to agree to double-day shift-working in re-equipped mills and to co-operate in schemes to improve the efficiency of labour utilization. The scheme gained union support for the changes in work practices, but largely foundered on employers' limited willingness to amalgamate into large groups, even though the minimum size was eventually reduced (Singleton 1991*a*: 106–7; Dupree 1992: 28–31).

In one influential view the systems of labour organization moved from being a major reason for Lancashire's comparative advantage in the Victorian heyday to becoming a central contributor to its competitive weakness in the twentieth century. Lazonick (1986: 45) argues that under this system a deal had been effectively struck in the late nineteenth century whereby 'the fragmented employers had been willing to grant workers substantial shopfloor control and earnings stability in exchange for labour peace and uninterrupted production'. But in his view this system was no longer viable in the new competitive conditions after the First World War, when a revolution in the corporate structure was required involving vertical integration of the various processes in the industry coupled to an effective displacement of power over patterns of work away from the workers to management. Unions and workers thus contributed significantly to restricting the options available to the industry in trying to make itself more competitive:

Attempts to raise productivity and cut costs by redivision of labour on the *traditional* technologies were stymied by the desire and power of the unions to protect their positions of job control. At the same time, firms that contemplated the introduction of new technologies, such as the ring-frame and automatic loom, had to contend with the power of the

ring spinners' union or the weavers' union to determine the level of
piece-rates and the number of machines per worker (Lazonick 1986: 20–1).

But as Lazonick himself suggests, in his analysis the labour
aspect was only part of the institutional conditions which obstructed the move to a vertically integrated, truly mass-production cotton industry. The key problem was the heavy investment
(both financial and psychic) in the highly vertically disintegrated
system of nineteenth-century Lancashire, in which flexibility and
responsiveness to market conditions were purchased at the expense of the low production costs available from a mass-production system. Faced with competition from low-wage producers,
the necessary technological and productive changes could not be
pursued because of the institutional blockage—the unwillingness
and incapacity of the owners to give up their separate corporate
identities to form modern, large-scale, and vertically integrated
corporations (Lazonick 1986; Mass and Lazonick 1990: 50–7).

As we have seen, this linkage between forms of corporate
organization and labour practices was made explicitly by the
Labour government in the 1948 proposals. In this they gained
considerable support from the trade unions, but rather little from
employers. However, the one major attempt by the government
to couple the modernization of the industry to a reform of labour
practices proved ineffectual. The problem was not the unwillingness of the state to involve itself in issues concerning labour and
productivity but the obduracy of employers. Whether employers
were right to resist such a strategy is returned to in the discussion
of investment and company organization.

THE EFFICIENCY OF INVESTMENT

One of the best known features and criticisms of the British
cotton industry was its failure to invest significantly in the new
technologies of ring-spinning and automatic looms before the
First World War. In 1913 in the United States 87 per cent of all
spindles were rings, while only 19 per cent were in Britain, the
traditional mule-spindle making up the remainder. At the same
date automatic looms made up 40 per cent of all looms in the
United States, but only 1–2 per cent of those in Britain. (Robson
1957: 355–6).

Much debate has gone into the reasons for this difference. Was it due to entrepreneurial failure or to differences in the constraints facing employers in the two countries? There is now a broad consensus that in terms of the market conditions facing individual employers, the British failure to adopt the new technology was a rational one, though the reasons for this failure, and whether it represented a failure in some broader, national sense remain matters of dispute[4] (Sandberg 1974: chs. 2–4; Mass and Lazonick 1990).

Britain's failure to adopt the new technology on a large scale did not of course mean there was no investment in Lancashire in the boom years before 1914. But most of this investment aimed at increasing capacity along existing lines rather than embodying new techniques. Total capacity in the industry continued to expand in the period from 1914 through to the end of the post-war boom, and assuming that one ring-spindle was equivalent to 1.33 mules, spinning capacity peaked in 1927. In fact given the scale of the drop in demand the reduction in capacity in Lancashire was very limited, perhaps 5 per cent between 1924 and 1930. Gross investment in about 800,000 spindles was made in this period (compared with 57.6m. total capacity in 1924). In the 1930s by contrast capacity fell sharply, by almost 40 per cent between 1930 and 1939. At the same time gross investment declined almost to vanishing point (Sandberg 1974: 123).

One of the striking features of the 1930s was that the number of ring-spindles fell by 20 per cent, though their share of total capacity rose. A major reason for this was the possibility of profitable (or loss-minimizing) sales of second-hand rings abroad, whilst second-hand mules had nothing but scrap value. The likelihood of such sales increased markedly with bankruptcies, which became much more common in the 1930s. As commentators had lamented even earlier, Lancashire was not only equipping its competitors with new machines (most ring-spindles were made in Lancashire) but also with second-hand equipment from Lancashire's mills (Bowker 1928).

---

[4] The dispute partly depends on whether entrepreneurs are seen as successful in so far as they respond rationally to given constraints, or whether they change the constraints. The former may be called a neo-classical approach, the latter Schumpeterian, after Joseph Schumpeter.

In general Lancashire's investment behaviour in the 1920s and 1930s is perfectly explicable in terms of demand conditions and the very low realized and, presumably, expected profits in the period. More controversial is that behaviour in the later 1940s. In the war period total capacity was stable, concentration leading to mothballing rather than scrapping. The 1946 Working Party recommended that in order to respond to likely continuing labour shortages and to increased competitiveness there should be a major re-equipment of the industry coupled to a big programme of amalgamations. The programme of re-equipment was linked to the Platt Committee's (1944) emphasis on the lack of ring-spindles and automatic looms in Lancashire, and the Working Party recommended that the programme be financed by a levy on the industry and administered by a Re-Equipment Board (Working Party 1946: ch. 6).

These proposals were subject to much discussion between industry representatives and the Board of Trade, and eventually the government came forward with the 1948 Act (Dupree 1992: 28–31). This substituted a 25 per cent grant for a levy to encourage spinning re-equipment. As noted above, this aid was made conditional on reforms in labour practices and amalgamations. However the amalgamation proposals met substantial resistance. The minimum number of spindles in an amalgamation necessary to qualify for the grant was reduced from one-half to one-quarter of a million under pressure from the employers, but even then few new amalgamations took place. The expectation was that £12m. might be needed to finance the subsidy, but in the event only £2.6m. was claimed (Singleton 1991a: 107).

A number of factors conditioned this outcome. Demand conditions were leading to high profits with existing equipment, much of which had long since been written off. Capacity was plentiful, the constraint on output largely being labour supply. Singleton (1990b, 1991a: ch. 2) sees this failure to invest in new equipment as a rational response to prevailing conditions and expectations, especially, he argues, Lancashire's well-founded belief that in the medium term prospects for the industry were poor.[5] On the other hand it may be asked whether this is not too deterministic a view

---

[5] Dupree (1987, ii, xvi) asserts, however, that Raymond Streat's diary shows that important figures in the industry in the late 1940s did not regard the resumption of the downward trend in its fortunes as inevitable.

of the industry's future. Whilst it is clearly difficult to see Lancashire hanging on to its old low-quality markets in the face of revived competition from low-wage producers in the 1950s, perhaps something more might have been rescued if some attempt had been made to invest in order to move the industry up-market, as was done with some success by other high-wage, Western European producers (Tomlinson 1991*e*; Singleton 1991*b*).

The proposals of the Working Party and the government of the 1940s were basically for an Americanization of the industry in terms of technology and working practices, but it is doubtful how far this would have been successful if attempted. The US industry itself came under very heavy competitive pressures after 1950, and so perhaps did not provide a model which in the long run would have been viable for Lancashire.

THE EFFICIENCY OF TECHNICAL CHANGE

As noted above, the British cotton industry throughout the twentieth century was characterized by very limited technical change. The basic spinning and weaving processes did not change radically, though there was more innovation in the finishing (dyeing, bleaching, printing) parts of the industry. Research and development expenditure seems to have been very limited, most of it being spent through the Shirley Institute, headquarters of the British Cotton Industry Research Association, this Association having been set up in the enthusiasm for industrial research brought about by the First World War.[6] In 1946 the Shirley Institute spent £140,000 and employed 70 graduates full-time on research. A survey of research by individual firms in 1946 revealed a 'far from reassuring' position where only 108 (out of over 2,000) firms in the industry indicated that they employed between them 86 graduates engaged full-time on research (Working Party 1946: 132).

[6]   The founding document of the Association (Provisional, 1917) is a classic of the type produced in the war. It proposes more research so that Britain can win the 'war of commerce' once the 'war of iron and steel' is over (5). Germany is both the threat to British economic supremacy, but also the model of how things could be better.

Before the 1940s this area does not seem one to which either the industry itself or government had devoted much attention. Whilst important breakthroughs were made in artificial fibres, the cotton industry itself remained a low-tech entity, with what R & D did occur focused on 'the refinement and improvement of existing machines and processes rather than to the discovery or invention of fundamentally different ones' (Working Party: 132).

The Working Party called for a major enhancement of this R & D activity as part of its project for modernizing the industry. This included proposals for experimental mills to test out new methods and practices, with an especial emphasis on new methods of labour deployment. Most effort in the late 1940s went into these latter efforts, organized by both the Cotton Board and the Shirley Institute. Despite encouraging results, the technologies developed did not spread widely in the industry (Singleton 1991*a*: 72–5). A similar fate befell efforts by the Board of Trade's Special Research Unit, which attempted to spread OR techniques into industry, including the cotton industry.

THE EFFICIENCY OF COMPANY STRUCTURE AND ORGANIZATION

The cotton industry of the pre-1913 years had a very particular form of industrial organization which evolved slowly through the period of pre-eminence in the nineteenth century. This form of organization was highly unintegrated, both horizontally or vertically. Broadly the industry can be divided into spinning, weaving, and finishing sections plus agents and merchants, and each of these consisted of a large number of small firms specialized in their own activities. Indeed, there were major subdivisions within these sectors, commonly geographically based: for example, the Oldham area concentrated on spinning coarse yarns while Bolton concentrated on fine yarns. Jewkes and Jewkes (1966: 120) calculated that in 1911 77 per cent of spindles were owned by firms that only spun, 65 per cent of looms in firms that only wove.

There seems to be general acceptance that this pattern of organization was well suited to competitive success in the nineteenth century. In a rapidly expanding but changing market this pattern allowed the agents and merchants to feed back customer requirements to firms who produced largely to order on the basis of highly specialized machinery, workers, and managers. Connections between independent firms were maintained by informal networks, creating significant external economies of scale in the South Lancashire area where the industry was concentrated (Lazonick 1986: 22–3; Singleton 1991*a*: 4–5).

How far this structure was an obstacle to responding to the competitive challenge after 1913 has been much debated (Lazonick 1983; Saxonhouse and Wright 1984; Mass and Lazonick 1990). Broadly put, Lazonick and his co-workers argue that to transform itself the British industry required transformations in its techniques across the board, and that vertical disintegration was a crucial obstacle to that. For one section, say spinning, to shift to new techniques only made sense if parallel changes were being made elsewhere, or the new levels of throughput of yarn would not find a market. On the other hand Saxonhouse and Wright suggest that factor cost rather than organizational factors accounted for the failure to adopt technological changes. In this view Britain's loss of competitiveness reflected the underlying shift in comparative advantage in cotton production as Britain became a capital-rich, high-wage country trying to compete with low-wage countries in a sector where wage costs were crucial.

How far major changes in company organization were needed in response to the decline in demand in the inter-war period was much debated at the time, though the beginnings of this debate largely began in the late 1920s rather than earlier in that decade. At the beginning of the slump in demand after the post-war boom the main response by the industry was the traditional one of short-time working, based on the assumption that the problem was temporary and expansion would recommence in due course. As noted in Chapter 4, this was a common view in the staple industries and government circles in this period.

But from the late 1920s an enthusiasm for rationalization emerged, a term which in the context of the cotton industry meant amalgamations aimed at securing closure of marginal concerns and concentration of production in the most efficient concerns. This enthusiasm even tempted Keynes into are uncharacteristic intervention into industrial politics (Keynes 1981*a*).

Schemes for such amalgamations partly flowed from the failure of attempts at voluntary control of output and prices, such as that attempted by the American Yarn Association covering the American spinning section (Kirby 1974: 149, 154–5). Such attempts suggest how far the fragmented nature of the industry was an obstacle to collective action, and this meant that any process of voluntary amalgamation was likely to be difficult to secure. This problem was resolved, at least in part, by the role of an outside agency—the Bank of England—in amalgamations and scrapping.

Whilst reacting to initiatives from within the industry, the prime motive for the Bank to get involved at all was to secure the position of the commercial banks. As noted above the local banks in Lancashire had unwittingly become big creditors of cotton firms in the wake of the collapse of the post-war boom. Between 1921 and 1927 these banks had been reluctant to 'pull the plug' on the indebted mills, partly for fear of losing custom from such an attitude, partly from a long tradition of non-interference in the firms they lent to. However, the Bank of England was worried that such indebtedness threatened the viability of the Lancashire banks, who unlike nationwide banks were unable to offset losses in cotton from profits elsewhere.

It was in an attempt to resolve the interrelated structural problems of the Lancashire banks and the cotton industry that Norman [Governor of the Bank] intervened in the late 1920s, when he marshalled most of the creditor banks into coercing a large number of their debtor mill companies into a new merger, the Lancashire Cotton Corporation (LCC) (Bamberg 1988: 87).

The promoters of the LCC saw it as a first move towards vertical integration in the industry, but in the short run saw the amalgamation as more or less automatically producing significant economies of scale. But the actual mills acquired by the LCC, whilst not necessarily the least efficient, were a random collection, many of which were old and inefficient and scattered over Lancashire. The commercial banks saw the LCC not so much as the spearhead of a revival of the industry but more as a useful way of unloading some of their most dubious assets. The Corporation, far from moving into vertical integration, rapidly got bogged down into trying desperately to make this heterogeneous set of spinning capacity into an efficient horizontal amalgamation. After many travails the LCC in the later 1930s did manage to scrap a considerable number of spindles and integrate the rest into a profitable firm. But the outcome was much less than the original ambition to reorganize the whole of the industry (Bamberg 1988: 87–94).

The Bank of England's role in the cotton industry was partly designed by Norman to pre-empt state intervention (Kirby 1974: 149). In fact the Labour government of 1929, about which such concerns might be thought most relevant, was extremely reluctant to get involved in direct intervention in industry, and backed the Bank's role in the LCC (Edgerton 1986: ch. 7).

Various other attempts to get finance for amalgamations, especially in the spinning section, were made in the 1930s. The problem was that finance was hard to obtain unless amalgamations were likely to enhance profitability. This was unlikely unless they led to substantial capacity reductions, and it was very difficult to secure agreement on such reductions. Amalgamations thus became unlikely unless underpinned by statutory measures of control. In the event the government was only willing to provide such measures in a very limited form, that of scrapping surplus capacity, under the 1936 Cotton Spinning Industry Act: 'Whilst a reduction in spinning capacity was undoubtedly desirable, the primary objective of the 1936 Act was distinct from that of the earlier rationalization movement in so far as it was aimed, not at overcoming adverse market conditions, but at easing and hastening the operation of market forces' (Bamberg 1988: 96).

Structural change in the cotton industry in the 1930s was much faster than in the 1920s. In the 1920s there was virtual stagnation, as both labour and capital were reluctant to leave the industry. In the 1930s a substantial reduction in capacity took place via market and non-market forces. But this still (in 1938) left capacity utilization at 75 per cent in spinning and 66 per cent in weaving (Kirby 1974: 157–8). Equally, whilst there had been a substantial process of horizontal amalgamation, especially on the spinning side of the industry, there was little evidence of a process of vertical integration. Some at least in the industry saw the desirability of such a structure, but the obstacles to its achievement remained considerable.

Structural changes during the Second World War were very limited. The concentration of production policy was explicitly a temporary measure, and was largely reversed after the war so that total capacity and its structure were little altered. The firms mothballed during the war were not necessarily the least efficient, as an important criterion in the concentration process was how far labour in a particular area was in demand for munitions production. This meant closures related to this factor which did not necessarily correlate with inefficiency (Edgerton 1986: 291–3; Lacey 1947: 32–5).

When the Working Party made its report the industry remained vertically unintegrated. It calculated that 'less than a fifth of the spindles and less than a quarter of the looms are owned by firms which both spin and weave' (37). In terms of horizontal concentration, the top five firms owned about one-third of total capacity (39) in spinning, whilst in weaving the top sixteen firms only owned just over 5 per cent of total capacity (41). In response to these figures, and its desire to see a major re-equipment of the industry, the Working Party argued for amalgamation and for vertical integration. In both cases, however, the recommendations were quite strongly qualified to emphasize that these changes were called for not from a general belief in the virtues of size, but as necessary to facilitate re-equipment and the possibility of a concerted policy for the industry as a whole (175).

As noted already, the 1948 Act designed to encourage re-equipment was conditional on a minimum size of plant in the spinning sector. In 1946 there were over 250 spinning firms (almost 90 per cent of the total) with less than 250,000 spindles, which the government agreed to regard as that minimum (39). But very few of these were willing to give up their independent existence for the sake of the investment grant.

Some movement towards vertical integration took place in the late 1940s, but most of it was delayed until the 1950s and 1960s (Table 13.4). Vertical integration eventually came about when the fate of the industry was sealed, and developed largely from a defensive response to what had become an overwhelming collapse of the industry. It was also part of the process whereby cotton became absorbed in the man-made fibre industry and ceased to exist as a separate entity (Singleton 1991*a*: ch. 10).

TABLE 13.4. *Vertically integrated spinning-weaving firms, 1939–65*

	% of total spindles	% of total looms
1939	23	24
1953	32	31
1955	36	33
1959	58	35
1965	67	41

Source: Jewkes and Jewkes (1966), p. 122.

STATE CAPACITY AND STATE ACHIEVEMENTS

Prior to the Second World War governments of all persuasions were extremely reluctant to become involved in the affairs of the cotton industry. During the First World War a Cotton Control Board had been established on a statutory basis, but this had been explicitly for the duration of the war, and largely concerned with the allocation of scarce raw cotton amongst firms in the industry. It was wound up at the war's end (Henderson 1922).

The reasons for this reluctance to become involved resulted partly from a general unwillingness to break with the tenets of economic liberalism. This doctrine regarded such intervention as likely to do more harm than good, both by reducing the free response to changing circumstances held to be the economic keystone of a free enterprise economy, and by unleashing all kinds of undesirable political pressures for the expansion of government into areas where it was incompetent and likely to be at the mercy of vested interests. Apart from such general doctrinal objections there were more specific problems that such intervention would raise. First, there was the problem of what agency of the government could play a role in industry. In the case of the cotton industry a significant government interest was shown by the 1929 Labour government. A Committee was established first under the Committee for Civil Research and later the Economic Advisory Council. The Board of Trade became involved in discussions over the Committee's report. At about the same time Sir Horace Wilson became Chief Industrial Adviser to the Board of Trade and actively pursued proposals for capacity reduction with employers from Lancashire. But the Board of Trade was not equipped for an active interventionist role and its actions were linked to 'industrial diplomacy' (Ch. 4). Partly because of the absence of an agency appropriate for the purpose the government was unwilling to attempt any legislation or to intervene publicly in the industry. In consequence it welcomed the role of the Bank of England as a way of doing something without being directly involved (Edgerton 1986: ch. 7; Roberts 1984).

Another problem for any greater interventionist role was the absence in this period of a body able to speak for the consensus of Lancashire's views, especially as regards any changes in the structure of the industry. As Robson (1957: 214) remarks, 'In the cotton industry, collective action in regard to labour relations, price arrangements and raw material supplies emerged at an early stage and were, in general, dealt with by the sections of the industry directly concerned'. Only in the mid-1920s was there a groping towards more general representative bodies. In 1925 a Joint Committee of Cotton Trades Organizations (JCCTO) emerged, partly following from the example of the Cotton Control Board, embracing most employers in the industry, and from 1928 the trade unions were included. However this body found it difficult to agree on common action, and in the 1920s attempts to change the structure of the industry were mainly made by particular sections of the industry, for example, the spinners of American yarn (Dupree 1987: i, xxiii).

The government was reluctant to involve itself in the industry unless proposals appeared to have widespread support. Such support did eventually emerge for the reduction of capacity in spinning, and this led to the 1936 Act, and similarly with the legal enforcement of wages in weaving in 1934. But the proposals put forward by the printers and dyers in 1936 to control prices and output were rejected by the government, both as too restrictive and also because not all sections of the industry agreed with them (Robson 1957: 216–17). Overall 'for much of the nineteen thirties the industry, sectionally and in general, was confused and uncertain as to the appropriate courses of action to adopt and was by no means unanimous in its demands for statutory assistance' (Kirby 1974: 156).

Other factors which may have lessened the willingness of government to intervene in the organization of cotton in comparison with other staples like coal and iron and steel include the limited strategic importance of the industry, the lack of a strong push from the trade-union side for intervention, and the absence of a breakdown in industrial relations (Kirby 1974: 156–7).

In the area of markets for its products the Manchester Chamber of Commerce eventually emerged as an effective representative body for the industry (Dupree 1987: i: xxiv). Here also there was a body—the Board of Trade—with a clear remit to act in this area, and though not regarded as sufficiently active by the MCC the Board did pursue the industry's interests in the tariff and quota bargaining that characterized the decade. However there was little the Board could do in relation to the key Indian market, where broader political considerations ruled out any attempt to prevent the growth of Indian tariff autonomy.

Just before the Second World War the JCCTO came forward with proposals for a statutory Cotton Board with powers to operate an elaborate system of price controls and other services for the industry. These proposals were embodied in the Cotton Industry Act of 1939, though this became a dead letter on the outbreak of war. However this proposal did help shape the rather less elaborate wartime Cotton Board (Dupree 1987: ii: xix).

Originally largely concerned with promoting exports, later in the war the Board co-operated closely with the cotton control (a department of the Ministry of Supply) in such matters as the concentration policy and the utility scheme for standard cloths for consumers under wartime rationing and price controls. Most importantly, from early on in the war the Board was involved in discussions about post-war policy for the industry. It put forward statutory minimum prices as a key foundation for reform of the industry, but this was not popular with the Board of Trade, who wanted a movement away from the restrictionist policies of the 1930s (Dupree 1992: 6–10).

No clear policies for the post-war period emerged from wartime discussions, and the new Labour government came to power with a strong commitment to start afresh with tripartite (employer–union–independent) scrutiny of industries like cotton through what became Working Parties. This cut across the activities of the by now well-established Cotton Board and also undercut the good relations that Stafford Cripps, President of the Board of Trade, had initially established with the employers

in the industry, partly by reassuring them that cotton nationalization was not on the government's agenda.

The setting up of the Working Party tended to divide opinion
in the cotton industry, and its report showed some of those
divisions very clearly. Half of the members of the Working Party
refused to support the report's recommendations for compulsory amalgamations, enforced scrapping, and a levy-financed
re-equipment of the industry. Whilst opposed to neither amalgamation nor re-equipment they believed that entrepreneurs were the
best judge of their desirability, and they regarded the Working
Party's proposals as bureaucratic and stifling to the recovery of
the industry. In broad terms they stood by traditional economic
liberalism or *laissez-faire*, headed by the well-known liberal
economist, John Jewkes (Working Party 1946).

The Working Party also recommended a permanent tripartite
body for the industry, and this approach to cotton was repeated
in proposals for other sections, and led to the Industrial Organization and Development Act of 1947 with its proposals for
Development Councils. Under this Act a Cotton Board was
established in 1948, which essentially continued the old Board,
the main difference being that the number of trade-union representatives was increased to equal the number of employers. The
Board lacked compulsory powers, save those of registration of
firms, collection of statistics, and a levy to cover its expenses
(Dupree 1992: 24–5).

Once established the new Cotton Board was important in
getting agreement on the re-equipment subsidy under the 1948
Act. This grant was used as a carrot to encourage amalgamations, rather than the Working Party idea of the stick of
compulsion. Edgerton (1986: ch. 8) has argued that the Attlee
Government's commitment to consensus and co-operation with
the private industries such as cotton inhibited more radical and
necessary reforms. Certainly the commitment of the government
to tripartism was strong and this could be an inhibition on
action. On the other hand it is not obvious that policies could
have been pursued against the wishes of the majority of employers, perhaps especially a fragmented industry like cotton
with a long history of divergent opinions and recalcitrance in the
face of schemes of reorganization. This is the classic dilemma of
industrial policy.

The Attlee Government had the most comprehensive policies for cotton of any administration. These covered a range of areas already discussed in this chapter—labour recruitment and deployment, amalgamation, and re-equipment underpinned by investment grants. Plainly all this action failed to stem the tide of long-run decline. Whilst the labour-force did expand significantly, modernization in any sense was generally very limited. In part this may have been due to ambiguity in the government's own policy, torn between a desire to modernize for long-run competitiveness and a desire to maximize output and exports in the short run.

But at the centre of the failure of this project must lie the limited response by the employers. In the face of strong demand and high profits from existing practices they lacked the stick of necessity to change their ways. Perhaps they may be regarded as rational in their pessimism about the industry's future, though such pessimism was certainly not universal (Singleton 1991a; Tomlinson 1991a). What does seem clear is that this was the last chance for the industry, a breathing-space before strong competition revived and easy profits disappeared, never to return.

The Conservative government after 1951 took a much less sustained interest in the cotton industry. Its election roughly coincided with the return of the buyers' market, but the government was extremely reluctant to respond to industry pressure to make a protectionist response to this new situation. Whilst eventually some trade controls did re-emerge, they did little to alter the trend towards not only loss of export markets but increasing import penetration at home.

In 1958, largely for short-term political reasons, the government brought forward plans to finance the scrapping of excess capacity and re-equipment of the industry. But in the face of market pressures this measure gave only a small and brief boost to the industry's prospects. Thoroughgoing protectionism was not a viable option by the 1950s. Cotton was not longer important enough to justify the harm such a policy was likely to do to British exports from retaliation. And whilst willing to bend the rules, the Conservatives had become a party strongly committed to a liberal international trade regime (Miles 1968: chs. 4, 5; Harris 1972: 211–16).

CONCLUSIONS

The position of the British cotton industry in 1913 was unsustainable. It was a low-tech producer of mainly low-quality cloths for export markets mainly in poor countries. Whilst it had a highly flexible form of organization and, in their given tasks, highly skilled workers and managers, the industry in that form was extremely vulnerable to forces which were already well established in 1913. Given protection against imports (a necessary condition because of the low transport costs relative to the value of cotton goods) almost any country could enter the cotton industry and at least conquer its domestic market. World trade relative to output was on a long-term downward path, and a country like Britain, a rich country dominating the world export market by exporting most of its output, was an anomaly. Once India, the key market by 1913, was granted tariff autonomy the decline of the industry in its 1913 form was inevitable.

Change in the industry was therefore unavoidable. The might-have-been question is, therefore, not whether the industry could have been preserved in something like its 1913 form, but whether subsequent changes could have made the decline of the industry less calamitous. In particular, the concern of this chapter has been the government's role in the process of decline: could government have brought about a happier outcome?

The first point to be made on this issue is that overall the government's impact on the industry over the whole period was quite small. On the structure of the industry, the government's tacit support for amalgamations and later explicit support for scrapping in the inter-war period may have aided their processes, but they would probably have largely taken place in any event. After the traumas of the 1920s, and then again the slump of the early 1930s the industry was slowly able to organize itself to change.

During the Second World War the concentration-of-industry policy could have been the basis for a radical reconstruction of the industry. But in fact the deal was explicitly that the closure of mills would be on a temporary basis, and indeed a levy was collected from the producing firms for the maintenance of those mothballed.

In terms of the cotton industry, the Attlee Government was by far the most interventionist of any in the twentieth century.

This was part of its role as a 'government of industrial modernization', and also the result of a short-run imperative to raise output and exports. These two aspects could conflict, for example over how far investment should be aimed at immediate output gains or longer-term competitiveness. But for the most part the government seems to have (eventually) evolved a clear modernization programme, linking grants for re-equipment to amalgamations and changes in work practices. But the impact of this was much smaller than the government hoped. Finally, after a hands-off period, the Conservatives leapt in with the 1959 Act for scrapping and re-equipment, but this was a much less comprehensive approach than that attempted in the late 1940s, and like the earlier effort did not generate a large-scale response. Whether the reaction of Lancashire employers to these government actions be counted as bone-headedness or rational responses to market realities may be disputed. But both episodes showed the weakness of government in the face of indifference or hostility from the employers to policy initiatives.

Until the 1950s the other main area where the government was involved was in trying to secure export markets. Here again the government's impact was small. Little could be done about the loss of Indian outlets, and the only time other British markets received much protection from Japanese competition was in the generally protectionist 1930s. Even then the fate of Lancashire mainly reflected an accentuation of the decline in total world trade in cotton, a context in which only a few export markets mainly in the Empire could be secured by government action. In the 1950s attention switched to imports from Commonwealth producers. The government's response was extremely limited, and the restraints which were eventually negotiated slowed rather than reversed the decline of Lancashire even in its home markets.

Could government have done more? In the inter-war period the problem of the decline of the staples was of course new, and both the industries and government only slowly realized their decline was permanent and required a new style of response. In some industries—for example coal and iron and steel—the government in the 1930s became more heavily involved than in cotton. This partly reflected the strategic importance of those industries but also the industries' own abilities to get together with a plan of action. In cotton this latter condition was very slow to be realized, and the government, probably wisely, was reluctant to intervene where there were serious differences of opinion amongst sectors of the industry.

The Attlee Government could have nationalized the cotton industry as a prelude to more radical reorganization. But this was always unlikely. The unions in cotton had supported nationalization from the 1930s, but usually with limited enthusiasm. The industry was not, in the language of the times, a 'commanding height'. It had not had its capital stock seriously run down, like coal and the railways. Its industrial relations had never reached the low points of those in coal. Overall it lacked the features which underlay most of Labour's list for nationalization (Barry 1965: 135–40).

In the absence of nationalization, any attempt to change the industry had to be with the consent if not active support of the owners. For whatever reason, their active enthusiasm for modernization was very limited by the 1940s. Finally the Conservative government of the 1950s prided itself in its belief in free-market competition, and though exceptions were made, such as the 1959 Act, more coercive forms of policy were never likely to appear.

On the market side, the government was constrained by the realities of the broad political situation in India in the 1920s and 1930s. In the latter decade it did partake in the worldwide trend to protectionism, but in the 1940s and especially the 1950s the growth of a multilateral, liberal-trade regime meant Lancashire's problems became only a small part of a much wider calculation about the benefits of free trade (and about the Commonwealth) which allowed little help for Lancashire. As Raymond Streat argued (1968: 18–19) 'What was done by public action was on the whole too small in scope and too late in date to effect materially a sequence of events already set in motion by political and industrial developments in the world at large'.

Should the government have done more? Singleton (1991*b*) has argued that the post-1945 attempts to bolster the industry were mistaken, and that the resources tied up in the industry should have been encouraged to move to other uses. Two brief points may be made on this. First, the argument would not apply to the inter-war period, when the alternative use for resources would have been unemployment, unlike in the post-war period. Second, whilst in economic efficiency terms straightforward arguments can be made for not preserving resources in uses where there are uses which will yield greater returns, this begs the question about whether resources in cotton were necessarily to be used inefficiently. A radical programme of modernization, for example, aimed at moving up-market into higher quality, better-designed, and more elaborate products might have preserved a little more of the industry, and reduced the scope of the process of post-war deindustrialization.

Further Reading

Bamberg, J. (1988), 'The Rationalization of the British Cotton Industry in the Interwar Years', *Textile History*, 19: 83–102.

Dupree, M. (1987) (ed.), *Lancashire and Whitehall: The Diary of Sir Raymond Streat, 1931–57*, 2 vols., Manchester.

Dupree, M. (1992), 'The Cotton Industry: A Middle Way Between Nationalization and Self Government?', in H. Mercer, N. Rollings, and J. Tomlinson (eds.), *Labour Government and Private Industry: The Experience of 1945–51*, Edinburgh: 137–61.

Kirby, M. (1974), 'The Lancashire Cotton Industry in the Interwar Years: A Study in Organisational Change', *Business History*, 16: 145–59.

Lazonick, W. (1983), 'Industrial Organisation and Technical Change: The Decline of the British Cotton Industry', *Business History Review* 57: 195–236.

Robson, R. (1957), *The Cotton Industry in Britain*, London.

Sandberg, L. (1974), *Lancashire in Decline*, Columbus, Oh.

Singleton, J. (1991), *Lancashire on the Scrapheap*, Oxford.

14

A Case-Study: Cars

INTRODUCTION

The cotton industry discussed in the previous chapter may be seen as symbolic of Britain's industrial pre-eminence in the nineteenth century, fallen on hard times in the twentieth. In contrast, the car industry, whose life only began right at the end of the nineteenth century, symbolizes the problems of those new industries central to industrial performance through much of the twentieth century.[1] The literature on British economic decline commonly treats cars as reflecting (perhaps in exaggerated form) the general difficulties the country has had in matching the industrial performance of major competitors. Certainly that decline has been striking. Although always well behind the Unites States as a car producer in the first half of the century, Britain was the first or second largest European producer. As late as 1955 she produced more cars than Germany, and at that date was the world's largest exporter (Table 14.1). But by the beginning of the 1990s Britain was the only major industrial country without a domestically owned mass-production car manufacturer, and was running a major deficit on trade in cars.

Unsurprisingly, with an industry as important as cars, governments have been concerned with its fortunes almost from the beginning. This chapter focuses on how that concern has been expressed in policy, the effects on the fortunes of the industry, and whether there were obvious policy alternatives which might have yielded better results.

---

[1] This chapter focuses on cars, though this does not of course cover the whole of the motor industry. The story of commercial vehicles seems distinct and is therefore not dealt with at the same time.

CONTEXT

The first British car company is usually said to be Daimler, established in 1896. Before the First World War the industry in Britain was small, with a high birth and death rate for firms and without a dominant pioneer like Ford in the United States to force through rapid changes in techniques of production (Saul 1962: 40–4). The market for cars consisted of rich consumers, and only in the inter-war period did the market expand to embrace the middle classes. At the same time the industry's structure changed, so that by the end of the 1930s there was a clear dominance by the 'big six' (Austin, Morris, Ford, Vauxhall, Rootes, and Standard), two of which, Ford and Vauxhall, were American-owned. These companies increasingly competed with each other largely by producing new models rather than by direct price competition, though the trend in prices throughout the 1920s and 1930s was significantly downwards.

TABLE 14.1. *UK car output and exports 1913–89* (000s)

	Output	Exports
1913	34	—
1920	—	4
1929	182	24
1937	390	54
1945	17	70
1955	898	322
1965	1,772	627
1975	1,272	528
1985	1,056	204
1989	1,267	276

Sources: 1913–55, Maxcy and Silberston (1959), pp. 223, 226; 1955–89, *Economic Trends*.

The British car industry rode the effects of the slump of the 1930s very well, and output continued to expand in all but the worst years. By the end of that decade the industry was little more than a tenth the size of that in the United States, but in a European context Britain was the major player, with output equal to France and Germany combined, and with 16 per cent of world exports (Foreman-Peck 1982: 868, 871).

In both World Wars car output was cut back severely to direct resources to war uses, but after the Second World War, unlike the First, the post-war boom was sustained for a long period in the face of pent-up demand and destruction and disorganization of competitors. Never previously a significant purchaser of car imports, Britain now became a major exporter, greatly aided by the dollar shortage, which reduced many countries' capacity to purchase US cars.

But this export and production boom peaked in relative terms in the mid-1950s. Absolute levels of output and exports continued to expand, but Britain's share of the world totals of both shrank. From the early 1970s this relative decline was turned into an absolute one in the face of massive import penetration (including, increasingly, imports by multinationals with production facilities in Britain). The number of domestically owned producers shrank until only British Leyland survived, encompassing the two volume car companies, Austin and Morris, which had originally merged in 1952. Alongside BL were the American majors—Ford, Vauxhall (General Motors), and (briefly) Chrysler, plus from the 1970s Peugeot. In the 1980s these were added to by the Japanese producers, Nissan and Honda.

By the beginning of the 1990s Britain's only domestically owned producer with any pretensions to size (now called Rover) was reduced to output of the Metro, successful in the UK but with a limited market on a world scale, and semi-luxury cars partly based on Rover's links with Honda. 'In the 1980s the British automobile industry had been transformed from a sector where British-owned firms and foreign direct investors competed against one another to one where the British firms were all either wholly or partially owned by foreign competitors' (Reich 1990: 1).

MARKETS

Until the 1970s the British industry was largely immune from significant import penetration (Table 14.2). For much of its early history the industry produced cars significantly different from the main potential sources of imports, the United States. This difference partly arose naturally, from the short distances travelled on relatively good but congested roads typical of

Britain. This can be seen as creating a demand for small, light cars with small engines, in considerable contrast to the typical American heavy and powerful car.

TABLE 14.2. *Car imports into the UK market 1913–85* (% share of total market)

1913[a]	1.6
1920	1.6
1929	12.8
1937	5.9
1945	negligible
1955	2.2
1965	5.2
1970	14.3
1975	33.2
1980	41.1
1985	48.2
1989	54.6

[a] including CVs.

Source: Society of Motor Manufactures and Traders, Annual Statistics.

But much comment on the industry in the first half of the century emphasizes the government's role in creating a demand for such cars by the tax system. From 1910 to 1947 car taxation was based on the cubic capacity of the car engine, providing an incentive for small-bore, long-stroke engines. This system was often attacked as forcing British producers to make a car with little foreign appeal, on the assumption that in most countries a larger, more powerful car would be favoured (Plowden 1971: ch. 8). In this way, it was alleged, exports were reduced, though so also, by the same logic, was the demand for imports, especially from the United States.

However this argument may be exaggerated. Unlike most commentators, Maxcy and Silberston (1959: 49–50) make some simple calculations on this issue and these suggest that the tax was limited in impact. They calculate that the difference between running a 'small' (8 h.p.) and 'big' (12 h.p.) car under the pre-1947 tax regime was only 6*d.* per week, which even in 1930s prices was a small proportion of the total costs of running a car. Their conclusion seems apt: 'On balance, the truth may be that the form of motor taxation before the war imposed some bias towards lower-powered cars, and hence some hardship on exports, but that other factors were more important' (50; see also Silberston 1958: 23–4). They back this up by pointing out that the changes of 1947/8 (basically to a flat-rate tax) were not followed by any significant shifts in the distribution of engine size in cars brought by British consumers, though the issue is clouded by a rise in petrol tax at the same time (50–1).

Tax may have played a role in shaping the demand for cars in Britain, but probably through the relatively high total tax burden (purchase tax, car tax, petrol tax) raising the costs of running a car than through the engine size basis of car tax. In any event, total international trade in cars whilst this tax regime was in operation was quite small, so that Britain was not strongly deviant from the world pattern, except for the success of US exporters in countries without indigenous car industries.

Much more important than the domestic tax regime in shaping the import levels in cars was the tariff. This was first imposed as one of the McKenna Duties in 1915 at $33\frac{1}{3}$ per cent, ostensibly to save shipping space but which was then maintained (with a short break in 1924/5) until the 1960s. In that decade, under the Kennedy Round of GATT, the tariff was reduced in stages from $33\frac{1}{3}$ per cent to 17 per cent by 1969, and to 11 per cent in 1972 (Dunnett 1980: 96, 129).

This protectionism had a number of consequences. First, it added to the underlying economic forces making for an overall low level of international trade in cars, and the natural forces distinguishing the pattern of British demand from the products of the major exporter up to the 1960s, the United States. It thus reinforced the limits on Britain's export potential, imposed by producing car types closely geared to the particular needs of the national market. Second, it encouraged multinational investment in the UK to circumvent the tariff barriers—a point returned to in the section below on Company Structure and Organization. Third, it formed the basis for a system of Imperial preference and tariff bargaining which provided the industry with access to some foreign markets on privileged terms. This was especially the case in the 1930s when exports grew almost entirely on the basis of sales in such protected markets. Maxcy and Silberston (1959: 111) calculate that such sales—domestic and foreign—covered 97 per cent of all cars sold in 1938. For exports before the Second World War this meant a domination by Empire markets. In 1937 the four biggest car export markets for Britain by value were New Zealand, Australia, South Africa, and India and Pakistan, and the Commonwealth as a whole accounted for 85 per cent of the total (PEP 1950: 83).

Overall, protectionism probably raised output in the car industry before the Second World War, first and most obviously by directly reducing imports. The impact of the duties comes out quite strongly from the period in 1924/5 when, following Snowden's fanatical commitment to free trade, they were abolished. In cars this led to a surge in imports which took their share in home sales from 15 per cent in 1924 to 28 per cent in the following year. 'The implication of the observed effects is that the duty was very important in restricting the sales of Continental cars of similar design to British products . . .' (Miller and Church 1979: 194). Second, it encouraged the granting of preferences in Empire countries, where in the absence of preferences demand would probably almost entirely have been met by US and other foreign producers. Allen's (1939: 180) conclusion for the 1920s seems apt on the British industries' export performance right up to 1939: 'The British car has made its way only into markets where the British sympathies of the population and the preferential duties have favoured it, and even in those markets the Americans are far ahead'.[3]

The war fundamentally altered the British export situation. Whilst the US dominance of world output was increased by the war, its ultimate effect was to curtail US exports because of the shortage of dollars which characterized the late 1940s and early 1950s. British exports rose from 70,000 cars in 1946 to 344,000 in 1950, more than 3 times the US level by the latter date (Maxcy and Silberston 1959: 226). The combination of a world-wide dollar shortage and the virtual absence of competition from continental European suppliers meant this export expansion was in part autonomous of government efforts. But in addition to these forces the government was desperate to maximize car exports for balance of payments reasons. They therefore badgered

[3] The depreciation of sterling in the early 1930s also boosted exports, though this obviously did not help competitiveness in the markets where currencies were tied to sterling.

the industry to increase its exports and backed this up with steel allocations which broadly speaking went only to those who met export quotas (PRO 1951*a*). The industry was therefore forced to divert supply away from the intense demand of the home market. This policy was continued until 1952 and was undoubtedly government's most forceful intervention in the car market ever.

Unfortunately the appetite for British cars abroad reflected not so much their inherent desirability as the problems of obtaining alternatives. Hence, as the dollar shortage diminished and the European producers revived (and the steel shortage diminished) the British car-makers shifted back to greater reliance on the home market. Whilst in 1950 exports were almost 70 per cent of output, by 1956 they were only 40 per cent, and this downward trend continued thereafter. The absolute number of cars exported continued to expand in the 1950s and 1960s, but Britain's share of the world market reached an all-time peak of 52 per cent in 1950 and fell continuously thereafter.

Explanations for the failure to take advantage of this market dominance to build a continuing strong position in export markets can be seen as the same as general, long-run explanations for the industry's decline. But there were also specific factors. First, many of these exports were of pre-war models, so exports were very vulnerable to competition from post-war models produced by reviving industries elsewhere. Second, most British exporters seem to have regarded the export expansion as unavoidably temporary and therefore not to be pursued with vigour. Parts and service networks were extremely poor, and this had a self-fulfilling effect of reducing demand when alternative sources of supply appeared (Dunnett 1980: 36–7).

In the 1950s and 1960s the failure to maintain export markets did not prevent a rapid expansion of the industry. Home demand boomed, and only a small proportion was fed by imports. Whilst demand expanded rapidly in the wake of the long-boom expansion of incomes—the income elasticity of demand for cars being around 2.5 (Maxcy and Silberston 1959: 40)—demand also fluctuated sharply. This was the era of stop-go, and many authors have seen this policy as imposing significant costs on the industry by increasing uncertainty and inhibiting investment. In its strongest version stop-go is blamed for the loss of export markets, as the policy was said to encourage a stop-go approach to selling abroad, which was treated as a vent for cars surplus to the fluctuating needs of the home market (Dunnett 1980: ch. 4). Another version of the same story, popular with producers at the time, was that a stable home market was a necessary base for launching into export markets.

Undoubtedly the form of stop–go macro management did bear particularly heavily on consumer durables in general and cars in particular. This was because of the use of credit controls and, especially, hire-purchase regulations to affect the level of demand for cars. However, detailed studies of this issue suggest that the impact of hire-purchase controls has generally been exaggerated, the main determinant of demand for new cars being incomes not hire-purchase (Silberston 1963). This means that the general impact of stops on demand was probably more important than hire-purchase *per se*, but even then the fluctuations in output and income brought about by policy in this period should not be exaggerated. Studies (e.g. Whiting 1976) have shown that these fluctuations were no greater in Britain than in other Western European countries without such a policy regime. The key point about the demand for cars is that it can readily be postponed, big fluctuations in current demand resulting from relatively small numbers of consumers deciding to retain existing vehicles rather than purchase new ones (Jones and Prais 1976).

The long period of expansion of demand and output and the golden age of the British car industry ended quite abruptly at the beginning of the 1970s. Problems arose initially not from a collapse of total demand but an incapacity to respond to the demand stimulus of the 'Barber boom' (1971–3). Imports, which had run at around 6 per cent of the home market on average in the 1960s rose in 1971 to 19 per cent; by 1975 it was 33 per cent and by the end of the decade over half. The home market, on which the domestic producers had become overwhelmingly reliant, ceased to be captive.

This is partly to be explained by the reduction of tariff duties. The cuts in the McKenna duties already noted were added to by the free access of EC produced cars once Britain entered in 1973. However the timing of the import increases suggests a key role was played by the unavailability of the domestic product in a time of sharp demand increase—it is otherwise difficult to account for the step-increase (a doubling in the share of the British market) between 1971 and 1973. Equally this increase undoubtedly built on the declining reputation of the British product, strongly evident in the late 1960s. Once imports achieved this breakthrough they never looked back: 'The apparent loyalty, or possibly habit, of many Britons for British cars, which had been a feature of the market since before World War Two, was permanently weakened' (Dunnett 1980: 123).

The picture on imports is complicated by the growing role of tied or captive imports—imports of cars by producers who made some cars in Britain, but nevertheless increasingly supplied the British market from overseas. Particularly in the context of growing European integration, the major multinational car companies developed European strategies which often involved supplying the whole of the West European market from one factory. At the beginning of the 1970s probably only around 3 per cent of the British market was served by such imports, but this figure grew to over 20 per cent by 1982, almost three-quarters of this accounted for by Ford (Wilks 1984: 71–2). In principle this was a two-way street—British-based multinationals could also be a source of exports in this new division of labour. In practice the balance of production and trade was against Britain, so that captive trade exacerbated the effects of straightforward demand for foreign cars by British consumers.

Another complicating feature of the demand picture in this period was the sharp division between cars bought by individuals and those bought by companies. The latter source of demand expanded rapidly from the mid-1960s to the mid-1970s. Williams (1983: 233) suggests that such sales rose from under 10 per cent in 1964 to around 50 per cent a decade later. This rapid growth seems to have resulted from a combination of an increasingly favourable tax regime for company cars and the desire of company managements to circumvent pay controls in an era of income policies.

Initially this peculiar pattern of car purchase served to assist domestically produced cars, as it was the declining numbers of individual purchasers who first developed a sharp appetite for the imported product. In 1974 imports had only 4 per cent of the company fleet market, but 45 per cent of that of private purchases (CPRS 1975). The fleet market was dominated by Fords in the 1970s, with inroads by Vauxhall in the 1980s, and these companies increasingly supplied that market from tied imports, so that by the latter decade the benefits to British trade from this different pattern of demand had been substantially eroded.

The other importance of this market structure is suggested by the dominance of Ford and Vauxhall of the fleet market. British Leyland[4] never made a successful entry into this market. Its dealer network was geared to the individual purchaser and it found it difficult to produce the car to suit fleet-purchaser demands. In the 1970s this formed a significant problem for Leyland—it was locked into a market which was being squeezed in size by the growth of the fleets, and where the buyers were rapidly developing a taste for the overtly foreign product (Williams 1983: 234–5).

The trends established in the 1970s developed in magnified form in the following decade. Import penetration continued to rise sharply. This was a feature common to Western European countries at this time, but what greatly added to the process in Britain was the unique dependence on tied imports. After 1972 this was accompanied by an absolute fall in car production. In the recession of the early 1980s output was less than half of a decade earlier, and by the end of the 1980s it was only a little larger. This was, of course, accompanied by a plummeting in employment levels, from over 300,000 in the early 1970s to little more than a third of that number by 1990.

The stark decline of the British-produced car in the 1970s and 1980s arose from the loss of market share in the home market plus the failure to develop a significant export trade. It must be emphasized that growing levels of imports and exports have been a feature of all major industrial countries in this period. What distinguished the British position was not the growing taste for Volkswagens and Renaults, but the fact that the Fords and Vauxhalls increasingly came from abroad. On the other hand the defining problem of the domestically owned producer, British Leyland, was not that it faced enhanced competition from abroad,

---

[4] Unless otherwise stated this name is used to cover the various forms of the Austin-Morris mass car producer, from the foundation of the British Motor Corporation (BMC, in 1952), British Motor Holdings (in 1966), British Leyland Motor Corporation (in 1968), British Leyland (BL, in 1975), and Rover Group (in 1986).

but that it failed to capture a significant export market as competing European companies did (Williams *et al.* 1987a: ch. 4).

PROFITS

Before the First World War the car industry in Britain was a picture of anarchic competition, with firms entering the industry in large numbers and most exiting within a short time. For example, between 1902 and 1913 thirty-five companies entered the industry, but thirty-seven left it, leaving a net figure of 48 still producing (Maxcy 1958: 365). Profits for those who stayed in the race seem to have been quite respectable, though most were paid out in dividends, and to a much greater extent than in the contemporary US industry, capital was raised externally (Lewchuk 1986: 141 and app., table 1).[5] Profits arose from gaining a competitive edge in an expanding market not from market dominance.

The inter-war period was characterized by large fluctuations in the output of cars and parallel fluctuations in profits for the car producers taken as a whole, especially in the slump after 1920 and to a lesser extent after 1929 (Maxcy and Silberston 1959: 159–61). These sharp fluctuations were one factor in weeding out many of the small producers, so that by the end of the 1920s the big six were taking over 70 per cent of the market, and the big three (Austin, Ford, Morris) almost two-thirds (Church and Miller 1977: 180). With fixed costs generally only 10–15 per cent of the total, price-cutting was very bad for profits, so the emphasis was on competition by model characteristics rather than price. Firms which did badly in such competition, like Ford in the 1920s or Morris in the early 1930s, tended to do badly overall. Ford's attempt to rectify its position by producing the £100 car in the 1930s saw its market share expand but this did not restore its profits (Maxcy and Silberston 1959: 73–4: 160–1).

Broadly speaking the inter-war period saw the creation of a quite stable oligopoly of (predominantly British-owned) car producers who were able to make respectable profits: 'Between

---

[5] Though this was not true of Morris (not included in Lewchuk's table), on which see Overy (1976): 4–5.

1922 and 1939 Austin's average gross profits were 19 per cent on net tangible assets. The average per annum yield on ordinary shares issued by British motor vehicle firms was 8.4 per cent between 1921 and 1932, while the yield on US shares held in British portfolios over the same period was only 5 per cent' (Lewchuk 1986: 142). As before the war, however, these profits were not tied to high levels of investment (with the exception of Ford) but to high pay-out rates, averaging 66 per cent of net earnings (Maxcy and Silberston 1959: 161).

The early post-1945 period was the most profitable ever for British car companies (Table 14.3). Whilst some caution needs, as always, to be exercised in relation to such figures, the trends seem clear. In the face of the sellers' market, both at home and overseas, and despite the much-trumpeted supply difficulties, until the early 1950s profits were readily to be had. But from various years in the early 1950s the trend altered for the different companies. In fact the car companies followed a similar but accentuated profits pattern to that of most British manufactures—high profits in the early post-war years, followed by a long decline thereafter, dwindling to almost nothing in the early 1980s.

TABLE 14.3. *Rates of return on capital 1947–56*

	1947	1948	1949	1950	1951	1952	1953	1954	1955	1956
Austin	28	16	17	44	51	—	—	—	—	—
Morris	21	12	21	48	—	—	—	—	—	—
BMC	—	—	—	—	—	—	31	38	34	19
Ford	22	23	19	34	28	26	35	36	30	15
Standard	7	14	18	18	31	22	22	28	27	5
Vauxhall	29	25	23	21	20	35	59	56	32	14

Source: Maxcy and Silberston (1959), p. 175.

British Leyland profits in the long boom show sharp fluctuations paralleling the sharp fluctuations in output, but a general declining trend, and this was a pattern probably mirrored in the other British-owned producers (Standard was acquired by Leyland in 1961, Rootes by Chrysler in 1964). Williams (1983: 223–5) argues that this low profitability on the basis of rapidly expanding output reflected British Leyland's strategy of producing very basic cars with low margins by low-capital-intensive methods which meant economies of scale were limited: 'The economics of the business were such that volume in itself would not generate profit for a firm like BMC where there was under-investment' (224). This low-investment strategy was combined with a continuation of the high pay-outs from profit. As Lewchuk (1986: 150) argues 'In the highly profitable years before World War I, during the profitable years of the 1930s, and during the lean years of the late 1960s and early 1970s, distribution from profits seems to have exceeded the level consistent with long run growth'. After the early 1970s there were to be few profits for Leyland, the £76m. loss of 1975 leading to nationalization, but being only a prelude to the record loss of £380m. in 1980, equivalent to 13.5 per cent of revenue (Williams 1983: 260–1). After that date creative accounting only barely disguised continuing losses (Williams *et al.* 1987*a*: app. I).

British Leyland was not all of the British industry, though by the end of the long boom it was the only significant British-owned mass producer. Its main competitor for most of the post-war period was Ford, whose profits seem to have been more respectable, though with a similar trend to that of Leyland. However it should be noted that to a significant extent Ford in Britain faced similar pressures to those of Leyland, and this was a major reason why the captive import situation developed so unfavourably: 'The key to Ford's strong market share and profitability lay not so much in its superior performance as a British producer but in its capacity as a multinational to bring large quantities of imports into Britain' (Tolliday 1991: 108).

THE EFFICIENCY OF LABOUR

Governments have made no direct attempts to affect the quantity or composition of labour in the car industry, unlike in cotton. On the other hand, much of the complex history of British governments' attempts to intervene more generally in the labour-market and especially in industrial relations have been linked to an understanding of the car industry in which such relations are believed to have been the key to the industry's performance. One could, without too much exaggeration, write a whole history of the debate about British industry in the twentieth century which focused on 'the labour question' and in which the car industry would figure as the pre-eminent example of this version of 'the British disease'.

Labour relations didn't appear as the centre of public debate about the car industry until the 1960s. But this does not mean government actions had had no effect before that date. Tolliday (1987*b*) argues that in the 1940s and early 1950s the government's search for an agreement with national union leaders had played an important role in encouraging the growth of local bargaining outside formal channels, rather than this being seen as simply the consequence of union strength (e.g. Donnelly and Thoms 1989). Equally in the 1950s the government played a crucial role in the attempts by motor industry employers to 'roll back' the unions, and an equally important one in the following decade in forcing even the most recaltricant to come to some *modus vivendi* with the unions. Throughout this period cars were too important to be ignored, and the government was an important if somewhat unstable element in establishing the industrial relations pattern in the industry.

As late as 1959 a Board of Trade report on the industry made no mention of industrial relations as a significant issue in the prospects for the industry (PRO 1959). However, in the late 1960s the combination of the Labour government's extreme sensitivity to industrial disputes, the tough macroeconomic environment, and the growth of strikes in the car industry combined to put industrial relations and especially those in cars close to the top of the political agenda. The Donovan Report of 1965–8 encapsulated much of the dominant view and one which saw cars as symptomatic of most of British industry. The analysis offered by Donovan was that national, formal bargaining systems were paralleled by informal, local, usually shop-steward based systems which led to conflicts, and in which the latter system was seen by many as allowing an anarchic system of leap-frogging claims and productivity-reducing practices. The ill-fated proposals of *In Place of Strife* were also aimed, albeit in a different fashion, at changing industrial relations in a way deemed crucial to Britain's industrial efficiency and the performance of its car industry in general.

However there is little empirical evidence from the 1960s and early 1970s that industrial relations were crucial to the industry's fortunes. Strikes did rise in number in the 1960s, but these usually small, dispersed stoppages had little impact on overall production levels, whilst longer stoppages tended to be associated with recessions (Turner *et al.* 1967). Shop stewards were highly active, though differentially so between companies, but usually their

bargaining horizons remained very narrowly focused on wages, and stewards continued to respect surprisingly large areas of unilateral management control and the 'right to manage' especially over issues such as hire and fire, plant closures and information disclosures, labour mobility, and the use of overtime and short-time to cover fluctuations in production (Tolliday 1991: 95).

Equally, union resistance to technical change, in cars as in most industries, appears largely a myth (Willman 1986, esp. chs. 3, 7, 9).

In the 1970s the debate over industrial relations and industrial performance, with cars at the centre, was rekindled by the collapse and subsequent nationalization of British Leyland. In 1975 three reports on the industry (Ryder 1975; CPRS 1975; House of Commons 1975) all to a greater or lesser extent blamed the industry's failings on a combination of low investment and bad working practices. It was the latter which most commentators focused upon, the sophisticated arguing that low investment was the consequence of poor industrial relations.

Part of the reason for this focus on labour was the undoubted fact that labour productivity in British car production was significantly below that of the United States, as indeed it had been throughout the industry's history (Willman 1986: 152–3). But this disparity is an obvious consequence of the low-investment strategy of the industry, and in itself neither an index nor an explanation of relative efficiency. As in the 1940s, labour productivity was used in the 1970s, especially in the car industry, to draw extremely disingenuous conclusions. The argument that labour productivity differences resulted in part from low investment was countered by the argument (e.g. CPRS 1975) that even with the same capital equipment, productivity in British car firms was significantly below that of similar factories abroad. However Nichols (1986) has shown how frail this argument was, relying on management opinion and inadequate matching of allegedly similar products.

These debates of the 1970s were an important element in forming public policy on the car industry. The initial government response to the collapse of British Leyland was to back a massive investment-led strategy, but this rapidly failed, and by 1977 a quite new direction was initiated in the nationalized firm under the direction of Michael Edwardes. He, believing British Leyland 'presents a microcosm of the issues affecting British industry as a whole' (Edwardes 1983: 9) pursued a strategy of re-establishing managerial prerogatives as central to the revival of the company.

The immediate objectives of this strategy were largely achieved. Managerial control was re-exerted over a slimmed-down work-force, with militants sacked and shop stewards neutered. Work practices were extensively reformed (Willman and Winch 1985). This process eventually raised labour productivity significantly, but only in the sense of getting the level back to where it had been ten years previously. 'By the early 1980s, the company was making about half the number of cars it had made ten years previously; the company then shed half the work-force and the company ended up more or less where it was originally in terms of labour productivity' (Williams *et al.* 1987*a*: 25).

As Williams *et al.* (1987*a*) persuasively argue, whilst labour productivity in British Leyland was low as a consequence of the low level of output, the belief that this was due to labour practices led to a wholly disproportionate focus on this issue by management under Edwardes. They argue persuasively that the company, whilst pursuing a mistaken investment strategy (a point returned to below), was fatally deflected from the key problem of securing a market for the new products they brought forward.

The post-1977 strategy was unreasonably pre-occupied with the work-force who were (at worst) the minor internal obstacle to productive continuous full utilisation of the company's production facilities. It neglected the major external constraints in the market place outside the factory which would remain when the work-force had been reduced to compliance and docility (33).

From one point of view the Edwardes strategy was perfectly rational. The Labour government which appointed him and its Conservative successor made it clear that financial support for the enterprise would only be forthcoming if it tackled the labour problem. As Tolliday (1991: 107) rightly suggests 'whatever their rationale in terms of the efficiency of production, aggressive policies towards labour were a political *sine qua non* for survival'. On the other hand this approach fitted the prejudices of much of British management, long accustomed to demonology as a sub-stitute for positive analysis.

The focus on the labour question in cars has gained more interesting and nuanced support from writers such as Lewchuk (1986, 1987) in the context of a broad attempt to explain Britain's relative industrial decline in institutional terms. The broad thrust of this view, most explicit in Elbaum and Lazonick (1986) though having much in common with Chandler (e.g. 1990), is that in the nineteenth century Britain developed a range of institutions—trade unions, companies, financial bodies—which were ill-fitted to deal with the demands of the mass-production technology of the twentieth century. In Lewchuk's view, as applied to cars, the basic problem was that Britain never adopted the labour and managerial practices which would have allowed a full use of American production techniques. Instead there emerged a hybrid 'British system of mass production' in which a key feature was limited managerial control over labour effort, and hence the concession to labour and its institutions of a much greater say in production processes than under the American way.

Whilst free from most of the vulgar anti-labourism of much literature in this area, and with many interesting things to say, Lewchuk's arguments do suggest a 'one best way' approach, which believes that the US car companies found the way to produce cars efficiently, and the British were deficient in not following this route. The implication is that labour practices, especially those at British Leyland, whilst not the fault of the workers were nevertheless the major hindrance to better compet-itive performance. But as already suggested the direct evidence for such effects is thin. More generally the implication that Ford and General Motors got it right is not at all clear, at least in the British case, where Ford's practices at least were not the royal road to success (Tolliday 1991). Finally, as Lewchuk (1987: 220) himself hints, the enormous American interest in Japanese car-production methods in the 1980s throws backward doubts on the one best way view of car production.

THE EFFICIENCY OF CAPITAL

Until the 1970s capital for investment was rarely seen as a significant constraint on the car industry either by the car companies or the government. For most of the years up to that decade profits had been generally healthy if fluctuating. In many cases this was linked to high pay-out levels and relatively low fixed investment. But this strategy was not seen by those involved as forced on an unwilling industry by niggardly capital markets. The high pay-outs kept those markets generally sweet, and capital-raising did not appear as an issue.

The first direct role of government in car company investment seems to have occurred in the wake of the Second World War. Contrary to the assertions of writers like Dunnett (1980: ch. 3) or Reich (1990: ch. 6), British policy at this time was willing to discriminate between different car producers in favour of those who seemed to be fulfilling government policy objectives. This particularly took the form of easing controls on those firms believed to be best fulfilling the export drive, but it also took the form of *de facto* investment subsidies (Reich: 227). One striking example is Standard, a favourite of the time, who were given a wartime factory at an almost peppercorn rent to help them produce their Vanguard. This was quite a different policy to that pursued at the same time in cotton, where a general investment subsidy was offered, subject to conditions (Ch. 13).

This was part of a wider interventionism, returned to in the next section, and it did not set a trend for the next decades. After the return of the Conservatives in 1951 a return to liberalism prevailed which ruled out such interventionism. But the nagging worries about the scale of British car companies, which was evident in the 1950s (and prevented any opposition to the Austin–Morris merger of 1952) came to the fore in the 1960s. As emphasized in Chapter 10, the 1964–70 Labour government was obsessed with creating 'national champions' via merger, aided by the IRC, and this body was instrumental in encouraging the formation of British Leyland in 1968, by merging British Motor Holdings with Leyland. The overall logic of such policies is discussed in the following section, but it is significant to note that the government was willing to back its support for this merger with money, if only to the extent of a £25m. loan.

However it is not clear that the merger would not have gone ahead without this sweetener.

Much the most important intervention in the investment levels of the industry came around the time of the nationalization of British Leyland in 1974/5. As Wilks (1984: 290) notes 'for a brief period during 1975/6 the British government had a coherent, well-reasoned policy for the motor industry. It came and went in the blink of an eye'. Unfortunately, along with parallel policies in coal and steel, the basis for government action was a belief that massive investment almost by itself would secure a profitable and productive future for the enterprise. This was predicated on very positive and under-calculated projections of future markets, which in all three cases, including cars, eventually proved highly optimistic. In British Leyland real assets per person rose by 160 per cent between 1976 and 1983, but the returns on this investment were negative, and only continual write-offs sustained the balance-sheet. As Williams *et al.* (1986) argue, the Ryder plan accepted by the government for British Leyland rested on the unrealistic assumption that investment could succeed in turning the enterprise around without measures to secure markets for that output.

Under Edwardes the wilder excesses of the Ryder plan were rejected and the focus was on slimming down the enterprise, whilst investing heavily in new, especially robotic techniques to produce new models and focusing managerial attention on reforming labour practices. This led eventually to much lower levels of investment as operations were slimmed down at least to some extent to match the realities of the market. But if Ryder was a huge gamble on an unlikely success, Edwardes and his successors ultimately presided over an implicit acceptance of failure.

Leyland, along with many British industries, did have an investment problem by the early 1970s (Table 14.4). But figures of capital per worker could not sensibly be used as an argument for more investment *per se*. Investment is part of the overall strategy of an enterprise involving product design and mix, production strategies, and market opportunities. Low investment compared to roughly comparable firms may be an index of a problem (though not invariably) but investment levels are not a helpful place to begin thinking about company strategy. Why did the government tend to fall into this trap in the 1970s in particular? Partly because the truth of low investment often alleged against British companies was, in turn often linked to high dividends. In this way to focus on investment was ideologically convenient because it tied the solution of industrial issues to redistributive concerns (i.e. hostility to unearned incomes) and most broadly still to a critique of the City as an ineffectual provider of investment funds for industry. Again, a nuanced version of this allegation is plausible (Williams *et al.* 1983: ch. 1) but unfortunately it, too, could be used as a way of avoiding the key issues of enterprise governance and strategy which the failure of companies like British Leyland in the 1970s posed.

TABLE 14.4. *Fixed capital per worker, various dates* (£.)

1960 (Ford UK)	1427
1965 (Ford UK)	2903
1969 (British Leyland)	882
1970 (Ford UK)	3035
1973 (Ford UK)	2957
1974 (British Leyland)	1155

Source: Lewchuk (1986), p. 157.

THE EFFICIENCY OF TECHNICAL CHANGE

Technical change has never been central to the debate about the deficiencies of the British car industry, despite its well-known lag in productivity behind the United States. This perhaps partly reflected the structure of the industry, which has both included US producers as major participants almost from the beginning, and consisted of a small number of producers. Thus, in contrast to cotton, it could be argued neither that the industry was ignorant of US methods nor that it was too small and fragmented for individual firms to be able to afford to adopt American techniques. There were no obvious parallels in cars to the British cotton industry's failure to adopt ring-spinning or automatic looms. Critics of the industry such as Lewchuk, who use the American industry as a standard, have emphasized the lack of organizational rather than strictly technological borrowing.

However, again in that heyday of industrial policy activism, the 1940s, the government did articulate to the industry worries about the technological gap between producers in Britain. It was a common theme of debates at this time that a large part of Britain's productivity problem stemmed from the gap between the most and least efficient. To bridge this gap the government urged firms to share know-how and one of the industries to take this up most explicitly was motor cars—not obviously an industry where the gap was likely to be large, given the small number of firms and the highly competitive conditions under which they operated. Under some pressure from the government via the National Advisory Council for the Industry, the SMMT in 1948, announced a plan for 'mutual aid', providing that manufacturers would make available for inspection by one another and by suppliers of raw materials and equipment, their factory premises, their plant, and their technical and administrative resources. The focus of attention was primarily standardization, one of the other great themes of 1940s industrial policy (ch. 7), particularly the standardization of components (PEP 1950: 136).

Collective research has always been very limited in the car industry. As already noted, unlike cotton the oligopolistic structure has undermined any argument that only collective action can achieve the necessary scale of research. Even more importantly, new product (as opposed to process) developments have been the centre of competitive strategy in the industry for most of its existence, so the space for collective action has been very limited. Nevertheless, under the aegis of the DSIR a Motor Industry Research Association was built up in the 1940s, helped by £25,000 from the DSIR—but this was no more than a drop in the ocean of R & D expenditure in the industry (PEP 1950: 55; Reich 1990: 236).

After the nationalization of 1975, and especially under Edwardes, the government accepted it would have to provide major funds for new model developments at British Leyland. But equally the very high costs of such developments is one of the major reasons why the company was encouraged to collaborate with Honda in the mid-1980s—development costs were now so high that many European producers were beginning to collaborate in sharing the cost, and for such a small-scale producer as British Leyland had become such collaboration was very difficult to avoid.

THE EFFICIENCY OF COMPANY STRUCTURE AND ORGANIZATION

Few economists' concepts have the beguiling apparent simplicity of economies of scale. Equally no industry has been supposed to be subject to such economies as much as cars. Perhaps there is no more potent rhetoric of twentieth-century industry than mass production symbolized above all else by the Ford production line. Yet empirically economies of scale, including those in the car industry, have been difficult to measure and assess. In 1959 Maxcy and Silberston (87) wrote of the 'astonishingly small amount of published quantitative evidence pertaining to such an important question as that of economies of scale' and went on to refer to that 'shyest and most retiring of all economic concepts— the long run average cost curve'.

Whilst this gap has been partially filled by later work (especially Pratten 1971; also Silberston 1972), the whole area remains contentious, and the contention has been given an extra twist by the recent debate about 'flexible specialization' and whether the age of mass production and economies of scale has been superseded by one in which new technology enables small producers to compete effectively. The evidence on this would seem to suggest that, whilst in some parts of car production such economies may have been reduced, e.g. body assembly, in others, such as engines they may have actually increased as development costs have soared (Williams *et al.* 1987*b*).

Whatever the empirical problem of measuring economies of scale in the car industry, belief in their existence has been a key feature of government approaches to the industry. But this is not to say that the development of the industry from a highly competitive structure with a large number of competitors into an oligopoly dominated by the few has been the result of government policy. This concentration of the industry, a large part of which was in place by the end of the 1920s, was largely the natural consequence of competition in the industry rather than government policy. The key period seems to have been between 1922 and 1929, when only 5 new firms entered the industry and 62 left. Whilst this still left 31 firms in production, the top five of them had over 80 per cent of output (Maxcy 1958: 365–7). This process provides strong *prime facie* evidence that economies of scale were significant at this time—indeed some have argued that the market test or 'survivor technique' is the best way of judging the existence of such economies (Stigler 1958).

This view is reinforced perhaps by noting that this process of concentration was not mainly by merger (and therefore linked to the exigencies of the capital market, like most merger booms) but by internal growth on the one hand and bankruptcy on the other. Mergers did occur, such as that of Morris in the 1920s and Rootes in the 1930s (Maxcy 1958: 366–7, 373), but in neither case was it the main basis for the company's expansion.

Up to the Second World War the government took little interest in structural change in the industry: even if it had had an anti-Trust and merger policy it would have mattered little given the competitive if oligopolistic nature of the industry. But during and at the end of the Second World War serious doubts came to the surface in civil service and ministerial circles about the future of the industry (Tiratsoo 1992). These worries did not lead to any clear policy of reform, but to a number of initiatives largely focused on trying to get the industry itself to reform, prodded, as in so many other areas of industry, by the energetic figure of Cripps.[6] The industry reluctantly accepted a National Advisory Council for the Motor Manufacturing Industry (NACMMI) with minority union representation but much of the pressure from governments seems to have been informal, as well as some public urging of reform on the industry by Cripps (Plowden 1971: 312–16).

The government believed in the need for reform to secure the long-term competitiveness of the industry, but at the same time it wanted to maximize the industry's exports. Some have argued that these policies were contradictory, and that in practice pursuit of short-term export maximization damaged the industry's long-run performance. Dunnett (1980: 35–6) in particular has argued that

Government export policy had a profound effect on the structure of the UK motor industry. In effect it supported the weak and outdated manufacturers at the expense of the more efficient . . . the steel quota

---

[6] Strictly speaking the car industry in this period came under the aegis of the Ministry of Supply, but 'Officials at Supply appear to have worked directly to Cripps, often virtually by-passing their own Minister, the ineffectual Wilmot' (Plowden 1971: 313).

system, in striving to be fair, effectively froze industry structure . . . [and] frustrated the forces of the market operating to achieve a needed rationalisation and standardisation of the industry.

This view has little basis in the evidence. Whilst not having a policy of 'national champions', the government did discriminate between producers in steel quotas and in other ways, largely according to how they seemed to be performing in export markets i.e. by competitive criteria (Tiratsoo 1992). Rather than simply spreading supplies equally amongst firms, the Ministry of Supply wrote to Sir William Rootes quite explicitly denying any idea that the government would allow the industry itself to decide on steel allocations, and stressing that the government would use discretion in the matter (PRO 1951*a*). This is not to say the government got it right; in the medium term the favoured Standard company was a poor bet (though this was far from obvious in the late 1940s). But the idea that the government prevented the forces of competition from working seems ill-founded. Reich (1990: 236–40) wavers between saying the government did not discriminate and saying it discriminated in favour of Ford.

The government does not seem to have actively pursued rationalization via merger in this period—but then the case for this was surely poor, the number of significant firms already being so small. The top five firms controlled over 70 per cent of output, so this was in no sense a fragmented industry like cotton, where such pressure for rationalization made much more sense.

Instead, and reasonably enough, the government focused on standardization as a major route to greater efficiency. This meant a reduction in the number of models produced by the industry and a standardization of components. The general response of the industry was to accept the need for these changes, but to argue that it had already progressed a long way and that too rapid changes could disrupt the maximization of exports (PEP 1950: ch. 10; NACMMI 1947). But it does seem likely that the government did have some effect in galvanizing the industry into action, not least because of the leverage given at this time by the control of steel supplies.

In 1952, in by far the most important merger so far, Austin and Morris combined to create BMC, which was then the fourth largest car company in the world. The motives for this move seem to have been largely defensive—to fight the US threat to the UK and Dominion popular-priced car market (Maxcy 1958: 380–1). The merger was basically an initiative from within the industry, though one encouraged by the government, but without any financial carrot.

The subsequent history of BMC provides a classic reminder of the caution with which notions of economies of scale need to be deployed in either analysis or policy. This is true at two levels. First, as is well known, the new BMC remained for many years little more than a holding company in which Austin and Morris continued to be run as largely separate entities, with separate model ranges and minimum rationalization of productive capacity (Reich 1990: 240–3). Second, there is a real question about how large, given the low investment strategy, economies of scale in this period really were. Maxcy and Silberston (1959: 67–9) suggest that at target volumes fixed costs were only 10–15 per cent of total cost in an average car company in this period. Given its low investment strategy BMC was probably at the bottom of this range. Consequently, the benefits of scale were likely to be very limited. Substantial 'economies could only be obtained by firms, like VW, which invested heavily in capital-intensive mass production. The economics of the business were such that volume in itself would not generate profit for a firm like BMC where there was under-investment' (Williams 1983: 224).

The dependence of economies of scale on both corporate organization and strategy was not well recognized in the 1960s when 'find the most efficient company and merge everything with it' is not too unfair a description of the driving force of policy (Ch. 10). On the other hand the objective force of enhanced international competition as trade barriers fell seemed to make the creation of national champions, able to compete with all-comers almost unavoidable. From such concerns came the government's active support for the creation of British Leyland, by the merger of British Motor Holdings with the truck producers Leyland, though most of this support was high-level prodding, including a dinner party at Chequers, rather than money, which was limited to a £25m. loan. The merger was a striking piece of financial engineering, with Leyland paying with its own paper and gaining support on the basis of past opportunistic profit-making. 'The rise of Leyland provides us with a classic merger boom example of how the ability to pay in paper allowed a small company to buy its way into the big time' (Williams 1983: 226). Just as after 1952, the merger of 1968 was not pursued into a clear rationalization of production facilities. This partly reflected the lack of investment funds when the costs of new model development and tooling were rising sharply. The result was a series of new products (though with old engines)—the Marina, Allegro, and Princess—which failed to fulfil consumers' desires which increasingly favoured imported cars.

Having played some part in creating British Leyland as the national champion in the 1960s, governments in the 1970s felt obliged to sustain it when collapse came. The nationalization of 1975 had no necessary corollary in strategy for the enterprise. In the event the first phase (1975–7) saw an ill-fated attempt to maintain the scale of the enterprise, but when this became unsustainable the slimming down of the enterprise was accepted and this was pursued with vigour until the company could, after much creative accounting and debt write-offs, be sold back to the private sector in 1988.

The 1980s then saw the end of the idea that British Leyland should be a privatized national champion. For the Conservative government it was just another company with no special claims, a view symbolized by the willingness to sell the company to Ford. Equally this attitude was symbolized by the courting of Japanese producers, who established production facilities in Britain in the 1980s. Though hardly a point to be emphasized by economic liberals, the decision of the Japanese to set up such facilities was greatly encouraged by the continued protectionism of European countries towards Japanese cars. Japanese companies were particularly welcomed as purveyors of a 'new realism' in industrial relations, with their enthusiasm for single-union deals and flexible work systems.[7] But the total contribution to domestic output, employment, and value added of Japanese firms by the end of the 1980s remained small.

---

[7] Just what exactly the 'Japanese system of production' is, especially as applied in overseas subsidiaries, and how far it conformed with the managerialist rhetoric of 1980s economic liberalism remains unclear, and the subject of lively debate: see, for example, Williams *et al.* (1990).

STATE CAPACITY AND STATE ACHIEVEMENTS

In formulating policies for the car industry in Britain one major issue faced by governments has been their attitude to multinational enterprises (MNEs). Almost from its beginnings the British car industry has been multinational. British Leyland and its various components were never major producers outside the UK, but Ford established a plant in Manchester as early as 1911 and has held a significant market share with British-produced goods since the 1930s. General Motors took over Vauxhall in the 1920s, though remained a rather marginal player until the 1980s. Chrysler entered the fray only briefly in the 1960s and 1970s with its acquisition of Rootes, quickly sold on to Peugeot.

Throughout these years the British government has pursued an unusually liberal policy by international standards, with few controls over the activities of the foreign-owned companies. Generally speaking the perceived benefits in the form of employment and economic dynamism have outweighed any doubts governments might have entertained on the impact of such companies. The only reasonably systematic criterion employed has related to the foreign exchange aspects of such companies coming to Britain. Once established, firms have been treated as if indigenous (Jones 1990). A major incentive for such siting of MNE facilities in Britain has been tariffs and other controls over imports, plus in more recent years proximity to European markets (Maxcy 1981: ch. 13). In addition British governments in more recent years have offered financial incentives, sometimes on a lavish scale, to attract such investment, as for example in the deal with Ford to site its new engine plant at Bridgend in South Wales in the early 1980s (Wilks 1984: 250).

Occasionally British governments have expressed doubts about the desirability of the expanding multinational role in the car industry. In the mid-1960s when Chrysler took over Rootes, the Minister of Technology Tony Benn expressed anxiety whether 'Britain, looking ahead over a period of years, might not be able to sustain three large American corporations and a British corporation when the United States which is three times our size and has a much larger output can only sustain three corporations' (cited in Maxcy 1981: 227). But such doubts have always been overridden by worries over the employment consequences of any rebuff for the multinationals. This stance reached its nadir in 1976–9, when the government bailed out Chrysler-UK at substantial cost, only to have the production facilities sold to Peugeot three years later (Wilks 1984: chs. 6, 7).

Reich (1990) argues that this welcoming of the multinationals in Britain, especially Ford, has been at the expense of the putative national champions, Austin-Morris and British Leyland. He draws fair contrast with the less liberal policies pursued in West Germany, though whether this difference can explain the success of the German national champion, Volkswagen, and the failure of British Leyland seems doubtful. It is difficult to argue that the exclusion of Ford from Britain would have necessarily changed the strategy of Leyland in the 1950s and 1960s, and in the 1970s and 1980s all British-based producers have suffered from the upsurge of imports, and the British position has suffered from Ford's running down of production facilities in the UK, and the growth of captive imports.

This point raises a basic problem in talking about multinationals —how far does ownership matter? If the basic British desire has been to maximize efficient domestic output and employment in cars, should this have lead to any concern over whether the facilities were British or foreign-owned? Of course, there will be foreign exchange consequences, though these can easily be exaggerated. Otherwise the crucial issues would seem to be those of domestic content, i.e. how much of a car produced in this country is actually built from domestically produced components, and the location of activities such as R & D with the implications for the value-added impact of the activity.

In this context, it is interesting to note that it was only in relation to the Japanese companies coming in in the 1980s that explicit content-regulation was imposed, though how effective such regulation was remains a moot point. The tide of internationalization of the car industry would seem to make any policy hinging on ownership increasingly anachronistic in the 1990s, but that is not an argument against forms of regulation concerned with the activities of all firms active within national boundaries.

Unsurprisingly, perhaps, the failure of the British car industry has led many to ask whether the government has not played a part in that demise, by sins of commission or omission. Dunnett (1980) provides a good summary of the critical arguments. He strongly criticizes the capacity-based tax system as a major inhibition to the development of export-competitive cars between the wars. But as already suggested the evidence does not support this view, and this argument was by and large a rather desperate attempt by the producers to blame others for their problems. It is of interest to note that in Germany small cars also dominated production in this period, although the tax regime was quite different (Plowden 1971: 168).

Equally the policies pursued in the 1940s were less ill-judged than he suggests (ch. 3), and indeed the Attlee Government seems to have had a more considered policy for the industry than possibly any other in the twentieth century, though one complicated by the possible conflict between short-term export promotion and long-run efficiency. Similarly the impact of the policy of stop-go in the 1950s and 1960s, whilst hardly helping the industry, has been exaggerated. As Maxcy and Silberston (1959: 191) argued at the time 'the motor industry is not so exceptionally tender a flower that the Government should at all costs hesitate to reduce its sales temporarily by such devices as raising purchase tax or the minimum hire purchase deposit'.

Another policy criticized by Dunnett (79–80) is that of government encouragement of the car companies to locate in development areas in the 1960s in the cause of reducing regional unemployment. The implication here is that such locations imposed higher costs on the companies and thus lowered their efficiency. But there is no clear evidence for this, and in fact wage costs were significantly lower in these areas than in the favoured southern and Midland locations (Silberston 1965: 264–5). Indeed these policies are probably best regarded as failures of regional rather than industrial policy, as the government only persuaded the companies to establish branch plants in high unemployment areas which subsequently proved prone to rapid closure.

Finally, the governments of the post-war period stand condemned for not solving the industrial-relations problems in the car industry in the 1960s and 1970s (Dunnett 1980: 110–11). Two points may be made on this issue. First, as previously argued, the whole industrial relations/labour issue has been exaggerated as a problem for the industry. When it was solved in British Leyland in the 1980s it did little to help that company's survival. Second, quite what governments could have done in these decades remains unclear. Governments did affect industrial relations undoubtedly, but equally they were only one player, and not obviously the most important. Legislation, perhaps the easiest option for the government, was tried in 1971, but proved a notable failure. Third, it seems unhelpful to regard industrial relations as a separate issue from the whole strategy of the companies in the industry.

Overall, the government's alleged sins of both commission and omission as outlined by Dunnett appear exaggerated. Government has simply been less important than he suggests in shaping the performance of the industry. But this is not to say the appropriate verdict is (largely) 'not guilty'. Governments, it can be argued, could have done more.

In making this point it is first of all important to note the powers of government. As Plowden (1971: conclusion) argues on the general issue of regulation of the industry, governments have had room for manœuvre. They have faced powerful pressure groups, but by no means could it be said that these have entirely hamstrung policy. Government, arguably, could and should have done more. Whilst as suggested above the issue of multinationals is a complex one, some harder bargaining might have been employed[8]—this idea gained some support in the 1970s, though the planning agreement with Chrysler had no legal force and highlights the difficulty of a government bargaining from weakness based on a desperate desire to maintain employment. But earlier attempts at content-regulation might have been deployed to give Britain a better position in the growth of tied imports.

In relation to MNEs the government at least in principle has some leverage. In relation to domestically owned producers this has only rarely been the case. It was most obviously true in the 1940s when the control over steel was used to try to change the industry, though in a context where the desperate need for exports gave the companies a ready riposte to any attempts to try to move them faster than they wanted to go.

The basic problem of British Leyland in the 1950s and 1960s, the failure to rationalize production and to build a smaller range of cars by more capital-intensive methods, was something which, directly at least, governments could do little about. Even

---

[8]   Ford's threats in the 1930s to abandon production in Britain unless the system of car tax was reformed seem to have been ignored (Plowden 1971: 173).

Cripps-style admonishments were unfashionable for most of this period, the attitude of the Conservative government being well summarized by the President of the Board of Trade's statement in 1956 that 'It is not for any Government to export motor cars; it is for the motor industry to do that' (cited Plowden 1971: 343). It was this period which we may regard as the lost opportunity for the British car industry, when its expanding output disguised its poor competitive performance, which was then exposed when free trade came in the late 1960s and 1970s.

The nationalization of 1975 (like that of Rolls Royce under the previous Conservative government) was politically inescapable given the importance of British Leyland to the British economy. Unfortunately it was a change which, initially, provided only a means to pump more money into the enterprise in pursuit of a doomed strategy. When this failed it became a shell within which a (relatively) orderly retreat could be pursued, little different from what was happening in much of British manufacturing industry.

Whether there were ready alternatives to these policies by the mid-1970s may be doubted. Consumer tastes for imported cars, conditioned by a long history of poor-quality British products, made the market constraints on the enterprise extremely difficult to overcome by any means. Perhaps a little less blind faith in shibboleths like economies of scale (in the 1960s) or investment-led recovery (in the 1970s) might have helped, though perhaps the only viable alternative at company level was that eventually taken of almost complete withdrawal from any claim to be a major producer of mass-produced cars.

CONCLUSIONS

By the end of the 1980s some of the most acute commentators on the British car industry were arguing that the key issue for that industry was the market (Williams *et al.* 1987a: ch. 5). As in other key trading sectors like white goods, the level of import penetration and lack of domestic exporting capacity combined to make it difficult to see how any British-based producer could do much to expand unless the market was secured by some means, their own suggestion being a regime of tough content-regulation for key sectors including cars.

As Williams and his co-authors are well aware, such proposals fly in the face of the whole trend towards international economic liberalization of recent years, sustained not only by the long-held theories of economists, but by the politically much more important interest of consumers in buying in the cheapest markets. With consumerism rampant across the ideological spectrum, and producer interests politically very difficult to articulate by the early 1990s, the possibility of such a protective regime in however mild a form appeared extremely remote. Yet in its absence it is difficult to see where any revival of the British car industry could come from.

This conclusion must therefore end on a very gloomy note as regards the prospects of the British car industry. The best that can be hoped for is that by suitable agreement at Western European level the distribution of multinational (European, American, and Japanese) production, regulated as to content, can be more equally distributed within the EC. Politically however this appears only marginally less unlikely than the kind of regime which would protect the home market in order to allow some revival of domestic production in a safeguarded market.

It may be suggested that cars, like cotton, is an old industry, doomed to be replaced by others in the changing patterns of demand and suppliers cost-driven comparative advantage, just like the industries of the first Industrial Revolution. But such an argument is impossible to apply to cars. On the demand side, though the industry is always subject to sharp cycles, there is no evidence that consumers have satiated their desire for cars. On the other hand the supply of imported cars is increasingly not from low-wage countries, but from high(er)-wage Western European producers. Britain is the only major Western European country whose output of cars falls below sales—in 1989 output was 1.27m. but sales were 2.3m. (Rhys 1990: 14).

The most striking consequence of this is of course for the balance of payments. In 1989 the vehicle industry (cars and commercial vehicles) generated a deficit of £6.55bn., equivalent to 35 per cent of the overall deficit on manufactured goods, and almost 80 per cent of this derived from the car sector. Of course, there is no reason why any individual sector of the balance of payments should yield a surplus. But cars remain a huge trade sector, and to compensate for this scale of deficit elsewhere is extraordinarily difficult. Furthermore cars do seem to typify problems across the range of consumer and business durables, notably IT equipment and consumer electronics. These big, expanding sectors together generate the manufacturing deficit (Rhys 1990: 11–12).

Cars then typify the process of deindustrialization which has played a significant part in the debate about the British economy since the 1970s. The use of this term needs considerable care (Blackaby 1978). There is nothing inherently desirable in having large proportions of employment and output in manufacturing industry, and successful industrial countries would expect to satisfy their demand for manufactured goods from a falling proportion of the work-force if productivity rose rapidly (Rowthorn and Wells 1987). On the other hand, this has not been the case in Britain. Deindustrialization, signalled not only by proportional but also by rapid absolute falls in the numbers employed in industry, has been the consequence of failure not of success. It has not been the realization of a comparative advantage in services, but a comprehensive (but not universal) failure to compete in those goods in which every other major industrial country (though obviously to varying degrees) has a major presence.

Deindustrialization is best defined, following Singh (1977), as a failure of the manufacturing sector to generate sufficient net exports to pay for the imports demanded at socially acceptable levels of output, employment, and exchange parity. Unfortunately since Singh first wrote, what is socially acceptable has shifted radically, not least in terms of unemployment. Nevertheless, his definition still stands. Deindustrialization is not a problem of nostalgia for days when a much larger proportion of the population worked producing tangible products to the rhythm of factory whistles. It is a problem of being unable to find an acceptable combination of economic policy outcomes, combining above all growth and employment. Thus by 1990 the problem of industrial inefficiency could best be seen in this light, as a broad problem of the British polity to find a way of reinvigorating industry in the name of these broad but essential aims.

Further Reading

Dunnett, P. (1980), *The Decline of the British Motor Industry: The Effects of Government Policy, 1945–1979*, London.

Lewchuk, W. (1987), *American Technology and the British Vehicle Industry*, Cambridge.

Maxcy, G., and Silberston, A. (1959), *The Motor Industry*, London.

PEP (1950), *Political and Economic Planning Engineering Reports II—Motor Vehicles*, London.

Saul, S. B. (1962), 'The Motor Industry in Britain to 1914', *Business History*, 5: 22–44.

Wilks, S. (1984), *Industrial Policy and the Motor Industry*, Manchester.

Williams, K. (1983), 'BMC/BLMC/BL—A Misunderstood Failure', in K. Williams, J. Williams, and D. Thomas (eds.), *Why Are the British Bad at Manufacturing?*, London

Williams, K., Williams, J., and Haslam, C. (1987), *The Breakdown of Austin Rover*, Leamington Spa.

References

(The place of publication is London, unless otherwise stated.)

Addison, P. (1977), *The Road to 1945*.

Ady, P. H. (1962), 'The Terms of Trade', in G. D. N. Worswick and P. H. Ady (eds.), *The British Economy 1945–51*, Oxford: 147–72.

Aldcroft, D. H. (1962), 'The Early History and Development of Export Credit Insurance in Britain, 1919–1939', *Manchester School*, 30: 69–85.

Alford, B. W. E. (1986), 'Lost Opportunities: British Business and Businessmen During the First World War', in N. McKendrick and R. B. Outhwaite (eds.), *Business Life and Public Policy*, Cambridge: 205–27.

—— (1988), *British Economic Performance 1945–75*.

Allen, G. C. (1939), *British Industries and their Organization*.

—— (1948), *Economic Thought and Industrial Policy*.

—— (1951), 'The Concentration of Production Policy', in D. N. Chester (ed.), *Lessons of the British War Economy*, Cambridge: 167–81.

—— (1968), *Monopoly and Restrictive Practices*.

Allsopp, C. (1991), 'Macroeconomic Policy: Design and Performance', in M. Artis and D. Cobham (eds.), *Labour's Economic Policies 1974–79*, Manchester: 19–37.

Amery, L. S. (1946), *The Washington Loan Agreements: A Critical Study of American Economic Policy*.

Arndt, H. W. (1978), *The Rise and Fall of Economic Growth*, Melbourne.

Artis, M., and Cobham, D. (1991) (eds.), *Labour's Economic Policies 1974–79*, Manchester.

—— —— and Wickham-Jones, M. (1992), 'Social Democracy in Hard Times: The Economic Record of the Labour Government 1974–1979', *Twentieth Century British History*, 3: 32–58.

Ashworth, W. (1960), *An Economic History of England 1870–1939*.

—— (1986), *The History of the British Coal Industry*, v. *1946–1982: The Nationalised Industry*, Oxford.

—— (1991), *The State in Business 1945 to the mid-1980s*.

Atkin, J. (1970), 'Official Regulation of British Overseas Investment 1914–1931', *Economic History Review*, 23: 324–35.

BPC (1972/3), *British Productivity Council, Annual Review*.

Bailey, B. (1990), 'Technical Education and Secondary Schooling', in E. Evans and P. Summerfield (eds.), *Technical Education and the State*, Manchester: 97–119.

Balfour (1926), *Committee on Industry and Trade: Industrial Relations.*

—— (1927), *Committee on Industry and Trade: Factors in Commercial and Industrial Efficiency.*

Balogh, T. (1947), 'Money Incentive and the Production Drive', in Oxford Institute of Statistics (ed.), *Studies in War Economics*: 13–16.

—— (1948), *Dollar Crisis: Causes and Cure*, Oxford.

—— (1949), 'Britain's Economic Problem', *Quarterly Journal of Economics*, 58: 32–67.

—— (1958), 'Differential Profits Tax', *Economic Journal*, 68: 528–33.

Bamberg, J. (1988), 'The Rationalisation of the British Cotton Industry in the Interwar Years', *Textile History*, 19: 83–102.

Bank of England (1981), 'Profitability and Company Finance', *Bank of England Quarterly Bulletin*, 21: 228–31.

Bannock, G., and Albach, H. (1991), *Small Business Policy in Europe.*

Barker, R. (1972), *Education and Politics 1900–51*, Oxford.

Barlow, M. (1901), 'The New Companies Act 1900', *Economic Journal*, 11: 180–92.

Barna, T. (1949), 'Those "Frightfully High" Profits', *Bulletin of the Oxford University Institute of Statistics*, 11: 213–26.

Barnett, C. (1986), *The Audit of War.*

Barry, E. E. (1965), *Nationalisation in British Politics.*

Beckerman, W. (1974) (ed.), *The Labour Government's Economic Record.*

Beer, S. (1982), *Modern British Politics.*

Begg, D., Dornbusch, R., and Fischer, S. (1991), *Economics*, 3rd edn.

Benn, C. and Fairley, J. (1986) (eds.), *Challenging the M.S.C. on Jobs, Education and Training: Enquiry into a National Disaster.*

Benn, T. (1989), *Against the Tide: Diaries 1973–6.*

Bennett, A., and Smith-Gavine, S. (1988), 'The Percentage Utilization of Labour Index', in D. Bosworth (ed.), *Working Below Capacity*: 326–63.

Berghoff, H. (1990), 'Public Schools and the Decline of the British Economy 1870–1914', *Past and Present*, 129: 148–67.

Beveridge, W. H. (1928), *British Food Control*, Oxford.

Bevin, E. (1942), *The Job to be Done.*

Blackaby, F. T. (1978) (ed.), *De-Industrialisation.*

Blank, S. (1972), *Government and Industry in Britain: The F.B.I. in Politics 1945–65*, Farnborough.

Blaug, M. (1958), 'The Classical Economists and the Factory Acts', in A. W. Coats (ed.), *The Classical Economists and Economic Policy*: 104–22.

Bonavia, M. (1971), *British Rail.*

Booth, A. (1987), 'Britain in the 1930s: A Managed Economy?', *Economic History Review*, 40: 499–522.

Booth, A. (1989*a*), *British Economic Policy 1931–49: A Keynesian Revolution?*

—— (1989*b*), 'Britain in the 1930s: A Managed Economy? A Reply to Peden and Middleton', *Economic History Review*, 42: 548–56.

—— and Pack, M. (1985), *Employment, Capital and Economic Policy: Great Britain 1918–1939*, Oxford.

Boothby, R., Macmillan, H., Loder, J., and Stanley, A. (1927), *Industry and the State: A Conservative View.*

Boswell, J. S., and Johns, B. R. (1982), 'Patriots or Profiteers? British Businessmen and the First World War', *Journal of European Economic History*, 11: 423–45.

Bowen, A. (1991), 'Labour Market Policies', in M. Artis and D. Cobham (eds.), *Labour's Economic Policies 1974–79*, Manchester: 190–212.

Bowker, B. (1928), *Lancashire Under the Hammer.*

Boyce, R. (1987), *British Capitalism at the Crossroads*, Cambridge.

Brady, R. (1950), *Crisis in Britain.*

Braverman, H. (1974), *Labour and Monopoly Capital*, New York.

Brech, M. J. (1985), 'Nationalised Industries', in D. Morris (ed.), *The Economic System in the UK*, Oxford: 771–97.

Brennan, E. J. T. (1975), *Education for National Efficiency: The Contribution of Sidney and Beatrice Webb.*

Briggs, A. (1961), *Social Thought and Social Action: A Study of the Work of Seebohm Rowntree 1871–1954.*

British Employers Confederation (1950), 'Restrictive Practices . . . Summary of Replies Received', Modern Records Centre, University of Warwick, MSS200/B/3/2/C 821, pt. 2.

Brittan, S. (1964), *The Treasury Under the Tories, 1951–1964.*

Britton, A. (1991), *British Macroeconomic Policy 1974–1987.*

Broadberry, S., and Crafts, N. (1990), 'Explaining Anglo-American Productivity Differences in the Mid-Twentieth Century', *Bulletin of the Oxford University Institute of Economics and Statistics*, 52: 375–402.

—— —— (1992), 'Britain's Productivity Gap in the 1930s: Some Neglected Factors', *Journal of Economic History*, 52: 531–58.

Brooke, S. (1989), 'Revisionists and Fundamentalists: The Labour Party and Economic Policy During the Second World War', *Historical Journal*, 32, 157–75.

—— (1991), 'Problems of "Socialist Planning": Evan Durbin and the Labour Government of 1945', *Historical Journal*, 34: 687–702.

Brown, C. J. F., and Sheriff, T. D. (1978), 'De-Industrialisation: A Background Paper', in F. T. Blackaby (ed.), *De-Industrialisation*: 233–62.

Brown, W. (1991), 'Industrial Relations', in M. Artis and D. Cobham (eds.), *Labour's Economic Policies 1974–1979*, Manchester: 213–28.

Buckley, C. M., and Day, R. (1980), 'Nuclear Reactor Development in Britain', in K. Pavitt (ed.), *Technical Innovation and British Economic Performance*: 252–66.

Bullock, A. (1967), *The Life and Times of Ernest Bevin*, ii. *Minister of Labour 1940–45*.

Burk, K. (1982) (ed.), *War and the State*.

—— (1988), *The First Privatisation: The Politicians, The City and The Denationalisation of Steel*.

Burn, D. (1958), *The Structure of British Industry*, ii, Cambridge.

Burnham, J. (1940), *The Managerial Revolution*, New York.

Buxton, N. (1970), 'Entrepreneurial Efficiency in the British Coalmining Industry between the Wars', *Economic History Review*, 23: 476–97.

—— (1982), 'Coalmining', in N. Buxton and D. H. Aldcroft (eds.), *British Industry Between the Wars*: 48–78.

C.4893 (1886), *Final Report of the Royal Commission . . . into the Depression of Trade and Industry*, PP 1886, vol. 23.

C.7421 (1894), *Report of the Royal Commission on Labour*, PP 1894, vol. 35.

Cd. 8005 (1916), *Scheme for the Organisation and Development of Scientific and Industrial Research*, PP 1914–16, vol. 50.

Cd. 8181 (1916), *Report of a Sub-Committee of the Advisory Committee of the Board of Trade on Commercial Intelligence*, PP 1916, vol. 15.

Cd. 8271 (1916), *Recommendations of the Economic Conference of the Allies, held at Paris 14–17th June 1916*, PP 1916, vol. 34.

Cd. 8715 (1918), *Memorandum by the Board of Trade and the Foreign Office with Respect to the Future Organisation of Commercial Intelligence*, PP 1917/18, vol. 29.

Cd. 8912 (1918), *Memorandum with Respect to the Re-organisation of the Board of Trade*, PP 1917/18, vol. 29.

Cd. 9035 (1918), *Final Report of the Committee on Commercial and Industrial Policy After the War*, PP 1918, vol. 13.

Cd. 9065 (1918), *Health of Munitions Workers Committee: Final Report*, PP 1918, vol. 12.

Cd. 9236 (1918), *Ministry of Reconstruction Report of Committee on Trusts*, PP 1918, vol. 5.

Cd. 9346 (1918), *Report to the Board of Trade by the Committee Appointed to Investigate the Question of Financial Facilities for Trade*, PP 1918, vol. 15.

Cmd. 166 (1919), *Special Report from the Select Committee on High Prices and Profits, Together with Minutes of Evidence*, PP 1919, vol. 5.

Cmd. 514 (1920), *Findings by a Sub-committee of the Standing Committee on Trusts . . . on the Fish Trade*, PP 1920, vol. 23.

Cmd. 662 (1920), *Findings of a Committee Appointed to Inquire into the Principle of Fixed Retail Prices*, PP 1920, vol. 23.

Cmd. 983 (1920), *Findings of a Sub-committee Appointed by the Standing Committee on the Investigation of Prices . . . in Respect of Furniture*, PP 1920, vol. 23.

Cmd. 1645 (1922), *Report of the Committee Appointed to Enquire into the Working and Effects of the Trade Boards Acts*, PP 1922, vol. 10.

Cmd. 3615 (1930), *Report of the Committee of the Economic Advisory Council on the Cotton Industry*, PP 1929/30, vol. 12.

Cmd. 6311 (1941), *Correspondence Respecting the Policy of H.M.G. in Connexion with the Use of Materials Received under the Lend-Lease Agreement*, PP 1940/1, vol. 8.

Cmd. 6527 (1944), *Employment Policy*, PP 1943/4, vol. 8.

Cmd. 9474 (1955), *Royal Commission on the Taxation of Profits and Income*, PP 1955/6, vol. 27.

Cmd. 9504 (1955), *Monopoly and Restrictive Practices Commission: Collective Discrimination*, PP 1955/6, vol. 24.

Cmd. 9703 (1956), *Technical Education*, PP 1955/6, vol. 36.

Cmd. 9725 (1956), *The Economic Implications of Full Employment*, PP 1955/6, vol. 36.

Cmnd. 124 (1957), *Defence: Outline of Future Policy*, PP 1956/7, vol. 23.

Cmnd. 827 (1959), *Committee on the Working of the Monetary System: Report* (Radcliffe), PP 1958/9, vol. 17.

Cmnd. 1337 (1961), *Financial and Economic Obligations of Nationalised Industries*, PP 1960/1, vol. 27.

Cmnd. 1844 (1962), *National Incomes Commission*, PP 1962/3, vol. 31.

Cmnd. 1892 (1962), *Industrial Training: Government Proposals*, PP 1962/3, vol. 31.

Cmnd. 2154 (1963), *Report on the Future of Higher Education,* (Robbins), PP 1962/3, vol. 11.

Cmnd. 2299 (1964), *Monopolies, Mergers and Restrictive Practices*, PP 1963/4, vol. 26.

Cmnd. 2764 (1965), *The National Plan*, PP 1964/5, vol. 30.

Cmnd. 2874 (1965), *Investment Incentives*, PP 1965/6, vol. 13.

Cmnd. 2899 (1965), *Industrial Reorganisation Corporation*, PP 1965/6, vol. 13.

Cmnd. 3347 (1967), *Kennedy Round of Trade Negotiations, 1964–67*, PP 1966/7, vol. 38.

Cmnd. 3437 (1967), *Nationalised Industries: A Review of Economic and Financial Objectives*, PP 1967/8, vol. 39.

Cmnd. 3623 (1968), *Report of the Royal Commission on Trades Unions and Employers Organisation,* (Donovan), PP 1967/8, vol. 32.

Cmnd. 3888 (1969), *In Place of Strife: A Policy for Industrial Relations*, PP 1968/9, vol. 53.

Cmnd. 4237 (1969), *Productivity, Prices and Incomes Policy After 1969*, PP 1969/70, vol. 9.

Cmnd. 4811 (1971), *Small Firms: Report of the Committee of Inquiry on Small Firms* (Bolton), PP 1971/2, vol. 9.

Cmnd. 4814 (1971), *A Framework for Government Research and Development* (Rothschild), PP 1971/2, vol. 25.

Cmnd. 4942 (1972), *Industrial and Regional Development*, PP 1971/2, vol. 18.

Cmnd. 5710 (1974), *The Regeneration of British Industry*, PP 1974, vol. 7.

Cmnd. 6003 (1974), *Membership of the E.C.: Report on Renegotiation*, PP 1974/5, vol. 9.

Cmnd. 6315 (1975), *An Approach to Industrial Strategy*, PP 1975/6, vol. 17.

Cmnd. 6706 (1976), *Industrial Democracy* (Bullock), PP 1976/7, vol. 16.

Cmnd. 7131 (1978), *The Nationalised Industries*, PP 1977/8, vol. 37.

Cmnd. 7198 (1978), *A Review of Monopolies and Mergers Policy*, PP 1977/8, vol. 24.

Cmnd. 7439 (1979), *The Government's Expenditure Plans 1978/9 to 1982/3*, PP 1978/9, vol. 18.

Cmnd. 8455 (1981), *A New Training Initiative: A Programme for Action*, PP 1981/2, vol. 50.

Cmnd. 9474 (1985), *Employment: The Challenge for the Nation*, PP 1984/5, vol. 56.

Cmnd. 9571 (1985), *Lifting the Burden*, PP 1984/5, vol. 61.

Cmnd. 9734 (1986), *Privatisation of Water Authorities in England and Wales*, PP 1985/6, vol. 50.

Cmnd. 9794 (1986), *Building Businesses—Not Barriers*, PP 1985/6, vol. 53.

CM. 185 (1987), *Civil Research and Development*, PP 1987/8, vol. 49.

CM. 278 (1988), *D.T.I.—The Department for Enterprise*, PP 1987/8, vol. 54.

CM. 316 (1988), *Training for Employment*, PP 1987/8, vol. 56.

CM. 512 (1988), *Releasing Enterprise*, PP 1987/8, vol. 58.

CM. 540 (1988), *Employment for the 1990s*, PP 1988/9, vol. 44.

CPRS (1975), *The Future of the British Car Industry*.

Cadbury, E. (1914), 'The Case For and Against Scientific Management', *Sociological Review*, 7: 99–117.

Cain, P. (1979), 'Political Economy in Edwardian England: The Tariff Reform Controversy', in A.O. Day (ed.), *The Edwardian Age: Conflict and Stability 1900–1914*: 34–59.

Cairncross, A. (1985), *Years of Recovery: British Economic Policy 1945–51*.

Cairncross, A. (1990), *Planning in Wartime: Aircraft Production in Britain, Germany and the U.S.A.*

—— (1992), *The British Economy since 1945*, Oxford.

—— and Burk, K. (1992), *Goodbye, Great Britain: The 1976 I.M.F. Crisis.*

—— and Eichengreen, B. (1983), *Sterling in Decline*, Oxford.

—— and Watts, N. (1989), *The Economic Section 1939–1961: A Study in Economic Advising.*

Calder, A. (1971), *The People's War.*

Campbell-Kelly, M. (1989), *I.C.L.: A Business and Technical History*, Oxford.

Cannan, E. (1916), 'Report on British Industry after the War', *Economic Journal*, 26: 97–104.

Capie, F. (1981), 'Tariffs, Elasticities and Prices in Britain in the 1930s', *Economic History Review*, 34: 140–2.

—— (1983), *Depression and Protectionism.*

—— (1991), 'Effective Protection and Economic Recovery in Britain, 1932–37', *Economic History Review*, 44: 339–42.

—— and Collins, M. (1992), *Have the Banks Failed British Industry?*

Carew, A. (1987), *Labour under the Marshall Plan*, Manchester.

Carter, C. F., and Williams, B. (1957), *Industry and Technical Progress*, Oxford.

—— —— (1959), *Science in Industry: Policy for Progress*, Oxford.

Cassels, J. (1989), 'Reflections on Tripartism', *Policy Studies*, 9: 6–19.

Casson, M. (1983), *Economics of Unemployment: An Historical Perspective.*

Centre for Local Economic Strategies (1992), *Reforming the T.E.C.s: Towards a New Training Strategy.*

Chalmers, M. (1985), *Paying for Defence: Military Spending and British Decline.*

Chandler, A. (1990), *Scale and Scope: The Dynamics of Industrial Capitalism*, Cambridge, Mass.

Chatterji, B. J. (1981), 'Business and Politics in the 1930s: Lancashire and the Making of the Indo-British Trade Agreement, 1939', *Modern Asian Studies*, 15: 527–73.

Checkland, S. G. (1983), *British Public Policy 1776–1939*, Cambridge.

Chester, D. N. (1975), *The Nationalisation of British Industry 1945–51.*

Chick, M. (1990), 'Marginal Cost-Pricing and the Peak Hour Demand for Electricity 1945–51', in M. Chick (ed.), *Governments, Industries and Markets*, Aldershot: 110–26.

—— (1991), 'Competition, Competitiveness and Nationalisation', in G. Jones and M. Kirby (eds.), *Competitiveness and the State: Government and Business in Twentieth Century Britain*, Manchester: 60–77.

Chitty, C. (1986), 'T.V.E.I.: The M.S.C.'s Trojan Horse', in C. Benn and J. Fairley (eds.), *Challenging the M.S.C on Jobs, Education and Training: Enquiry into a National Disaster*: 76–98.

Church, R., and Miller, M. (1977), 'The Big Three: Competition, Management, and Marketing in the British Motor Industry, 1922–1939', in B. Supple (ed.), *Essays in British Business History*, Oxford: 163–86.

Clapham, J. (1938), *An Economic History of Modern Britain*, iii, Cambridge.

Clarke, P. (1988), *The Keynesian Revolution in the Making 1924–1936*, Oxford.

Clarke, R. W. B. (1982), *Anglo-American Economic Collaboration in Peace and War, 1942–49* (ed. A. Cairncross), Oxford.

Clegg, H. (1985), *A History of British Trade Unions since 1889*, ii, *1911–1939*, Oxford.

Cline, P. (1982), 'Winding Down the War Economy: British Plans for Post-War Recovery 1916–19', in K. Burk (ed.), *War and the State*: 157–81.

Coats, A. W. (1968), 'Political Economy and the Tariff Reform Campaign of 1903', *Journal of Law and Economics*, 11: 181–229.

—— (1971) (ed.), *The Classical Economists and Economic Policy*.

Cole, G. D. H. (1923), *Trade Unionism and Munitions*, Oxford.

Coleman, D. C. (1975), 'War Demand and Industrial Supply: The Dope Scandal, 1915–19', in J. Winter (ed.), *War and Economic Development*, Cambridge: 205–27.

—— (1980), *Courtaulds: An Economic and Social History*.

Collins, M. (1991), *Bankers and Industrial Finance in Britain 1800–1939*.

Collins, B., and Robbins, K. (1990) (eds.), *British Culture and Economic Decline*.

Colwyn, (1927), *Report of Committee on National Debt and Taxation*, Cmd. 2800, PP 1927, vol. 11.

Conservative Party (1947), *The Industrial Charter*.

—— (1958), *Onward in Freedom*.

Coopey, R., Spinardi, E., and Uttley, M. (1992), *Defence Science and Technology: Adjusting to Change*.

Cosh, A., Hughes, A., Singh, A., Carty, J., and Plender, J. (1990), *Takeovers and Short-Termism in the U.K.*, Institute for Public Policy Research, Industrial Policy Paper no. 3.

Cottrell, P. (1980), *Industrial Finance 1830–1914*.

Cowling, K., and Sugden, R. (1987), *Transnational Monopoly Capitalism*, Brighton.

Crafts, N. F. R. (1991), 'Reversing Relative Economic Decline? The 1980s in Historical Perspective', *Oxford Review of Economic Policy*, 7: 81–98.

—— (1992a), 'Productivity Growth Reconsidered', *Economic Policy*, 15: 388–414.

—— (1992b), *Was the Thatcher Experiment Worth It?: British Economic Growth in a European Context*, Centre for Economic Policy Research, Discussion Paper no. 710.

Crafts, N. F. R., Leybourne, S. J., and Mills, T. C. (1990), 'Measurement of Trend Growth in European Industrial Output before 1914: Methodological Issues and New Estimates', *Explorations in Entrepreneurial History*, 27: 442–67.

Crofts, S. (1989), *Coercion or Persuasion? Economic Propaganda, 1945–51.*

Cronin, J. (1991), *The Politics of State Expansion: War, State and Society in Twentieth Century Britain.*

Crosland, A. (1956), *The Future of Socialism.*

Cutler, T. (1992), 'Vocational Training and British Economic Performance: A Further Instalment of the "British Worker Problem"', *Work, Employment and Society*, 6: 161–83.

—— Williams, J., Williams, K. (1986), *Keynes, Beveridge and Beyond.*

—— —— —— (1989), *1992: The Struggle for Europe.*

Dahl, R. (1947), 'Workers Control of Industry and the British Labour Party', *American Political Science Review*, 41: 875–900.

Daniel, G., and Jewkes, J. (1928), 'The Post-War Depression in the Lancashire Cotton Industry', *Journal of the Royal Statistical Society*, 91: 159–92.

Daniels, W. W. (1987), *Workplace Industrial Relations and Technical Change.*

Davenport, N. (1974), *Memoirs of a City Radical.*

Davenport-Hines, R. (1984), *Dudley Docker: The Life and Times of a Trade Warrior*, Cambridge.

Davidson, R. (1985), *Whitehall and the Labour Problem in Late Victorian and Edwardian Britain.*

Davies, E. (1940), *National Capitalism.*

Davis, M. (1990), 'Technical Education, 1944–1956', in P. Summerfield and E. J. Evans (eds.), *Technical Education and the State Since 1850*, Manchester: 120–44.

Deakin, B. M., and Pratten, C. (1987), 'Economic Effects of YTS', *Employment Gazette*, 95: 491–7.

Dean, A. (1981), 'Public and Private Sector Pay and the Economy', in J. L. Fallick and R. F. Elliott (eds.), *Incomes Policies, Inflation and Relative Pay*, 45–71.

Denison, E. F. (1967), *Why Growth Rates Differ*, Washington, DC.

Devons, E. (1950), *Planning in Practice*, Cambridge.

—— (1951), 'The Problem of Co-ordination in Aircraft Production', in D. N. Chester (ed.), *Lessons of the British War Economy*, Cambridge: 102–21.

Diamond, J. (1948), 'The Private Sector', in D. Munro (ed.), *Socialism: The British Way*: 57–87.

Dicey, A. V. (1907), *Lectures on the Relations Between Law and Public Opinion in England During the Nineteenth Century.*

Dintenfass, M. (1984), 'The Politics of Producers Co-operation: The F.B.I./T.U.C./ N.C.E.O. Talks, 1929–33', in J. Turner (ed.), *Businessmen and Politics*: 76–92.

—— (1988), 'Entrepreneurial Failure Reconsidered: The Case of the Interwar British Coal Industry', *Business History Review*, 62: 1–34.

—— (1992), *The Decline of Industrial Britain 1870–1980.*

Donnelly, T., and Thoms, D. (1989), 'Trade Unions, Management and the Search for Production in the Coventry Motor Car Industry, 1939–75', *Business History*, 31: 98–113.

Dore, R. (1986), *Flexible Rigidities: Industrial Policy and Structural Adjustment in the Japanese Economy 1970–80.*

Dow, J. C. R. (1965), *The Management of the British Economy, 1945–60*, Cambridge.

Dowie, J. (1968), 'Growth in the Inter-War Period: Some More Arithmetic', *Economic History Review*, 21: 93–112.

—— (1975), '1919/20 is in Need of Attention', *Economic History Review*, 27: 429–50.

Driver, C. (1983), 'Import Substitution and the Work of the Sector Working Parties', *Applied Economics*, 15: 165–76.

Dunnett, P. (1980), *The Decline of the British Motor Industry: The Effects of Government Policy, 1945–1979.*

Dupree, M. (1987), (ed.), *Lancashire and Whitehall: The Diary of Sir Raymond Streat, 1931–57*, 2 vols., Manchester.

—— (1990), 'Struggling with Destiny: The Cotton Industry, Overseas Trade Policy and the Cotton Board, 1940–1959', *Business History*, 32: 106–28.

—— 'Fighting against Fate: The Cotton Industry and the Government during the 1930s', *Textile History*, 21: 93–112.

—— (1992), 'The Cotton Industry: A Middle Way Between Nationalisation and Self Government?', in H. Mercer, N. Rollings, and J. Tomlinson (eds.), *Labour Government and Private Industry: The Experience of 1945–51*, Edinburgh: 137–61.

Durbin, E. (1985), *New Jerusalems: The Labour Party and the Economics of Democratic Socialism.*

Economic Journal (1930), 'Symposium on Rationalisation', 40: 351–68.

Edgerton, D. E. H. (1986), 'State Intervention in British Manufacturing Industry 1931–51: A Comparative Study of Policy for Military Aircraft and Cotton Textile Industries' (unpublished Ph.D. dissertation, University of London).

—— (1987), 'Science and Technology in British Business History', *Business History*, 29: 84–103.

Edgerton, D. E. H. (1991), *England and the Aeroplane.*

—— (1992), 'Whatever Happened to the Warfare State? The Ministry of Supply 1945–51', in H. Mercer, N. Rollings, and J. Tomlinson (eds.), *Labour and Private Industry: The Experience of 1945–51*, Edinburgh: 91–116.

—— and Hughes, K. (1989), 'The Poverty of Science: A Critical Analysis of Scientific and Industrial Policy Under Mrs. Thatcher', *Public Administration*, 67: 419–33.

Edwardes, M. (1983), *Back From the Brink.*

Edwards, R. S., and Townsend, H. (1956), *Business Enterprise.*

Eichengreen, B. (1981), 'Sterling and the Tariff, 1929–32', *Princeton Studies in International Finance*, 48.

—— (1984), 'Keynes and Protection', *Journal of Economic History*, 44: 363–73.

Elbaum, B., and Lazonick, W. (1986) (eds.), *The Decline of the British Economy*, Oxford.

Elger, T. (1991), 'Task Flexibility and the Intensification of Labour in U.K. Manufacturing in the 1980s', in A. Pollert (ed.), *Farewell to Flexibility?*, Oxford: 46–66.

Elliott, J. (1978), *Conflict or Co-operation? The Growth of Industry Democracy.*

Elliott, R. (1978), 'Industrial Relations and Manpower Policy', in F. Blackaby (ed.), *British Economic Policy 1960–74*, Cambridge, 564–618.

Estrin, S., and Holmes, P. (1983), *French Planning in Theory and Practice.*

Evans, E., and Summerfield, P. (1990) (eds.), *Technical Education and the State*, Manchester.

FBI (1943), *Industry and Research.*

Fairburn, J. (1989), 'The Evolution of Merger Policy in Britain', in J. Fairburn and J. Kay (eds.), *Mergers and Merger Policy*, Oxford: 193–230.

Farrer, T. H. (1883), *The State in its Relation to Trade.*

Feinstein, C. H. (1972), *National Income, Expenditure and Output of the UK*, Cambridge.

—— (1990), 'Britain's Overseas Investments in 1913', *Economic History Review*, 43: 288–95.

Fels, A. (1972), *The British Prices and Incomes Board*, Cambridge.

Fetherston, M., Moore, B., and Rhodes, J. (1979), 'E.E.C. Membership and U.K. Trade in Manufactures', *Cambridge Journal of Economics*, 3: 399–407.

Fforde, J. (1992), *The Bank of England and Public Policy 1941–1958*, Cambridge.

Fielding, S. (1992), 'Labourism in the 1940s', *Twentieth Century British History*, 3: 138–53.

Fine, B. (1990*a*), 'Economies of Scale and a Featherbedding Cartel?: A Reconsideration of the Interwar British Coal Industry', *Economic History Review*, 43: 438–49.

—— (1990*b*), *The Coal Question*.

Finn, D. (1987), *Training Without Jobs*.

Fishbein, W. H. (1984), *Wage Constraint by Consensus: Britain's Search for an Incomes Policy by Agreement, 1965–1979*.

Fitzgerald, R. (1988), *British Labour Management and Industrial Welfare 1846–1939*.

Flanders, A. (1964), *The Fawley Productivity Agreements*.

Florence, P. S. (1933), *The Logic of Industrial Organization*.

—— (1957), *Industry and the State*.

Flux, A. W. (1894), 'The Commercial Supremacy of Great Britain', *Economic Journal*, 4: 595–605.

——(1904), 'Britain's Place in Foreign Markets', *Economic Journal*, 14: 356–71.

Fogarty, M., and Brooks, D. (1989), *Trade Unions and British Industrial Development*, Oxford.

Foreman-Peck, J. (1981), 'The British Tariff and Industrial Protection in the 1930s: An Alternative Model', *Economic History Review*, 34: 132–9.

—— (1982), 'The American Challenge of the 1920s: Multinationals and the European Motor Industry', *Journal of Economic History*, 41: 865–81.

Foster, J. (1974), *Class Struggle and the Industrial Revolution*.

Foxwell, H. S. (1917*a*), 'The Nature of the Industrial Struggle', *Economic Journal*, 27: 315–29.

—— (1917*b*), 'The Financing of Industry and Trade', *Economic Journal*, 27: 502–22.

Freeman, C. (1979), 'Technical Innovation and British Trade Performance', in F. Blackaby (ed.), *De-Industrialisation*: 56–73.

—— (1982), *The Economics of Industrial Innovation* (2nd edn.).

—— and Young, A. (1965), *The Research and Development Effort in Western Europe, North America and the Soviet Union*, Paris.

French, D. (1982), 'The Rise and Fall of "Business as Usual" ', in K. Burk (ed.), *War and the State*: 7–31.

Friedberg, A. L. (1988), *The Weary Titan: Britain and the Experience of Relative Decline 1895–1905*, Princeton, NJ.

Friedlander, K. T. (1946), 'Export Advertising', in M. Abrams (ed.), *Britain and Her Export Trade*: 303–16.

Frost, R. (1991), *Alternating Currents: Nationalised Power in France, 1946–70*, Ithaca, NY.

Furniss, H. S. (1918) (ed.), *The State and Industry during the War.*

Gaitskell, H. (1956), *Socialism and Nationalisation*, Fabian Tract no. 300.

Gardner, N. K. A. (1976), 'Economics of Launching Aid', in A. Whiting (ed.), *The Economics of Industrial Subsidies*: 141–55.

Garside, W. R. (1990), *British Unemployment 1919–1939: A Study in Public Policy*, Cambridge.

Giffen, R. (1900), 'Our Trade Prosperity and the Outlook', *Economic Journal*, 10: 295–307.

Glyn, A. (1988), 'Colliery Results and Closures After the 1984/85 Coal Dispute', *Oxford Bulletin of Economics and Statistics*, 50: 161–73.

—— (1992), 'The "Productivity Miracle", Profits and Investment', in J. Michie (ed.), *The Economic Legacy 1979–1992*: 77–87.

—— and Sutcliffe, B. (1971), *The Profits Crisis.*

Gordon, L. (1938), *The Public Corporation in Great Britain*, Oxford.

Gospel, H. (1979), 'Employers Labour Policy: A Study of the Mond–Turner Talks 1927–33', *Business History*, 21: 180–97.

—— (1991) (ed.), *Industrial Training and Technological Innovation.*

Gourvish, T. (1986), *British Railways 1948–73: A Business History*, Cambridge.

—— (1991), 'The Rise (and Fall?) of State-Owned Enterprise', in T. Gourvish and A. O'Day (eds.), *Britain Since 1945*: 111–34.

Gower, E. (1979), *Gower's Modern Company Law*, 4th edn.

Graham, A. (1972), 'Industrial Policy', in W. Beckerman (ed.), *The Labour Government's Economic Record*: 178–217.

Grant, A. T. K. (1967), *A Study of the Capital Market in Britain from 1891–1936*, 2nd edn.

Green, E. (1985), 'Radical Conservatism: The Electoral Genesis of Tariff Reform', *Historical Journal*, 29: 667–92.

Green, F. (1989) (ed.), *The Restructuring of the UK Economy.*

—— and Ashton, D. (1992), 'Skill Shortages and Skill Deficiencies—A Critique', *Work, Employment and Society*, 6: 287–301.

Grieves, K. (1988), *The Politics of Manpower, 1914–1918*, Manchester.

Grove, J. W. (1962), *Government and Industry in Britain.*

Guenault, P. H., and Jackson, J. M. (1960), *The Control of Monopoly in the United Kingdom.*

Guest, D. E. (1990), 'Have British Workers Been Working Harder in Thatcher's Britain? A Re-Consideration of the Concept of Effort', *British Journal of Industrial Relations*, 28: 293–312.

Hague, D. and Wilkinson, G. (1983), *The I.R.C.: An Experiment in Industrial Intervention*.

Hakim, C. (1987), 'Trends in the Flexible Workforce', *Employment Gazette*, 95: 549–60.

Hall, M. (1962), 'The Consumer Sector 1950–60', in G. D. N. Worswick and P. H. Ady (eds.), *The British Economy in the Nineteen Fifties*, Oxford, 429–60.

Hall, P. (1986), *Governing the Economy: The Politics of State Intervention in Britain and France*, Oxford.

Hancock, W. K. (1970), 'The Reduction of Unemployment as a Problem of Public Policy', in S. Pollard (ed.), *The Gold Standard and Employment Policy Between the Wars*: 99–121.

—— and Gowing, M. (1949), *British War Production*.

Hannah, L. (1979), *Electricity Before Nationalisation: A Study of the Development of the Electricity Supply Industry to 1948*.

—— (1982), *Engineers, Managers and Politicians: The First Fifteen Years of Nationalised Electricity Supply in Britain*.

—— (1983), *The Rise of the Corporate Economy* (2nd edn.).

—— (1990), 'Economic Ideas and Government Policy on Industrial Organisation in Britain Since 1945', in M. Furner and B. Supple (eds.), *The State and Economic Knowledge*, Cambridge: 354–75.

—— (1993), 'The Socialist Experiment: The Economic Consequences of the State Ownership of Industry in the UK', in R. Floud and D. McCloskey (eds.), *The Economic History of Britain since 1700*, 2nd edn., vol. iii, Cambridge.

Hansard (1955/6), *House of Commons Debates*, vol. 549, cols. 1943–58.

Hare, P. (1980), 'Import Controls and the C.E.P.G. Model of the U.K. Economy', *Scottish Journal of Political Economy*, 27: 183–96.

—— (1985), *Planning in the British Economy*.

Harnetty, P. (1962), 'The Indian Cotton Duties Controversy 1894–1896', *English Historical Review*, 77: 684–702.

Harris, J. (1972), *Unemployment and Politics*, Oxford.

—— (1977), *William Beveridge*, Oxford.

—— (1990), 'Economic Knowledge and British Social Policy', in M. Furner and B. Supple (eds.), *The State and Economic Knowledge*, Cambridge: 379–400.

Harris, N. (1972), *Competition and the Corporate Society: British Conservatives, the State and Industry 1945–1964*.

Harrison, M. (1990), 'A Volume Index of the Total Munitions Output of the United Kingdom, 1939–44', *Economic History Review*, 48: 657–66.

Hart, P. (1987), 'Small Firms and Jobs', *National Institute Economic Review*, 121: 60–3.

Hart, P., and Prais, S. J. (1956), 'The Analysis of Business Concentration: A Statistical Approach', *Journal of the Royal Statistical Society*, Series A, 119: 150–76.

Hatfield, M. (1978), *The House the Left Built.*

Hay, J. R. (1983), *The Origins of the Liberal Welfare Reforms 1906–1914*, 2nd edn.

Hayek, F. (1960), *The Constitution of Liberty.*

—— (1980), *1980s Unemployment and the Unions.*

Heald, D. (1980), 'The Economic and Financial Control of the U.K. Nationalised Industries', *Economic Journal*, 90: 243–65.

—— (1983), *Public Expenditure: Its Defence and Reform*, Oxford.

Healey, D. (1990), *The Time of My Life.*

Heim, C. (1984), 'Limits to Intervention: The Bank of England and Industrial Diversification in the Depressed Areas', *Economic History Review*, 37: 533–50.

Helm, D., Mayer, C., Mayhew, K. (1991), 'The Assessment: Microeconomic Policy', *Oxford Review of Economic Policy*, 7: 1–12.

Hemming, M. F. W., Miles, C. M., and Ray, G. F. (1958), 'A Statistical Summary of the Extent of Import Control in the U.K. Since the War', *Review of Economics and Statistics*, 26: 75–109.

Henderson, H. D. (1922), *The Cotton Control Board*, Oxford.

Henderson, P. D. (1952), 'Development Councils', in G. D. N. Worswick and P. H. Ady (eds.), *The British Economy 1945–50*, Oxford: 452–62.

—— (1962), 'Government and Industry', in G. D. N. Worswick and P. H. Ady (eds.), *The British Economy in the Nineteen Fifties*, Oxford: 326–77.

Hendry, J. (1989), *Innovating for Failure: Government Policy and the Early British Computer Industry*, Cambridge, Mass.

Hicks, J., Hicks, U., and Rostas, L. (1941), *The Taxation of War Wealth*, Oxford.

Hicks, U. (1970), *The Finance of British Government 1920–46*, 2nd edn., Oxford.

Hill, D. W. (1950), *Co-operative Research in Industry.*

Hills, J. (1989), *Changing Tax.*

Hilton, B. (1988), *The Age of Atonement: The Influence of Evangelicism on Social and Economic Thought, 1785–1865*, Oxford.

Hilton, J., Mallon, J. J., Manor, S., Rowntree, S. B., Salter, A., and Stuart, F. D. (1935), *Are Trade Unions Obstructive? An Empirical Inquiry.*

Hirst, P. (1979), *On Law and Ideology.*

—— and Zeitlin, J. (1989) (eds.), *Reversing Industrial Decline.*

—— —— (1991) (eds.), 'Flexible Specialisation versus Post-Fordism', *Economy and Society*, 20: 1–56.

Hobson, J. (1894), *The Evolution of Modern Capitalism.*

Hoffman, R. (1964), *Great Britain and the German Trade Rivalry*, New York.

Holland R. F. (1981), 'The Federation of British Industries and the International Economy, 1929–39', *Economic History Review*, 34: 287–300.

Holland, S. (1975), *The Socialist Challenge*.

Holmes, M. (1985), *The Labour Government 1974–79*.

House of Commons (1975), *Expenditure Committee, 14th Report: The Motor Vehicle Industry*, PP 1974/5, vol. 25.

House of Lords (1991), *Select Committees on Science and Technology: Innovation in Manufacturing Industry, Report*, HL, 18–1.

Howlett, P. (1993*a*), 'The Wartime Economy, 1939–45', in R. Floud and D. McCloskey (eds.), *The Economic History of Britain Since 1900*, vol. 3, Cambridge.

—— (1993*b*), 'New Light Through Old Windows: A New Perspective on the British War Economy', *Journal of Contemporary History*, 28: 361–79.

Howson, S. (1973), 'A Dear Money Man? Keynes on Monetary Policy 1920', *Economic Journal*, 83: 456–64.

—— (1975), *Domestic Monetary Management in Britain 1919–39*, Cambridge.

—— (1988), 'Socialist Monetary Policy', *History of Political Economy*, 20: 543–64.

—— and Winch, D. (1977), *The Economic Advisory Council, 1930–1939*, Cambridge.

Hughes, A. (1989), 'Small Firms, Merger Activity and Competition Policy', in J. Barker, J. S. Metcalfe, and M. Porteous (eds.), *Barriers to Growth in Small Firms*: 128–72.

—— (1992), 'Big Business, Small Business and the Enterprise Culture', in J. Michie (ed.), *The Economic Legacy 1979–1992*: 296–311.

Hunt, E. H. (1981), *British Labour History 1815–1914*.

Hunter, A. (1966), *Competition and the Law*.

Hutton, G. (1953), *We Too Can Prosper*.

ILO (1944), *Joint Production Machinery*, Geneva.

ILP (1926), *The Living Wage*.

Inman, P. (1957), *Labour in the Munitions Industries*.

Jamieson, A. G. (1991), 'Credit Insurance and Trade Expansion in Britain, 1820–1980', *Accounting, Business and Financial History*, 1: 163–76.

Jefferys, K. (1987), 'British Politics and Social Policy During the Second World War', *Historical Journal*, 30: 123–44.

Jewkes, J. (1946), 'Is British Industry Inefficient?', *Manchester School*, 14: 1–16.

—— (1958), 'British Monopoly Policy 1944–56', *Journal of Law and Economics*, 1: 1–19.

—— and Jewkes, S. (1966), 'A Hundred Years of Change in the Structure of the Cotton Industry', *Journal of Law and Economics*, 9: 115–34.

—— Sawers, D., and Stillerman, R. (1958), *The Sources of Invention*.

Johnman, L. (1991), 'The Labour Party and Industrial Policy, 1940–45', in N. Tiratsoo (ed.), *The Attlee Years*: 29–53.

—— (1992), 'The Shipbuilding Industry', in H. Mercer, N. Rollings, and J. Tomlinson (eds.), *Labour Governments and Private Industry: The Experience of 1941–1951*, Edinburgh: 186–211.

Johnson, C. (1991), *The Economy Under Mrs. Thatcher*, Harmondsworth.

Johnson, P. B. (1968), *Land Fit for Heroes: The Planning of British Reconstruction*, Chicago.

Johnson, P. S. (1969), 'Research in Britain Today', *Lloyds Bank Review*, 94: 34–49.

Johnson, S. (1991), 'The Small Firm and the U.K. Labour Market in the 1980s', in A. Pollert (ed.), *Farewell to Flexibility*, Oxford: 219–55.

Jones, D., and Prais, S. (1976), 'Plant Size and Productivity in the Motor Industry', *Bulletin of the Oxford University Institute of Statistics*, 40: 131–52.

Jones, D. T. (1976), 'Employment and Productivity in Europe Since 1955', *National Institute Economic Review*, 77: 72–85.

Jones, G. (1981), *The State and the Emergence of the British Oil Industry*.

—— (1990), 'The British Government and Foreign Multinationals Before 1970', in M. Chick (ed.), *Governments, Industries and Markets*, Aldershot: 194–214.

Jones, G. S. (1971), *Outcast London*, Oxford.

Jones, H. (1983), 'Employers Welfare Schemes and Industrial Relations in Inter-War Britain', *Business History*, 25: 61–75.

Jones, L. (1957), *Shipbuilding in Britain: Mainly Between the Two World Wars*, Cardiff.

Jones, R. (1987), *Wages and Employment Policy 1936–87*.

Joseph, K. (1975), *Reversing the Trend*.

Kaldor, N. (1966), *The Causes of the Slow Rate of Growth of the United Kingdom*.

Kaplan, J. J., and Schleiminger, G. (1989), *The E.P.U.: Financial Diplomacy in the 1950s*, Oxford.

Keith, S. T. (1981), 'Inventions, Patents and Commercial Development from Governmentally Financed Research in Great Britain: The Origins of the N.R.D.C.', *Minerva*, 19: 92–122.

Kennedy, C. (1962), 'Monetary Policy', in G. D. N. Worswick and P. H. Ady (eds.), *The British Economy in the Nineteen Fifties*, Oxford: 301–25.

Kennedy, W. P. (1987), *Industrial Structure, Capital Markets and the Origins of British Economic Decline*, Cambridge.

Kenworthy, L. (1990), 'Are Industrial Policy and Corporatism Compatible?', *Journal of Public Policy*, 10: 233–65.

Keynes, J. M. (1914), 'War and the Financial System', *Economic Journal*, 24: 460–86.

—— (1925/72), 'The Economic Consequences of Mr. Churchill', in *Essays in Persuasion, Collected Writings*, ix. 207–230.

—— (1926/72), 'The End of Laissez-Faire', in *Essays in Persuasion, Collected Writings*, ix. 272–94.

—— (1981*a*), 'Industrial Reorganisation: Cotton', in *Collected Writings*, xix, pt. 2. *Activities 1922–1929: The Return to Gold and Industrial Policies*.

—— (1981*b*), *Collected Writings*, xx. *Activities 1929–31: Rethinking Employment and Unemployment Policies*.

Kilroy, A. (1954), 'The Task and Methods of the Monopolies Commission', *Manchester School*, 22: 37–61.

Kindleberger, C. P. (1964), *Economic Growth in France and Britain 1851–1950*, Cambridge.

King, D. (1987), *The New Right*.

King, M. (1975), 'The U.K. Profits Crisis: Myth or Reality?' *Economic Journal*, 85: 33–54.

Kirby, M. (1974), 'The Lancashire Cotton Industry in the Interwar Years: A Study in Organisational Change', *Business History*, 16: 145–59.

—— (1977), *The British Coal Mining Industry 1870–1946*.

—— (1979), 'The Politics of Coercion in Inter-War Britain: The Mines Department of the Board of Trade, 1920–42', *Historical Journal*, 22: 373–96.

—— (1987), 'Industrial Policy', in A. Booth and S. Glynn (eds.), *The Road to Full Employment*: 93–109.

—— (1992), 'Institutional Rigidities and Economic Decline: Some Reflections on the British Experience', *Economic History Review*, 45: 637–60.

—— and Rose, M. (1991), 'Productivity and Competitive Failure: British Government Policy and Industry, 1914–19', in G. Jones and M. Kirby (eds.), *Competitiveness and the State*, Manchester: 20–39.

Kirkaldy, A. W. (1918) (ed.), *Industry and Finance: War Expedients and Reconstruction*.

Kitson, M., and Solomou, S. (1990), *Protectionism and Economic Revival: The British Interwar Economy*, Cambridge.

Kitson, M., Solomou, S., and Weale, M. (1991), 'Effective Protection and Economic Recovery in Britain during the 1930s', *Economic History Review*, 44: 328–38.

Kramer, D. (1988), *State Capital and Private Enterprise: The Case of the U.K. National Enterprise Board.*

Krause, L. B. (1968), 'British Trade Performance', in R. Caves (ed.), *Britain's Economic Prospects*, Washington, DC: 198–230.

Kuehn, D. (1975), *Takeovers and the Theory of the Firm: An Empirical Analysis for the U.K. 1957–1969.*

Labour Party (1918), *Labour and the New Social Order.*

—— (1934), *For Socialism and Peace.*

—— (1937), *Labour's Immediate Programme.*

—— (1945), *Let Us Face the Future.*

—— (1946), *Criteria for Nationalisation*, (Research Department paper, RD 33).

—— (1947), *Public Ownership: The Next Step* (Research Department paper, RD 38, by Michael Young).

—— (1948*a*), *Production: The Bridge to Socialism.*

—— (1948*b*), *Future Nationalisation Policy* (Research Department paper, RD 161, by Douglas Jay).

—— (1949*a*), *Competitive Public Enterprise* (Research Department paper, RD 300).

—— (1949*b*), *Labour Believes in Britain.*

—— (1950*a*), *Labour and the New Society.*

—— (1950*b*), *Let Us Win Through Together.*

—— (1963), *Report of the Annual Conference of the Labour Party.*

—— (1973*a*), *Labour's Programme 1973.*

—— (1973*b*), *The N.E.B.: Labour's State Holding Company.*

—— (1975), *Labour and Industry: The Next Steps.*

Lacey, R. W. (1947), 'Cotton's War Effort', *Manchester School*, 15: 26–74.

Layard, R. (1987), *How to Beat Unemployment*, Oxford.

Lazonick, W. (1983), 'Industrial Organisation and Technical Change: The Decline of the British Cotton Industry', *Business History Review*, 57: 195–236.

—— (1986), 'The Cotton Industry', in B. Elbaum and W. Lazonick (eds.), *The Decline of the British Economy*, Oxford: 18–50.

League of Nations (1945), *Industrialisation and World Trade*, New York.

Lee, M. (1980), *The Churchill Coalition, 1940–45.*

Lees, D., and Chiplin, B. (1970), 'The Economics of Industrial Training', *Lloyds Bank Review*, 96: 29–41.

Lemon, C. (1949), *Report of the Committee on Standardisation in the Engineering Industry.*

Lewchuk, W. (1986), 'The Motor Vehicle Industry', in B. Elbaum and W. Lazonick (eds.), *The Decline of the British Economy*, Oxford: 135–61.

—— (1987), *American Technology and the British Vehicle Industry*, Cambridge.

Liberal Party (1928), *Britain's Industrial Future* (the 'Yellow Book').

Little, I. M. D. (1962*a*), 'Higgledy, Piggledy Growth', *Bulletin of the Oxford University Institute of Statistics*, 24: 387–412.

—— (1962*b*), 'Fiscal Policy', in G. D. N. Worswick and P. H. Ady (eds.), *The British Economy in the Nineteen Fifties*, Oxford: 231–300.

Littlechild, S. (1989), 'Myths and Merger Policy', in J. Fairburn and J. Kay (eds.) *Monopoly and Merger Policy*, Oxford: 301–21.

Littler, C. R. (1982), *The Development of the Labour Process in Capitalist Societies.*

Lloyd, E. M. H. (1924), *Experiments in State Control*, Oxford.

Lowe, R. (1978), 'The Failure of Consensus in Britain: The National Industrial Conference 1919–21', *Historical Journal*, 21: 647–75.

—— (1982), 'A Still, Small Voice? The Ministry of Labour 1916–19', in K. Burk (ed.), *War and the State*: 108–34.

—— (1986), *Adjusting to Democracy: The Role of the Ministry of Labour in British Politics 1916–1939*, Oxford.

—— (1990), 'The Second World War, Consensus, and the Foundation of the Welfare State', *Twentieth Century British History*, 1: 152–82.

Lynch, F. (1991), 'France', in A. Graham and A. Seldon (eds.), *Government and Economics in the Postwar World*: 54–78.

MacBriar, A. (1962), *Fabian Socialism and British Politics, 1884–1918*, Cambridge.

McClelland, K. (1990), 'Apprenticeship in Engineering and Shipbuilding', in E. Evans and P. Summerfield (eds.), *Technical Education and the State*, Manchester: 19–36.

Macdonagh, O. (1975), 'Government, Industry and Science in the Nineteenth Century: A Particular Study', *Historical Studies*, 65: 503–17.

Macdonald, G. W., and Gospel, H. F. (1973), 'The Mond–Turner Talks, 1927–33', *Historical Journal*, 16: 807–29.

MacGregor, D. H. (1909), 'Shipping Conferences', *Economic Journal*, 19: 503–16.

—— (1927), 'Rationalisation of Industry', *Economic Journal*, 37: 521–50.

—— (1934), *Enterprise, Purpose and Profit*, Oxford.

MacKenzie, F. A. (1901), *The American Invaders: Their Plans, Tactics and Progress.*

McKinlay, A. (1990), 'A Certain Short-Sightedness: Metal Working, Innovation, and Apprenticeship, 1897–1939', in H. Gospel (ed.), *Industrial Training and Technological Innovation*: 93–111.

Macleod, R., and Macleod, K. (1975), 'War and Economic Development: Government and the Optical Industry in Britain, 1914–18', in J. M. Winter (ed.), *War and Economic Development*, Cambridge: 165–204.

Macmillan (1931), *Committee on Finance and Industry*, Cmd. 3897, PP 1930/1, vol. 13.

Macmillan, H. (1938), *The Middle Way*.

Macrosty, H. (1901), *Trusts and the State*.

—— (1907), *The Trust Movement in Great Britain*.

—— (1927), 'Inflation and Deflation in the U.S. and U.K. 1919–1923', *Journal of the Royal Statistical Society*, 90: 45–122.

McKibbin, R. (1974), *The Evolution of the Labour Party, 1910–1924*, Oxford.

McWilliams-Tollberg, R. (1975), 'Marshall's Tendency to Socialism', *History of Political Economy*, 7: 75–111.

Maguire, P. (1991), 'Designs on Reconstruction: British Business, Market Structures and the Role of Design in Post-War Recovery', *Journal of Design History*, 4: 15–30.

Maier, C. S. (1987), *In Search of Stability*, Cambridge.

Marrison, A. J. (1983), 'Businessmen, Industries and Tariff Reform in Great Britain, 1903–1930', *Business History*, 25: 148–78.

Marshall, A. (1890), *Principles of Economics*.

—— (1899), *Elements of Economics of Industry*.

—— (1903/26), 'Memorandum on the Fiscal Policy of International Trade', in *Official Papers*.

—— (1907), 'The Social Possibilities of Economic Chivalry', *Economic Journal*, 17: 7–29.

—— and Marshall, M. (1884), *The Economics of Industry*, 2nd edn.

Marwick, A. (1964), 'Middle Opinion in the Thirties: Planning, Progress and Political Agreement', *English Historical Review*, 79: 285–98.

Mason, T., and Thompson, P. (1991), ' "Reflections on a Revolution?": The Political Mood in Wartime Britain', in N. Tiratsoo (ed.), *The Attlee Years*: 54–70.

Mass, W., and Lazonick, W. (1990), 'The British Cotton Industry and International Competitive Advantage: The State of the Debates', *Business History*, 32: 9–65.

Matthews, R. C. O. (1968), 'Why Has Britain Had Full Employment since the War?', *Economic Journal*, 78: 555–69.

—— Feinstein, C. H., and Odling-Smee, J. (1982), *British Economic Growth 1856–1973*, Oxford.

Maxcy, G. (1958), 'The Motor Industry', in P. L. Cook and R. Cohen (eds.), *Effects of Mergers*: 353–422.

—— (1981), *The Multinational Motor Industry*.

—— and Silberston, A. (1959), *The Motor Industry*.

Mayer, C., and Alexander, J. (1990), *Banks and Securities Markets: Company Financing in Germany and the U.K.*, Centre for Economic Policy Research, discussion paper 117.

Mayhew, C. (1939), *Planned Investment*, Fabian Research Series, 45.

—— (1946), *Socialist Economic Planning: The Overall Picture*, Fabian Discussion Series, no. 1.

Maynard, G. (1988), *The Economy under Mrs Thatcher*, Oxford.

Meadows, P. (1978), 'Planning', in F. T. Blackaby (ed.), *British Economic Policy 1960–74*, Cambridge: 402–17.

Meeks, G. (1977), *Disappointing Marriage: A Study of the Gains from Merger*, Cambridge.

Mercer, H. (1991*a*), 'The Monopolies and Restrictive Practices Commission, 1949–56: A Study in Regulatory Failure', in G. Jones and M. Kirby (eds.), *Competitiveness and the State*, Manchester: 78–99.

—— (1991*b*), 'The Labour Governments of 1945–51 and Private Industry', in N. Tiratsoo (ed.), *The Attlee Years*: 71–89.

—— (1992), 'Anti-Monopoly Policy', in H. Mercer, N. Rollings, and J. Tomlinson, (eds.), *Labour and Private Industry: The Experience of 1945–51*, Edinburgh: 55–73.

—— (1993), *Constructing a Competitive Order: The Hidden History of Anti-Trust*, Cambridge.

—— Rollings, N., and Tomlinson, J. (1992), *Labour Governments and the Private Sector: The Experience of 1945–51*, Edinburgh.

Metcalf, D. (1989), 'Water Notes Dry Up: The Impact of the Donovan Proposals and Thatcherism at Work on Labour Productivity in British Manufacturing Industry', *British Journal of Industrial Relations*, 27: 1–32.

—— (1990), 'Union Presence and Labour Productivity in British Manufacturing: A Reply to Nolan and Marginson', *British Journal of Industrial Relations*, 28: 249–66.

Michie, J. (1992) (ed.), *The Economic Legacy 1979–1992*.

Middlemas, K. (1979), *Politics in Industrial Society*.

—— (1983), *Industry, Unions and Government: 21 Years of N.E.D.C.*

—— (1986), *Power Competition and the State*, i. *Britain in Search of Balance, 1940–61*.

Middleton, R. (1985), *Towards the Managed Economy: Keynes, the Treasury and the Fiscal Policy Debate of the 1930s*.

Miles, C. (1968), *Lancashire Textiles: A Case Study of Industrial Change*, Cambridge.

Mill, J. S. (1896), *Principles of Political Economy*.

Miller, M., and Church, R. (1979), 'Motor Manufacturing', in N. Buxton and D. Aldcroft (eds.), *British Industry between the Wars*: 179–215.

Miller, P. (1991), 'Accounting Innovation Beyond the Enterprise: Problematising Investment Decisions and Programming Economic Growth in the U.K. in the 1960s', *Accounting, Organisations and Society*, 16: 733–62.

Millward, R. (1991), 'The Nationalised Industries', in M. Artis and D. Cobham (eds.), *Labour's Economic Policies 1974–79*, Manchester: 138–57.

—— (1993), 'Industrial and Commercial Performance Since 1950', in R. Floud and D. McCloskey (eds.), *The Economic History of England Since 1700*, iii (2nd edn.), Cambridge.

Milward, A. S. (1984), *The Economic Effects of the World Wars on Great Britain* (2nd edn.).

—— (1987), *War, Economy and Society, 1939–1945*.

Minford, P. (1991), *The Supply-Side Revolution in Britain*.

Ministry of Labour (1927), *Report of an Inquiry into Apprenticeship*.

—— (1945), *The Cotton Spinning Industry: Report of a Committee set up to Review the Wages Arrangements and Methods of Organisation of Work*.

—— (1958), *Training for Skills*.

—— (1959), *Practices Impeding the Full and Efficient Use of Manpower*.

Ministry of Munitions (1922), *History of the Ministry of Munitions*, vii, viii.

Mitchell, B. R. (1988), *British Historical Statistics 1750–1870*, Cambridge.

Mitchell, J. (1963), *Crisis in Britain, 1951*.

Moggridge, D. (1972), *British Monetary Policy 1924–31*, Cambridge.

Molyneux, R., and Thompson, D. (1987), 'Nationalised Industry Performance: Still Third Rate?', *Fiscal Studies*, 8: 48–82.

Mond, A. (1927), *Industry and Politics*.

More, C. (1980), *Skill and the English Working Class, 1870–1914*.

Morgan, A. (1978), 'Commercial Policy', in F. T. Blackaby (ed.), *British Economic Policy 1960–74*, Cambridge: 515–63.

Morgan, E. V. (1952), *Studies in British Financial Policy, 1914–25*.

Morgan, K. O. (1984), *Labour in Power, 1945–51*, Oxford.

—— (1987), 'The Rise and Fall of Public Ownership in Britain', in J. M. W. Bean (ed.), *The Political Culture of Modern Britain*: 277–98.

Morrison, H. (1933), *Socialisation and Transport*.

Moseley, R. (1978), 'The Origins and Early Years of the National Physical Laboratory: A Chapter in the Pre-History of British Science Policy', *Minerva*, 16: 222–50.

Mosley, O. (1925), *Revolution by Reason*.

Mottershead, P. (1978), 'Industrial Policy', in F. T. Blackaby (ed.), *British Economic Policy 1960–74*: 418–83.

Mowery, D. (1987), 'Industrial Research, 1900–1950', in B. Elbaum and W. Lazonick (eds.), *The Decline of the British Economy*, Oxford: 189–222.

Murphy, M. E. (1945), *The British War Economy 1939–43*, New York.

NACMMI (1947), *National Advisory Council for the Motor Manufacturing Industry: Report of Proceedings*.

NEDO (1962), *Growth of the UK Economy to 1966*.

—— (1963), *Conditions Favourable to Faster Growth*.

National Audit Office (1987), *Assistance to Industry under Section 8 of the Industrial Development Act 1982,* HCP, 329, PP 1985/6, vol. 33.

New, C., and Myers, A. (1987), *Managing Manufacturing Operations in the U.K. 1975–1985*, Cranfield.

Newbould, G. (1970), *Management and Merger Activity*, Liverpool.

Newton, C., and Porter, D. (1988), *Modernisation Frustrated*.

Nichols, T. (1986), *The British Worker Question: A New Look at Workers and Productivity in Manufacturing*.

Niven, M. M. (1967), *Personnel Management 1913–1963*.

Nolan, P. (1989), 'Walking on Water: Performance and Industrial Relations under Thatcher', *Industrial Relations Journal*, 20: 81–92.

OECD (1991), *Industrial Policy in O.E.C.D. Countries: Annual Review 1991*, Paris.

O'Brien, P. (1990), 'Marshall's Work in Relation to Classical Economics', in J. R. Whitaker (ed.), *Centenary Essays on Alfred Marshall*, Cambridge: 127–63.

Ormerod, P. (1991), 'Incomes Policy', in M. Artis and D. Cobham (eds.), *Labour's Economic Policies 1974–79*, Manchester: 56–72.

Ostergaard, G. N. (1954), 'Labour and the Development of the Public Corporation', *Manchester School*, 22: 192–216.

Oulton, N. (1987), 'Plant Closures and the Productivity Miracle in Manufacturing', *National Institute Economic Review*, 121: 53–9.

—— (1990), 'Labour Productivity in U.K. Manufacturing in the 1970s and in the 1980s', *National Institute Economic Review*, 132: 71–91.

Overy, R. J. (1976), *William Morris: Viscount Nuffield*.

—— (1980), *The Air War, 1937–1945*.

—— (1984), *Goering: The 'Iron Man'*.

Oxford (1947), *Studies in War Economics*, prepared at the Oxford University Institute of Statistics, Oxford.

Oxford Review (1988), *'Long Run Economic Performance in the U.K.'*, Oxford Review of Economic Policy, 4/1 (special issue).

PEP (1950), *Political and Economic Planning Engineering Reports*, ii. *Motor Vehicles*.

—— (1951), *Manpower*.

—— (1952), *Government and Industry*.

—— (1953), *Technological Education*.

—— (1957), *Industrial Trade Associations: Activities and Organisation*.

—— (1960), *Growth in the British Economy*.

PRO (1919*a*), RECO 1/881, Min. of Reconstruction, Reconstruction Problems Pamphlets 16–23.

—— (1919*b*), RECO 1/882, Min. of Reconstruction, Reconstruction Problems Pamphlets 24–31.

—— (1919*c*), RECO 1/883, Min. of Reconstruction, Reconstruction Problems Pamphlets 32–8.

—— (1930), CAB 24/214 C. Attlee, 'The Problems of British Industry', 29 July 1930.

—— (1943*a*), AVIA 15/1945, *Ministry of Aircraft Production response to the Select Committee on National Expenditure Report on Aircraft Production*, August 1943.

—— (1943*b*), CAB 87/63, *Committee on Postwar Employment*, Board of Trade, 'General Support of Trade', October 1943.

—— (1943*c*), CAB 87/13, Reconstruction Priorities Committee, Treasury, 'Influences Affecting the Level of the National Income', June 1943.

—— (1946), CAB 130/2, *Atomic Energy*, Minutes of Meeting, 25 October 1946.

—— (1949*a*), CAB 134/690, Socialisation of Industries Committee, 'Management–Worker Relationships in the Socialised Industries', 7 April.

—— (1949*b*); CAB 134/690, Socialisation of Industries Committee, 'Government Control over Socialised Industries', 26 April.

—— (1950*a*), CAB 134/691, Socialisation of Industries Committee, Minutes, 12 May.

—— (1950*b*), PREM 8/1183, Memo by the President of the Board of Trade (Harold Wilson) 'The State and Private Industry', 4 May 1950.

—— (1951*a*), CAB 134/691, Socialisation of Industries Committee, 'Report of Sub-Committee on Relationships with Workers in Socialised Industries', 10 May.

—— (1951*b*), SUPP 14/331, Ministry of Supply 'Motor Industry, Steel Allocation 1951'.

—— (1956), CAB 134/1230, Board of Trade, 'British Institute of Management', 16 March 1956.

—— (1959), T230/486, Committee on Future Prospects of the Motor Industry, Board of Trade, 'Recent Development and Present Position of the Motor Industry', July.

Paish, G. (1951), 'The London New Issue Market', *Economica*, 18: 1–17.

Panitch, C. (1976), *Social Democracy and Industrial Militancy*, Cambridge.

Parker, H. M. D. (1957), *Manpower: A Study of Wartime Policy and Administration*.

Parris, H. (1965), *Government and the Railways in Nineteenth Century Britain*.

Pavitt, K. (1980) (ed.), *Technical Innovation and British Economic Performance*.

Peacock, A., and Bannock, G. (1991), *Corporate Takeovers and the Public Interest*, Aberdeen.

Peck, M. (1968), 'Science and Technology', in R. Caves (ed.), *Britain's Economic Prospects*, Washington, DC: 448–86.

Peden, G. (1985), *British Economic and Social Policy: Lloyd George to Margaret Thatcher*, Deddington.

Penn, R. (1983), 'Trade Union Organisation and Skill in the Cotton and Engineering Industries in Britain, 1850–1960', *Social History*, 8: 37–56.

Perry, P. J. C. (1976), *The Evolution of British Manpower Policy*.

Phelps-Brown, E. H. (1959), *The Growth of British Industrial Relations*.

Piercy, W. (1959), Memorandum and Evidence to Radcliffe: 194–201 and Qs. 12674.

Pigou, A. C. (1903), *The Riddle of the Tariff*.

—— (1947), *Aspects of British Economic History 1918–1925*.

Piore, M., and Sabel, C. (1984), *The Second Industrial Divide, Possibilities for Prosperity*, New York.

Platt (1944), *Report of the Cotton Textile Mission to the USA, March–April 1944*.

Platt, D. C. M. (1968), *Finance, Trade and Politics in British Foreign Policy, 1815–1914*, Oxford.

Plowden, W. (1971), *The Motor Car and Politics*.

Polanyi, K. (1944), *The Great Transformation*, New York.

Pollard, S. (1970) (ed.), *The Gold Standard and Employment Policies Between the Wars*.

—— (1978), 'The Nationalisation of the Banks: The Chequered History of a Socialist Proposal', in D. Martin and D. Rubinstein (eds.), *Ideology and the Labour Movement*: 167–90.

—— (1990), *Britain's Prime and Britain's Decline*.

—— (1992), *The Development of the British Economy 1914–90,* 4th edn.

Pollert, A. (1991) (ed.), *Farewell to Flexibility?*, Oxford.

Ponting, C. (1990), *Breach of Promise: Labour in Power 1964–1970*.

Posner, M., and Pryke, R. (1965), *New Public Enterprise*.

Postan, M. M. (1952), *British War Production*.

Prais, S. (1976), *The Evolution of Giant Firms in Great Britain*, Cambridge.

—— and Steedman, H. (1986), 'Vocational Training in France and Britain: Construction', *National Institute Economic Review*, 116: 45–56.

Pratten, C. (1971), *Economies of Scale in Manufacturing Industry*, Cambridge.

—— (1976), *Labour Productivity Differences within International Companies*, Cambridge.

—— (1991), *The Competitiveness of Small Firms*, Cambridge.

Pressnell, L. (1986), *British External Economic Policy,* i. *The Post-War Financial Settlement.*

Prest, A. R., and Coppock, D. C. (1972), *The U.K. Economy: A Manual of Applied Economics*, 4th edn.

—— —— (1980), *The U.K. Economy: A Manual of Applied Economics,* 8th edn.

Price, G. L. (1978), 'The Expansion of British Universities and their Struggle to Maintain Autonomy', *Minerva*, 16: 357–81.

Provisional (1917), Provisional Committee on Research and Education for the Cotton Industry, 'Scientific Research in Relation to Cotton and the Cotton Industry', Manchester.

Pryke, R. (1971), *Public Enterprise in Practice.*

—— (1981), *The Nationalised Industries: Policies and Performance Since 1961*, Oxford.

Public Money (1987), 'Does Selective Support for Industry Work', *Public Money*, 7: 47–51.

Rainbird, H. (1991), 'The Self-Employed: Small Entrepreneurs or Disguised Wage Labourers', in A. Pollert (ed.), *Farewell to Flexibility?*, Oxford: 200–14.

Rainnie, A. (1989), *Industrial Relations in Small Firms: Small Isn't Beautiful.*

Ramsden, J. (1980), *The Making of Conservative Party Policy: The Conservative Research Department Since 1929.*

Ray, G. F. (1960), 'Britain's Imports of Manufactured Goods', *National Institute Economic Review*, 8: 12–29.

Reader, W. (1975), *Imperial Chemical Industries, A History: The First Quarter Century 1926–52*, Oxford.

—— (1977), 'Imperial Chemical Industries and the State, 1926–1945', in B. Supple (ed.), *Essays in British Business History*, Oxford: 227–43.

Reddaway, W. B., and Smith, A. D. (1960), 'Progress in British Manufacturing Industries in the Period 1948–54', *Economic Journal*, 70: 17–37.

Rees, J. F. (1921), *A Short Fiscal and Financial History of England 1815–1918.*

Reich, S. (1990), *The Fruits of Fascism: Postwar Prosperity in Historical Perspective*, Ithaca, NY.

Reid, A. (1985), 'Dilution, Trade Unionism and the State in Britain During the First World War', in S. Tolliday and J. Zeitlin (eds.), *Shopfloor Bargaining and the State*, Cambridge: 46–74.

Rempal, R. (1972), *Unionists Divided: Arthur Balfour, Joseph Chamberlain and the Unionist Free-Traders*, Newton Abbot.

Rhys, G. (1990), 'The Motor Industry and the Balance of Payments', *The Royal Bank of Scotland Review*, 168: 11–27.

Richardson, R. (1991), 'Trade Unions and Industrial Relations', in N. F. R. Crafts and N. Woodward (eds.), *The British Economy Since 1945*, Oxford: 417–42.

Riesman, D. (1987), *Alfred Marshall: Progress and Politics*.

Robbins, L. (1978), *The Classical Economists and Economic Policy*, 2nd edn.

Roberts, B. (1958), *National Wages Policy in War and Peace*.

Roberts, R. (1984), 'The Administrative Origins of Industrial Diplomacy: An Aspect of Government–Industry Relations, 1929–35', in J. Turner (ed.), *Businessmen and Politics*: 93–104.

—— (1992), 'Regulatory Responses to the Market for Corporate Control in Britain in the 1950s', *Business History*, 34: 183–200.

Robinson, D. (1972), 'Labour Market Policies', in W. Beckerman (ed.), *The Labour Government's Economic Policies*: 300–34.

Robinson, E. A. G. (1986), 'The Economic Problem of the Transition from War to Peace', *Cambridge Journal of Economics*, 10: 165–85.

Robson, R. (1957), *The Cotton Industry in Britain*.

Robson, W. A. (1937) (ed.), *Public Enterprise: Developments in Social Ownership and Control in Great Britain*.

Roderick, G., and Stephens, M. (1974), 'Scientific Studies and Scientific Manpower in the English Civic Universities 1870–1914', *Science Studies*, 4: 41–63.

Rodgers, T. (1986), 'Sir Allan Smith, the Industrial Group and the Politics of Unemployment 1919–1924', *Business History*, 28: 100–23.

Rogow, A. A., and Shore, P. (1955), *The Labour Government and British Industry, 1945–51*, Oxford.

Rollings, N. (1988), 'British Budgetary Policy, 1945–54: A Keynesian Revolution?', *Economic History Review*, 41: 283–98.

—— (1990), 'The Control of Inflation in the Managed Economy: Britain 1945–53' (unpublished Ph.D. diss., Bristol University).

—— (1992), ' "The Reichstag Method of Governing?": The Attlee Governments and Permanent Economic Controls', in H. Mercer, N. Rollings, and J. Tomlinson (eds.), *Labour and Private Industry: The Experience of 1945–51*, Edinburgh: 15–36.

Roseveare, H. (1969), *The Treasury*.

Ross, D. (1990), 'The Clearing Banks and Industry—New Perspectives on the Interwar Years', in J. J. Van Helten and Y. Cassis (eds.), *Capitalism in a Mature Economy: Financial Institutions, Capital Exports and British Industry 1870–1939*, Aldershot: 52–70.

Rostas, L. (1952), 'Changes in the Productivity of British Industry', *Economic Journal*, 60: 15–24.

Rowlinson, M. (1988), 'The Early Applications of Scientific Management by Cadbury's', *Business History*, 30: 377–95.

Rowntree, S. B. (1902), *Poverty: A Study of Town Life*.

Rowthorn, B., and Wells, J. (1987), *De-Industrialisation and Foreign Trade*, Cambridge.

Rubery, J. (1989), 'Labour Market Flexibility in Britain', in F. Green (ed.), *The Restructuring of the U.K. Economy*, 155–76.

Ryan, P. (1989), 'Youth Interventions, Job Substituting and Trade Union Policy', in S. Rosenberg (ed.), *The State and the Labour Market*, New York: 175–96.

Ryder, D. (1975), *British Leyland: The Next Decade*, PP 1974/5, vol. 14.

Sabel, C., and Zeitlin, J. (1985), 'Historical Alternatives to Mass Production', *Past and Present*, 108: 133–76.

Sandberg, L. (1974), *Lancashire in Decline*, Columbus, Ohio.

Sanderson, M. (1972*a*), *The Universities and British Industry*.

—— (1972*b*), 'Research and the Firm in British Industry, 1919–39', *Science Studies*, 2: 107–51.

—— (1988), 'Education and the British Economy', *Oxford Review of Economic Policy*, 4: 38–50.

Saul, S. B. (1962), 'The Motor Industry in Britain to 1914', *Business History*, 5: 22–44.

—— (1965), 'The Export Economy 1870–1914', *Yorkshire Bulletin of Economic and Social Research*, 17: 5–18.

—— (1985), *The Myth of the Great Depression*, 2nd edn.

Sawyer, M. (1985), *The Economics of Industries and Firms*, 2nd edn.

—— (1991*a*), 'Industrial Policy', in M. Artis and D. Cobham (eds.), *Labour's Economic Policies 1974–79*, Manchester: 158–75.

—— (1991*b*), 'Prices Policy', in M. Artis and D. Cobham (eds.), *Labour's Economic Policies 1974–79*, Manchester: 176–89.

Saxonhouse, G., and Wright, G. (1984), 'New Evidence on Stubborn English Mules and the Cotton Industry, 1878–1920', *Economic History Review*, 37: 507–19.

Sayers, R. S. (1956), *British Financial Policy, 1939–1945*.

—— (1976), *The Bank of England 1891–1944*, 3 vols., Cambridge.

Schenk, C. (1991), 'British Management of the Sterling Area 1950–1958' (unpublished Ph.D. dissertation, London University).

Schumpeter, J. (1954), *History of Economic Analysis.*

Schuster, G. (1909), 'The Patents and Designs Act 1907', *Economic Journal*, 19: 538–51.

Scott, J. D. (1962), *Vickers: A History.*

Scott, M. (1962), 'The Volume of British Imports', in G. D. N. Worswick and P. H. Ady (eds.), *The British Economy in the Nineteen Fifties*, Oxford: 133–46.

Searle, G. R. (1971), *The Quest for National Efficiency*, Oxford.

Seers, D. (1949), *Changes in the Cost of Living and the Distribution of Income Since 1938*, Oxford.

—— (1950), 'The Levelling of Incomes', *Bulletin of the Oxford University Institute of Statistics*, 12: 271–98.

Select Committee (1868), *Report from the Select Committee on Scientific Instruction*, PP 1867/8, vol. 15.

—— (1877), *Report from the Select Committee on the Companies Acts, 1862 and 1867*, PP 1877, vol. 8.

—— (1941), Select Committee on National Expenditure, 21st Report *Output of Labour*, PP 1940/1, vol. 3.

—— (1942), Select Committee on National Expenditure, 7th Report *Supply of Labour*, PP 1941/2, vol. 3.

—— (1952/3) on the Nationalised Industries, *Report and Minutes*, HCP 235, PP 1952/3, vol. 6.

Sells, D. (1923), *The British Trade Boards System.*

Semmel, B. (1960), *Imperialism and Social Reform.*

Shadwell, A. (1906), *Industrial Efficiency: A Comparative Study of Industrial Life in England, Germany and America.*

Shanks, M. (1961), *The Stagnant Society.*

—— (1963) (ed.), *The Lessons of Public Enterprise: A Fabian Society Study.*

Sheldrake, J., and Vickerstaff, S. A. (1987), *The History of Industrial Training in Britain*, Aldershot.

Sheringham, G. (1981), *English Education, Social Change and War, 1911–20*, Manchester.

Shonfield, A. (1959), *British Economic Policy Since the War.*

—— (1965), *Modern Capitalism: The Changing Balance of Public and Private Power.*

Silberston, A. (1958), 'The Motor Industry', in D. Burns (ed.), *The Structure of British Industry: A Symposium*, ii, Cambridge: 1–44.

—— (1963), 'H.P. Controls and the Demand for Cars', *Economic Journal*, 73: 32–53.

—— (1965), 'The Motor Industry 1955–1964', *Bulletin of the Oxford University Institute of Statistics*, 27: 253–86.

—— (1972), 'Economies of Scale: A Survey', *Economic Journal*, 82: 369–91.

Silberston, A. (1981), 'Industrial Policies in Britain, 1960–80', in C. Carter (ed.), *Industrial Policy and Innovation*: 39–51.

Silverman, H. A. (1946) (ed.), *Studies in Industrial Organisation*.

Singh, A. (1977), 'UK Industry and the World Economy: A Case of De-Industrialisation?', *Cambridge Journal of Economics*, 1: 113–36.

Singleton, J. (1986), 'Lancashire's Last Stand: Declining Employment in the British Cotton Industry, 1950–70', *Economic History Review*, 39: 92–107.

—— (1990*a*), 'Showing the White Flag: The Lancashire Cotton Industry, 1945–1965', *Business History*, 32: 129–49.

—— (1990*b*), 'Planning for Cotton, 1945–1951', *Economic History Review*, 43: 62–78.

—— (1991*a*), *Lancashire on the Scrapheap*, Oxford.

—— (1991*b*), 'The Crisis in Postwar Lancashire: A Rejoinder', *Economic History Review*, 44: 527–30.

—— (1992), *The Cotton Industry and the British War Effort, 1914–1918*, University of Manchester Working Papers in Economic and Social History, no. 12.

Smith, A. (1759/1976), *Theory of Moral Sentiments* (ed. D. D. Raphael and A. L. Macfie), Oxford.

—— (1776/1976), *The Wealth of Nations* (ed. R. H. Campbell and A. S. Skinner), Oxford.

Smith, A. D. (1992), *International Financial Markets: The Performance of Britain and its Rivals*, Cambridge.

Snyder, R. (1944), *The Tariff Problem in Great Britain 1918–23*, Stanford, Calif.

Solow, R. M. (1956), 'A Contribution to the Theory of Economic Growth', *Quarterly Journal of Economics*, 70: 65–94.

Stanworth, J., and Gray, C. (1991) (eds.), *Bolton 20 Years On: The Small Firm in the 1990s*.

Starkey, K., and McKinlay, A. (1989), 'Beyond Fordism? Strategic Choice and Labour Relations in Ford U.K.', *Industrial Relations Journal*, 20: 93–100.

Statistical Digest (1975), *History of the Second World War: Statistical Digest of the War*.

Steedman, H. (1988), 'Vocational Training in France and Britain: Mechanical and Electrical Craftsmen', *National Institute Economic Review*, 126: 57–71.

—— and Wagner, K. (1989), 'Productivity, Machinery and Skills: Clothing Manufacture in Britain and Germany', *National Institute Economic Review*, 128: 40–57.

Steedman, I. (1991), 'The Economic Journal and Socialism, 1890–1914', in J. D. Hey and D. Winch (eds.), *A Century of Economics*, Oxford: 65–91.

Steel, D. (1982), 'Review Article: Government and Industry in Britain', *British Journal of Political Science*, 12: 449–503.

Stewart, M. (1972), 'The Distribution of Income', in W. Beckerman (ed.), *The Labour Government's Economic Record 1964–70*.

Stigler, G. (1958), 'The Economies of Scale', *Journal of Law and Economics*, 1: 54–71.

Stout, D. (1978), 'De-Industrialisation and Industrial Policy', in F. T. Blackaby (ed.), *De-Industrialisation*: 171–95.

—— (1979), 'Capacity Adjustment in a Slowly Growing Economy', in W. Beckerman (ed.), *Slow Growth in Britain: Causes and Consequences*, Oxford: 103–17.

Strange, S. (1971), *Sterling and British Policy*, Oxford.

Streat, R. (1968), 'The Cotton Industry in Contraction', *District Bank Review*, 127: 1–20.

Streeten, P. (1962), 'Commercial Policy', in G. D. N. Worswick and P. H. Ady (eds.), *The British Economy in the Nineteen Fifties*, Oxford: 76–113.

Supple, B. (1986), 'Ideology or Pragmatism? The Nationalisation of Coal, 1919–46', in N. McKendrick and R. B. Outhwaite (eds.), *Business Life and Public Policy*, Cambridge: 228–50.

—— (1987), *The History of the British Coal Industry, iv. 1913–46: The Political Economy of Decline*, Oxford.

—— (1988), 'The Political Economy of Demoralisation: The State and the Coalmining Industry in Britain between the Wars', *Economic History Review*, 44: 566–91.

—— (1990), 'Official Economic Inquiry and Britain's Industrial Decline: The First Fifty Years', in M. Furner and B. Supple (eds.), *The State and Economic Knowledge*, Cambridge: 325–53.

—— (1993), 'British Economic Decline Since 1945', in R. Floud and D. McCloskey (eds.), *The Economic History of England Since 1700*, iii, 2nd edn., Cambridge.

Swann, D., Howe, W. S., Maunder, P., and O'Brien, D. P. (1974), *Competition in British Industry: Restrictive Practices Legislation in Theory and Practice*.

TUC (1931), *Annual Report of the Trades Union Congress*.

—— (1932), *Annual Report of the Trades Union Congress*.

Tawney, R. H. (1914), *The Establishment of Minimum Rates in the Cabinet-Making Industry Under the Trade Boards Act of 1909*.

—— (1943), 'The Abolition of Economic Controls 1918–21', *Economic History Review*, 13: 1–30.

Taylor, A. J. (1972), *Laissez-Faire and State Intervention in Nineteenth Century Britain*.

Taylor, F. W. (1911), *Scientific Management*.

—— (1914), 'Scientific Management: Reply', *Sociological Review*, 7: 266–9.

Tew, B., and Henderson, R. F. (1959), *Studies in Company Finance*, Cambridge.

Thatcher, A. R. (1979), 'Labour Supply and Employment Trends', in F. Blackaby (ed.), *De-Industrialisation*: 26–48.

Thirlwall, A. (1987), *Nicholas Kaldor*.

Thomas, D. (1983), 'G.E.C.: An Outstanding Success?', in K. Williams, J. Williams, and D. Thomas, *Why Are the British Bad at Manufacturing?*: 133–78.

Thomas, I. (1937), 'The Coal Mines Reorganisation Commission', in W. A. Robson (ed.), *Public Enterprise: Developments in Social Ownership and Control in Great Britain*, 209–46.

Thomas, W. A. (1973), *The Provincial Stock Exchanges*.

—— (1978), *The Finance of British Industry 1918–1976*.

Thompson, G. (1990), *The Political Economy of the New Right*.

Thoms, D. (1990), 'Technical Education and the Transformation of Coventry's Industrial Economy', in E. Evans and P. Summerfield (eds.), *Technical Education and the State since 1850*, Manchester: 37–54.

Tiratsoo, N. (1990), 'Popular Politics, Affluence and the Labour Party in the 1950s', in A. Gorst, L. Johnman, and W. Scott Lucas (eds.), *Contemporary British History 1931–61: Politics and the Limits of Policy*, 44–61.

—— (1991) (ed.), *The Attlee Years*.

—— (1992), 'The Motor Car Industry', in H. Mercer, N. Rollings, and J. Tomlinson (eds.), *Labour Governments and Private Industry: The Experience of 1945–51*, Edinburgh: 162–85.

—— and Tomlinson, J. (1993a), *Industrial Efficiency and State Intervention: The Experience of 1939–51*.

—— —— (1993b), 'Mancur Olson and the Mirage of Restrictive Practices', *Business History*, forthcoming.

Tolliday, S. (1984), 'Tariffs and Steel, 1916–34: The Politics of Industrial Decline', in J. Turner (ed.), *Businessmen and Politics*: 50–75.

—— (1986), 'Steel and Rationalisation Policies 1918–1950', in B. Elbaum and W. Lazonick (eds.), *The Decline of the British Economy*, Oxford: 82–108.

—— (1987a), *Business, Banking and Politics: The Case of British Steel, 1918–1939*, Cambridge, Mass.

—— (1987b), 'Government, Employers and Shopfloor Organisation in the British Motor Industry 1939–69', in S. Tolliday and J. Zeitlin (eds.), *Shopfloor Bargaining and the State*, Cambridge: 108–47.

—— (1991), 'Ford and "Fordism" in Postwar Britain: Enterprise Management and the Control of Labour', in S. Tolliday and J. Zeitlin (eds.), *The Power to Manage?*: 81–114.

Tomlinson, B. R. (1975), 'India and the British Empire 1880–1935', *Indian Economic and Social History Review*, 12: 339–80.

Tomlinson, J. (1977), 'Anglo–Indian Economic Relations 1913–28, with Special Reference to the Cotton Trade', (unpublished Ph.D. diss., University of London).

—— (1979), 'The First World War and British Cotton Piece Exports to India', *Economic History Review*, 32: 494–506.

—— (1980), 'Socialist Politics and the "Small Business" ', *Politics and Power*, 1: 165–74.

—— (1981), *Problems of British Economic Policy 1870–1945*.

—— (1982), *The Unequal Struggle? British Socialism and the Capitalist Enterprise*.

—— (1983), 'Regulating the Capitalist Enterprise: The Impossible Dream?', *Scottish Journal of Political Economy*, 30: 54–68.

—— (1985), *British Macroeconomic Policy since 1940*.

—— (1986), 'Democracy Inside the Black Box? Neo-classical Theories of the Firm and Industrial Democracy', *Economy and Society*, 15: 220–50.

—— (1987*a*), *Employment Policy: The Crucial Years 1939–55*, Oxford.

—— (1987*b*), *The 1945 Labour Government and Industrial Democracy*, Brunel University Discussion Paper, no. 8706.

—— (1990*a*), *Public Policy and the Economy Since 1900*, Oxford.

—— (1990*b*), *Hayek and the Market*.

—— (1991*a*), 'The Attlee Government and the Balance of Payments, 1945–51', *Twentieth Century British History*, 2: 47–66.

—— (1991*b*), 'A Missed Opportunity?: Labour and the Productivity Problem 1945–51', in G. Jones and M. Kirby (eds.), *Competitiveness and the State in Twentieth Century Britain*, Manchester: 40–59.

—— (1991*c*), 'The Labour Government and the Trade Unions', in N. Tiratsoo (ed.), *The Attlee Years*, 90–105.

—— (1991*d*), 'The Failure of the Anglo-American Council on Productivity', *Business History*, 33: 82–92.

—— (1991*e*), 'Planning for Cotton, 1945–1951', *Economic History Review*, 44: 523–6.

—— (1992), 'Productivity Policy', in H. Mercer, N. Rollings, and J. Tomlinson (eds.), *Labour and Private Industry: The Experience of 1945–51*, Edinburgh: 37–54.

—— (1993*a*), 'Mr. Attlee's Supply Side Socialism', *Economic History Review*, 46: 1–22.

—— (1993*b*), 'The Politics of Economic Measurement: The Rise of the Productivity Problem in the 1940s', in A. Hopwood and P. Miller (eds.), *Accounting in its Social Context*, Cambridge.

Tomlinson, J. (1993c), 'The Iron Quadrilateral: Political Constraints on Economic Reform Under the Labour Government', *Journal of British Studies* (forthcoming).

Trebilcock, R. C. (1966), 'A "Special Relationship"—Government, Re-armament and the Cordite Firms', *Economic History Review*, 19: 364–79.

Turner, H. A. (1969), 'The Donovan Report', *Economic Journal*, 79: 1–10.

—— Clack, G., and Roberts, G. (1967), *Labour Relations in the Motor Industry*.

Turner, J. (1984), 'The Politics of Organised Business in the First World War', in J. Turner (ed.), *Businessmen and Politics*: 33–49.

—— (1988), 'Servants of Two Masters: British Trade Associations in the First Half of the Twentieth Century', in H. Yamazaki and M. Miyamoto (eds.), *Trade Associations in Business History*, Tokyo: 173–98.

Tyson, R. E. (1968), 'The Cotton Industry', in D. H. Aldcroft (ed.), *The Development of the British Industry and Foreign Competition 1875–1914*: 100–27.

Urwick, L. (1929), *The Meaning of Rationalisation*.

Varcoe, I. (1981), 'Co-operative Research Associations in British Industry, 1918–34', *Minerva*, 19: 433–63.

Vickers, J., and Yarrow, G. (1988), *Privatisation: An Economic Analysis*, Cambridge, Mass.

Vickerstaff, S. (1985), 'Industrial Training in Britain', in A. Lawson (ed.), *Organised Interests and the State*: 45–64.

Vig, N. (1968), *Science and Technology in British Politics*.

Vlaeminke, M. (1990), 'The Subordination of Technical Education in Secondary Schooling, 1870–1914', in E. Evans and P. Summerfield (eds.), *Technical Education and the State*, Manchester: 55–76.

Wadhwani, S. (1990), 'The Effects of Unions on Productivity Growth, Investment and Employment: A Report on Some Recent Work', *British Journal of Industrial Relations*, 28: 371–85.

—— and Brown, W. (1990), 'The Economic Effects of Industrial Relations Legislation since 1979', *National Institute Economic Review*, 131: 57–70.

Waine, B. (1991), *The Rhetoric of Independence: The Ideology and Practice of Social Policy in Thatcher's Britain*, Oxford.

Walters, A. (1986), *Britain's Economic Renaissance*, Oxford.

Webb, B., and Webb, S. (1902), *Problems of Modern Industry*.

—— —— (1920), *Constitution of a Socialist Commonwealth of Great Britain*.

Webb, S. (1891), 'The Difficulties of Individualism', *Economic Journal*, 1: 360–81.

—— (1901*a*), *Twentieth Century Politics: A Policy of National Efficiency*, Fabian Tract no. 108.

—— (1901*b*), 'Lord Rosebery's Escape from Houndsditch', *The Nineteenth Century*, repr. in E. J. T. Brennan (1975), (ed.), *Education for National Efficiency: The Contribution of Sidney and Beatrice Webb.*

—— (1918), *Labour and the New Social Order.*

Wedderburn, W. (1989), 'Freedom of Association and Philosophies of Labour Law', *Industrial Law Journal*, 18: 1–38.

Weiner, H. E. (1960), *British Labour and Public Ownership.*

Wells, S. J. (1966), 'E.F.T.A.—The End of Transition', *Lloyds Bank Review*, 82: 18–33.

West, E. G. (1965), *Education and the State: A Study in Political Economy.*

—— (1975), 'Education Slowdown and Public Intervention in 19th Century England', *Explorations in Economic History*, 12: 61–87.

—— (1983), 'Nineteenth Century Educational History: The Kiesling Critique', *Economic History Review*, 36: 426–34.

Whiteside, N. (1979), 'Welfare Insurance and Casual Labour: A Study of Administrative Intervention in Industrial Employment, 1906–26', *Economic History Review*, 32: 507–22.

—— (1980), 'Industrial Welfare and Labour Regulation in Britain at the Time of the First World War', *International Review of Social History*, 25: 307–31.

Whiting, A. (1976), 'An International Comparison of the Instability of Economic Growth', *Three Banks Review*, 66: 26–46.

Wiener, M. (1985), *English Culture and the Decline of the Industrial Spirit 1850–1980*, Harmondsworth.

Wilks, S. (1984), *Industrial Policy and the Motor Industry*, Manchester.

—— and Wright, M. (1987), *Comparative Government–Industry Relations*, Oxford.

Williams, E. É. (1896/1973), *Made in Germany.*

Williams, J., Haslam, C., and Williams, K. (1990), 'Bad Work Practices and Good Management Practices: The Consequences of the Extension of Management Control in British and Japanese Manufacturing Since 1950', *Business History Review*, 64: 657–88.

Williams, K. (1983), 'BMC/BLMC/BL—A Misunderstood Failure', in K. Williams, J. Williams, and D. Thomas (eds.), *Why Are the British Bad at Manufacturing?*

——Williams, J. and Thomas, D. (1983), *Why Are the British Bad at Manufacturing?*

—— —— and Haslam, C. (1987*a*), *The Breakdown of Austin Rover*, Leamington Spa.

—— Cutler, T., Williams, J., and Haslam, C. (1987*b*), 'The End of Mass Production', *Economy and Society*, 16: 405–39.

Williams, K., Haslam, C., Wardlow, A., and Williams, J. (1986), 'Accounting for Failure in the Nationalised Enterprises', *Economy and Society*, 15: 167–219.

Williams, P. (1978), *The Emergence of the Theory of the Firm*.

—— (1990), 'The Attitudes of the Economics Professions in Britain and the U.S. to the Trust Movement, 1890–1914', in J. D. Hey and D. Winch (eds.), *A Century of Economics*, Oxford: 92–108.

Williamson, P. (1984), 'Financiers, the Gold Standard and British Politics, 1925–31', in J. Turner (ed.), *Businessmen and Politics*: 105–29.

Willman, P. (1986), *Technological Change, Collective Bargaining and Industrial Efficiency*, Oxford.

—— and Winch, G. (1985), *Innovation and Management Control: Labour Relations at BL Cars*, Cambridge.

Wilson, H. (1980), *Committee to Review the Functioning of Financial Institutions*, Cmnd. 7937.

Wilson, T. (1945), 'Price and Outlay of State Enterprise', *Economic Journal*, 55: 454–61.

—— (1966), 'Instability and the Rate of Growth', *Lloyds Bank Review*, 83: 16–32.

Winch, D. (1972), *Economics and Policy*.

—— (1990), 'Economic Knowledge and Government in Britain', in M. Furner and B. Supple (eds.), *The State and Economic Knowledge*, Cambridge: 40–70.

—— (1992), 'Scottish Moral Philospher as Political Economist', *Historical Journal*, 36: 91–113.

Winter, J. (1974), *Socialism and the Challenge of War*.

Wood, S. (1989) (ed.), *The Degradation of Work?*

Working Party (1946), *Cotton*.

Worswick, G. D. N. (1962), 'The British Economy 1950–1959', in G. D. N. Worswick and P. H. Ady (eds.), *The British Economy in the Nineteen Fifties*, Oxford: 1–75.

—— and Ady, P. H. (1952) (eds.), *The British Economy 1945–50*, Oxford.

Wright, J. F. (1962), 'The Capital Market and the Finance of Industry', in G. D. N. Worswick and P. H. Ady (eds.), *The British Economy in the Nineteen Fifties*, Oxford: 461–501.

Wrigley, C. (1976), *David Lloyd George and the British Labour Movement*, Brighton.

—— (1979), *The Government and Industrial Relations in Britain 1910–1921*.

—— (1982a), 'The Government and Industrial Relations', in C. Wrigley (ed.), *A History of British Industrial Relations 1875–1914*: 135–58.

—— (1982*b*), 'The Ministry of Munitions: An Innovatory Department' in K. Burk (ed.), *War and the State*: 32–56.

—— (1987), 'The First World War and State Intervention in Industrial Relations 1914–18', in C. Wrigley (ed.), *A History of British Industrial Relations*, ii. *1914–1939*: 23–70.

Young, S., and Lowe, S. V. (1978), *Intervention in the Mixed Economy: The Evolution of British Industrial Policy 1964–72*.

Zebel, S. (1967), Joseph Chamberlain and the Genesis of Tariff Reform', *Journal of British Studies*, 7: 131–57.

Zweiniger-Bargielowska, I. (1993), 'Rationing, Austerity and the Conservative Party Recovery After 1945', *Historical Journal* (forthcoming).

Zwerg, F. (1951), *Trade Unions and Productivity*, Oxford.

Index